Discourse and Discrimination

'No other book on racism combines the urgency of today's news with the comprehensiveness of a robust empirical base and a religiously developed theoretical framework ... This is an important book for anyone with interests from the discursive theory of racism to today's Austrian/European political crisis.'

Ron Scollon, *Georgetown University*

Discourse and Discrimination is a study of how racism, antisemitism and ethnicism are reflected in discourse.

Reisigl and Wodak first survey four established discourse-analysis approaches, discussing the strengths and weaknesses of each, and then provide their own model of critical discourse analysis. Using this model, the authors present three case studies. While the focus of these studies is on racism in Austria, the approach is relevant for the study of discrimination in any context.

Drawing on a wide range of sources – from political speeches and legal documents to newspaper articles, television broadcasts and everyday conversations – Reisigl and Wodak question why even today, in a post-World-War-II society, racism and antisemitism are still virulent.

Martin Reisigl is based at the University of Vienna and is co-author of *The Discursive Construction of National Identity*. **Ruth Wodak** is Professor of Applied Linguistics in the Department of Linguistics at the University of Vienna, and Director of the Discourse, Politics, Identity Research Center at the Austrian Academy of Sciences. Her English books include *Disorders of Discourse, Gender and Discourse*, and *Language, Power and Ideology*, and she is also co-author of *The Discursive Construction of National Identity*.

305.8

Discourse and Discrimination

Rhetorics of racism and antisemitism

**Martin Reisigl and
Ruth Wodak**

London and New York

First published 2001
by Routledge
11 New Fetter Lane, London EC4P 4EE

Simultaneously published in the USA and Canada
by Routledge
29 West 35th Street, New York, NY 10001

Routledge is an imprint of the Taylor & Francis Group

© 2001 Martin Reisigl and Ruth Wodak

Typeset in Baskerville by
HWA Text and Data Management, Tunbridge Wells
Printed and bound in Great Britain by
TJ International Ltd., Padstow, Cornwall

British Library Cataloguing in Publication Data
A catalogue record for this book is available from the British Library

Library of Congress Cataloging in Publication Data
Reisigl, Martin, 1969–
    Discourse and discrimination : Rhetorics of racism and
    antisemitism / Martin Reisigl and Ruth Wodak,
        p. cm.
    Includes bibliographical references and index.
     1. Racism–Austria–History. 2. Antisemitism–Austria–History.
    I. Wodak, Ruth, 1940– II. Title.

DB47 .R38 2000
305.8′009436–dc21   00-038259

ISBN 0-415-23149-3 (hbk)
ISBN 0-415-23150-7 (pbk)

Contents

Tables

Figures

Acknowledgements

The authors wish to express their gratitude to many people and institutions.

First of all, we especially want to thank four people who made an important contribution bringing the manuscript into a readable form of English. We are greatly indebted to Carolyn Straehle for correcting the English of the manuscript's first draft and for translating most of the German data analysed in chapters 3 and 4 into English. We are also very grateful to Peter Muntigl and Birgit Huemer for translating most of the German data analysed in chapter 5. Further, we would particularly like to thank Bryan Jenner for correcting the English grammar and style of the final version of the manuscript.

For assistance in providing data and expertise for analysis we would like to express our gratitude to the anti-racist Austrian organisation Helping Hands – and especially to Verena Krausneker – to the Viennese Fund for Integration and to the Viennese Liberal Forum.

We owe very special thanks to Teun A. van Dijk, Theo van Leeuwen, Jim Martin, Maria Sedlak and Ineke van der Valk for their constructive comments on earlier versions of chapters 1 and 2. We are also very grateful to Karin Wetschanow for productive discussions about the referential categories and for her suggestion to introduce the categories of 'criminonyms' and 'genderonyms'. Further, we are extremely grateful to the critical readers for the their valuable reports and suggestions for improvement of both content and style of an earlier version of the book. We are happy to be able to thank two of the readers by name, viz. Christina Schäffner and Ron Scollon, who were willing to divulge their anonymous identity as critical readers. Despite their invaluable contributions, we remain completely responsible for any remaining errors and deficiencies the book might possess.

We are also very grateful to the *Annual Review of Anthropology* and to the Austrian publisher Drava for their permission to reprint several parts of the articles 'Discourse and Racism: European Perspectives' and 'Discourse and Racism' (see Wodak and Reisigl 1999, Wodak and Reisigl 2000) in a slightly different version in some sections of chapters 1 and 2 of the present book.

One of the two authors, viz. Martin Reisigl, owes very many thanks to the Austrian Academy of Sciences that awarded him a generous two-year grant that, among other things, allowed him to invest some of his time and energies into the present book project.

We would like to thank Lieselotte Martin for all her efficient organisational support that accompanied the genesis of the book and the search for a publisher.

Finally, we are very grateful to Routledge for their interest in our work and the decision to publish the book. In particular, we wish to express our warmest thanks to Katharine Jacobson, Louisa Semlyen and John Hodgson for all their editorial efforts and prompt organisational assistance.

Martin Reisigl and
Ruth Wodak

Preface

With the present book, the authors pursue at least six objectives, which are all closely interrelated. First, we aim at a critical approach to the phenomenon of social discrimination, especially of racism, antisemitism and ethnicism from a discourse-analytical point of view. As it is one of our key assumptions that racism, ethnicism and antisemitism are – to a large extent – produced and reproduced discursively, the discourse-analytical approach is very rewarding when dealing with these forms of social discrimination. Second, we give a critical overview of the concepts of 'race' and 'racism' and critically discuss their culture and language dependence, which is often neglected and can therefore lead to misunderstandings in inter- and cross-cultural communication. Third, we seek to provide a critical synopsis of various scientific explanations that point to economical, social, political, cultural, social psychological and cognitive roots of racist, antisemitic and ethnicist prejudices. Fourth, we offer an introduction to five important discourse-analytical approaches to racism, antisemitism and ethnicism, thereby proposing possible methods of linguistic analysis that permit the identification of manifest and latent discriminatory meanings of texts and discourses. Fifth, we present three illustrative case studies of so-called 'everyday antisemitism', political 'xenophobia' and 'institutional racism', which should facilitate understanding of how concrete discourse analysis works with authentic discursive data. Although the data stem from the Austrian context, we believe that the theoretical and methodical approach will also be fruitfully applicable to the discourse-analytical investigation of other parts of the world. Finally, we make a tentative proposal for a promising model of critical discourse analysis that works within the political framework of deliberative democracy and illustrates how deliberative democracy should facilitate successful engagement in anti-discriminatory, anti-racist politics and policy-making.

In contrast to many of the books concerned with topics similar to those treated in our book, we endeavour to offer an approach that is theoretically clear and encompassing, conceptually rigorous, thematically broad, methodically and analytically relatively stringent, and empirically comparatively rich.

In view of our triangulatory and crossdisciplinary perspective, we hope that our readership will be as crossdisciplinary as the book itself. Apart from linguists, and in particular text and discourse analysts interested in the topic of social discrimination, we assume that the book is of potential interest for anybody concerned with ethnic studies, racism and antisemitism, especially for researchers, students and teachers of sociology, political sciences, history and media studies.

The present book is a further result of the many years of productive discussion and cooperation between the two authors. The discursive teamwork and exchange of ideas is reflected in all six chapters of the publication. The authors mutually commented and discussed the different versions of each chapter in several phases of revision and complementation. As far as the actual, final form, content and writing of the single chapters is concerned, both authors had equal parts in the writing of chapters 1 and 6. Martin Reisigl is the author of chapters 2 and 5, and Ruth Wodak is the author of chapters 3 and 4.

In order to assist readers to formulate their reading expectations, we offer a brief overview of the content of each chapter in advance.

Chapter 1 is a theoretical and methodical introduction to the notions of 'race', 'racism' and 'antisemitism' and to the study of racism, antisemitism and ethnicism. It provides an overview of four European discourse-analytical approaches to the analysis of racist, antisemitic and ethnicist utterances. First, it discusses the concepts of 'race' and 'racism' etymologically, historically and from the point of view of different cultures and languages. Second, it deals with some of the most significant explanations from various disciplines, which – more or less alternately – try to reflect on the material, economical, social, political, cultural, social psychological, cognitive and other causes and motives for racism, antisemitism and ethnicism, and which, in selectively focusing on one cause and motive or another, have an important and sometimes biasing impact on the choice of specific anti-racist strategies. Third, the chapter presents four discourse-analytical approaches to racism, viz., first, the theory about prejudices and stereotypes of Uta Quasthoff, second, the sociocognitive approach of Teun A. van Dijk, third, the discourse theory about collective symbols and discourse strands of Jürgen Link and the Duisburg Group and, fourth, the sociopsychological approach of the Loughborough Group.

Chapter 2 is a theoretical and methodical introduction to the approach to the linguistic and rhetorical analysis of racism and antisemitism that has been developed by the two authors of the book, who promote the Viennese discourse-historical analysis. After a brief summarising critique of the four discourse-analytical approaches discussed in chapter 1, the discourse-historical approach is presented as a context-sensitive theory that follows a complex concept of social critique and focuses on the historical and political dimension of discursive actions. The chapter gives an overview of the history of the discourse-historical approach and discusses the key notions of 'discourse', 'genre', 'fields of action', 'intertextuality' and 'interdiscursivity'. It describes some of the discourse-analytical tools useful in the analysis of discourses about 'racial', 'national' and 'ethnic' issues. The presentation of the discursive elements and strategies which, in our discourse-analytical view, deserve special attention in the analysis of racist, antisemitic and ethnicist discrimination through language, is orientated to five simple questions:

- How are persons named and referred to linguistically? (*referential strategies*).
- What traits, characteristics, qualities and features are attributed to them? (*predicational strategies*).
- By means of what arguments and argumentation schemes do specific persons or social groups try to justify and legitimate the exclusion, discrimination, suppression and exploitation of others? (*argumentation strategies*, including *fallacies*).
- From what perspective or point of view are these namings, attributions and arguments expressed? (*perspectivation* and *framing strategies*).
- Are the respective discriminating utterances articulated overtly, are they even intensified or are they mitigated? (*mitigation* and *intensification strategies*).

After the theoretical, methodical and exemplifying presentation of the categories of analysis, the chapter finally illustrates some of the analytical means of the discourse-historical approach with an example of racist political discourse, taken from an interview with Jörg Haider, the leader of the Austrian Freedom Party (FPÖ).

Chapter 3 is the first of three case studies. It deals with antisemitic discourse in postwar Austria and summarises aspects of the revival of and resistance to Austrian antisemitism since 1945, focusing especially on linguistic manifestations of prejudices towards Jews as they emerged in public discourse in the 1986 Austrian presidential campaign of Kurt Waldheim. The strategies and linguistic realisations of antisemitic discourse in the so-called 'Waldheim affair' are made explicit, taking the notion of 'syncretic antisemitism' – meaning that the old boundaries between a racist or ethnicist or religious antisemitism are no longer important, and that antisemitic stereotypes are produced and functionalised whenever a political context seems suitable for it – as theoretical background. The data analysed in this chapter are taken from the media (television and radio news broadcasts, newspapers and journals), from speeches of politicians and – in particular – from everyday conversations on the street. Complementary data from opinion polls are also integrated in the analysis. Apart from rather direct and explicit manifestations of antisemitic prejudices, the detailed analysis of the narrow 'co-text' and context of the 'everyday conversations' also reveals latent and implicit antisemitic meanings.

Chapter 4 presents a second discourse-historical case study. It is a triangulatory analysis of the 'Austria first' petition – also known as the 'anti-foreigner petition' – which was initiated in 1992 and 1993 by the FPÖ and its leader Jörg Haider, and which proposed very severe political measures to 'curb' immigration. Situated within the framework of critical discourse analysis, this chapter critically analyses the discriminatory text of the petition and its official rationale ('*Begründung*'), as well as the media debates, the political advertising campaign and its slogans promoting the support or refusal of the petition, and the petition-related polemical discussions about the so-called 'foreigner issue' in parliament. Before analysing the argumentation strategies and manipulative rhetorical devices used in the different genres in order to construct 'the foreigner' and to disguise explicitly racist contents, we provide some information about the histori-cal, sociopolitical and legal context. We conclude the chapter by illustrating the present discriminatory discourse on the so-called 'foreigner problem' with some sequences from a more recent TV interview with Jörg Haider, in which he discusses the new party program that attempts to align itself with Christian values in order to argue fallaciously for discrimination against 'foreigners'.

Chapter 5 contains a third case study on 'institutional' and 'culturalist racism'. Its topic is the political administration of social exclusion, the attempt to legiti-mise as well as to de-legitimise institutional measures of immigration control – strictly speaking, the expulsion of 'aliens', most of them Turkish citizens – within the legal framework of modern nation-states like Austria. The discourse about the authorities' refusals of residence permits for aliens in Austria in 1996, 1997 and 1998 is analysed against the methodical and theoretical background presented in chapter 2. First, the chapter gives an overview of the whole public discourse in Austria about residence permits for aliens and about family reunion. Then, it informs the readers about the Austrian policy on 'aliens' and demo-graphic developments in Austria. The sections conveying this context information, which may be illuminating for the subsequent analysis, are followed by a discourse and text analytical description of the official notifications in question as a legal genre that has the performative force to regulate directively a specific aspect of the life of an applicant – in our case, the temporally limited permit to reside legally in a specific part of a specific country or not. After this genre-theoretical embedding, the administrative practice of the Municipal Authorities is analysed from a linguistic and argumentation analytical perspec-tive, against the background of the analytical tools described in chapter 2. Further, in the present case study of discriminatory administrative notifications, the focus of analysis also lies on judgements of the Administrative Court, on the uncovering and public critique by opposition parties, and on the 'deliberative democratic' function of media coverage as an important political instrument of control. Finally, the chapter discusses the possible tension between legality and legitimacy and the anti-discriminatory potential of a democratic model based on a strong civil society.

Chapter 6, in conclusion, summarises the possible discourse-analytical contri-bution to the study of racism and the engagement in anti-discrimination policy and politics. The concluding outline takes up the critical and politically control-ling function of critical discourse analysis within a model of deliberative democracy, focusing on the reconstructive, diagnostic and prospective potential of the linguistic and rhetorical approach to discriminatory discourse proposed in this book.

Vienna, January 2000

1 'Race', racism and discourse

An interdisciplinary, historical and methodical overview

What exactly are we supposed to take 'racist' and 'racism' to mean? What specific forms of 'genetic', 'cultural' and 'institutional racism' do we face today and what causes them? How do these different forms of racism manifest themselves in discourse? Is it possible to distinguish racism from adjacent or possibly overlapping discriminatory phenomena like antisemitism, nationalism, ethnicism and sexism? What analytical – including discourse-analytical – criteria, if any, can be used to set at least relatively clear boundaries between these different '-isms'? These are only a small number of questions that still await satisfactory answers, despite the vast amount of specialist literature in the areas of social science, history, philosophy and even discourse analysis (see Van Dijk *et al.* 1997 for a recent discussion).

In view of the multifaceted nature of the issue and its theoretical complexity we will not be able in this chapter to give comprehensive answers to all these questions, especially as regards a thorough discussion of the relationship between the above-mentioned '-isms'. What we hope to achieve is an overview of influential concepts of 'race' and 'racism' and to give a synopsis, illustrated with a few short examples, of four discourse-analytical approaches to the problem of racism. Our own discourse-analytical approach will be discussed in chapter 2.

The starting point of a discourse-analytical approach to the complex pheno-menon of racism is to realise that racism, as a social practice, and as an ideology, manifests itself discursively. On the one hand, racist opinions and beliefs are produced and reproduced by means of discourse; on the other hand, through discourse, discriminatory exclusionary practices are prepared, promulgated, and legitimised. In order to gain an insight into the social and historical structure and dynamics of racist (nationalist, ethnicist, sexist) prejudices that could be conceived as specific mental states composed of – normally negative, emotion-ally very loaded and rigid – generalising attitudes towards social groups (cf. Quasthoff 1987: 787), discourse analysts have to relate the discriminatory linguistic features to the social, political and historical contexts of the analysed 'discursive events'. This obviously holds for the terms and concepts of 'race' and 'racism' as well.

On the other hand, discourse serves to criticise, delegitimise, and argue against racist opinions and practices – that is, to pursue anti-racist strategies. As far as this is concerned, the tasks of critical discourse analysts are at least two: first, critical discourse analysts can try to describe, socio-diagnostically, the actual anti-racist discursive practices and their efficiency or inefficiency. Second, if critical discourse analysts themselves want to act politically and to participate in the fight against racism and discrimination, they may engage in civil society and express a prospective critique that aims at optimising anti-racist policy. Particularly in the fifth and sixth chapters of the present book, we offer an outline of the anti-discriminatory potential of critical discourse analysis within a political model of 'deliberative democracy'.

In this introductory chapter, we dispense with detailed and extensive analyses of concrete discursive examples that help to show and reconstruct the discursive production and reproduction of racism and the accompanying discursive counter-actions. For that, we refer to the three case studies in chapter 3, 4, and 5, but also to chapter 2, in which we illustrate the concrete discursive manifestation of racism by analysing a short excerpt from an interview with an Austrian politician.

The concepts of 'race' and 'racism'

'Race'? 'race'? 'race': a historical-political etymological overview

Today it is an undeniable fact for geneticists and biologists that the concept of 'race', with reference to human beings, has nothing to do with biological reality (Jacquard 1996: 20). From a social functional point of view, 'race' is a social construction. On the one hand, it has been used as a legitimising ideological tool to oppress and exploit specific social groups and to deny them access to material, cultural and political resources, to work, welfare services, housing and political rights. On the other hand, these affected groups have adopted the idea of 'race'. They have turned the concept around and used it to construct an alternative, positive self-identity; they have also used it as a basis for political resistance (Miles 1993: 28) and to fight for more political autonomy, independence, and participation.

From a linguistic point of view, the term 'race' has a relatively young, although not precisely clear, etymological history. The Italian 'razza', the Spanish 'raza', the Portuguese 'raça' and the French 'race' have been rarely documented from the thirteenth century onwards and with more frequent occurrences beginning in the sixteenth century. There is some documentation from the sixteenth century, when the term also appeared in English. The term has, at different times, entered different semantic fields, for example:

- the field of ordinal and classificational notions that include such words as 'genus', 'species', and 'varietas'

- the field that includes social and political group denominations such as 'nation' and 'Volk' (in German) and, more rarely, 'dynasty', 'ruling house', 'generation', 'class' and 'family'
- the field that includes notions referring to language groups and language families such as 'Germanen' (Teutons) and 'Slavs' (Conze and Sommer 1984: 135).

Particularly as far as the last semantic field and the related construction and taxonomisation of 'races' – treated as equivalent to language families – as well as the related legitimation of racism are concerned, the ideological contribution of philology and linguistics was an extraordinarily inglorious one. Apart from the racialising usurpation, the synecdochical generalisation and the mythicalisation of the 'Aryan' – originally, 'Aryan' was the self-designating name for Persians living in Iran and in north-west India (Poliakow 1993, Römer 1985, Conze and Sommer 1984: 159) – philology and linguistics are responsible for at least three serious errors that provided the basis for the connection and approximation of race and language classifications (Römer 1985: 41 ff.). First, they are guilty of having confused language relationship and speaker relationship – that is to say, of having assumed till the second half of the twentieth century that a specific 'language family' is firmly bound to a distinctive and coherent group of persons, and that linguistic 'kinship' automatically implies a 'blood relationship' between the speakers of a certain language and language family. Such a biologising view clearly neglects all the historical and geographical contingencies and factors of 'linguistic imperialism' that heavily influence language choice, language change and language spread, and have nothing to do with natural developments. Second, linguistics and philology are responsible for a discriminatory hierarchy of languages and language types. They are responsible for supposing, in Eurocentric, ethnocentric and evolutionary terms, that there exists a development of languages and language types from lower to higher levels, and that this descent and ranking can still be proved if one looks at the 'actual' relationship between languages and language types. Third, and in close relation with the second point, linguistics and philology must be called to account for the metaphorical, naturalising and personifying description of languages as organisms and quasi-human beings, and for mixing up the forms and types of language with an alleged cultural level and ability of the speakers. The wrong parallel was drawn, until the second half of the twentieth century, that people with an allegedly 'primitive' culture speak an allegedly 'primitive' language, whereas people with a supposed 'high' culture were considered to speak highly developed languages, so-called 'languages of the civilised world'. The more different the structure of an 'exotic' language – 'exotic' from a one-sided European point of view – from the type of inflectional Indo-European languages, the more this language and its speakers were regarded as 'deviant' and 'primitive'. In the worst cases, such an 'exotic' language was animalised – that is to say, made analogous with animals giving tongue.

The pre-scientific (up to the eighteenth century) meaning of 'race' with regard to human beings – we omit discussion of language-specific usage of the term 'race' with reference to animals, plants, and even extrabiological groupings of things, such as 'type' or 'sort' (*Il Nuovo Dizionario di Garzanti* 1984: 725, and *Duden* 1989a: 1214 ff.) – was mainly associated with aristocratic descent and membership of a specific dynasty or ruling house. The term primarily denoted 'nobility' and 'quality', and had until then no reference to somatic criteria. However, in the eighteenth and nineteenth centuries the pseudobiological and anthropological systematisations soon related its meaning to over-generalised, phenotypic features designed to categorise people from all continents and countries. The idea of 'race' became closely incorporated into political-historical literature and was conceptually transferred to the terminology of human history. In the second half of the nineteenth century, the concept, now with historical and national attributes, was linked to social Darwinism – which can be traced to Darwin's theory of evolution only in part – and became an 'in-word' outside the natural sciences. 'Race theorists' interpreted history as a 'racial struggle' within which only the fittest 'races' would have the right to survive. They employed the political catchword with its vague semantic contours almost synonymously with the words 'nation' and 'Volk' for purposes of their biologistic, political population programs of 'racial cleansing', eugenics and birth control.

The extremely radicalised 'race' theory of the German antisemites and National Socialists in the tradition of Arthur de Gobineau, Houston Stewart Chamberlain and Georg Ritter von Schönerer tied together synchretistically (i.e. intermingling different doctrinal pieces without any strict internal coherence) the religious, nationalist, economist, culturalist, and biologistic antisemitism, which then served as the ideology to legitimise systematic, industrialised genocide.

Apropos 'antisemitism': the terms 'antisemitism' and 'antisemitic', which in retrospect cover the whole range of religious, economist, nationalist, socialist, Marxist, culturalist and racist prejudicial aversion and aggression against Jews, were most probably coined in 1879 in the agitational, antisemitic circle of the German writer Wilhelm Marr (Nipperdey and Rürup 1972). At that time the word 'antisemitic' was employed as a self-descriptive, political 'fighting word'. In 1935, the National Socialist Ministry of Propaganda (*'Reichspropaganda-ministerium'*) issued a language regulation in which it prescribed that the term should be avoided in the press and replaced with the term 'anti-Jewish' (*'anti-jüdisch'*), '[...] for the German policy only aims at the Jews, not at the Semites as a whole' (quoted from Nipperdey and Rürup 1972: 151). Undoubtedly, the term 'antisemitic' has been used in postwar Germany and in postwar Austria more often than during the National Socialist reign of terror. This is because the term has become a politically 'stigmatic' word for describing others and its meaning has been expanded in the analysis of anti-Jewish aggression throughout history.

It was the German antisemites' and National Socialists' use of 'race theory' that 'stimulated a more thorough critical appraisal of the idea of "race" in

Europe and North America and the creation of the concept of racism in the 1930s' (Miles 1993: 29). The term 'racism', with its suffix '-ism', which denotes a theory, doctrine or school of thought as well as the related behaviour (Fleischer and Barz 1992: 190), was probably first used in the title of a temporarily unpublished German book written by Magnus Hirschfeld in 1933/4. In this book, which was translated and published in English in 1938, Hirschfeld argued against the pseudoscientifically backed contention that there exists a hierarchy of biologically distinct 'races' (Miles 1993: 29). The actual linguistic 'career' of the term started in the postwar period (Sondermann 1995: 47).

Since 1945, use of the term 'race' in the German-language countries of Germany and Austria has been strictly taboo for politicians, for academics, and even for the general public. In France, the expression *'relations de race'* would also be regarded as racist (Wieviorka 1994: 173). On the other hand, the term 'race relations' is still commonly used in the United Kingdom and in the United States. Research about racism must take into account these differences in language usage. Misinterpretations can lead to difficulties in translation and even to mistakes in shaping different analytical categories used when dealing with the issue of racism (Wieviorka 1994: 173).

Defining racism

'Racism', the stigmatising headword and political 'fighting word', is on almost everyone's lips today, probably because its meaning has become extraordinarily expanded and evasive. There is talk of a 'genetic', 'biological', 'cultural', 'ethno-pluralist', 'institutional' and 'everyday racism', of a 'racism at the top', of an 'elite racism', of a 'racism in the midst', of an 'old' and a 'new' or 'neo-racism', of a 'positive racism', and of an 'inegalitarian' and a 'differentialist racism'. Because of this inflationary use, there is no commonly acknowledged definition of the term. Therefore we will consider only seven recent terminological approaches to the concept – including our own approach.

According to Albert Memmi (1992: 103), 'racism' refers to the generalised and absolute evaluation of real or fictitious differences that is advantageous to the 'accuser' and detrimental to his or her victim. With this negative judgement, the accuser wants to legitimise his or her privileges or aggressions. In this characterisation, the meaning of racism in the very strict sense is lost. Thus, Memmi offers a narrow and a broad definition of 'racism'. He suggests using the term 'racism' exclusively to denote the form of discriminatory judgement that encompasses the evaluation of both real or fictitious biological differences. In contrast to this, his neologism 'heterophobia' – coined in analogy to 'xeno-phobia' – is designated to denote all 'phobic' and aggressive constellations that are directed against others, and that are legitimised by different psychological, cultural, social, or metaphysical arguments (Memmi 1992: 121). According to Memmi, 'racism' in its strict sense has to be understood as a special variety of 'heterophobia', bearing a co-hyponymical relation to 'antisemitism' or 'Jew-phobia', 'Arab-phobia', 'black-phobia', 'sexism', 'homophobia', 'youth-phobia' and 'phobia against differently abled persons'. There can be no objection to Memmi's attempt to find a cover term for different forms of ideological and socio-practical discrimination. However, the literal meaning of the term 'hetero-phobia' – and this critique is valid for terms like 'xenophobia' as well – is rather problematic. First, it neglects the active and aggressive aspect of discrimination and, second, it pathologises racism (and all the other forms of discrimination covered by 'heterophobia') through the 'disease metaphor' of 'phobia', which, as such, plays down racism and, at least implicitly, exculpates racists.

According to Colette Guillaumin (1991: 164; 1992) and Detlev Claussen (1994: 5), every racism is a syncretism (for the analysis of antisemitism as a syncretic phenomenon see Mitten 1992 and Mitten 1997), an ideological muddle of different pseudoscientific doctrines, religious and confessional beliefs, and stereotypical opinions, that constructs a pseudocausal connection between phenotypic, social, mental, symbolic, and fictitious traits. Guillaumin refers to four types of features – the morphophysiological, social, symbolic and fictitious ones – which together characterise the construction of 'race'. The juxtaposition of these features unfortunately suggests at least an analytically discrete separa-tion, though the four criteria are by no means separable from each other, because there is no social without symbolic. Moreover, fictionality can be and, as far as 'race' is concerned, has always been, an ingredient of morphophysiological, social as well as symbolical ascription.

For Guillaumin, 'racism' means, simultaneously,

- a practical behaviour (on the street, in the workplace, in institutions, etc.)
- a political program
- a legal structure (e.g. citizenship conferred according to *jus sanguinis*)
- a practical horizon of a state (e.g. the projection of a 'clean race' or an apartheid policy).

Here too, the distinction between the last three points seems to be arbitrary and questionable, because both the legal structure and the 'horizon of a state' are political affairs and concerns.

Philomena Essed (1991 and 1992) holds the view that

> racism must be understood as ideology, structure and process in which inequalities inherent in the wider social structure are related, in a deterministic way, to biological and cultural factors attributed to those who are seen as a different 'race' or 'ethnic group'.
>
> (Essed 1991: 43)

Apart from the fact that Essed's definition intermingles 'racism' with 'ethni-cism' – a mixing that is as common in current theories about racism as the mixing of 'racial' with 'ethnical' – there are good reasons for replacing the abstract and barely tangible notion of 'process' in her definition with the terms 'action' or 'practice'. Even Essed herself points to the practical dimension when she explains why she chose the term 'process': '[...] racism is a "process" because structures and ideologies do not exist outside the everyday practices through which they are created and confirmed. These practices both adapt to and themselves contribute to changing social, economic, and political conditions in society' (Essed 1991: 44)

One of the most interesting points in Essed's approach is the theoretical elaboration of 'everyday racism'. The concept of 'everyday racism' is intended to integrate, by definition, macro- and microsociological dimensions of racism (Essed 1991: 16). After having criticised the dichotomic distinction between 'institutional' and 'individual racism' as erroneously placing the individual outside the institutional (even though 'structures of racism do not exist external to agents – they are made by agents – but specific practices are by definition racist only when they activate existing structural racial inequality in the system' [Essed 1991: 36]), Essed explains her understanding of the term 'everyday':

> [...] the 'everyday' can be tentatively defined as *socialised meanings making practices immediately definable and uncontested so that, in principle, these practices can be managed according to (sub)cultural norms and expectations.* These practices and meanings belong to our familiar world and usually involve routine or repetitive practices.
>
> (Essed 1991: 48–9)

Building on this definition, she goes on to say that everyday racism can be characterised as the integration of racism into everyday situations through practices (cognitive and behavioural) that activate underlying power relations. In other words:

> [...] everyday racism can be defined as *a process in which (a) socialised racist notions are integrated into meanings that make practices immediately definable and manageable, (b) practices with racist implications become in themselves familiar and repetitive, and (c) underlying racial and ethnic relations are actualised and reinforced through these routine or familiar practices in everyday situations.*
>
> (Essed 1991: 52)

One of the most systematic and radical approaches to the issue of 'race' and 'racism' is that of Robert Miles. In his view, in order to analyse 'race problems' adequately, one must eliminate all conceptions of 'race' as a thing in itself, with the power to have effects. One must do this in spite of the fact that the idea of 'race' constitutes an element of everyday common sense:

> There are no 'races' and therefore no 'race relations'. There is only a belief that there are such things, a belief which is used by some social groups to construct an Other (and therefore the Self) in thought as a prelude to exclusion and domination, and by other social groups to define Self (and so to construct an Other) as a means of resisting that exclusion. Hence, if it is

used at all, the idea of 'race' should be used only to refer descriptively to such uses of the idea of 'race'.

(Miles 1993: 42)

Miles' analysis of racism unfolds around five key concepts. First, the notion of *'racialisation'* denotes the dynamic and dialectical representational process of categorisation and meaning construction in which specified meanings are ascribed to real or fictitious somatic features (Miles 1992: 100–3 and Miles 1989: 74–7).

Second, in order to avoid a semantic overstretch of the term, Miles wants to regard 'racism' exclusively as an ideological and representational phenomenon analytically distinguished from *'exclusionary practice'*. The concept of 'exclusionary practice' is thought to refer to concrete intentional actions as well as to unintentional material consequences, both of which lead to an unequal (hierarchical) treatment and disadvantaging of persons in the allocation of resources and services. Miles suggests this distinction in order to avoid conclusions that assume a mono-causal explanation of discriminatory practices and do not take into account that a concrete exclusionary practice might be multi-determinational and that racism is but one of its various causes.

Third, *'racism'*, as an ideology both of exclusion and inclusion, can be either a relatively coherent, pseudological theory or a quite incoherent accumulation of prejudiced clichés, images, attributions and arguments. Whatever the case, it presupposes racialisation, though the racialisation of the involved social groups does not constitute a sufficient condition to qualify a statement or occurrence as racist. An explicit negative judgment of a racialised group must also be present for such a qualification to be made. In this judgement, the deprecatory features ascribed to the constructed 'race' can be both biological and cultural.

The fourth key concept in Miles' theory about racism is that of *'institutional racism'*. Miles defines this idiosyncratically as racism under circumstances marked by exclusionary practices, which developed from a racist discourse that has become silent (because it was no longer accepted as a legitimisation of the exclusionary practices), or that has been replaced with a new discourse (also as a result of a taboo). It is difficult to see why the 'silence' should be the prerequisite for labelling something as 'institutional racism'. In the case of the acquisition of citizenship according to *jus sanguinis*, for example, the 'racist discourse' has not been silenced, and the aspect of political institutionalisation is by no means denied by the fact that the law is explicitly oriented towards the racist categorisation by 'blood'.

However, the phrase 'institutional racism' should, in our view, always be used carefully, and it is often better to speak about 'institutionalised' or 'institutionally supported or favored racism' instead, because these phrases leave an (admittedly backgrounded) syntactical trace of actors in the form of the passive verbal processes, whereas the former, in simply attributing to 'racism' the quality of being 'institutional', does not contain any linguistic hint of actors (for a different critique of the term 'institutional racism' see also Krausneker [1999:

26 ff.], who proposes replacing the term by 'structural racism'). Since the terminological phrase 'institutional racism' implies a de-personalising, abstract and often metonymic perspective, one easily runs the risk of oppressing and making anonymous the responsible social actors who perform the discriminatory practices in the name of an institution or as its representatives. At the level of the implementation and execution of laws or regulations, there is almost always a need for individuals who personally act as members of, and with the authority of, the institution or organisation. From the normative ethical point of view that we adopt, these individuals are responsible for their actions, although there is no doubt that – in an institution – the organisational differentia- tion and segregatory division of labour can lead to a parcelling out of the responsibility. Also, an institution may often gather momentum in the sense that the organisational frame and partition of labour favors administrative procedures which, only in combination, bring about systematic discriminations that may even be unintended at the level of the individual action of the institution's members.

Miles' fifth concept is that of '*ideological articulation*'. This concept is used to illuminate how ideologies – for example, racism, nationalism, sexism, and ethnicism – verge on each other, how they are connected, and how they overlap (for the ideological connection of 'race' and 'nation' see Miles 1993: 79).

The chronological distinction between the '*old*' and the '*new racism*' was introduced by Barker (1981) and taken up by Taguieff (1987), Balibar and Wallerstein (1990[1988]), Balibar (1991), and Kalpaka and Räthzel (1986). Miles prefers the chronologically neutral distinction (proposed by Taguieff 1987) between an 'inegalitarian' and a 'differentialist racism', 'although acknowl- edging that this distinction is not as precise as its creator presumes' (Miles 1994: 199). The reason why Miles understandably refuses to speak in terms of 'old' and 'new racism' lies in the uncertainty regarding the concept of 'neo- racism' – characterised as racism grounded in the stress of cultural differences – and whether this racism is really fundamentally 'new' and different. Because of the basic syncretist nature of racism, which can be described in terms of 'ideological articulation', even the classical, pseudoscientific racism of the nineteenth and twentieth centuries always included a reference to the cultural or national 'character' and 'uniqueness' (Rattansi 1994: 55).

Apropos '*inegalitarian*' and '*differentialist racism*': the concept of 'inegalitarian racism' is intended to denote the legitimisation of domination, discrimination, and separation based on overt doctrines in support of genetic, biological inferiority, whereas 'differentialist racism' emphasises cultural differences, including lifestyles, habits, customs and manners, and paints a threatening picture of the mixing and interbreeding of cultures and ethnic groups. This latter concept is more or less synonymous with the notion of 'cultural racism', better labelled 'culturalist racism'. 'Cultural racism' seems tautological, because every racism is undeniably a cultural phenomenon, whereas the suffix '-ist' in the qualification as 'culturalist' more exactly names the explicit ideologising orientation towards and reference to culture. 'Differentialist racism' seems to avoid explicit hierarchisation. Implicitly, however, an inferiorisation of the cultures of the 'others' is always presupposed by the social, economic and political inequality between the members of the 'own' culture and the members of the 'other' culture(s). '*Ethnopluralist racism*', which tries to legitimise strict segregation and discrimination by claiming that multiculturalism threatens 'cultural and ethnic purity' and leads to 'contamination', 'degeneration', and 'decline', can be categorised as a specific type of culturalist or differentialist racism. For a discussion of the 'two logics of racism' as described here see Wieviorka (1994: 182 ff.).

As far as our own concept of racism is concerned, we take note of Miles' caveat regarding hasty monocausal assumptions of a relationship between exclusionary practices and racist opinions. Nevertheless, we assume that racism is both an ideology of a syncretic kind and a discriminatory social (including discursive) practice that could be institutionalised and backed by hegemonic social groups. Racism is based on the hierarchical construction of groups of persons who are characterised as communities of descent and to whom are attributed specific collective, naturalised or biologically labelled traits that are considered to be almost invariable. These traits are primarily related to biological features, appearance, cultural practices, customs, traditions, language, or socially stigmatised ancestors. These are – explicitly or implicitly, directly or indirectly – evaluated negatively, and this judgement is closely in accord with hegemonic views. As an ideological mix, racism combines different, and sometimes even contradictory, doctrines, religious beliefs and stereotypes, thereby constructing an almost invariable pseudocausal connection between – possibly fictitious – biological (genetic and phenotypic), and social, cultural and mental, traits.

How to explain 'racism'

Many approaches from different disciplines reflect on the material, economical, social, political, sociopsychological, cognitive and other causes and motives for racism. The explanations offered by each have an important impact on the choice of specific anti-racist strategies. Let us briefly consider nine of the most significant approaches, to which, unfortunately, we cannot do complete justice in this general survey (for an overview of theoretical accounts see, for example, Poliakov, Delacampagne and Girard 1992: 145–96, Bader 1995: 14–81, Zerger 1997: 99–164, whose systemisations and accounts all clearly leave their mark on the following explanations).

Social cognitive accounts focus on social categorisation and stereotyping, relying on the cognitive concepts of 'prototypes', 'schemas', 'stereotypes' and 'object classification'. They deal with discriminatory prejudices as being primarily a problem of social perception. Some social cognition researchers, for example Hamilton and Trolier (1986), argue that 'the way our minds work, the way we process information, may *in itself* be sufficient to generate a negative image of a group. They point to several strands of evidence but, most notably, to the illusory correlation studies' (Wetherell and Potter 1992: 38). Their concepts of society and social environment are quite static, a-historical and context-insensitive, and they assume that prejudicial apperceptions and categorisations (inherent in all persons) are inevitable and cognitively 'useful'. In presuming this, they risk playing down and even – at least implicitly – justifying racism as a 'survival strategy'. In addition, they cannot explain why some people are more susceptible to racist ideology than others, and how the relationship between attitudes and actions is to be viewed – that is to say, why some people convert their racist prejudices into materialised violence and discrimination while others shy away from physical aggression.

Social identity theory (Hogg and Abrahams 1988, Tajfel 1981, Tajfel and Turner 1985, Turner 1981, Turner 1985, Turner and Giles 1981, Turner *et al.* 1987) places the concepts of social identity and social categorisation at the center of its socio-psychological theory of intergroup relations. In contrast to the above-mentioned approach, it recognises the importance of socialisation and group experiences in the development and acquisition of social categories. From the perspective of social identity theory, social structures and relations shape the individual perception, identity and action. Categorisations are assumed to be necessary for reducing the complexity of the social world. Individual perception is formed by patterns aligned with group memberships and non-memberships. Self-stereotyping is the basic psychological process of group phenomena like social cohesion, ethnocentrism, cooperation, altruism and acting together. The socially learned patterns of perception tend to favour the own ingroup and to derogate the outgroups. The image of the own ingroup is more differentiated than the images of the others' groups, which, all in all, are much more characterised by 'internal attributions' than the ingroup. The outgroups' actions and behaviour are seldom explained by reference to external factors of communicative situation and historical, social, political and economic context, but primarily by pointing to alleged inherent and essential traits. Racism and ethnocentrism are, in large part, seen as the interpersonal result of group membership and as the psychological effects of identifying with a specific group in economic and social competition with other groups. According to this theory, self- and other-categorisation follows the relativistic 'principle of metacontrast': on the one hand, similarities between the members of a group are exaggerated, whereas similarities between different groups are understated; on the other hand, differences within a group are played down and perceived as being smaller than differences between groups, which are overemphasised. Social identity theorists assume that especially persons with a weak individual identity, with insecurities in acting and experiences of powerlessness and loneliness, tend towards evaluating the 'own' group highly positively and towards strongly disparaging the groups of others. Some of the causal assumptions of this theory are rather too simple and reductionist: apart from the simplistic frustration-aggression hypothesis and the hasty analogical generalisation of the results of small-group-experiments, the relationship between experiences, thinking and practices is simply assumed without any closer differentiation. Like the social cognition approach – and here we follow Wetherell's and Potter's critique –

social identity theory suffers from 'a tendency to universalise the conditions for racism and a lingering perceptualism' (Wetherell and Potter 1992: 47). The implications for anti-racism are therefore very pessimistic.

Several nativist *psychoanalytical theories* (for psychoanalytical accounts of racism see also Loewenstein 1952, Poliakov, Delacampagne and Girard 1992: 175– 82, Brainin, Ligeti and Teicher 1993 and Ottomeyer 1997: 111–31; for psychological accounts see Mecheril and Thomas 1997) hold this universalistic viewpoint in common with the two approaches already referred to. Allport is right to criticise some psychoanalytical theories for tending to ascribe to all persons the same dependency on unconscious aggressions and fixations which undoubtedly characterise the inner life of neurotic and psychotic persons (1993: 10). In positing the 'thanatos' – that is to say, innate death instincts, which include the auto- and allo-destructive or auto- and allo-aggressive instinct – certain varieties of psychoanalysis naturalise aggressions against 'the other' as an anthropological invariant rooted in biology, and thus relinquish their political potential to be critical of society and to argue for an improvement of the social conditions that have a strong impact on the inner-psychic conflicts related to racism and ethnicism (see Masson 1984 and especially Jacoby 1983 for his critique of the politically self-disarming and self-immunising medicalisation and professionalisation of conformist psychoanalysis). The overemphasis of the biological determination of aggressions against 'others' was already criticised by the early Erich Fromm (1988[1941]: 159 ff.), who stresses that destructiveness is not at all an unchanging and equal part in everyone's life. Moreover, Fromm believes that the degree of destructiveness is heavily dependent on social conditions and indirectly proportional to the degree of social repression of the individual's development as a whole, including her or his creativity and spontaneity and the fulfillment of her or his sensual, emotional and intellectual desires and capacities: 'Destructiveness is the result of unlived life' (Fromm 1988: 161).

Apart from the 'aggressive' and 'destructive instinct', central psychoanalytical conceptualisations that are employed to analyse and account for racist, ethnicist and chauvinist aggression include 'projection and rationalisation', 'anti-super-ego-aggression', 'sado-masochism', 'narcissism', 'projection of oral greed or avarice', 'projection of jealousy against the younger sisters and brothers', 'anal aggression and cleaning mania', 'phallic threatening, envy of sexual potency and Oedipus complex' and 'repression of homosexuality' (Ottomeyer 1997). Both racism and antisemitism are analysed psychoanalytically in terms of conflicts between the ego and the super-ego and conflicts between the ego and the id. The former conflicts are considered to be involved in 'Christian anti-semitism', in which the Jews are hated by the Christians as the bearers and representatives of the divine law that is part of the Christian super-ego. The conflicts between the ego and the super-ego are also assumed to be entangled in postwar antisemitism in Germany and Austria, which, more and more, seems to be developing into an 'anti-super-ego-antisemitism'. By that psychoanalysts mean an antisemitism based on the prejudiced victim–victimiser-reversal that tries to abolish the subject's own bad conscience for the Nazi crimes by projecting the notion that the former prosecutors are persecuted by vindictive and avaricious Jews who are not willing to forgive and who never stop demanding financial and symbolic 'reparations' and 'compensations'. The antisemitic anti-super-ego-aggression is currently directed against all who advocate remembrance of the racist Nazi crimes and their victims and who are therefore perceived as annoying parent-like figures that aim at ruining one's zest for life. Psychoanalytic researchers of racism today presume that right-wing populists subsequently demolish or suspend the super-ego by persuasively propagating rationalising scapegoat-prejudices against ethnic minorities and immigrants. Thus, aggression is no longer impeded by internal monitoring.

The second form of inner-psychic conflicts related to racism and antisemitism, that is to say, conflicts between the ego and the id, are described by reference to the three stages of libido development distinguished in psychoanalysis. Against the conceptual background of these three stages, racism, antisemitism and ethnicism against racialised or ethnicised groups, Jews and foreigners are projection surfaces for unwanted libidinous, aggressive and narcissist stirrings (Ottomeyer 1997: 120 ff.). Discriminatory prejudices, like that of Jews being avaricious and of 'foreigners' and refugees being spoilt 'socio-parasites' and 'economic refugees' ('*Wirtschaftsflüchtlinge* ') who exploit the welfare system, are analysed as the projection of the subject's own oral greed and avarice combined with the projection of one's own jealousy of younger sisters and brothers. Derogatory metaphors like 'dirt' and 'vermin', fears of 'miscegenation' and the metaphor of 'ethnic and racial cleansing' employed in racist, antisemitic and ethnicist utterances are interpreted by psychoanalysts in terms of anal aggression and cleanliness mania. The prejudices towards male 'foreigners' as being inclined to sexual harassment, the prejudice towards 'the foreigners' as having sexual superiority, higher fertility and birth rates, and being the carriers of Aids and venereal diseases, are related in psychoanalytic theories to fantasies of phallic threatening, to the envy of sexual potency and the Oedipus complex. Some psychoanalytic approaches, finally, also assume that ambivalence and repressed homosexual desire are involved in racism and antisemitism (see below, p. 17).

In contrast to nativist variants of psychoanalytic approaches, which are inclined to legitimise the social status quo, *critical theory* (e.g. Adorno 1973[1950], Adorno 1993, Adorno *et al.* 1950, Fromm 1988, Horkheimer 1992, Horkheimer and Flowerman 1949 f., Horkheimer *et al.* 1987, Fenichel 1993, Simmel 1993 [1946], and Reich 1986[1933], and more recently Outlaw 1990), in combining neo-Marxism, politically committed psychoanalysis and sociopsychology, connects economic, political and cultural structures as well as social dynamics with the character structure of a person fundamentally coined in her or his childhood socialisation. Thus, critical theory does not merely describe racist, and especially antisemitic, prejudice, but tries primarily to explain its genesis in order to illuminate the conditions for the emergence and social maintenance of Nazi fascism and antisemitism and in order to help to eradicate authoritarianism and racist prejudice. Adorno (1973[1950]: 8) regards insight into character structure as the best protection against the tendency to ascribe constant traits to individuals as 'innate' or 'racially determined'. Since a specific character structure – the authoritarian personality – makes an individual susceptible to antidemocratic propaganda, the social and economic conditions under which the potential turns into active manifestation have to be uncovered.

In order to characterise the authoritarian personality, early critical theory, and especially Erich Fromm, takes up the psychological and psychoanalytic concepts of 'sadism' and 'masochism'. Fromm (1988: 181) is convinced that Nazism is not just a political problem that has to be understood against the background of socioeconomic factors. He holds the view that the fact that a whole people can be seised by racist Nazism, must, in addition, be explained in terms of psychological motivation and reasons, and that includes a de-sexualised sado-masochist inclination prepared by a particular type of social-isation. Authoritarian personalities – that is to say, persons who, on the one hand, are receptive to blind obedience, subordination and execution of orders, and who, on the other hand, are capable of discriminatory, racist, antisemitic and ethnicist aggression – can be seen as sado-masochistic characters, who readily submit to the powerful and despise the weak, since they have a strong desire for super-ego domination and want to escape from the uncertainty of autonomy, self-determination and freedom of decision into irrational, security-giving authoritarianism and totalitarianism that are closely connected to destructive-ness and conformism.

Horkheimer and Adorno (1991[1944]) analyse antisemitism from a psycho-logical perspective as a projection of socially tabooed emotions, wishes and stirrings onto 'the Jews', and, from an economic viewpoint, as the veiling of and evasive averting from the capitalist relationship of exploitation by inventing a scapegoat. They interpret antisemitic prejudices as part of a more general syndrome of attitudes that is closely connected with character dispositions (Zerger 1997: 122 ff.). The main interest of Adorno, Horkeimer, Frenkel-Brunswik, Fromm, Levinson, Marcuse, Standford and all the other researchers collaborating on the extensive interdisciplinary research project on antisemitism that was published in several volumes under the general title 'Studies in Prejudice' from 1949 onward, is the potentially fascist individual. With the help of numerous sets of standardised questions, the researchers aim at grasping the opinions about and attitudes towards antisemitism (A-Scale), ethnocentrism (E-Scale), political-economical conservativism (PCE-Scale) and fascism (F-Scale). To measure the proneness to fascism, they take into consideration nine variables (Adorno 1973: 45 and 71–5):

- conventionalism
- authoritarian subordination
- authoritarian aggression
- anti-intraception (i.e. the defence of subjectivity, fantasy and sensibility)
- superstition and stereotyping

- attitudes towards power and 'robustness'
- destructiveness and cynicism
- projectivity (a disposition to believe in absurd and dangerous occurrences in the world)
- sexuality (exaggerated interest in sexual 'events')

The researchers stress that character structure and behaviour cannot be treated as equivalent. Character is, rather, a reaction potential that determines ideological preference, and strongly depends on the socioeconomic and political conditions as well as the general intellectual climate within a society. Early critical theorists conceptualise the genesis of the authoritarian character as the sado-masochistic solution of the Oedipus complex by a weak ego that cannot deal differently with the decline of paternal authority in late bourgeois society. The critical theorists' problematic assumption of the bourgeois paternal authority as a positive point of reference for a critique of totalitarianism has been criticised by Jessica Benjamin (1982: 426 ff.) (see Zerger 1997: 126 ff.).

Taking up early critical theory, Lucius Outlaw (1990: 72 ff.) propagates a critical theory of 'race' which challenges the common-sense assumption that 'race' is a self-evident, organising, explanatory concept. Stressing the socio-historical constructivist dimensions of 'race', Outlaw points to the danger, particularly widespread in the United States, of taking an essentialising and objectivising concept of 'race' as the focal point of contention, thereby supplying a shorthand explanation for the source of contentious differences. A similar critique is put forward by Claussen (1994: 2), who complains that in the 'public world' ('*Weltöffentlichkeit*') almost all violent social tension in the United States – for example the street fights in Los Angeles in 1992 – are reported as 'race riots' – 'a headword that seems to make superfluous every analysis'. In contrast to such simplistic explications, Outlaw pleads for emancipatory projects informed by traditions of critical thought which might help to move beyond racism, without reductionism, to pluralistic socialist democracy.

The '*colonial paradigm*' or '*race-relations approach*' (Cox 1970, Szymanski 1985, Wallerstein 1979, Fox-Genovese 1992, Genovese 1995) – a notion coined by Miles – views racism within the classical Marxist tradition as the consequence of colonialism and imperialism in the context of capitalism. It analyses racism in the light of the development of a capitalist world economic system. One of the first to analyse 'race relations' within this framework is Cox (1970) (see Miles 1993: 30 ff.). He characterises 'race relations' as 'behaviour which develops among people who are aware of each other's actual or imputed physical differences' (1970: 320). Although Cox claims that 'races' are social constructions, he reifies them as distinctive, permanent, immutable collectivities distinguished by skin colour. As Miles (1991 and 1994) points out, however, the 'colonial paradigm', assuming that racism was created to legitimise colonial exploitation, externalises the problem of racism one-sidedly, one consequence being its inability to explain antisemitism and the negative racialisation of other 'interior' minorities (e.g. 'gypsies') in Europe before and after the Second World War.

The '*political economy of migration paradigm*' (Castles and Kosack 1972 and 1973, Nikolinakos 1975, Lawrence 1982, Sivanandan 1982 and 1990, Miles 1993) analyses the processes of 'racialisation' in the capitalist centres in connection with migration, capital accumulation and class formation. Rejecting the sociological paradigm of 'race relations', Castles and Kosack (1972 and 1973) focus on worldwide migration after 1945 as a consequence of uneven capitalist development on a world scale. They identify immigrant workers

> as having a specific socio-economic function found in all capitalist societies, namely to fill undesirable jobs vacated by the indigenous working class in the course of the periodic reorganisation of production. This stratum of immigration workers thereby came to constitute a 'lower stratum' of the working class, which was thereby fragmented.
>
> (Miles 1993: 36)

In common with the proponents of the 'race relations approach', Castles and Kosack do not reject the idea of 'race' as an analytical concept. 'Rather, they subordinated it to a political economy of labour migration and class relations: that is, they retained the category of "race" in order to deny its explanatory significance' (Miles 1993: 36).

The analyses by Sivanandan (1982 and 1990) also suffer from the absence of any critical evaluation of 'race' and 'race relations' as analytical concepts. They suggest at least indirectly that the human population is composed of a number of biological 'races'. Beyond that, they ascribe to 'race' more or less the same status of reality as to 'social class' and reduce racism primarily to economic factors.

The *postmodern* approaches and the *cultural studies perspective* – which except for its neo-Marxist orientation relies, at least partly, on postmodernism – (Center for Contemporary Cultural Studies 1982, Hall 1978, 1980, 1989, and 1994, Gilroy 1987, Rattansi and Westwood 1994, Rattansi 1994, Westwood 1994, Bhabha 1990, Said 1978 and 1993, Fanon 1986, Bauman 1989 and 1991) seek primarily to analyse the cultural, ideological and political construction of racism. They emphasise 'that ethnicities, nationalisms and other forms of collective identity are products of a process to be conceptualised as a cultural politics of representation, one in which narratives, images, musical forms and popular culture more generally have a significant role' (Rattansi 1994: 74; for a critique of the notion of 'collective identity' see Berger and Luckman 1980: 185, and Wodak *et al.* 1998: 58; for a critique of the terminological confusion see below). Rejecting Western 'metanarratives' constructed around particular 'collective subjects' like 'nations', 'races', 'ethnic groups' and 'classes', Rattansi and Westwood (1994: 2) point out that the conceptual vocabulary of 'nationalism', 'racism', 'ethnicism' and 'class struggle' can no longer provide the basis for a viable taxonomy of violent social antagonisms and clashes. In their view, these concepts no longer permit the creation of convincing, all-encompassing explanatory frameworks, since subjectivities and identifications are multiple and shifting under the 'postmodern condition' (Lyotard 1984) of chronic disembedding, decentering, de-essentialisation and reinvention of traditions and 'collective' identities. Although they want to do without 'metanarratives', postmodernists are not completely consistent in their refusal of 'metanarratives' and large-sized 'collective subjects'. Rattansi (1994), for example, makes use of the abstract and undifferentiated notion of 'Western identities' as completely unquestioned reified entities.

It is quite a common topos to relate racism in one or another form with modernity. Already Horkheimer and Adorno (1991 [1944]) describe Nazi fascist antisemitism as the about-turn of modern Enlightenment into its opposite – a reversal that they consider to be closely related to the myths of the Enlightenment, to the modern development of instrumental reasoning and capitalist exploitation. However, they aim at defending modernity, rationalism and the humanist ideas by revealing some of their inherent pernicious implications. Wieviorka (1991, 1994) also relates racism to modernity. He holds the view that the current spread of racism has to do with the actual de-structuration of industrial societies, with increasing difficulties of state and public institutions and with the ongoing transformations of national identities (for a critique of Wieviorka's post-industrial framework, see Miles 1994). Cultural studies and postmodern approaches also associate modernity with racism. Unlike critical theorists, who believe modernity to be an incomplete project that should not be given up (Habermas 1981[1980]), they bid farewell to modernity, as the name 'postmodernity' itself already implies. Postmodern researchers in racism regard Western genocide against aboriginal people, slavery, imperialist and colonial domination and exploitation, and the Holocaust, in all of which Western doctrines of 'racial' and cultural superiority have played a constitutive role, as the other side of Western modernity. Relying on poststructuralist psychoanalysis (e.g. Lacan, Kristeva), they link racism to sexuality, considering racism to be one response of the generically fragile, split, fragmented ego (Frosh 1987, 1989 and 1991) and of the repressed homosexual desire leading to ambivalence and projection of unwanted feelings about the body toward others, whether Jews, 'black' people or Asians (Fanon 1986: 163–78).

Abstaining from attempts to give a clear definition of 'race' and 'racism', they personify or reify the idea of 'race' (Miles 1993 and 1944). Within this theoretical framework, problematical reification is also applied to terms such as 'modernity', 'discourse', 'power' and 'cultural' or 'collective identity'. Furthermore, the postmodern refusal to offer a distinct terminology sometimes leads to the confusion of '-isms' and identities. Although Rattansi (1994: 21) is quite aware of these theoretical implications of postmodernism, he simply brackets the issue.

Miles proposes the *'racism-after-race-relations'* paradigm (Miles and Phisacklea 1979, Guillaumin 1991, Guillaumin 1992, Goldberg 1993, and Taguieff 1987) as an alternative neo-Marxist theorisation of racism. It is not his intention to revive the classical argumentation that racism is 'only' a utilitarian invention of the bourgeoisie to divide the working class and to legitimise colonialism

(Miles 1994: 204). Rather, he locates the explanation for racism in the 'disorganisation of capitalism', strictly speaking, in a field of several contradictions 'between, on the one hand, universalism and humanism, and, on the other, the reproduction of social inequality and exploitation' (Miles 1994: 207). Miles sees the first contradiction in the conflict between the universalising and equalising tendencies embodied in the 'commodification of everything' (Wallerstein 1990[1988]) and the capitalist necessity to reproduce social inequality. Here, racism mediates ideologically by attributing specified social collectivities with essential, naturalising traits, thereby justifying social inequality and uneven development. The second contradiction Miles identifies is that

> between these same universalising tendencies and the reality of extensive cultural diversity rooted in the disaggregation of social formations, within which material reproduction was socially organised prior to the development of the capitalist mode of production, and which have been reproduced parallel with that development while those social formations have not been fully incorporated into the capitalist world economy.
>
> (Miles 1994: 205)

Here, racism makes it possible to racialise social groups resisting capitalist 'progress' as primitive and inferior. The third contradiction Miles points out is that between the tendencies towards economic globalisation and the nationalisation of social formations – that is to say, the partial confinement of capitalist relations of production within the political form of nation-states in which political subjects are nationalised and racialised. While strictly rejecting the concept of 'race' as an analytical one, Miles hardly questions the actual analytical force of the 'traditional' concepts of 'class' and 'class relations', which in view of current social change ought to be reconceptualised (for a similar critique see Wetherell and Potter 1992: 72). However, Miles (1994: 207) does not propose a holistic explanation for the expression of contemporary racism in Europe. He recognises the multiple determination of racism, with which we completely concur.

No monocausal and monodimensional approach is adequate to grasp the complexity of racism. Racialisation is crisscrossed by ethnic, national, gender, class and other social constructions and divisions, thus making highly short-sighted a separating view on 'race' or 'racialisation' as an isolated determinant of social relations. Multidimensional analysis is required in order to obtain adequate historical reconstructions, actual diagnoses and anticipatory prognoses, all of which are necessary to develop promising anti-racist strategies. Among many other things, a multidimensional analysis of racism must take into account adjacent and overlapping phenomena such as antisemitism, nationalism and ethnicism. We shall not discuss the intricate relationship between these discriminatory ideologies and practices here. We will only refer the reader to Aegerter (1996a and 1996b), Bergmann and Erb (1990), Bergmann, Erb and Lichtblau (1995), Geiss (1988), Mitten (1997), Mosse (1990), Pauley (1993),

Poliakov (1979–89 and 1993), Spörk (1996: 23–30), Wippermann (1997), Wistrich (1996: 31–46) and Wodak *et al.* (1990) for discussion of the issue of antisemitism and racism; to Balibar and Wallerstein (1990 [1988]), Fischer and Wölfsingseder (1995), Miles (1993), Silverman (1994) and Wiegel (1995) for discussion of the connections and differences between nationalism and racism; and to Altermatt (1996), Bader (1995), Brumlik (1990: 179–90), Dittrich and Radtke (1990), Erikson (1993), Feagin (1990: 85–118), Heckmann (1991), Lentz (1995), Rex (1990: 141–54) and van Dijk *et al.* (1997) for discussion of the relationship between ethnicity/ethnicism and racism. Apart from these important analyses, however, which focus on only two or three of the '-isms', an accurate and comprehensive study that tries to compare all of them integrally as well as with each other, still remains an urgent need for future research on racism. We cannot comply with this need in the present study, since we are fully occupied with our objective of approaching the phenomena of racism and antisemitism from a discourse-analytical point of view and of analysing the discursive production and reproduction of these discriminatory ideologies and practices.

Four discourse-analytical approaches to racism

Prejudices and stereotypes

Uta Quasthoff (1973, 1978, 1980, 1987, 1989, 1998) was one of the first discourse analysts to attempt to study and categorise prejudiced discourse. Her first major analysis of social prejudices (Quasthoff 1973) does not completely transcend – with a few exceptions – the sentence level, but it opens the field for further research. Quasthoff distinguishes between 'attitudes', 'convictions' and 'prejudices'. She defines *'attitudes'* as the affective position taken towards a person one relates to and to whom one can express dislike or sympathy. *'Convictions'* ascribe qualities to others and often provide rationalisations for negative attitudes (e.g. that 'blacks smell bad'). *'Prejudices'* are mental states defined (normally) as negative attitudes (the affective element) towards social groups with matching stereotypic convictions or beliefs (for the concepts of 'social' and 'linguistic prejudice' see also Heinemann 1998).

For the purposes of linguistic access, Quasthoff defines the term *'stereotype'* as the verbal expression of a certain conviction or belief directed towards a social group or an individual as a member of that social group. The stereotype is typically an element of common knowledge, shared to a high degree in a particular culture (Quasthoff 1987: 786, Quasthoff 1978). It takes the logical form of a judgement that attributes or denies in an oversimplified and general-ising manner, and with an emotionally slanted tendency, particular qualities or behavioural patterns to a certain class of persons (Quasthoff 1973: 28).

To explain the function of social prejudice, Quasthoff considers several psychological approaches that, on the one hand, describe prejudice as an inte-gral part of authoritarian systems (inner psychic functions of stereotypes)

(Adorno *et al.* 1950, Mitscherlich and Mitscherlich 1977) and that, on the other, maintain a scapegoat theory explanation (social functions of stereotypes). Quasthoff also stresses that the externalisation of prejudices in the form of stereotypes functions socially as a unifying and cohesive means for phatic communion. In addition, she rightly argues that social prejudices also have a cognitive-linguistic orientating function. They simplify communication within one's own group, strengthen the sense of belonging, and delineate the outgroup. This is particularly the case during periods of inner resistance and in times of rapid social change. As to the changeability of stereotypic beliefs, Quasthoff's investigations suggest that specific (frequent, relatively close and permanent) forms of personal contact with members of the respective outgroup can positively influence attitudes and beliefs with respect to that outgroup.

Quasthoff's investigations cover all kinds of social prejudices and stereotypes, not only racist and nationalist ones. On the basis of semantic and formal logical criteria, Quasthoff (1973) distinguishes four types of stereotypic expressions according to different degrees of directness:

- 'Analytical' propositions that claim to express a truth are the basic forms of stereotypes. All stereotypes can be traced back to this structure. A quality or behaviour pattern is ascribed to a group. The group is the subject, and the quality or behaviour pattern the predicate. A stereotype of this type takes the form of a statement. From the point of view of logic it is a general-isation that can be formalised by use of a universal quantifier as the specific 'analytical judgement' (e.g. 'Germans are industrious and hard-working'), which suggests that the predicate ascribed to the subject is intentional on the part of the subject and is an essential, inherent, and intrinsic feature of the group.

- Modified (restricted) statements are limited in force or, strictly speaking, in the possibility of fixing the speaker's or writer's own perspective, through the use of certain signals like the subjunctive or the interrogative mood, or impersonal constructions with verbs of saying (*verba dicendi*) or verbs of feeling (*verba sentiendi*) in the surface structure of the utterances (e.g. 'Gypsies are said to have a reputation for stealing'; 'Turks are believed not to be interested in decent housing'). The semantic level of such statements does not show whether the speaker is simply reporting a hegemonic prejudiced opinion or subscribes to it personally.

- Directly expressed stereotypes are utterances in which the speaker explicitly refers to herself or himself by means of personal constructions that consist of the deictic expression 'I' and a verb of believing (*verbum putandi*) or a verb of thinking (*verbum cogitandi*) (e.g. 'I don't think that the Americans are up to our intellectual depth at all').

- In the case of the 'text linguistic type', the stereotype is expressed implicitly (e.g. 'He is Jewish, but he's very nice'), and the prejudiced meaning (that 'Jews are normally not nice') is being presupposed or inferable. The interpretation of 'text linguistic' stereotypes relies on knowledge of context and transcends the sentence level. Inference-triggering devices such as specific adverbs (e.g. the adversative conjunction 'but' in the example mentioned above) suggest this interpretation.

Quasthoff's four categories cover a broad range of verbal expressions and nuances. Since the four types express different grades of directness, their occurrence depends to a great extent on situation and setting. Because of tolerance norms, the second and fourth types occur most frequently.

According to Quasthoff (1973), sentences are the linguistic units most amenable to her type of analysis. However, Quasthoff herself points out that

> [t]he definitional quality that the grammatical unit of the linguistic description of stereotypes is the sentence does not mean that stereotypes empirically have to appear in the form of complete sentences. It solely implies that the semantic unit of a stereotype is a proposition, i.e. reference and predication, as opposed to a certain form of reference as such.
>
> (Quasthoff 1987: 786 and 1989: 183)

A categorisation according to the sentence structure of the most obvious prejudices is only partially able to grasp latent meanings, allusions, indirect strategies, vague formulations, implications, and forms of argumentation, all of which can extend beyond a single sentence and characterise written texts or oral discourse connected with prejudice and racism. In fact, Quasthoff's fourth type of stereotypical expressions already transcends the single-sentence perspective. In addition, since 1973, Quasthoff herself has investigated the role of stereotypes in different kinds of discourse – among other types in everyday argumentation (Quasthoff 1978, 1998) and narratives (Quasthoff 1980) – thus broadening her linguistic horizons towards social prejudice. When, for example, she applied Toulmin's schematism (1969) to the microstructural level of argumentation, Quasthoff came to the conclusion that stereotypes do not exclusively, or even primarily, appear as warrants. If they are used to support a claim, they appear usually as a backing (Quasthoff 1978: 27). Moreover, stereotypes can themselves be either data or claims, supported, in their turn, by other kinds of propositions.

The sociocognitive discourse-analytical approach (van Dijk)

Teun van Dijk does not neatly distinguish between ethnicism, racism and adjacent forms of discrimination (for a recent discussion of these concepts see also van Dijk *et al.* 1997), as he believes that these are fuzzy and overlapping concepts. The model of prejudice used by van Dijk is partially based on sociopsychological considerations similar to those of Quasthoff. According to van Dijk, prejudice is not merely a characteristic of individual beliefs or emotions about social groups, but a shared form of social representation in group members, acquired during processes of socialisation and transformed and enacted in social communication and interaction. Such ethnic attitudes have social functions, e.g. to protect the interests of the ingroup. Their cognitive structures and the strategies of their use reflect these social functions.

(van Dijk 1984: 13)

While Quasthoff most generally stresses the marking of distance toward outgroups and the establishment of ingroup solidarity (and phatic communication) as social functions of prejudice, van Dijk focuses on the 'rationalisation and justification of discriminatory acts against minority groups' in more detail (van Dijk 1984: 13). He designates the categories used to rationalise prejudice against minority groups as 'the 7 D's of Discrimination'. They are dominance, differentiation, distance, diffusion, diversion, depersonalisation or destruction, and daily discrimination. These strategies serve in various ways to legitimise and enact the distinction of 'the other': for example, by dominating the minority groups, by excluding them from social activities, and even by destroying and murdering them (van Dijk 1984: 40).

For the elaboration of a discourse-analytical theory about racist discourse, one of the most valuable contributions of van Dijk's model is the heuristic assistance it provides in linking the generation of prejudice to discursive units larger than the sentence. Van Dijk's initial assumption is that those parts of the long-term memory directly relevant to the production and retention of ethnic prejudices (recognition, categorisation and storage of experience) can be divided into three memory structures: semantic memory, episodic memory and the control system.

According to van Dijk, *semantic memory* is social memory: It is here that the collectively shared beliefs of a society are stored. These beliefs are organised as attitudes, and as such are fitted into group schemata that provide the cognitive basis of our information processing about members of outgroups. Our perception of individual experiences is influenced by these cognitive representations, which are always adapted to pre-existing models. The models themselves are initially acquired during socialisation. The attitudes stored in the group schemata are of a generalised and abstract nature and are determined by their organisation in socially relevant categories of the group that is being evaluated. In van Dijk's view, national origin and/or appearance, socioeconomic status, and sociocultural norms and values, including religion and language, are decisive categories for ethnic prejudice (here again, van Dijk does not distinguish between racist, nationalist and ethnicist beliefs; see Mitten and Wodak 1993: 193 ff.). In linguistic utterances, such attitudes appear as generally accepted statements divorced from the current context (e.g. 'Jews are good business people').

Moreover, continues van Dijk, *episodic memory* retains personal or narrated experiences and events as well as patterns abstracted from these experiences.

The listener constructs a textual representation of a story in episodic memory. This representation allows the listener to reproduce, if necessary, what was told and also how it was told. The listener constructs a model of the story (situation model) that is richer than the discourses about it. Such a model also features previous experiences about the same or similar situations and will also embody instantiated information from general group schemata (van Dijk 1984: 25). The general situational models are the link between narrated events or personally retained experiences and the structures of the semantic memory. Consequently (still in reference to the example quoted above), one unfavorable experience of doing business with a Jewish merchant becomes a situational model that states that 'doing' business with Jews will always have negative results.

In his new context model (van Dijk 1998a), van Dijk distinguishes between specific *event models* and *context models*. He views both types of models as being personal and not shared by a group. Accordingly, van Dijk conceptualises the third structure of long-term memory, the *control system*, as a personal model of the social situation. The task of the control system is to link communicative aims and interests (e.g. persuasion) with the situational and individual social conditions (e.g. the level of education, gender, and relationship to the person one is addressing). Van Dijk calls the processes involved in the perception, interpretation, storage, use, or retrieval of ethnic information about minority groups and their actions 'strategies'. The control system coordinates these various strategies and at the same time monitors the flow of information from long-term memory to short-term memory as well as the storage or activation of situation models in episodic memory.

One of the main strategies of the control system is to link a positive self-presentation – i.e. one acceptable to society and signalling tolerance – with an existing negative attitude to foreigners. Positive self-presentations are expressed in phrases such as 'Personally, I have nothing against Jews, but the neighbours say ...'. The interaction of these three memory systems thus both directly and indirectly influences the decoding and encoding – that take place in the short-term memory – of the received and/or self-produced remarks about minorities. Van Dijk's model can thus explain the cognitive processes of the text recipients: isolated experiences, statements, and symbols, are assigned to general schemata and confirm existing prejudices.

Van Dijk (1984 and 1991) analyses prejudice stories that were elicited systematically at certain points in interviews with different groups of informants in Amsterdam and in the United States. These stories are often introduced by procataleptic disclaimers, which allow a positive self-presentation for the speaker: *apparent denials* ('I have nothing against Blacks/Turks/Jews, but ...'.), *apparent admission* ('Of course, there are also smart Blacks/Turks/Jews, but ...'.), *transfer* ('I don't mind so much, but my neighbour/colleagues ...'.), and *contrast* ('We always had to work a lot, but they ...'). In such cases, the interviewee projects herself or himself as an absolutely tolerant person, who conforms to the explicit and implicit norms of the official policy and morals in the Netherlands or the United States. The alleged negative experience with a singular person or specific group is embedded into a discriminatory narrative discourse as an illustrative example and provides ostensible empirical evidence for the character of the defamed group as a whole. Van Dijk is able to show in a thorough analysis of such stories that the narrative schema developed by Labov and Waletzky (1967) is used, with the sole exception that a resolution is often missing. Consequently, the listener should draw her or his own conclusions. This 'openness' is another profession to the official norm and exempts the speaker from any responsibility. The speakers do not suggest that any measures be taken, they only relate a story. Such narratives cluster around a very small and precise number of topics. Immigrants threaten the population, they are criminal, and their cultural traditions are alien.

Though van Dijk's model can probably account for a wider range of discursive manifestations of prejudice than can Quasthoff's, at times his explicit cognitive approach does not seem to accord sufficient weight to the affective and sociohistorical aspects of prejudiced discourse that can influence the schematic categorisation and perception of 'reality'. Prejudice becomes comprehensible only within its psychological, social, historical and linguistic context, and van Dijk's model could perhaps differentiate more in these areas. Yet the insights gained by van Dijk's analysis of prejudice stories are considerable.

More recently, van Dijk (1991, 1993, 1998a, 1998b) has turned to the analysis of 'elite racism' and to the integration of the concept of 'ideology' into his sociocognitive model, in which he distinguishes analytically between social cognition, discourse and society (the latter including social structures, culture, politics and history). He focuses mainly on the investigation of newspaper editorials, school books, academic discourse, interviews with managers, political speeches and parliamentary debates, with the basic assumption that 'the elite' produces and reproduces the racism that is then implemented and enacted in other social fields. We certainly believe that 'the elite' plays a significant role in the production and reproduction of racism, but we prefer to assume a more reciprocal, less monocausal and unidirectional top-down relationship of influence between the 'elite' and other social groups and strata within a specific society.

Discourse strands and collective symbols

Siegfried and Margret Jäger and the Duisburg group are probably the most prominent researchers in Germany dealing with issues of racism and discourse (S. Jäger 1992 and 1993, M. Jäger 1996a, S. Jäger and M. Jäger 1992, S. Jäger and Januschek 1992, S. Jäger and Link 1993, Kalpaka and Rhätzel 1986, Link 1990 and 1992). Their research was triggered largely by the violent racism that started shortly after 1992, when new and stricter immigration laws were implemented in Germany. Simultaneously, the unification of West Germany and the former communist East Germany erupted in racist violence against many foreigners who were physically attacked and whose asylum homes were set alight. Among other factors, this violence was and continues to be connected to the fact that the unification poses tremendous cultural and economic problems for the Germans and that foreigners provide a comfortable scapegoat (e.g. that millions of people lost their jobs post-unification) for these problems. The Duisburg group has been very active not only in its research and documentation of racism and hostility against foreigners, but also in proposing strategies against it (e.g. see M. Jäger, Cleve, Ruth and S. Jäger 1998: 167–236; Duisburger Institut für Sprach- und Sozialforschung 1999).

In several respects, the group follows and extends the research of van Dijk. Their research technique includes interviewing different groups of people to elicit their attitudes towards 'foreigners' and 'Jews'. In contrast to standard methods for conducting interviews, their method leads people to tell their personal stories in-depth. Besides studying everyday racism, the Duisburg group also conducts media analysis, in particular of the German tabloid, *Bildzeitung*, which launches large-scale campaigns against 'foreigners', but also of the conservative quality daily *Frankfurter Allgemeine Zeitung*, the regional daily newspapers *Frankfurter Rundschau*, *Westdeutsche Allgemeine Zeitung*, *Rheinische Post*, and the social liberal weekly *Der Spiegel*. A primary interest in the analysis of all these newspapers is the press coverage of criminal acts. A recent analysis (M. Jäger, Cleve, Ruth and S. Jäger 1998) shows that most of the papers tend to singularise and individualise (alleged) German perpetrators, and tend to collectivise 'foreigners' who (allegedly) have committed criminal offences. Moreover, 'foreign perpetrators' are marked by reference to their national or ethnic origin in half of the press articles of all newspapers except *Der Spiegel*.

Margret Jäger adopts the same theoretical and methodical framework as Siegfried Jäger. One of her main interests is the relationship between culturalist racism or ethnicism and the discourse about gender (in)equality. In her analysis of fifteen interviews with seven German women and eight German men, she shows that sexism and racism or ethnicism are interconnected in multiple ways, especially in discourse about Turkish men and women, in which the seemingly democratic and, in fact, often rationalising critique of Islamic patriarchy leads to the 'ethnification of sexism' – that is to say, to a view that constructs and stresses misogynous and sexist behaviour as an ethnic feature (M. Jäger 1996a: 10). In pretending that the matter of concern is the suppression of women and the equality of rights for both genders, the women and men interviewed for Margret Jäger's research project tended to fall back upon prejudices such as 'foreigners like Turks are culturally and religiously too different', 'male foreigners are inclined to sexual harassment', 'male foreigners are misogynists, sexists and patriarchal despotic oppressors who despise women' and 'female foreigners are mentally immature and retarded and willingly accept their suppression (visually symbolised by the headscarf) and exploitation by men'. These negative prejudices against 'the others' imply a bundle of positive 'we-are-better-than-they' prejudices towards one's 'own' ingroup, including the prejudice that 'we are democratic, enlightened, non-patriarchal, non-sexist, correct in our sexual contacts and all have equal rights'. Margret Jäger concludes that such racist and ethnicist sweeping generalisations and homogenisations can – at least partly

– be countered by clearly analysing the intricate folding of the discourse on female emancipation and the discourse on migrants and 'foreigners' and by singling out the fatal racist and ethnicist effects of the fallacious generalisations inherent in both discourses.

The main focus in many of the Duisburg studies is discourse semantics, and especially the uncovering of 'collective symbols' that are tied together in 'discourse strands', best explained as thematically interrelated sequences of homogeneous 'discourse fragments' – a 'discourse fragment' is a text or a part of a text that deals with a specific topic, for example with the topic of 'foreigners' (S. Jäger 1993: 181) – which appear on different 'discourse levels' (e.g. science, politics, the media, education, everyday life, business life and administration). 'Collective symbols' are designated as 'cultural stereotypes' in the form of metaphorical and synecdochic symbols that are immediately understood by the members of the same speech community (Link 1982, 1988, 1990 and 1992). Water, natural disasters like avalanches and flood disasters, military activities like invasions, all persuasively representing immigration or migrants as something that has to be 'dammed', are examples of collective symbols, just as the 'ship' metaphor symbolises the effects of immigration as an 'overcrowded boat', and the 'house-and-door' metaphor symbolises the ingroup's (e.g. 'national') territory as a house or building and the stopping of immigration as 'bolting the door'.

In addition, the above-mentioned 'headscarf' serves as a collective symbol that is open to several interpretations, including the reading as a symbol of sexist suppression of Islamic women, as a symbol of the acceptance of this male suppression by the suppressed, and, in general, as a symbol of the cultural and religious difference of Moslems.

The Duisburg group also analyses the construction of 'the Other' with a focus on the pronominal system, on the connotations of specific nouns, verbs, and adjectives, on stylistic features, on tense, mood, and modality, on specific syntactic means and structures, and on argumentation strategies, which are all employed in the presentation of self and other through discourse (S. Jäger 1993).

The results of the Duisburg studies are astounding and disturbing: both latent and manifest racism in Germany are growing and the 'interdiscourse' (the synchronic totality of shared interdiscursive elements like collective symbols, which are acquired through socialisation) is larded with racist utterances and allusions. Antisemitism seems to have been widely replaced by racism against Turks living in Germany, and some of the same racist stereotypes used against Jews in previous times are now used against 'foreigners', and especially against Turks. This does not mean that Germany is free of antisemitism (Stern 1991, Bergmann and Erb 1991, Bergmann, Erb and Lichtblau 1995). Antisemitism has widely been covered by a philosemitic inversion in public discourse.

The Duisburg researchers use Michel Foucault's theory of power and discourse, and elements of van Dijk's sociocognitive model (see above), for their theoretical basis. In contrast to van Dijk and similarly to the discourse-historical approach, the social, political and historical contexts are integrated into the analysis of discourse. They have developed an elaborate method for studying the macro- and micro-levels of discourse (S. Jäger 1993, M. Jäger 1996a, Titscher, Wodak, Meyer and Vetter 1998). They adhere to a wide concept of 'racism' that denotes the exclusion of others because of certain biological or cultural characteristics. The group in power is considered to be employing collective symbols to stigmatise, marginalise and exclude minority groups. In the Duisburg group's analysis, racism is tied to power and hegemony. The analysis does not label exclusionary utterances as racist when verbalised by groups that are not in power (M. Jäger 1996a: 15, see also Mitten and Wodak 1993). Theoretically, the researchers' understanding of 'racism' relies on the approaches of Miles (1992)[1989], Meulenbelt (1993), Hall (1989 and 1994) and Kalpaka and Räthzel (1986):

> We always then call something racism when persons who look differently and practice different customs and traditions and/or speak a different language – they are, all in all, considered to be different from the majority of the population – are judged negatively, and if, in addition, this judgement is in accord with the hegemonic discourse of the respective society.
>
> (M. Jäger 1996b: 35)

Within this paradigm, 'discourse' is defined as a social, not an individual, behaviour: 'I understand discourse as institutionalised language behaviour, this language behaviour determines actions and possesses power. This discourse is also real, constitutes reality' (Link 1983: 60). Consequently, discourse does not manifest actions: it is action. Thus, discourse analysis has to be conceived as analysis of society that aims at disentangling the net of the entire discourse of a society by bringing out the single discourse strands at the single discourse levels (S. Jäger 1993: 184). 'Interdiscourse' – in which the culture and traditions of a society at a certain time are sedimented – is opposed to the (scientific) 'specialised discourses' and, as mentioned above, conceptualised as systems of collective symbols connected to each other through certain 'ruptures in the images' (catachreses). The contradictions that arise from the clash of different systems of collective symbols are most significant for this type of analysis (S. Jäger 1993: 157 ff.). Although each single text is seen as a 'discourse fragment' that may be a part of the 'interdiscourse', more than one 'discourse fragment' can be contained in a single text. This is the case if a text refers to different, clearly separable topics.

The Duisburg researchers analyse their materials primarily in a qualitative way. They argue that the precise and differentiated study of discourse fragments gives insight into the interdiscourse and that quantitative analyses are therefore necessary only in certain cases. An accurate analysis of a specific racist discourse fragment, belonging to a specific discourse strand at a specific discourse level, may serve as an illustration of the entire racist discourse in Germany.

Interesting findings might result if researchers applied this form of analysis in other situations and arrived at intercultural comparisons that could explain the common and different nature, history and manifestation of racism, even in neighbouring and culturally similar countries.

The Loughborough group

The sociopsychologists Margaret Wetherell and Jonathan Potter (1992) oppose sociocognitive approaches that give absolute priority to the cognitive dimension in the analysis of racism and tend to universalise the conditions for racism (see the second section of this chapter, 'How to explain "racism" '; see also Potter and Wetherell 1987). They reject social identity theory and the social cognition approach for their 'lingering perceptualism' (Wetherell and Potter 1992: 47). Wetherell and Potter argue from a constructivist point of view that attitudes and stereotypes are not simply mediated via cognition, but that discourse is actively constitutive of both social and psychological processes, and thus also of racist prejudices. In the manner of Billig (1978, 1985, 1988) and Billig *et al.* (1988), Wetherell and Potter (1992: 59) posit that racism must be viewed as a series of ideological effects with flexible, fluid and varying contents. Racist discourses should therefore not be viewed as static and homogeneous, but as dynamic and contradictory. Even the same person can voice contradictory opinions and ideological fragments in the same discursive event. Consequently, Wetherell and Potter take up Billig's notion of 'ideological dilemmas'. Further-more, they also reject the concept of an immutable identity (see also Wodak *et al.* 1998 for a dynamic conceptualisation of 'identity'). As in the preceding sections, we can only summarise some important aspects of the work of the Loughborough Group and discuss it in the light of the other approaches analysing discriminatory discourse.

Wetherell and Potter (1992: 70) sympathise with, and adopt, the concepts of the 'politics of representation' and the 'definitional slipperiness' of theoreticians like Stuart Hall (1989 and 1994). In part, they have been influenced theoretically by some of Foucault's theses and remarks on discourse, power and truth, as well as by neo-Marxist theoreticians, although they criticise the approaches of Robert Miles and of critical theory (see above) for their Marxist 'determinism' (Wetherell and Potter 1992: 18 ff.) and for a traditional Marxist concept that refers to 'ideology' as 'false consciousness' (Wetherell and Potter 1992: 69) – a critique that, in our view, is at best only partly valid.

Like the Duisburg group and discourse-historical theorisation, the Lough-borough group stresses the context-dependence of racist discourse. They analyse interviews with people from New Zealand from a social-psychological, ethnographic and post-structuralist perspective, apply a detailed method in the investigation of discourse, and try to make the dynamics of racist ideologies explicit by including context information. They bring out the ideological dilemmas and the manifest and latent argumentation patterns (Wetherell and Potter 1992: 178 ff. and 208 ff.).

The two researchers define their task as 'mapping the language of racism' in New Zealand, and draw up a 'racist topography' by charting themes and ideologies through exploration of the heterogeneous and layered texture of racist practices and representations that make up a part of the hegemonic taken-for-granted in this particular society. That which is assumed to be obvious and widely unquestioned characterises a culture and society: against the background of the obvious characteristics, the members of a society specify what political actions will be considered legitimate, what will be considered merely 'trouble-making', what counts as social progress, how can it be impeded, what is racism and how it should most appropriately be countered.

Wetherell and Potter argue that racism is organised through discursive patterns of signification and representation. Therefore, it has to be investigated through the analysis of discourse. Nevertheless, they state that

> [w]e are not wanting to argue that racism is a simple matter of linguistic practice. Investigations of racism must also focus on institutional practices, on discriminatory actions and on social structures and social divisions. But the study of these things is intertwined with the study of discourse. Our emphasis will be on the ways in which a society gives voice to racism and how forms of discourse institute, solidify, change, create and reproduce social formations.
>
> (Wetherell and Potter 1992: 3)

In New Zealand, the history of racism is largely interrelated with the history of colonisation (Wetherell and Potter 1992: 22). In the main, the Māori people become members of the working class. Racist ideology is the means used by the ruling class to consolidate and reproduce its advantage. It does this by presenting its partial and sectional interests as the universal interests of the entire community. On the other hand, '[t]he experience of racism can produce a cohesive, effective and even a powerful platform as Māori people, in the New Zealand case, recognise some crucial joint interests, despite their different positions in an economic hierarchy' (Wetherell and Potter 1992: 73).

Wetherell and Potter argue that ideology misrepresents the functions of the State in creating the conditions for capitalist production. In their neo-Marxist or post-Marxist view, the classical assumption of a causal connection between the economic base and the superstructure is given up, and social determination comes to mean not cause and effect, but the setting of limits and the exerting of pressures on patterns of ideas, so that in some social contexts some chains of thought become more persuasive and more prevalent than in others (Wetherell and Potter 1992: 26). Wetherell and Potter state that many cognitive researchers believe the 'reality', but also the 'ideology', to be separate from discourse, which is individually and socially perceived. In social cognition analysis, they point out, the perceiver often remains a lone individual who forms, apparently in isolation, her or his account of 'racial' traits on the basis of actual similarities and differences between the individuals she or he encounters.

The social-cognitive model of the representational process pits a self-contained individual against the complexities of the real environment. Wetherell and Potter complain that cognition theory suffers from an absence of social theory – which actually seems to be the case. Nevertheless, some of the social-cognitive researchers – for example, van Dijk – stress that they are referring to 'group cognitions' and not to individuals.

Similarities between the Loughborough and Duisburg approaches go beyond emphasis on context-dependence and post-structuralist alignment. The Duisburg concept of 'interdiscourse', at least partly, has its counterpart in the Loughborough concept of 'interpretative repertoire', i.e.

> broadly discernible clusters of terms, descriptions and figures of speech often assembled around metaphors or vivid images. In more structuralist language we can talk of these things as systems of signification and as the building blocks used for manufacturing versions of actions, self and social structures in talk. They are some of the resources for making evaluations, constructing factual versions and performing particular actions.
>
> (Wetherell and Potter 1992: 90)

However, in its concrete analyses, the Loughborough group focuses mainly on narratives and argumentation and does not pay as much attention to metaphors or symbols as do Jürgen Link, Siegfried and Margret Jäger, and their associates.

Another parallel between the two approaches is that both criticise the concepts of 'the individual' and 'the subject'. But whereas the Duisburg group sometimes risks reification of the concept of discourse and, thus, of opening the way to relativism and determinism, Wetherell and Potter, although themselves not neatly protected from relativism, warn explicitly against viewing discourses

> as potent causal agents in their own right, with the processes of interest being the work of one (abstract) discourse on another (abstract) discourse, or the propositions or 'statements' of that discourse working smoothly and automatically to produce objects and subjects.
>
> (Wetherell and Potter 1992: 90)

However, the issue of agency and the question of the dialectics between individual actions and 'social formations' cannot be answered adequately here. This should be pursued in future research on discourse and racism.

2 The discourse-historical analysis of the rhetoric of racism and antisemitism

A context-sensitive, discourse-historical approach

Critique, discourse and context

To a certain extent, the four discourse-analytical approaches presented in chapter 1 have all influenced – either through more or less favourable reception or critical discussion – the theoretical and methodical approach introduced in this section.

We agree with many of Quasthoff's general sociopsychological assumptions of the social function of prejudices as a sociocohesive means for obtaining ingroup solidarity and 'phatic communion', but surpass the single-sentence perspective prevailing in her early work and also try to take into consideration the more latent and allusive meanings of discourses. To a certain degree, but not totally, we share the constructivist approach of Wetherell and Potter as well as their critique of universalising the conditions for racist discrimination, though without adopting their relativist postmodernist viewpoint. We share the Duisburg Group's 'transtextual', interdiscursive, sociopolitical and historical perspective as well as their interest in the analysis of collective symbols and metaphors, but we do not align ourselves with their affiliation with Foucaultian and postmodernist theories of discourse and power, which reify or personify language and discourse as autonomous, collusive actors which steer the speakers and hold the reins. And we adopt several of Teun van Dijk's concepts and categories (e.g. the notions of 'positive self-presentation' and 'negative other-presentation'), but place no emphasis on his sociocognitivism, the latter being incompatible with the hermeneutic basis of our model. Moreover, our assumptions of the relationship of influence between different social groups and strata within a specific society are less monocausal and unidirectional than those of van Dijk, for we do not want to overemphasise a top-down causality of opinion-making and manipulation (i.e. a manipulative impact from the allegedly homogenous 'elite' on the allegedly homogenous masses of ordinary people). In our view – and we have already emphasised this in the second section of chapter 1, 'How to explain "racism"' – the complexities of modern societies can only be grasped by a model of multicausal, mutual influences between different groups of persons within a specific society. That is to say: if we take, for example, politicians as specific and not at all homogeneous groups of elites, then they are best seen both as shapers of specific public opinions and interests and as seismographs that reflect and react to the atmospheric anticipation of changes in public opinion and on the articulation of changing interests of specific social groups and affected parties.

In addition to the four approaches mentioned in chapter 1, in recent years, the discourse-historical approach has increasingly been influenced by other schools and sub-disciplines, especially British discourse analysis in the tradition of Hallidayan systemic functional linguistics (e.g. by Fairclough 1989, 1992, 1995a, Fowler 1996, Hodge and Kress 1991 and van Leeuwen 1993, 1995 and 1996), by classical and new rhetoric as well as argumentation theory (e.g. by Toulmin 1996, Perelman 1976, 1980, 1994, Kopperschmidt 1980, 1989, Kien-pointner 1992, 1996, Kindt 1992, Wengeler 1997) and by German 'politico-linguistics' (e.g. Dieckmann 1964, 1975, 1981, Burkhardt 1996, Jung, Wengeler and Böke 1997, Jarren, Sarcinelli and Saxer 1998, Klein 1998 and Sarcinelli 1998).

Apart from these mainly linguistic and communication theoretical subdis-ciplines, the discourse-historical approach, committed to critical discourse analysis, adheres to the sociophilosophical orientation of critical theory (see Horkheimer and Adorno 1991 [1944], Marcuse 1980, Horkheimer 1992, Bonß and Honneth 1982, Benhabib 1992a, Benhabib 1992b, Honneth 1989, 1990, 1994, Menke and Seel 1993, Calhoun 1995, Habermas 1996, 1998a). As such, it follows a complex concept of social critique that embraces at least three interconnected aspects, two of which are primarily related to the dimension of recognition and one to the dimension of action (for a different distinction between and conceptualisation of three forms of critique – the 'immanent critique', the 'unmasking critique' and the 'critique as crisis diagnosis' – see Benhabib 1992a: 77–110):

'*Text* or *discourse immanent critique*' aims at discovering inconsistencies, (self-) contradictions, paradoxes and dilemmas in the text-internal or discourse-internal, for example, logico-semantic, cohesive, syntactic, performative, presup-positional, implicational, argumentation, fallacious and interactional (e.g. turn-taking) structures. As it is based on a hermeneutic exegesis with the help of specific linguistic and discourse-analytical tools, 'immanent' is here, of course, not meant in the very strict sense of 'without previous knowledge', for no analyst can escape the hermeneutic circle that always implies a certain understanding and preconception (with at least implicit theoretical assumptions) of the specific analytical instruments employed in the interpretation.

In contrast to the still widely unpolitical 'immanent critique', the '*sociodiagnostic critique*' is concerned with the demystifying exposure of the – manifest or latent – persuasive, propagandist, populist, 'manipulative' character of discursive prac-tices. It aims at detecting problematic – 'problematic' from the analyst's normative-ethical perspective as we explain below – social and political goals and functions of discursive practices, at uncovering the responsibilities and the speakers' – sometimes – disguised, contradictory, opposing, ambivalent or 'polyphonic' intentions, claims and interests, which are either inferable from the (spoken or written) discourse itself or from contextual, social, historical and political knowledge.

Apropos 'detection' and 'manipulation': from the metaphorical concepts of 'exposure/uncovering/unmasking' and 'manipulation' there arise at least two epistemic problems that one must self-critically (!) take into account. In a certain sense, the notion 'unmasking' contains the overtones of a know-it-all or know-it-better attitude on the part of the analysts, which can be highly problematic if the concepts of 'truth', 'deception' and 'reality' thus implied remain unquestioned. To speak about 'manipulation', and this is related to the issue just mentioned, could imply reductionist, hardly provable causal assumptions about the effects of language use, about a simple and direct relationship between discursive and other forms of social practices. Apart from that, the meaning of the expression risks incapacitating the recipients (hearers or readers) as autonomous, self-aware and self-reflective psycho-physical organisms. Both these problems can be minimised by circumspection and the greatest possible accuracy on our part as critical analysts. That means that we have to look at the data carefully, to apply our analytical tools prudently and to reconstruct the context of the discursive events meticulously, in order to provide transparent and intersubjectively comprehensible interpretations and analyses.

With sociodiagnostic critique, the analyst exceeds the purely textual or discourse internal sphere. She or he makes use of her or his background and contextual knowledge and embeds the communicative or interactional structures of a discursive event in a wider frame of social and political relations, processes and circumstances. From this point of view, discursive practices are seen as specific forms of social practices (Fairclough 1992) that are related to other forms of social activities. Here, the critical gaze is directed at exposing, inter alia, contradictions and oppositions between discursive and related social practices: for example, between nice declarations that have the function of positive political self-presentation and discrimatory administrative exclusionary practices that conflict with these declarations (see chapter 5). In keeping a watch on discursive practices related to or concerned with social activities under legitimation-obligation (as they may, for example, be connected with exercise of power and hegemony, with the imposition of duties and burdens and with political decisions of restricting an individual's freedom), this critical diagnosis can be seen as a form of social control. This means that critical analysts position themselves politically, and this leads us to a third moment of critique.

While the two aspects of critique mentioned above are primarily, but – since social control is already a practical political matter – not exclusively, related to the epistemic and cognitive dimensions of 'seeing through', of 'illuminating' and 'making transparent' (to use optical metaphors typical of the Enlightenment), the '*prospective critique*' is associated with the ethico-practical dimension. Inasmuch as it is contra-present and seeks to become practical and to change and transform things – by attempting to contribute to the solution of specific social problems and dysfunctionalities – it is political in the action-related sense of 'politics'. This form of critique is practised by Viennese critical discourse analysts who, in the past twenty years, have repeatedly been engaged in the attempt to contribute to the transformation and improvement of communication within public institutions by elaborating proposals and guidelines for reducing language barriers in hospitals, schools, courtrooms, public offices, and media reporting institutions (see Wodak 1996a) as well as guidelines for avoiding sexist language use (Kargl, Wetschanow, Wodak and Perle 1997).

Such an engaged social critique is nurtured ethically by a sense of justice based on the normative and universalist conviction of the unrestricted validity of human rights and by the awareness of suffering, which both take sides *against* social discrimination, repression, domination, exclusion and exploitation and *for* emancipation, self-determination and social recognition (in the Habermasian sense of 'difference-sensible inclusion', Habermas 1996: 172 ff.; see also Honneth 1994 and Calhoun 1995: 193–230). Further, it is motivated by the – perhaps in part utopian – conviction that unsatisfactory social conditions can, and therefore must, be subject to methodical transformation towards fewer social dysfunctionalities and unjustifiable inequalities.

The political model that, in our view, would best help to institutionalise and unfold this form of critique is that of a 'deliberative democracy' based on a free public sphere and a strong civil society, in which all concerned with the specific social problem in question can participate. Within such a political frame – and we will try to illustrate this especially in chapters 5 and 6 of the present book – the communicative structures of the public sphere can be functionalised as a wide network of sensors that allow one to deal with, to differentiate and to react to social and political problems of legitimation and to control and influence the use of political – legislative, juridical, administrative and executive – power (Habermas 1996: 290). This model of democracy, which is also a theory of rational argumentation (see pp. 70–80 of the present book) and discursive conflict solving (Benhabib 1997: 37), particularly focuses on the concepts of 'deliberation' and 'discourse' as well as on the critical function of the public. Its proponents assume that language is the central medium of democratic organisation and that the free public discursive exchange of different interests, wishes, viewpoints, opinions and arguments is vital for a pluralistic democracy in a modern decentered society, since it is essential for deliberatively and justly organising the different preferences, and since it can also have a critical influence on the relationship between legality and democratic legitimation within a political system. The quality of legislative and administrative power changes if it remains bound to an ongoing, public discursive-democratic process of the formation of opinion and of will as well as of political control, by means of which political power is critically watched during all stages of its exertion, and through which the implementation of laws can even be swayed in advance (see Habermas 1996: 289 ff.)

A very specific form of critical social practice directed against the status quo is '*retrospective critique*'. In criticising the status quo ante – that is to say, in critically reconstructing the past, the effects of which are still related to the present – and, at the same time, in criticising the present way of dealing with the past – that is to say, in critising the status quo – it has the quality of prospective critique, since it aims at the revision of an actual 'picture' or 'narrative' of history and, in consequence and in the future, at a new, responsible way of dealing with the past and its effects.

Though critique implies a certain degree of social distance on the part of the observing critics, the endeavour to 'intervene' (in the sense of Adorno 1963) for a social change – for example towards more social justice – is always situated. Critics are not disembodied heremitic individuals, but interested members of specific societies and social groups with specific points of view (see Walzer 1990 [1987]: 43–79). In order to avoid an excessively simplistic and one-sided perspective, social critique has to be carefully and self-reflectively applied. It has to keep loyalty, first, to the empathy with the victims of discrimination, second, to the principles of justice and, third, to the principles of rationality (not to be understood in the negative and restricted sense of 'instrumental rationality') that can help to lead to a better future.

We will conclude these remarks on 'critique' with a quotation from one of the founding figures of critical theory: 'To translate critical theory into political action is the yearning of those who take it seriously. There is, however, no general recipe for this, except perhaps the necessity of recognising one's own responsibility' (Horkheimer, quoted by O'Neill 1979: 273).[1]

One methodical way for critical discourse analysts to minimise the risk of critical biasing and to avoid simply politicising, instead of accurately analysing, is to follow the principle of triangulation: one of the most salient distinguishing features of the discourse-historical approach, compared to most of the approaches already mentioned, is its endeavour to work interdisciplinarily, multi-methodically and on the basis of a variety of different empirical data as well as background information (see for example Wodak *et al.* 1998 and Wodak *et al.* 1999). Depending on the respective object of investigation, it attempts to transcend the pure linguistic dimension and to include, more or less systematically, the historical, political, sociological and/or psychological dimension in the analysis and interpretation of a specific discursive occasion.

In investigating historical and political topics and texts, the discourse-historical approach attempts to integrate much available knowledge about the historical sources and the background of the social and political fields in which discursive 'events' are embedded. Further, it analyses the historical dimension of discursive actions by exploring the ways in which particular genres of discourse are subject to diachronic change (Wodak *et al.*, 1990; Wodak *et al.*, 1994).

In accordance to other approaches devoted to critical discourse analysis, and this has already been touched upon above, the discourse-historical approach perceives both written and spoken language as a form of social practice (Fairclough and Wodak 1997). A 'discourse' is a way of signifying a particular domain of social practice from a particular perspective (Fairclough 1995a: 14). As critical discourse analysts we assume a dialectical relationship between particular discursive practices and the specific fields of action (including situations, institutional frames and social structures) in which they are embedded: on the one hand, the situational, institutional and social settings shape and affect discourses, and on the other, discourses influence discursive as well as non-discursive social and political processes and actions. In other words, discourses as linguistic social practices can be seen as constituting non-discursive and discursive social practices and, at the same time, as being constituted by them.

To put it more precisely: 'discourse' can be understood as a complex bundle of simultaneous and sequential interrelated linguistic acts that manifest themselves within and across the social fields of action as thematically interrelated semiotic, oral or written tokens, very often as 'texts', that belong to specific semiotic types, i.e. genres.

We conceive 'texts' as materially durable products of linguistic actions, as communicatively dissociated, 'dilated' linguistic actions that during their reception are disembodied from their situation of production (see Ehlich 1983, Graefen 1997: 26, Reisigl 2000 in print: 231), whereas a 'genre' may be characterised, following Norman Fairclough, as the conventionalised, more or less schematically fixed use of language associated with a particular activity, as 'a socially ratified way of using langauge in connection with a particular type of social activity' (Fairclough 1995a: 14).

It is recommended that a very general 'genre analysis' of the genres involved in a discourse precedes the detailed analyses of the selected, concrete linguistic tokens, for example, texts. In order to be able to identify the idiosyncratic peculiarities of a specific singular text, one has to know something about the general features and structures of the semiotic type, that is to say, of the institutionalised, codified pattern of linguistic (inter)action to which the concrete text belongs. In this respect, particularly the macro-structures of syntactic cohesion and semantic coherence, the global mood structure (the exchange of speech acts or speech functions) and genre-specific stylistic features, can be the focus of analysis. Only against the background of such an analysis – and we will tentatively exemplify such an analysis in chapter 5 with the genre of 'official notification' – can the analysts adequately capture a specific piece of written or spoken text.

'Fields of action' (Girnth 1996) may be understood as segments of the respective societal 'reality', which contribute to constituting and shaping the 'frame' of discourse. The spatio-metaphorical distinction among different fields of action can be interpreted as a distinction among different functions or socially institutionalised aims of discursive practices. Thus, in the area of political action – and all three case studies with which we are dealing in the present book are in a wider sense 'localised' within this area – we distinguish between the functions of legislation, self-presentation, manufacturing of public opinion, developing party-internal consent, advertising and vote-getting, governing as well as executing and controlling as well as expressing (oppositional) dissent (see the figure below). A 'discourse' about a specific topic can find its starting point within one field of action and proceed through another one. Discourses and discourse topics 'spread' to different fields and discourses. They cross between fields, overlap, refer to each other or are in some other way socio-functionally linked with each other.

These discursive characteristics are described under labels that include 'textual chains', 'intertextuality' (see Beaugrande and Dressler 1981, Fairclough 1992: 101–36), 'interdiscursivity' (Fairclough 1995a: 133), 'orders of discourse' and 'hybridity'. 'Hybridity' refers to the heterogeneous mixture of different genres or genre features in a concrete linguistic token (written or oral) or a new genre, and 'interdiscursivity' means both the mutual relationships of discourses and the connection, intersecting or overlapping, of different discourses 'within' a particular heterogeneous linguistic product. 'Textual chains', on the other hand, refers to the sequence or succession of thematically or/and functionally related texts, which is preshaped by the frame of particular configurations of conventionalised linguistic practices (i.e. the ordered relationship within and between the fields of action) that reflect the social order in its discursive facet, that is to say, the 'orders of discourse' (Fairclough 1995a: 10).

We can represent the relationship between fields of action, genres and discourse topics with the example of the area of political action in figure 2.1, which is an elaboration and extension of the model proposed by Girnth (1996: 69).

We will illustrate and explain this general, abstract figure by the three examples of our case studies in chapters 3, 4 and 5, in figure 3.1, figure 4.1 and figure 5.1. There, we respresent diagrammatically our respective objects of investigation of the three case studies, the primary data we are considering, and the interrelationships between the political fields of action, the genres involved and the discourse topics related to the three discourses analysed, viz. the discourse about the 'Waldheim Affair' that arose in 1986, the discourse about the 'Austria First Petition' or 'Anti-Foreigner Petition', which was initiated by the right-wing and populist Austrian 'Freedom Party' FPÖ in the early nineties, and the discourse about aliens' residence permits in Austria in 1996, 1997 and 1998.

Figure 2.2 further illustrates the interdiscursive and intertextual relationships between discourses, discourse topics, genres (as types) and texts (as tokens). In this diagram, interdiscursivity (e.g. the intersection of discourse A and discourse B) is indicated by the two big overlapping ellipses. Intertextual relationships in general – whether of an explicitly referential kind, a formally or structurally iconic (diagrammatical) kind, or in the form of topical correlations, evocations, allusions or (direct and indirect) quotations – are represented by dotted double arrows. The assignment of texts to genres is signalled by simple arrows. The topics to which a text refers are indicated by small ellipses to which simple dotted arrows point; the topical intersection of different texts is signalled by the overlapping small ellipses. Finally, the specific intertextual relationship of thematic reference of one text to another is indicated by simple broken arrows.

Let us briefly exemplify this abstract distinction in figure 2.3 by a constructed, but plausible example that illustrates selected, potential interdiscursive and intertextual relationships between the Austrian discourse about the 'Austria

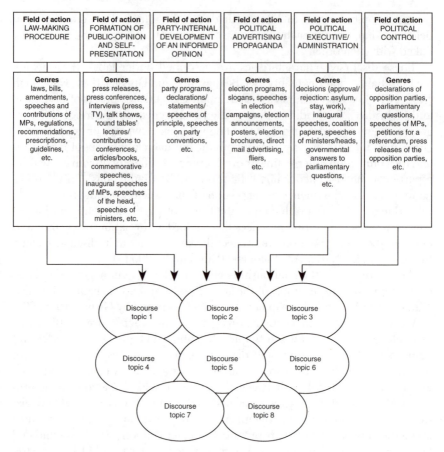

Field of action LAW-MAKING PROCEDURE	Field of action FORMATION OF PUBLIC-OPINION AND SELF-PRESENTATION	Field of action PARTY-INTERNAL DEVELOPMENT OF AN INFORMED OPINION	Field of action POLITICAL ADVERTISING/ PROPAGANDA	Field of action POLITICAL EXECUTIVE/ ADMINISTRATION	Field of action POLITICAL CONTROL
Genres laws, bills, amendments, speeches and contributions of MPs, regulations, recommendations, prescriptions, guidelines, etc.	**Genres** press releases, press conferences, interviews (press, TV), talk shows, 'round tables' lectures/ contributions to conferences, articles/books, commemorative speeches, inaugural speeches of MPs, speeches of the head, speeches of ministers, etc.	**Genres** party programs, declarations/ statements/ speeches of principle, speeches on party conventions, etc.	**Genres** election programs, slogans, speeches in election campaigns, election announcements, posters, election brochures, direct mail advertising, fliers, etc.	**Genres** decisions (approval/ rejection: asylum, stay, work), inaugural speeches, coalition papers, speeches of ministers/heads, governmental answers to parliamentary questions, etc.	**Genres** declarations of opposition parties, parliamentary questions, speeches of MPs, petitions for a referendum, press releases of the opposition parties, etc.

Discourse topic 1 Discourse topic 2 Discourse topic 3

Discourse topic 4 Discourse topic 5 Discourse topic 6

Discourse topic 7 Discourse topic 8

Figure 2.1 Selected dimensions of discourse as social practice

First Petition' and the Austrian discourse about 'national security' (for a detailed analysis of the discourse about the 'Austria First Petition' see chapter 4).

The two discourses partly overlap, and this is symbolised by the two big overlapping ellipses. The two specific texts selected from the whole discourse about the petition are the text of the petition itself and the text of a speech held by Jörg Haider during the campaign for the petition. The text of the 'Austria First Petition' can be assigned to the political genre of 'petition for a referendum' and is primarily situated in the field of political control. The text of Haider's speech may be a hybrid mixture that contains both elements of an election speech and of an alehouse conversation. This presupposed, it is primarily located in the field of political advertising or propaganda, but, in addition, also in the fields of political control and of formation of public opinion. This text may have been produced after the text of the petition itself and may explicitly refer to the petition text as a whole (as is indicated by the dotted double arrow), e.g. by a wording like 'as we demand in our petition', or simply

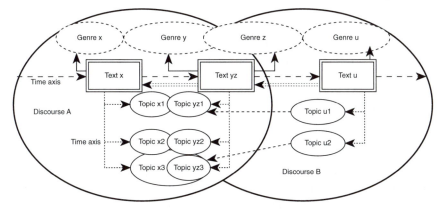

Figure 2.2 Interdiscursive and intertextual relationships between discourses, discourse topics, genres and texts

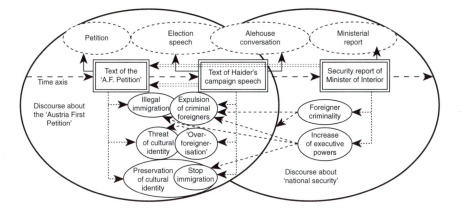

Figure 2.3 Interdiscursive and intertextual relationships between the discourse about the 'Austria First Petition' and the discourse about the 'national security'

share some topics with the petition text, without explicitly mentioning the petition (as indicated by the intersections of the small ellipses), or explicitly refer to specific topics of the petition text, by a wording like 'as we pick out as a central theme in point 6 of the petition' (as indicated by the simple, bending broken arrow). Let as further presume that this text speaks extensively about issues related to the topic of 'national security'. If this is the case, it also belongs to the political discourse about 'national security'. In this second discourse, we hypothesise, many other texts participate, including ministerial reports (genre), such as a specific security report of the Ministry of the Interior. As indicated by the dotted double arrow, this text may be intertextually related to the text of the petition. It may, for example, be related by explicit naming of the petition text in general, or by topical overlapping of the two texts without explicit reference. For reasons of clarity and comprehensibility, this latter intertexual relationship is not specifically indicated in figure 2.3, as it would be if there were overlapping small ellipses, for instance an ellipsis that represents the report's topic of internal national security and that overlaps with the ellipses standing for the topics of 'illegal immigration' and 'expulsion of illegal foreigners'. An intertextual relationship could also be established by the report's explicit thematic reference to topics of the petition: for example, by the report's reference to the demands in points 4 and 11 of the petition, in which the Austrian Freedom Party (FPÖ) requests an increase in executive powers (point 4) and the creation of the legal basis for the possibility of immediate expulsion and an imposition of residence prohibitions for foreign criminals (point 11; see chapter 4). We can hypothesise that the ministerial report refers to these two topics and points out that these claims are already fulfilled by the official Austrian governmental policy. Finally, we may assume that there could exist an explicit intertextual or interdiscursive relationship between the report's topic of 'foreigner criminality' and the discourse about the 'Austria First Petition' (as indicated by the arrow pointing from the small ellipse symbolising the topic of 'foreigner criminality' to the big ellipse indicating the whole discourse about the FPÖ-petition): for example, if the report were to tell us that in the public debate about the petition many of the prejudices about an allegedly high 'foreigner criminality' were reproduced, and that these prejudices are disproved by the criminal statistics contained in the report.

Discursive practices are socially constitutive in a number of ways. First, they play a decisive role in the genesis and production of certain social conditions. This means that discourses may serve to construct collective subjects like 'races', nations and ethnicities. Second, they might perpetuate, reproduce or justify a certain social status quo (and 'racialised', 'nationalised' and 'ethnicised' identities that are related to it). Third, they are instrumental in transforming the status quo (and 'racialising concepts', nationalities and ethnicities related to it). Fourth, discursive practices may have an effect on the dismantling or even destruction of the status quo (and of racist, nationalist and ethnicist concepts related to it). According to these general aims one can distinguish between constructive, perpetuating, transformational and destructive social macro-functions of discourses.

To explore the interconnectedness of discursive and other social practices as well as structures, we employ, as already mentioned, the principle of triangulation (cf. Cicourel, 1974); i.e. we combine various interdisciplinary, methodical and source-specific approaches to investigate a particular discourse phenomenon. In exploring the discursive construction of collective groups like 'races', nations and ethnicities, our interdisciplinary approach combines historical, sociopolitical and linguistic perspectives. Intradisciplinarily, we apply various methods of one and the same discipline. In addition, the principle of triangulation implies using various methods of data collection and the analysis of different corpora and genres, depending on the topic in question.

Our triangulatory approach is based on a concept of 'context' which takes into account

- the immediate language or text-internal co-text, i.e. the 'synsemantic environment' (see Bühler 1982[1934]) or 'semantic prosody' of a single utterance (lexical solidarities, collocational particularities and connotations, implications, presuppositions as well as thematic and syntactic coherence), and the local interactive processes of negotiation and conflict management (including turn-taking, the exchange of speech acts or speech functions, mitigation, hesitation and perspectivation)
- the intertextual and interdiscursive relationship between utterances, texts, genres and discourses (discourse representation and allusions or evocations)
- the extra linguistic social/sociological variables and institutional frames of a specific 'context of situation' (the formality of situation, the place, the time, the occasion of the communicative event, the group/s of recipients, the interactive/political roles of the participants, their political and ideological orientation, their sex or gender, age, profession, level of education as well as their ethnic, regional, national, religious affiliation or membership)
- the broader sociopolitical and historial context which the discursive practices are embedded in and related to; that is to say, the fields of action and the history of the discursive event as well as the history to which the discourse topics are related.

The history of the discourse-historical approach

The study in which this fourth dimension of context, and for which the discourse-historical approach was actually developed, first tried to trace in detail the constitution of an antisemitic stereotyped image, or '*Feindbild*', as it emerged in public discourse in the 1986 Austrian presidential campaign of Kurt Waldheim (Wodak *et al.* 1990, Mitten 1992, Gruber 1991). Since we will go into this investigation in more detail in chapter 3, here we will pass immediately to the subsequent study that was in neat topical connection with the study on Austrian postwar antisemitism.

The two-year research project of which this study was the result was carried out on the occasion of the Austrian '*Gedenkjahr* 1988', the year in which the 50th anniversary of Austria's occupation by the 'Third Reich' was commemorated. In the study, entitled 'Austria's languages of the past' (see Wodak *et al.* 1994), the main interests of investigation were

- the publication and the media treatment of the report by a commission of seven international historians on former president Waldheim's Nazi past in February
- the official political commemoration of the Austrian '*Anschluß*' in March
- the unveiling of a 'memorial against war and fascism' by the sculptor Alfred Hrdlicka in November, as well as the controversial discussions that preceded it for several months

- the premiere of the play 'Heldenplatz' by Thomas Bernhard in November, which deals with Austrian antisemitism then and now and its psycho-terrorising long-term impact on surviving Jewish victims
- the commemoration of the 50th anniversary of the November pogrom.

Specifically, the data base of this interdisciplinary discourse-historical study included a great variety of media genres (all kinds of printed media, radio reports, television news shows, television and newspaper series) as well as statements and addresses of Austrian politicians. The richness of the data allowed a differentiated examination of the official political and media recollection and critical reconsideration of the Austrian National-Socialist past, of the often conflicting narratives on Austrian history and of some related convenient myths, such as 'Austria was the first victim of the Nazi politics of dictatorship and territorial expansionism'.

The discourse-historical approach has been further elaborated in a number of more recent studies: for example, in a study on racist discrimination against immigrants from Romania and in a study on the discourse about nation and national identity in Austria.

The first study (see Matouschek, Wodak and Januschek 1995) focused on the changing of Austrians' attitudes towards their Eastern Central European neighbours. It studied the Austrian political and mass media discourse about Romania and Romanians before and just after the fall of the 'Iron Curtain' in 1989 and 1990. One of the most striking findings was that the politicians' debates, addresses and interviews as well as the mass media reports showed a tendency subsequently to shift from expressing and declaring compassion with the Romanians who were dictatorially terrorised, intimidated, tormented, and repressed by Ceauscescu's regime, to a more or less arrogant 'we-are-better' and patronising advising of how to reform Romania and implement democratic structures, and to the attempt to justify economically the rejection of the absorption and integration of Romanian asylum-seekers and refugees in Austria. After the Romanian 'revolution' in December 1989, the apparent initial sympathy soon gave way both to manifest protests against Romanian asylum seekers depicted negatively by manifest racist, that is to say, phenotypical, visible attributions of unpleasant appearance, criminal disposition and propensity to sexual violence, and to disguising rationalisations of the rejection by putting forward economic reasons – like costs, the 'unbearable' number of the refugees endangering Austria's socioeconomic stability, and the Romanians' non-vitally necessary economic motivation for migration (keyword: 'economic refugees') – as an excuse (for more details see the section 'Some historical information about Austria' in chapter 4).

The latter study was concerned with the analysis of the relationships between the discursive construction of national sameness and the discursive construction of difference leading to political and social exclusion of specific outgroups. In this study, we wanted to know how the imagined communities of nations and the respective national identities are constructed in discourse, and what topics, discursive strategies and linguistic devices are employed to construct national sameness and uniqueness on the one hand, and differences from other national collectives on the other. These questions were investigated in a series of case studies on the Austrian identity and nation. Taking several current social-scientific approaches as a point of departure, we developed a method of description and analysis which has applications beyond the discursive production of national identity in the specific Austrian examples studied. Our findings suggested that discourses about nations and national identities rely on at least four types of discursive macro-strategies (see the distinction between the four general social macro-functions): constructive strategies (aiming at the construction of national identities), preservative or justificatory strategies (aiming at the conservation and reproduction of national identities or narratives of identity), transformative strategies (aiming at the change of national identities) and destructive strategies (aiming at the dismantling of national identities). Depending on the context – that is to say, on the social field or domain in which the 'discursive events' related to the topic under investigation take place – one or other of the aspects connected with these strategies is brought into prominence.

In the light of this discourse-historical analysis, the traditional ideal-typical models of the '*Staatsnation*' (state-centred concept of nation) and the '*Kulturnation*' (culture-centred concept of nation) appeared to be inappropriate for the description of a specific empirical nation-state, on the assumption that the two concepts are strictly mutually exclusive. Both state and culture, in almost all of our data, played a role in the construction of national identity, though in official discourse – exemplified by political commemorative speeches as well as by press articles and political campaigns – culture was of slight importance. In semi-official and quasi-private discourse, however – the data studied were group discussions and interviews – cultural ideas reaching to the imagination of a common descent and ideas of an 'innate nationality' came to the fore. Thus, the study revealed that the distinction between the two concepts of nation is best understood as illuminating differences in national self-image *within* one and the same nation-state – strictly speaking, distinctions between different political and ideological orientations and affiliations within this state (for more details see Wodak *et al.* 1998, Reisigl 1998, de Cillia, Reisigl and Wodak 1999 and Wodak *et al.* 1999).

In all of the four studies taken from the Austrian context, discriminatory, racist and antisemitic as well as chauvinist utterances sometimes occurred simultaneously, especially in everyday conversations (which for the first study were tape-recorded in the streets; see chapter 3). In more official settings, nationalist, racist and antisemitic stereotypes occurred in a more vague form, mostly as allusions and implicit evocations triggered by the use of vocabulary that was characteristic of the historical period of National Socialism.

As explained in chapter 1, antisemitic and racist discourses are both of a syncretic nature. Their discursive strategies – e.g., of dissimilation (the discursive construction of the 'other' through the strategy of dissimilation is the precondition for every prejudiced discourse), of negative presentation and of exclusion

– and their linguistic realisations can be very similar, but the topics of the stereotypes partially vary. New immigrants from the former Eastern Bloc countries are seen as lazy, dirty, criminal and (as far as men are concerned) as sexually threatening. In general, the so-called 'foreigners' are seen as noisy and idle, as outrageous 'parasites' who take advantage of the social welfare system, as an economic threat by leading to an increase in unemployment rates, as being unwilling to integrate and assimilate, and thus as a threat of the national and cultural identity by 'over-infiltration' and 'inundation'. Jews very often are viewed as rich, intellectual and connected worldwide. Especially in Germany, antisemitic stereotypes often appear in the mask of philosemitism (Stern 1991): the previously negative prejudices are changed into extremely positive ones and appear the other way round in a new stereotypical discourse.

Categories of analysis

The specific discourse-analytical approach applied in the four studies referred to was three-dimensional. After having first established the specific *contents* or *topics* of a specific discourse with racist, antisemitic, nationalist or ethnicist ingredients, second, the *discursive strategies* (including argumentation strategies) were investigated. Then, third, the *linguistic means* (as types) and the specific, context-dependent *linguistic realisations* (as tokens) of the discriminatory stereotypes were looked into.

   In the following, we will describe abstractly some of the discourse-analytical tools useful in the analysis of discourses about 'racial', 'national' and 'ethnic' issues. There are several discursive elements and strategies which, in our discourse-analytical view, deserve to receive special attention. Picking five out of the many different linguistic or rhetorical means by which persons are discriminated against in an enthnicist or racist manner, we orientate ourselves to five simple, but not at all randomly selected, questions: How are persons named and referred to linguistically? What traits, characteristics, qualities and features are attributed to them? By means of what arguments and argumentation schemes do specific persons or social groups try to justify and legitimise the exclusion, discrimination, suppression and exploitation of others? From what perspective or point of view are these namings, attributions and arguments expressed? Are the respective discriminating utterances articulated overtly, are they even intensified or are they mitigated?

   According to these questions, we are especially interested in five types of discursive strategies, which are all involved in the positive self- and negative other-presentation. By 'strategy' we generally mean a more or less accurate and more or less intentional plan of practices (including discursive practices) adopted to achieve a particular social, political, psychological or linguistic aim. As far as the discursive strategies are concerned – that is to say, systematic ways of using language – we locate them at different levels of linguistic organisation and complexity.

First, there are *referential strategies* or *nomination strategies* by which one constructs and represents social actors: for example, ingroups and outgroups. This is done in a number of ways, such as membership categorisation devices, including reference by tropes, biological, naturalising and depersonalising metaphors and metonymies, as well as by synecdoches in the form of a part standing for the whole (*pars pro toto*) or a whole standing for the part (*totum pro parte*).

Second, once constructed or identified, the social actors as individuals, group members or groups are linguistically provided with predications. *Predicational strategies* may, for example, be realised as stereotypical, evaluative attributions of negative and positive traits in the linguistic form of implicit or explicit predicates. These strategies aim either at labelling social actors more or less positively or negatively, deprecatorily or appreciatively. They cannot neatly be separated from the nomination strategies. Moreover, in a certain sense, some of the referential strategies can be considered to be specific forms of predicational strategies, because the pure referential identification very often already involves a denotatively as well as connotatively more or less deprecatory or appreciative labelling of the social actors.

Third, there are *argumentation strategies* and a fund of *topoi* through which positive and negative attributions are justified, through which, for example, it is suggested that the social and political inclusion or exclusion, the discrimination or preferential treatment of the respective persons or groups of persons is justified.

Fourth, discourse analysts may focus on the *perspectivation*, *framing* or *discourse representation* by means of which speakers express their involvement in discourse, and position their point of view in the reporting, description, narration or quotation of discriminatory events or utterances.

Fifth, there are *intensifying strategies* on the one hand and *mitigation strategies* on the other. Both of them help to qualify and modify the epistemic status of a proposition by intensifying or mitigating the illocutionary force of racist, anti-semitic, nationalist or ethnicist utterances. These strategies can play an important role in the discursive presentation inasmuch as they operate upon it by sharpening it or toning it down.

Figure 2.4 sums up the selected strategic aspects of self- and other-presentation.

Referential and predicational strategies

The simplest and most elementary form of linguistic and rhetorical discrimination is that of identifying persons or groups of persons linguistically by naming them derogatorily, debasingly or vituperatively. Single anthroponymic terms like the German '*Neger*' and '*Nigger*', '*Zigeuner*', '*Jud*', '*Kanake*' and '*Tschusch*' (Austrian German) are sufficient to perform racist or ethnicist slurs on their own, as they connotatively convey disparaging, insulting meanings, without any other attributive qualification. Before we analyse and discuss some of these debasing appellative anthroponyms and 'collective proper names' in more detail and

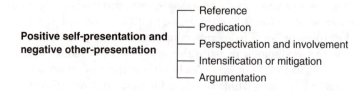

Figure 2.4 Strategies of self- and other-presentation

with concrete discursive examples, we want to give an overview – albeit very selective, provisional and summarising – of the general potential of personal reference for discriminating against people on the one hand and, on the other, for linguistically constructing or representing people, seemingly more or less 'neutrally', with respect or by holding them in esteem. In our incomplete typology, we cannot take into consideration the countless metaphoric and metonymic expressions by which people can be referred to. The mere attempt to systematise the metaphorical reference would easily fill a whole book. However, we will discuss at least some of the most frequent metaphors employed in discriminatory discourses about migrants and migration (see below pp. 58–60). The common feature of all the labellings listed in the following figure is that they are based on a referential identification procedure which is tropologically described as synecdochisation (see also Zimmerman 1989 and see below): a specific feature, trait or characteristic is selectively pushed to the fore as a 'part for the whole', as a representative depictor. Because of the descriptive quality of such referential categorisations, linguistic identification is already related to strategic predication and thus very often involves evaluation. And as we will see in the next section, reference can also be closely associated with argumentation. As far as the relationships among the different referential categories are concerned, we have to stress that they are not strictly disjunctive, as one can easily recognise by looking at figure 2.5. The terms between square brackets indicate that the expressions before the bracket can also be assigned to the referential category named by the term within brackets. The terminological labels listed in figure 2.5 in the column 'linguistic means' very often are hybrid compounds that combine Greek and Latin morphemes. In the following typology, the Greek morpheme 'onym', meaning 'name', can stand for both common and proper nouns.

Several referential strategies mentioned in figure 2.5 have been borrowed and adapted from Theo van Leeuwen's system network of representation of social actors in discourse (see van Leeuwen 1993 and 1996). Without extensively and exhaustively explaining the whole systematisation, we pick out those of van Leeuwen's analytical categories which are of great help for us in accurately describing some of the more subtle forms of discriminatorily, as well as positive-representatively, constructing, identifying or hiding social actors, viz. the categories of 'exclusion', 'inclusion', 'suppression', 'backgrounding', 'passivation', 'categorisation', 'specification', 'genericisation', 'assimilation', 'collectivisation', 'aggregation', 'impersonalisation', 'abstraction' and 'objectivation' (see also van Dijk and Rojo 1997).

The social actors' *exclusion from* or *inclusion in* the linguistic representations can serve many different psychological, social or political purposes or interests on the side of the speakers or writers. Linguistic exclusion is not only strategically employed to conceal persons responsible for discriminatory activities, it has clearly discriminating effects, as in cases of sexist ignoring of women by not naming them (pretending, for example, that the so-called 'generic masculine' in languages like German would linguistically include women, whereas its demonstrable interpretations by the majority of hearers or readers neglect them, and this leads to much actual disadvantaging of women in all societal domains), or in cases of linguistic underrepresentation of ethnic minorities by not giving them adequate access to mass media and by not reporting about them to an adequate extent. Linguistic inclusion – though it is very often an indicator of fair and just representation and treatment – can sometimes have a disguising, relativising or averting function. This is the case if the mention of many different social actors or groups of social actors (for example in the rhetorical form of a *totum pro parte*) hides the fact that a specific (advantageous or disadvantageous) treatment, a newly gained improvement or an accusation only concerns a subgroup of the persons mentioned and pretends that there is equal treatment, whereas inequalities and injustices remain in effect.

Van Leeuwen (1996: 38–41) distinguishes between two different forms of linguistic exclusion. While '*suppression*' means the radical, total exclusion that leaves no traces in the representation of specific social actors involved in a matter with which a text is dealing, as there is no reference to the social actors in question anywhere in the text, '*backgrounding*' refers to a less radical, de-emphasising exclusion, for the excluded social actors can be inferred with partial or total certainty from elsewhere in the text. Backgrounding can, among other strategies, be realised syntactically through '*passivation*'.

Among other concepts, the different degrees of more or less direct and explicit inclusion are analysed by van Leeuwen in terms of categorisation, specification/genericisation and impersonalisation.

'*Categorisation*' in the sense in which van Leewen uses it means the representation of social actors by functionalising, identifying or appraising them: in other words, by referring to them by virtue of ascribing to them identities, functions and positive or negative evaluations they share with others.

Though we adopt several of van Leeuwen's categories, we also redefine some of them. On the one hand, we understand 'identification' in a broader sense than Theo van Leeuwen does, taking it as hyperonym for all forms of personal reference by nomination. On the other hand, we conceive of 'classification' in the very strict sense of identifying a person by ascribing her or him a general status of social class membership. Van Leeuwen speaks about 'classification' – which he considers to be a specific form of identification – whenever

Selected strategies	Linguistic means	Examples of realisations (types)
COLLECTIVISATION	• deictics • collectives (they can also belong to the respective categories mentioned in the following rows)	we, us, they, them family, group, team, tribe, troupe/army, class, population, the people, 'ethnos', nation (literally and originally an origonym), race (originally possibly an origonym), '*Volk*', community, union, majority
SPATIALISATION	• toponyms used as metonymies or/and personifications (place/state/town for people)	*Deutschland* (Germany), *Österreich* (Austria), Turkey, Asia, Africa, America, *das Ausland* (the foreign countries)
	• anthroponyms referring to a person in terms of living on a place	resident, inhabitant, occupier, dweller
DE-SPATIALISATION	• de-toponymic anthroponyms (including reference based on local orientation)	*WienerIn* (Viennese), *EngländerIn* (Englishman/Englishwoman), Africans, '*AusländerIn*' ('foreigner', 'outlander'), *InländerInnen*, '*SüdländerIn*' ('southerner'), Europeans, 'Indians', Asians, Africans, Americans
	• de-adverbial anthroponyms	outsider, insider
EXPLICIT DISSIMILATION	• xenonyms	'alien' ('*FremdeR*'), stranger (*Fremdling*), the others,
ORIGINALISATION	• origonyms	allochthones, autochthones, natives, Aborigines, compatriots, ancestors
ACTIONALISATION/ PROFESSIONAL-ISATION	• actionyms/praxonyms and professionyms	asylum seekers, migrant, refugee, criminals, 'guest worker', workers, employees, clerks/officials, policeman/policewoman
SOMATISATION • racialisation (and especially 'colouring')	SOMATONYMS • 'racionyms' (often based on colour metaphors and selected body meronyms)	blacks, 'negros' ('*Neger*'), 'bush negros' ('*Buschneger*'), 'dark-skins' (*Dunkelhäutige*), 'red-skins' ('*Rothäute*'), 'redhead', 'slit eyes'/Chinks' ('*Schlitzaugen*'), coloured, whites, 'fairskins' ('*Hellhäutige*'), 'paleface' ('*Bleichgesicht*')

Figure 2.5 Selected referential potential with respect to personal reference

• 'engendering'	• 'genderonyms'	man, woman, girl, boy
• 'enageing'	• gerontonyms	the aged, youngsters, the youth [metonymy], child [relationym], parents [relationym], boy, girl, generation, '*Wehrmachts-generation*' [militarionym]
• specific body fragmentation	• specific (conspicuous) body meronyms like hair, weight and size standing for the whole person	blonde, fatty/fatso, beanpole, asshole [metaphor]
• reference in terms of the state of health	• anthroponyms describing the state of health	*GesundeR* (healthy person), *KrankeR* (sick person), patient, *InfizierteR* (infected)
• reference in terms of permanent or temporary bodily dysfunctionalities or handicaps	• anthroponyms denoting the dysfunction of senses or a bodily handicap	'cripple', *BlinderR* (blind person), *TaubeR/GehörloseR* (deaf), TaubstummeR (deaf-mute), *LahmeR* (lame person), stammerer, stotterer, invalid, disabled, 'handicapped'
• reference in terms of instruments and activities that help to compensate permanent or temporary bodily dysfunctionalities or handicaps	• anthroponyms denoting an instrument and activity that help to compensate permanent or temporary bodily dysfunctionalities or handicaps [actionyms]	*BrillenträgerIn* (person who wears glasses), *Brillenschlange* [metaphor: 'four-eyes'], *RollstuhlfahrerIn* (wheelchair user)
• reference in terms of bodily activities, including insufficient physical control	• anthroponyms denoting bodily activities, including insufficient physical control [actionyms] (partly also implicitly denoting the place of activity)	*Tölpatsch, Tölpel* (clumsy creature) [actionym], wanker [actionym], passer-by, hiker, rambler, traveller, climber
• reference in terms of mental deficiency	• anthroponyms denoting mental deficiency (including pathologonyms)	idiot, *Trottel* (dope), *Depp* (twit), *Blödmann* (stupid fool)
• reference in terms of temporary artificial alteration of bodily, sensual and mental capacities	• anthroponyms denoting an artificially produced alteration of bodily, sensual or mental capacities	drunk (*Besoffener*)
• reference in terms of 'bad', negatively sanctioned, abusive actions or habits	• negative habitonmys [actionyms]	*SäuferIn* (boozer), drug user, *DrogensüchtigeR* (drug addict), shrinker (*Faulpelz*)
• reference in terms of sexual orientation or habits	• anthroponyms referring to persons in terms of their sexual habits or orientation [most of them are relationyms]	heterosexual, homosexual, lesbian, gay, queer, bisexual, nymphomaniac, sado-masochist

Figure 2.5 (continued)

CULTURALISATION		
• ethnification	• ethnonyms	*TürkInnen* (Turks), *KanakInnen* (wops), *ZigeunerInnen* (gypsies), *TschuschInnen* (wops), Romanians, Poles, *Deutsche* (Germans), *ÖsterreicherInnen* (Austrians), nationals
• linguification	• linguonyms	*Deutsche, Deutschsprachige* (German-speaking persons), slaves, 'Indogermans', stammerer, stotterer
• religionisation	• religionyms	Christ, Muslims, Jews, 'ZigeunerInnen' (gypsies) (opaque)
• primitivisation	• synecdochising or metonymic anthroponyms denoting 'primitivity' or lack of civilisation	barefooted ('*Bloßfüßige*') [negationym/privatonym] barbarian (originally a Greek linguonym meaning 'stammerer' with reference to non-Greek speaking 'foreigners'), unskilled [negationym], 'bush negros', ('*Buschneger*')
ECONOMISATION	ECONONYMS	
• professionalisation	• professionyms	worker, labourer, employees, clerks/officials, policeman/ policewoman, workforce [metonymy]
• '(de-)possessivisation'	• anthroponyms referring to persons in terms of possession	rich, poor, *EigentümerIn* (owner), *BesitzerIn* (holder, proprietor)
• problematisation	• (negative) metaphorical anthroponyms	guest worker, *Schwarzarbeiter* (person doing illicit work) [criminonym]
• ideologisation	• ideologonyms	capitalist
'POLITICISATION'	POLITONYMS	
• nationalisation	'nationyms'	nationals, *Deutsche* (Germans), *ÖsterreicherInnen* (Austrians), *TürkInnen* (Turks), *KanakInnen* (wops), *ZigeunerInnen* (gypsies), (wops), Romanians, Poles, Hungarians
• 'classification'	• classonyms [in part, they are also politonyms]	*ProletInnen* (proles), prole-tarians, the rich [econonym], the poor [econonym], high society [metonymy], upper class [collective]

Figure 2.5 (continued)

• party political alignment	• party names [often metaphors and synecdoches]	*die Roten* (the Reds = Socialists), *die Schwarzen* (the Blacks), *die Blauen* (the Blues = Austrian Freedom Party), *die Grünen* (the Greens), National Socialists
• rough political alignment (polarisation)	• anthroponyms referring to persons in terms of rough political orientation [often orientational metaphors]	leftists, right-wing extremists [negative ideologonym]
• 'organisationalisation'	• names of political organisations (political organisationyms)	committee congress, parliament, government party
• 'professionalisation'	• anthroponyms referring to persons in terms of political professions (political professionyms)	politician, minister, major, president
• political actionalisation	• anthroponyms referring to persons in terms of political activities [actionyms]	voters, civilians, *ausländische/jüdische MitbürgerInnen* (foreign/Jewish fellow persons) [sociatives]
• granting or deprivation of political rights	• anthroponyms referring to persons in terms of assigning somebody political rights or of depriving somebody of rights	citizens, non-citizens, voters, refugees, bogus refugees
• ascription or denying of political membership to a national/state organisation	• anthroponyms referring to persons in terms of membership to a national/state organisation	citizens, nationals, non-citizens, *MitbürgerInnen* (fellow citizens)
• ascription of membership to supranational political organisations	• anthroponyms referring to persons in terms of membership to supra-national political organisations	third state nationals (*Drittstaatenangehörige*), EU citizens (*EU-BürgerInnen*)
• ascription of being or not being in need of political support	• anthroponyms referring to persons in terms of being or not being in need of political support	asylum-seekers, refugees, bogus refugees
• temporalisation	• anthroponyms with temporalising semantic features	*AltösterreicherIn* (old-Austrian), *NeoösterreicherIn* ('neo-Austrian')
MILITARISATION	• militarionyms	warrior, soldier [professionym], army, troupe, enemy [relationym], *SA* (*Sturmabteilung*), *SS* (*Schutzstaffel*), *Wehrmacht*

Figure 2.5 (continued)

SOCIAL
PROBLEMATISATION

• negation	• specific negative qualionyms, negationyms	illegals [criminonym], unemployed, unskilled, *Unmensch* (inhuman person)
• criminalisation	• criminonyms	criminals, illegals, dealers, mafiosi, delinquents, gang, murderer [relationym], '*Schubhäftling*' ('remand pending deportation prisoner/detainee'), '*Schübling*' (pejorative for 'remand pending deportation prisoner/detainee'), bogus refugee ('Scheinasylant'), perpetrator, culprit, victimiser, *SchwarzarbeiterIn* (person doing illicit work)
• negative ideologisation	• negative ideologonyms	racist, nationalist, ethnicist, sexist, misogynist, chauvinist, fascist, Nazi, imperialist, right-wing extremist
• pathologisation	• pathologonyms	psychopath, schizo, schizophrenic, nymphomaniac
• victimisation	• victimonyms	victim, *NotleidendeR* (person suffering deprivation)
RELATIONALISATION/ SOCIATIVISATION	• relationyms/sociatives (relational identification)	enemies/opponents, *ausländische/jüdische Mitmenschen* (foreign/Jewish fellow persons), guest, victim, victimiser, oppressor, oppressed, murderer, friends, neighbours, compatriots, *Mitmenschen* (fellow persons), children, (blood) relatives, ancestors

Figure 2.5 (continued)

social actors are referred to in terms of the major categories by means of which a given society or institution differentiates between classes of people. In our society these include age, gender, provenance, class, wealth, race, ethnicity, religion, sexual orientation, and so on.

(Van Leeuwen 1996: 54)

Analytically, we assume a strategy that represents social actors in terms of social activities. We name this strategy 'actionalisation', considering 'professionalisation' as a specific form of actionalisation, which, however, can also overlap with other categories: in the case of politicians, for example, with 'politicisation'. Accordingly, in the realm of onymic reference we distinguish between 'actionyms' and 'professionyms'.

Referential strategies, having to do with *relational identification*, i.e. the linguistic construction of social actors in terms of their personal, kinship or work relations etc. to each other, we label as *'relationalisation'* and *'sociativisation'* (we understand 'sociativisation' as the specific form of 'relationalisation' that consists in explicitly expressing the relationship by prefixes like 'co-' and 'fellow'), and the respective linguistic means as 'relationyms' and 'sociatives'. Out of all the different forms of *physical identification*, the representative construction of social actors in terms of physical characteristics that uniquely identify them in a given context, we especially focus on *'somatonyms'* and *'somatisation'*, the linguistic construction of social actors by synecdochisingly picking out a part or characteristic of their body: that is to say, by referring to a person on the basis of a meronymic semantic relationship. Van Leeuwen (1996: 60) regards 'somatisation' as a specific form of 'objectivation', a linguistic representation of social actors by means of reference to a place or a thing closely associated either with their person or with the activity they are represented as being engaged in – in other words, by metonymical reference. Van Leeuwen illustrates this conceptualisation with the example 'She put her hand on Mary Kate's shoulder'. Apart from the fact that within this utterance we cannot discern any metonymical (or synecdochical) reference, we do not consider 'somatisation' to be a form of objectivation, for the names of somatic parts of a person still carry the semantic feature '+ human' and these somatic parts are prototypically not called 'objects' in the sense of 'inanimate things', though we adopt van Leeuwen's general characterisation of 'somatisation'.

Specification or *genericisation* are two alternative aspects of representing social actors. While 'specification' means the reference to concrete individuals or specimens, 'genericisation' means generic reference by plural without article, as in the utterance 'Non-European immigrants make up 6.5 per cent of the population', by singular with a definite article (i.e. by a 'singularising synecdoche'), as in the example 'The foreigner has to adapt himself/herself', or by singular with an indefinite article, as in the sentence 'An Austrian will never accept that'. If specification is not realised as *'individualisation'*, for example by proper names, it is actualised by *'assimilation'*: that is to say, by reference to social actors as groups, realised by plurality. Van Leeuwen distinguishes between two forms of assimilation. *'Collectivisation'* is the reference to social actors as group entities, but without quantifying them, for example by means of deictics like 'we' or of collectives like 'family', 'group', 'team', 'tribe', 'troupe', 'class', 'mob', 'population', 'people', 'ethnicity', 'nation' and 'race'. *'Aggregation'* designates the quantification of groups of participants; it means the linguistic treatment of persons as numbers and statistics by means of definite or indefinite quantifiers.

According to van Leeuwen, the whole area of *'impersonalisation'*, i.e. of reference by (abstract) nouns whose meaning does not include the semantic feature '+ human', can be divided into *'abstraction'* and the already mentioned metonymical '*objectivation*'. '*Abstraction*' means the representation of social actors by means of a quality assigned to them: for example, the quality of being a problem (note that our understanding of 'problematisation', 'qualionyms', 'classonyms' etc., though these categories are all associated with abstractive processes, is still related to personalising reference). '*Objectivation*' is subdivided by van Leeuwen into '*spatialisation*' ('Austria is bringing in too many migrants'), '*utterance autonomisation*' ('The report notes that Austria's asylum policy is restrictive and inhuman'), '*instrumentalisation*' ('The bomb killed 110 civilians') and '*somatisation*' ('Her hand touched his shoulder').

Before we give a brief general overview of the different aspects of self- and other-presentation and try to complement Theo van Leeuwen's fruitful systematisation of '*representation* of social actors' with a tropological conceptualisation of metaphorical (e.g. anthropomorphising), metonymical and synecdochic construction or '*invention* of social actors' (for example of collective subjects), we would like to address a problem of the analysis of racism, ethnicism and nationalism that results from language-specific referential strategies.

In order to avoid vagueness and counter-productive, undifferentiated overgeneralisations, it is important, especially for multilingual analyses, to undertake contrastive terminological studies (including the diachronic dimension), which investigate the peculiarities of language use in different speech communities by comparing the different nomination potentials, including those for naming the phenomenal complex generally labelled as 'racism'. In German, the term 'racism' has until recently been used rather scarcely; instead, the notions '*Fremdenfeindlichkeit*' (hostility to strangers), '*Ausländerfeindlichkeit*' (hostility to foreigners) and '*Rechtsextremismus*' (right-wing extremism) were – and still are – used much more often whenever the respective discriminatory social practices (including discursive practices) were and are identified or criticised. Thus, language differences both in naming social actors and social practices in which the actors are involved (both as victims and as perpetrators) have to be accurately taken into account in the discourse analyses.

We noted above that reference can already bear the feature of predication, which is the second essential aspect of self- and other-presentation. 'Predication' is the very basic process and result of linguistically assigning qualities to persons, animals, objects, events, actions and social phenomena. Through predication, persons, things, events and practices are specified and characterised with respect to quality, quantity, space, time and so on. Predications are linguistically more or less evaluative (deprecatory or appreciative), explicit or implicit and – like reference and argumentation – specific or vague/evasive. Among other things, predicational strategies are mainly realised by specific forms of *reference* (based on explicit denotation as well as on more or less implicit connotation), by *attributes* (in the form of adjectives, appositions, prepositional phrases, relative clauses, conjunctional clauses, infinitive clauses and participial clauses or groups), by *predicates* or *predicative nouns/adjectives/pronouns*, by *collocations*, by explicit *comparisons*, *similes*, *metaphors* and other *rhetorical figures* (including *metonymies*, *hyperboles*, *litotes* and *euphemisms*) and by more or less implicit *allusions*, *evocations* and *presuppositions/implications*. Apropos 'connotation': So-called 'flag words' (*'Fahnenwörter'*), e.g. 'multiculturalism, 'integration', 'freedom' and 'democracy', and 'stigma words' (*'Stigmawörter'*), e.g. 'racism' and 'antisemitism', contain at least an implicit predication, as they connotatively convey a positive or negative deontic-evaluative meaning (see Hermanns 1982).

Among the most frequent prejudiced negative or (seemingly) positive traits, responsibilities and accusations explicitly or implicitly predicated to the discriminated groups of 'foreigners' (as far as the expression 'foreigner' is concerned, see the section 'The tropological construction and discrimination of ingroups and outgroups' below) in Austria we find the following ones (see Karl-Renner Institut 1990):

- 'Foreigners are to blame for high unemployment rates'
- 'Foreigners are bad, uncooperative work colleagues and workmates' (with contradictory attributions like 'They are lazy' versus 'They are addicted to overtime')
- 'Foreigners are "socio-parasites" ("*Sozialschmarotzer* ") who exploit the welfare system'
- 'Foreigners are always privileged in comparison with "us" '
- 'Foreigners are not willing to adapt themselves, to assimilate and to conform'
- 'Foreigners are too different in culture and religion. They are culturally less civilised and more primitive'
- 'Foreigners are careless and allow the flats and houses they are living in to fall into disrepair'
- 'Foreigners are dirty'
- 'Foreigners are bearers of infectious diseases'
- 'Male foreigners are inclined to sexual harassment'
- 'Male foreigners are sexists and patriarchal oppressors of women'
- 'Female foreigners are mentally immature and retarded and willingly accept their suppression and exploitation by men'
- 'Foreigners are always conspicuous and loud. They look physically different from national residents'
- 'Foreigners are aggressive and criminal'
- 'Foreigners are sexually more potent and more fertile and prolific'
- 'In contrast to "us", foreigners have too many children, which endangers the school success of "our" children and leads to infiltration of too many foreign influences'.

Most of these prejudices are used in argumentation, functionally employed as premises – strictly speaking, as first parts of the conclusion rules (see Toulmin 1996), or antecedents.

The main prejudiced traits, characteristics and responsibilities overtly or implicitly ascribed to Jews by antisemites then and now are the following ones (see Wodak *et al.* 1990):

- 'Jews are conspicuous; they are clearly discernible by their different physical appearance'
- 'Jews are different in culture and religion'
- 'Jews are restless, homeless and eternal migrants'
- 'Jews are the murderers of Jesus Christ; they are desecrators of hosts, ritual murderers and well-poisoners'
- 'Jews are power-hungry and powerful clandestine wire-pullers'
- 'Jews are criminal world conspirators'
- 'Jews are dishonourable, dishonest and false'
- 'Jews are business-minded, tricky and fraudulent; they are the prototypical capitalists'
- 'Jews are intelligent, intellectual and industrious' (a quite frequent philo-semitic positive stigmatisation)
- 'Jews are irreconcilable and always thirsting for vengeance'
- 'Jews are always privileged'
- 'Jews are social parasites'

The already mentioned syncretic character of antisemitism becomes very evident in view of all these prejudices recruited from such different areas as economics (including Marxist economics), Christian religion and biology. Though the explicit verbal externalisation of most of these debasing, humiliating and even dehumanising attributions has been taboo since the defeat of the National Socialists, some of them are even nowadays repeatedly uttered, at least implicitly and depending on the specific context (see chapter 3).

Of the numerous linguistic means and forms employed to realise these and the above-listed discriminatory predications – which, combined with the desired positive ascriptions to the 'own' ingroups, very often result in polarisations, black-and-white portrayals and manichean divisions into good and bad – the main rhetorical figures of tropes take an eminently significant role. The following section is dedicated to three of these, viz. to metaphors, metonymies and synecdoches.

THE TROPOLOGICAL CONSTRUCTION AND DISCRIMINATION OF INGROUPS AND
OUTGROUPS

For obvious reasons, the analysis of discriminating, racist, nationalist, ethnicist and sexist language use should focus critically on three of the four master-tropes. In linguistically constructing imagined communities (see Anderson 1988 [1983]) and collective subjects like 'races, 'nations' and 'ethnicities', synecdoches, metonymies and metaphors serve to create difference-levelling sameness and homogeneity, which are the basis on which people are treated uniformly and undifferentiatedly as non-individuals. De-individualisation, anonymisation, referential absorption and generalising selective foregrounding of common particularities are main discursive effects of metonymies and synecdoches, but also of many metaphors, although personifications, i.e. the group of anthropomorphising metaphors, grasping at evidentiality, vividness and identification, 'bring to life' or 'vitalise' abstract entities, phenomena, ideas and imaginations.

Tropes like metonymies, synecdoches and metaphors are related both to reference and predication. In discussing appellative reference and Theo van Leeuwen's systemic network of the linguistic representation of social actors, we already touched on synecdochising manoeuvres. Synecdoches (from the Greek: 'to take up with something else') are substitutions within one and the same field of reference: a term is replaced by another term, the extension of which is either semantically wider or semantically narrower (see Zimmerman 1989). According to the direction of substitution, there are two types of synecdoches. The particularising synecdoche (*pars pro toto*, that is to say, *a part standing for the whole*) or 'collective singular' (*the singular stands for the plural*), is a means of referential annexation, assimilation and inclusion, just as the generalising synecdoche (*totum pro parte*, that is to say, *the whole standing for a part*). Particularising synecdoches like the 'foreigner', the 'Jew', the 'Austrian' serve stereotypical generalisation and essentialisation that refer in a levelling manner to a whole group of persons (for examples see below). In languages like German, these are almost always realised in their masculine grammatical form (as far as party names as synecdoches are concerned, see Palonen 1995).

Metonymies (from the Greek: 'renaming', 'name change') are substitutions involving two semantically (and materially or cognitively) adjacent fields of reference: a name of a referent is replaced by the name of another referent, which semantically (abstractly or concretely) adjoins the referent of the replaced name. Depending on the relationship between the two neighbouring conceptual fields, one can distinguish between different metonymic replacements:

- the cause by the product (what van Leeuwen 1996: 60 named 'utterance autonomisation' – as a specific form of 'objectivating' social actors – also belongs to this type of metonymy): '*This nationalist discourse* [instead of its responsible creators] instigates people to acts of hostility against "foreigners" '
- the user of an object by the object: '*The trains* are on strike'
- the person/s by the place, for example the state/country, town, city, district or village where the person/s is/are living: '*Vienna* must not become *Chicago*' (for this slogan of the Austrian Freedom Party see chapter 4, pp. 164–5), '*Austria* is not willing to accept new immigrants'
- the person/s by the building in which the person/s is/are staying, working, imprisoned, etc.: '*The White House* decided to attack Saddam Hussein', '*The concentration camp Mauthausen* was liberated in May 1945'
- the action or event by the place where the action/s is/are performed or the event takes place: '*Auschwitz* must never ever happen again'
- the country or state by the persons living in this country or state: 'Cooperation is important because *we* are too small to allow disharmony in vital areas of our country' (as Wolfgang Schüssel said on 15 May 1995 in his speech commemorating the 50th anniversary of the signing of the international 'Austrian State Treaty')

- the persons by the time, time period or epoch they are living in: '*The twentieth century* has shaken the Austrians several times very heavily'
- the (responsible) representatives of an institution by the institution: '*The Parliament* passed a new alien act'. 'The *MA 62* (=*Magistratsabteilung* 62: that is to say, the 62nd department of the Viennese Municipal Authorities) implements the restrictive Residency Law extremely restrictively'
- the actions or events by the institution connected with these actions or events: '*The First Austrian Republic* can only be described as a history of failures'.

As one can see from the examples within brackets, metonymies enable the speakers to conjure away responsible, involved or affected actors (whether victims or perpetrators), or to keep them in the semantic background.

Personifications are, as mentioned above, specific forms of metaphors that bring together and link two different semantic fields, one with the semantic feature [− human], the other bearing the semantic feature [+ human]. Personifications or anthropomorphisations are rhetorically used to give a human form or to humanise inanimate objects, abstract entities, phenomena and ideas. They play a decisive role in animating imagined 'collective subjects' – as, for example, 'races', 'nations' and 'ethnicities'. Their apparent concreteness and vividness often invites hearers or readers to identify or to feel solidarity with the personified entity or against it.

Apart from personifications, there are many other forms of metaphors which are important in referentially and predicationally constructing ingroups and outgroups, whether they are imagined as 'races', 'nations', 'ethnicities and 'tribes' or as specific 'racialised', 'national', 'ethnic' or 'religious' majorities or minorities. Many of these metaphors function as 'collective symbols' (see chapter 1, p. 26). Very often, they are simultaneously used both as metaphors and representative synecdoches (see Gerhard and Link 1991: 18).

In discourses about 'races', 'nations' and 'ethnicities', these racialising, nationalising and ethnicising metaphors and synecdoches, but also the respective metonymies, are almost always connected with specific dychotomic, oppositional predications, which can form textual networks of semantic isotopes that help the speakers to polarise and to divide the world of social actors into 'black and white' and into 'good and bad'. The most frequent and conspicuous of these predications to 'real' or imagined social actors or groups of social actors, which serve positive or negative self-presentation and negative or positive other-presentation, are those of singularity/uniqueness/distinctiveness or individuality, of identity or similarity, of collectivity, of difference, of autonomy/independence/autarchy, of dependency/heteronomy, of continuity, of discontinuity, of (social) inclusion, of integration, of union or unity, of (social) cohesion, of (social) exclusion, of fragmentarisation, of multiplicity and of dissolution.

Apart from these basic identity-related attributions, 'national', 'racial' and 'ethnic' stereotypes or 'characters' are predicated on the basis of metaphors relying on the collective-symbolic concepts of materiality and body, of material status (e.g. the thermostatic status of 'warm' versus 'cold') and states of matter ('solid', 'fluid' and 'gaseous'), of material qualities like the weight ('heavy' versus 'light'), of spatiality, spatio-dynamics and temporality ('fast', 'fast-moving', 'ephemeral', 'persistent', 'tenacious', 'lively', 'mobile', 'flexible', 'slowly', 'inert', 'lethargic') and of the five sensorial concepts of visuality ('fair', 'pale', 'clear' and 'transparent' versus 'dark', 'gloomy' 'obscure'), audibility ('harmonious' versus 'loud' and 'noisy'), tactile sensation ('hard' versus 'soft'), olfactority ('nice-smelling' versus 'stinking') and taste ('tasteful' versus 'tasteless').

Racialising, nationalising and ethnicising metaphors of spatiality are primarily ordered around the symbolically and evaluatively loaded binary oppositions of 'internal' versus 'external' or 'internality' versus 'externality', of 'height/top' and 'up' versus 'bottom' and 'down/low', of 'foundations/ profundity/ground' versus 'bottomlessness', of 'superficiality' and 'flatness' versus 'depth', of 'centre' versus 'periphery/margin' as well as of 'boundary', 'limit' and 'extension/expansion' and 'spreading' (see Mayr and Reisigl 1998).

Metaphors of 'racial', 'national' and 'ethnic bodies' and 'materiality' are very often also recruited from naturalisations: that is to say, from meteoro-logisations, geologisations and biologisations. To the latter belong, besides the personifications already mentioned (both non-gendered and gendered), animal-isations (of both sexes) and florisations.

As far as German and Austrian discourses about migrants and 'racialised', 'national' and 'ethnic' minorities are concerned, the most frequent and stereo-typical metaphors employed in the negative referential construction or identifi-cation of social actors and in the negative predicational qualification of them, of their migration and of the alleged effects of immigration, are the following (the list closely follows Böke 1997; see also Gehard and Link 1991):

- *natural disasters:* immigration/migrants as avalanches or flood disasters
- *dragging/hauling:* illegal immigration as dragging or hauling (in German: 'schleppen')
- *water:* immigration/migrants as a water-course/current/flood that has to be 'dammed'
- *fire:* alleged effects of immigration/conflicts between 'racialised', 'national-ised' and 'ethnicised' groups as smoulding fire
- *thermostatics:* effects of immigration as pressure within the pot and conflicts between 'racialised, 'nationalised' and 'ethnicised' groups' as bubbling
- *plants and fertile soil:* migration and effects of migration as transplantation/ repotting, uprooting, or (alleged) causing of social conflicts as seeding
- *genetic material:* cultural and social traditions and 'heritage' as genetic material
- *growth/growing:* increasing immigration and increasing conflicts as growing
- *pollution and impurity:* intergroup contacts, exchanges and relations as pollu-tion and impurity
- *melting:* intergroup contacts, relations, exchanges and assimilation as melting
- *body:* racialised, nationalised, ethnicised groups are metaphorically ascribed 'collective (racial, national, ethnicity) bodies'; outgroups are metaphorised as 'foreign bodies' or alien elements

- *blood:* immigration as bleeding white or bloodletting of the imagined 'collective bodies'; intergroup relations as blood impurity
- *disease/infection:* immigration/migrants as an epidemic; intergroup contacts and relations as an infection
- *animals/animal-owning:* immigrants/minorities as parasites, as 'attracted like the moths to a flame', as herded together
- *war/fight/military:* immigration as military activity/invasion
- *goods/commodities and exchange of goods:* migration as import and export of workers/workforce; migrants as 'freight'
- *food*: 'good/welcome immigrants/minorities' versus 'bad/unwelcome immigrants/minorities' metaphorised as the wheat that has to be separated from the chaff
- *vehicle/boat/ship:* effects of immigration as overcrowded boat
- *house/building/door/gateway/bolt:* the ingroups' (e.g. 'national') territory as a house or building; stopping immigration as bolting the door.

It would be impossible to illustrate each of these metaphors exhaustively, or to illustrate the above-mentioned types of synecdoches and metonymies that are all employed in the tropological construction and discrimination of social actors by concrete examples, since this would greatly exceed our attempt simply to give an overview. We will encounter some of them in the three case studies to which chapters 3, 4 and 5 are dedicated. Some of them, however, we would like to present and discuss in the remaining part of this section, focusing particularly on Austrian and German examples, which illustrate the language-specificity of the discriminatory nomination of groups of social actors with which an English-speaking reader may not be very familiar.

Whereas the collective noun 'race' is still quite commonly used in English-speaking countries, this formerly terribly abused term has been widely taboo and replaced in German-speaking countries since 1945 by the peculiarly German term '*Ausländer*'. According to one of the most comprehensive German–English dictionaries (the dictionary edited by Reinhart von Eichborn, published in 1994, entitled *Die Sprache unserer Zeit. Wörterbuch in 4 Bänden*, vol. 3: 191), the term '*Ausländer*' is translated as 'foreigner', 'foreign subject', 'foreign national', 'alien', 'non-national', 'outlander', 'stranger' and 'nonresident alien'. Except for the expression of 'outlander', none of the English nouns really fits the corresponding German term as far as its literal meaning is concerned, which contains the local element of externality. The term '*Inländer*', for which it is even more difficult to find a corresponding English equivalent containing the meaning element of internality, the term is translated according to the same dictionary as 'native', 'subject', 'citizen', 'inhabitant', 'national resident' and, in Great Britain, as 'resident within the sterling area' (the anthroponym 'inlander' is not at all a very common term).

From these observations, it is clear that there is a problem of translation that must be taken into account whenever one wants to make a contrastive analysis of different discourses about discriminated social groups in different states where different languages are spoken. However, the analysis of the use of German expressions like '*Ausländer*' and '*Inländer*' reveals that these highly problematical, controversial and paradoxical terms reflect and serve to dismantle a paradoxical sociopolitical situation. As the German historian Klaus J. Bade (1994: 9–10) remarked, in normal everyday use, the usual German anthroponym '*AusländerIn*' ('foreigner' or 'alien') does not denote diplomats or North Atlantic Treaty Organisation (NATO) units residing or stationed in the country, nor tourists or rich 'foreigners' with an unearned capital income. It almost always denotes persons from former 'countries of recruitment' (so-called '*Anwerbeländern*') or their children (see also Engelmann 1984: 25–42 and Budzinski 1988: 12–14).

In other words, as far as the prototypical cognitive conceptualisation is concerned, the term '*Ausländer*' – which, by the way, almost exclusively appears androcentrically in its masculine grammatical form – is very often used as 'synecdoche', strictly speaking, as a *totum pro parte* by which the seemingly all-inclusive anthroponymical nomination actually refers only selectively to very specific groups of persons. Thus, the whole stands merely for a part.

From a legal point of view (see also Rittstieg 1997: IX–X) and presupposing Austria or Germany as the orientation starting-point, the German terms '*Ausländer*' and '*Ausländerin*' includes every person who does not have Austrian or German citizenship. In this sense, the terms '*Ausländerin*' and '*Ausländer*' correspond to the English 'alien' – apart from the fact that there are more restrictive naturalisation conditions in Austria and Germany than in most of the English-speaking countries. It includes all people of foreign citizenship; thus, not only persons who have been living in Austria or Germany for decades (that is to say the so-called 'first generation'), but also their children, who have been born and grown up in the country (the so-called 'second generation'), and very often even their grandchildren (the so-called 'third generation').

This legal definition is oriented towards the *jus sanguinis*. It has completely deviated and become estranged from the original meaning of the term '*AusländerIn*', which denotes persons who have their center of life and living, their main focal point of life, outside the country or state and who, thus, do not 'belong' to this country or state and its society (see Rittstieg 1997: IX). This means, as a result, that many so-called '*InländerInnen*' (as we said, there is hardly an English equivalent for this term) are considered to be foreigners, and this not only from a legal point of view, but also, as previously mentioned, in common everyday uses of the language. Some politicians, at times, quite 'gently', linguistically exclude this group of '*InländerInnen* without an Austrian or German citizenship' by using the euphemistic term of 'foreign fellow-citizens' ('*ausländische MitbürgerInnen*'). But this use of language cannot hide the fact that legally, they are not fellow citizens because they are not citizens at all.

The legal and everyday use of the term '*AusländerIn*' as well as the institutionalised exclusionary consequences related to it negate and disguise the fact that Austria – and the same holds true for Germany – has been, at least for several decades, a de facto immigration country. In contrast to the official phrasing of most of the parties who still deny Austria (or Germany) to be an immigration country, one finds in Austria and Germany more or less all the conditions and problems typical of immigration situations and immigration states. To quote Bade (1994: 10) (who himself refers to Germany, but in this case, one can extrapolate from the German situation to the Austrian one):

> In a further sense encompassing ways of life, mentalities and self-perception, however, the majority have already long been something like indigenous foreigners, foreign natives [*Inländer*, M.R. and R.W.], hyphenated-Germans (in reference to Germany), passport-foreigners, or Germans with a foreign passport. Definitions only 'stick' [literally, to 'grab', M.R. and R.W.] if they fit their subject. Therefore, paradoxical definitions reveal a paradoxical situation – in this case, an immigration-situation without an immigration-country.
>
> (Bade 1994: 10)[2]

Some of the problems inherent in the term '*AusländerIn*' (for example its synecdochic reference) obviously also relate to the term '*Ausländerfeindlichkeit*' as well as '*Fremdenfeindlichkeit*' which widely replace the term 'racism' in public discourses in the German-speaking countries. If one speaks of '*Ausländerfeindlichkeit*', one does not adequately name the problem, for the implied hostility is just directed towards specific groups of so-called '*AusländerInnen*', and not to all aliens – that is to say, to all people comprised by the legal definition of 'alien'.

We have included this rather lengthy discussion of terms to stress that in populist and everyday use of language the legal definition of foreigners – that is to say, of aliens – is almost always restricted to a much more specific and discriminatory meaning extension of the term. Primarily, people who do not speak German and come from the former 'Eastern Bloc', from former Yugoslavia or from Turkey are subsumed under this label in Austria and Germany, and a hierarchy is erected, as, for example, in a passage from the written document containing the reasons (in German it is called '*Begründung*') for the 'Anti-Foreigner Petition' initiated by the Austrian Freedom Party in 1992 (see chapter 4):

> The origin of the foreigners in Austria differs strongly from other European countries. In Switzerland about 70% of the foreigners come from the EC, in Sweden about half of them from the European economic area. In contrast, the majority of the foreigners in the FRG but also in Austria originate from areas outside the European economic area.
>
> (Reason 2/*Begründung* 2)[3]

In this example, the discursive construction of a hierarchy of 'foreigners' is restricted to a dichotomic division into 'foreigners from the European economic area' and 'foreigners originating from areas outside the European economic area', the latter being implicitly evaluated negatively by the comparison of Germany and Austria with Switzerland and Sweden, which presupposes that 'foreigners from the European area' are 'the lesser evil'. It is at least partly due to the formal requirements for political genres like petitions that here, the hierarchising evaluation of foreigners is rather moderate and implicit. In other, less formal contexts, this discriminatory hierarchy is linguistically also expressed by means of lexicalised (ethnonymic, nationymic or other) slurs like the Austrian '*Tschusch*' ('wop') and the German '*Kanake*' ('wop'), both denoting Turkish immigrants and immigrants from former Yugoslavia. These anthroponyms are – as others like German '*Neger*' ('negro') and '*Jud*' ('Jew') – already 'self-sufficient' for degrading persons just by naming them.

The collective singular or 'particularising synecdoche' is typical of stereotypes (see Quasthoff 1973: 267 and 282 ff.) and prejudiced discourse, in which statements about persons are made in a levelling, generalising, essentialising and eternalising manner, in which groups of social actors are presupposed to be homogeneous and are selectively ascribed a specific, allegedly shared, either negative or positive feature, trait, mentality and so on. A few decades ago, such tropes were, in general, much more common in formal, official discourses than they are now. Whereas, for example, until the 1950s, Austrian politicians quite often used the *pars pro toto* 'the Austrian' ('*der Österreicher*'), since then they have used in their speeches and addresses primarily both the distinguishing form '*die Österreicherinnen und Österreicher*' ('the female and male Austrians') or the abstractive toponym 'Austria' metonymically standing for 'the Austrians' (see Reisigl 1998: 250 and Reisigl 1999b: 305).

One of the historically most discriminating and incriminating collective singulars is the antisemitic German *pars pro toto* '*der Jude*', 'the Jew'. It was sometimes eternalisingly qualified as '*der ewige Jude*', 'the eternal Jew'. In everyday discourses, this particularising synecdoche was, and, if still used despite the verbal taboo, still is, phonologically often shortened by elision of the final vowel and realised as '*der Jud*'.

The blatant antisemitic abuse of the anthroponym 'Jew' still continues today to have the effect that quite a few, particularly German, non-Jews seem to have problems even to articulate the word 'Jew' or 'Jews' at all. For them, the word is still inseparably associated with massive negative associations and connotations.

Used as metaphorical antisemitic predication attributed to a specific person, and that means that it is not realised with a definite article, but with an indefinite one (e.g. '*er ist ein Jud*', 'he is a Jew'), 'a Jew' has the prejudiced meaning of 'a tight-fisted, greedy, cunning, business-minded man'. It is clear that this metaphorisation underlies the pragmatic fallacy of a *secundum quid*, of a 'hasty generalisation' (see the section below p. 73): strictly speaking, of the stereotype that 'all Jews are tight-fisted, greedy, cunning, business-minded persons'.

Of course, hasty generalisations are not only a characteristic of such metaphorical negative other-presentations or of many synecdoches. If one looks at the structure of prejudices from an argumentation theoretical perspective, one can ascertain that in every racist, antisemitic, nationalist, ethnicist and sexist prejudice or stereotype there is inherent a fallacious generalisation. Moses

Gercek, survivor of the Auschwitz concentration camp, in an interview describes antisemitic 'hasty generalisation' exemplarily as follows: 'We [= with "we" Moses Gercek means "the Jews"] also have criminals. If Mister Mueller is a criminal, they say, Mister Mueller is a criminal. But if Moses Gercek is a criminal, one says: "The Jews are criminals"' (Heenen-Wolff 1994: 26 f.).[4] Here, Gercek identifies a specific antisemitic prejudiced generalisation. While in this example the inadmissible generalisation is mimetically voiced as being linguistically performed by determination (by the definite article) and plural, in many cases fallacious generalisation directed against groups of discriminated 'others' can also be suggestively implied by the frequent referential foregrounding of specific features or 'traits'.

Some of the historically most incriminating anthroponyms are the 'racionyms' '*Neger* ', (German), 'negro' (English) and '*Nigger* ' (German) or 'nigger' (English). These pejorative racist somatonyms are based on the synecdochising Latin colour term '*niger* ', meaning 'black', and metaphorically denoting the skin colour (which, of course, is not 'black', just as the skin colour of so-called 'whites' is not white). In German, '*Neger* ' has been used since the seventeenth century, when it was borrowed from French '*négro* ', which is derived from Latin via Spanish and Portuguese '*negro* ' (Kluge 1999: 585, *Duden* 1989b: 482). The 'semantic degeneration' of the anthroponym is due to the extreme social discrimination lasting for centuries against those so named. The racist contempt for the group of persons linguistically referred to by '*Neger* ' has sedimented in the connotative meaning structure of the word, but the word was not taboo in German-speaking countries until the 1970s.

In spite of its hegemonic social banning, the metaphorising somatonym is sometimes still in use today (see also Matouschek 1999: 59-67). In Austria, there is a columnist of the *Neue Kronen Zeitung*, Staberl alias Richard Nimmer-richter (see chapter 4, pp. 175–8), who still writes about '*Neger* '. And also for parliamentary representatives like Erwin Rasinger, public health spokesperson of the conservative Austrian People's Party (ÖVP), it is no problem to speak about '*Neger* ' with reference to Afro-Americans (see an interview by Rasinger in the liberal-conservative daily *Die Presse*, 28 March 1997). Much worse still, the leader of the Austrian Freedom Party (FPÖ), Jörg Haider, on 9 October 1998 in a public discussion, in which he argued against the new liberal Act for Physicians that grants the right of free establishment, called foreign physicians who want to practice in Austria '*Buschneger* ' (literally: 'bush negros'): 'In future, every bush negro has the possibility to treat his collegues in Austria'. (see *Der Standard*, 13 October 1998, but also *Der Standard*, 24 April 1999 and *Der Standard*, 6 August 1999).[5] This intentionally debasing racist compound denomination metaphorically insinuates the discriminating prejudices of 'primitivity', 'under-development' and 'unculturedness'. These prejudices are suggested by the floronym 'bush', which symbolically encodes the opposite of 'civilisation' (see also Matouschek 1999: 63).

In everyday language use, in Austria and Germany, one can sometimes still hear the idiomatic and emphatic racist similitude, i.e. comparison, '*wie die Neger* ' ('like the negros'), which predicationally qualifies something as 'primitive', 'simple', 'chaotic' and 'junglelike'. Analogically, in everyday disourses one is sometimes still confronted with lexicalised ethnicist comparisons like *'wie die Türken '* ('like the Turks'), e.g heavy smokers are said 'to smoke like the Turks'. The most pejorative of the three German 'racionyms' referring to 'black' people, viz. *'nigger '*, is widely subjected to negative social sanctioning. However, if one looks in dictionaries, one can still find idiomatic phrases like 'so you're the nigger in the woodpile' and 'there's a nigger in the woodpile' (see Collins: 447). These phrases are, of course, explicitly marked as being 'pejorative'. Neverthe- less, the harmless German translations *'Sie sind es also, der querschießt '* (literally: 'so you are the one who spoils things') and *'irgend jemand schießt quer '* or *'da ist der Haken dran'* (literally: 'somebody is spoiling things' or 'there is a snag on it') leave no trace of the racist meaning of the English phrases: This must be considered to be problematic and raises the question of translation adequacy. Is a translation of a racist idiom satisfactory if it suggests that the literal meaning of the original phrase is unproblematic, or should one not try to find a somehow equivalent translation that to some extent also reflects the literal discriminatory meaning of the original? We plead for the second option, since it can help to sensitise the users of dictionaries to an awareness of linguistic discrimination.

Sensitisation is especially required if the linguistic discrimination is not performed so directly, as in cases where explicit onymic slurs are employed. The following example both contains explicit and implicit forms of linguistic discrimination. If the Austrian tabloid *Neue Kronen Zeitung* gives coverage of crimes and delicts committed by non-Austrian citizens, the (suspected) delin- quents are, in contrast to Austrian perpetrators, primarily and synecdochically referred to in terms of 'citizenship', 'nationality', 'ethnicity' and 'race', in de- toponymic terms of 'continental origin' or in terms of not being a 'national resident', an *InländerIn*. That means that these social actors are not identified as individuals but, completely undifferentiated, as 'the foreigners', 'the Africans', 'the Asians', 'the Poles', 'the Romanians' or 'the Turks' who have or who are suspected of having committed the crime. To illustrate, we will consider just one article taken from the *Kronenzeitung* of 15 November 1997. It is entitled 'Two Africans in detention. Drugs dealt 6000 times'. The lead goes as follows:

> A 'record' was achieved by two dealers from Africa. In just four-and-a- half months, the duo dealt cocaine and heroin more than 6,000 times to addicts in Vienna! Only hours before they were apprehended, they had transferred their 'weekly profit' of AS 150,000 to Senegal.

And the article's text itself goes as follows:

> Either the Döblinger Steg or the Friedensbrücke in Vienna served the men – daily exactly from 5 to 7 p.m. – as an 'office'. Two Viennese addicts were the look-out, giving a signal if police approached. According to the investigations, the Africans – in the scene they were known as 'Jimmy' and

'Ali' – had about 40 to 50 customers daily. And that was for a good 120 days. During questioning, the two, having forged identity cards with them, claimed not to know anything about it. Even their own names did not come to them. Just once, 'Ali' suddenly looked at a file, read the company name, and said: 'My name is 'Bene'... An accomplice named 'Rene' is still at large.[6]

In the headline, the two dealers are referred to in terms of their continental origin. In the lead and the main text they are referentially identified to as 'two dealers from Africa', 'the duo', 'they', 'the men', 'the Africans', 'Jimmy and Ali' and as 'the two'. Only once in the article can one read of the transfer of AS 150,000 to Senegal, from which the readers may infer that the two persons under arrest come from Senegal. Linguistically and, thus, also cognitively, the two suspected perpetrators are most present and prominent de-toponymically as 'Africans' – by the way, 'Africa' is a macro-toponym referring to a not particularly small geographic entity. One can assume with a high degree of certainty that this very rough reference foregrounding the feature of continental origin contributes substantially to the strengthening of the prejudice that 'all Africans in Vienna are dealers' and, in a broader sense, that 'many foreigners are criminals'. If one attempts to make a substitution test, the strangeness of this quite common persuasive discursive practice to refer to specific persons or groups of persons completely undifferentiatedly becomes clear and manifest. If the two arrested persons were two dealers with Austrian passports or with the passport of another member state of the European Union, the author of this press article would surely not have referred to them as 'the two Austrians arrested' or 'two dealers from Austria' or 'two dealers from Europe'. Such a substitution looks odd against the background of the underlying egocentrical, ethnocentrical, natiocentrical and eurocentrical perspective. This perspective implies that, the more distantly a person focused on in a specific context is located from the own geographical or 'national' origo or 'point of orientation' (see Bühler 1982 [1934]), the more unspecific, 'outlandish' and strange she or he is identified and probably also perceived as being.

What we learn from this example (for a very recent and detailed study on the linguistic representation of (presumed) criminal social actors in the press media coverage in Germany see M. Jäger, Cleve, Ruth and S. Jäger 1998) is that prejudices are not always expressed directly and by explicit ethnicist, racist or sexist slurs, as for example '*Neger*' ('negro'), '*Tschusch*' ('wop'), '*Kanake*' ('wop'), '*Zigeuner*' ('Gypsy')', *Schnalle*' ('tarty type'), or by debasing nominations which foreground in a fragmenting manner and stress a more or less stigmatised or negatively connotated fictitious or 'real' bodily feature, as for example 'the thick/fat one', 'the cripple', 'the blonde' (connotatively associated with stupidity and naivety), 'the red-head' (with reference to a woman, often connoting sexual availability and temperamentality) and so on. Negative predications can be expressed more suggestively, insinuatingly. But this is not the case in the last five examples we will present in this section, for within them, the discriminating predications are explicit.

The presupposition or emphasis of differences between nations often serves the negative, debasing delimitation from an outgroup considered to be a different national collective. In the next example taken from an exclusively male group discussion in Vienna on 'Austria' and 'Austrian identity', the male speaker emphasises the difference between Austrians and foreign residents with respect to mentality and form of life. The particularising synecdoche or collective singular 'the Southerner' ('*der Südländer*') indicates the stereotypical verbalisation of a specific prejudice to which the participant tries to give argumentative plausibility, by environmentalist interpretations aiming at explaining a possible conflict between 'Austrians' and 'foreigners' as a preprogrammed, unavoidable consequence resulting from the climatically determined differences in everyday forms of life and behaviour:

> There are really bas.../these basic – umm mentalities and because of the different ways of life I mean this is because – umm simply because probably the Southerner – because of the heat down there – is used to during the day – umm taking a siesta and lying around and he really only livens up in the evening. right? Of course those are differences that – automatically lead to conflict here.[7]

As already illustrated above, racist and ethnicist prejudices are not at all a peculiarity of private or semi-private discourse. Even highest political representatives can be suspected of having uttered racist, ethnicist or other slurs. This was the case in 1997 with the Austrian foreign minister Wolfgang Schüssel from the Austrian People's Party (ÖVP). Four accusations against Schüssel filled in the summer of 1997 the 'silly season' in Austrian press coverage (see the Austrian weekly *News*, No. 28 of 10 July 1997).

First, the foreign minister was accused of having called, at the end of October 1996, either the foreign minister of Uganda or the foreign minister of Burkina Faso as well as certain other person, 'barefooted' ('*Bloßfüßige*'). The synecdochic-metaphorical slur was allegedly uttered 'off record' and after dinner in the Hotel Interalp in Telfs in Tyrol, and that in the presence of six journalists. At this time, the Austrian People's Party was holding a party convention in Telfs. According to the journalists' record, Schüssel said: 'There was the foreign minister and also another barefooted one, and we wait until the labourers come in and bring in the camera ...'.[8] While '*Baraber*' is 'just' a condescending qualification of the members of a camera team, '*Bloßfüßige*' is clearly a racist metaphor eurocentrically implying the qualification 'primitive' in the very negative sense.

Second, the journalists accused Schüssel of having characterised the white Russian president Alexander Lukaschenko in debasing terms as '*Kümmeltürke*' ('wog'). In a briefing organised for Austrian EU correspondents in the bar of the Dorint Hotel in Brussels on 5 December 1996, immediately after the OSCE-summit conference, Schüssel described a situation during the conference in which he and Franz Vranitzky, in those days still Austria's chancellor, were sitting opposite Lukaschenko. According to the journalists' report, Schüssel said: 'He was sitting there like a *Kümmeltürk*, with his beard, and did not speak for hours'.[9] This predicational comparison, no matter whether it was really said or not, is clearly ethnicist. According to the *Duden* (1989a: 909), the expression '*Kümmeltürke*' was first used in the slang of German students to refer to those students who came from the surroundings of Halle an der Saale where a lot of caraway (German '*Kümmel*') was planted, which was the motive for ironically and metaphorically calling this geographic area '*Kümmeltürkei*', literally 'caraway Turkey'. It was metaphorically called 'Turkey' because in former times, many spices were imported from the Orient, meaning, inter alia, from Turkey. The slang word became increasingly negative-evaluative and was then employed to debase 'boring' and 'bourgeois' persons. Since the beginnings of labour migration, the term has been used especially to denote derogatorily so-called Turkish 'guest workers', but it is still used to refer to all Turks.

Third and fourth, the journalists accused Schüssel of having called, on the occasion of the EU-summit conference in Amsterdam, the president of the German Federal Bank a '*Sau*' or '*richtige Sau*', a '(female) pig' or a 'real (female) pig', and a Swedish delegate for the EU-summit conference in Amsterdam (either the premier or another member of the government) a '*Trottel*', an 'idiot'. During a breakfast in Amsterdam's Hilton Hotel on 17 June 1997, Schüssel was talking to journalists about a number of topics including the introduction of the Euro and the Swedish position regarding the establishment of environmental conservation in the Amsterdam Treaty. It is within this context that the Austrian foreign minister allegedly used the two insulting words. Though both the animalising metaphor and the insult denying mental or intellectual capacities are not racist or ethnicist, they are nevertheless slurs that do not fit the political function of a foreign minister, even if he or she performs them off record. However, Wolfgang Schüssel did not and was not forced to resign.

There are many other nouns or noun groups that are already discriminatory at very elementary levels of referential identification and of predication, and that are, thus, employed in racist, ethnicist name-calling. We will mention here only one more, which, in German-speaking countries, is quite controversially discussed, viz. the ethnonym '*Zigeuner*' or '*Zigeunerin*' ('Gypsy'). Its etymology is not completely reliably reconstructed, but Burgen (1998: 44) assumes that 'gitanes' or '*Zigeuner*' derives from Greek '*tsínganos*', which means 'heretic', 'infidel'. If this etymological reconstruction holds true, '*Zigeuner*' was originally a stigmatising religionym used by Christians. It was, to put it into the words of the historian Reinhart Kosellek (1989), an 'asymmetrical counter-concept', at the level of evaluative judgement unequally opposing 'the faithful', 'the Christians'. Used since the sixteenth century (see Grimm and Grimm 1991 [1877]: 1257), it was mostly employed as a heteronymic stigma-word connotatively associated with the negative, discriminatory prejudices of being tattered and ragged, roguish and wicked, thieving, vagrant, unsteady and antisocial (the Nazis apostrophised the group of Romany and Sinti victims imprisoned and murdered in concentration camps with a negationym as '*die Asozialen*', 'the antisocials'), false and mendacious, clairvoyant, inclined to cursing and witch-craft, and so on. Not least because of the National Socialist persecution and attempted genocide under the labels '*Zigeuner*' and 'antisocials', since 1945 the term has been widely taboo as being politically incorrect. However, this verbal taboo contrasts with the fact that the ethnonym has also been adopted by many Romany and Sinti people and re-evaluated positively, also for example by the German sintezza Theresia Seible. She lived in Würzburg during the time of National-Socialist dictatorship, was coercively sterilised and became a victim of the Nazis' medical experiments. Since then, her left leg has remained shortened by 2 cm. In an interview published in 1994, she explains her point of view regarding the term '*Zigeuner*':

> If I say it thus: *Zigeuner*. We have been persecuted by this name, and I think that one should bear the name by which one has been persecuted. They wanted to call us Sinti, but that is something that concerns us personally. Sinti, that is my moral law. But after Dachau it was demanded that '*Zigeuner*' should not be used anymore – as it is an insulting word and because it has still not been deleted by the vagrant office [*Landfahrerstelle*, M.R. and R.W.] – and to say the word 'Sinti' instead. But if one has been declared an outlaw since the 16th century and has been persecuted by this name, then I am proud to be a *Zigeunerle* [little Gypsy, M.R. and R.W.]. And I keep to the word *Zigeunerle*. Thousands of us have been persecuted and gassed by this name. One should really give respect to this word.
>
> (Ebbinghaus 1996: 377)[10]

What follows from this quotation is that the decision about whether a specific appellative denomination for persons or groups of persons is socially acceptable and politically correct or not can never be taken and abstractly prescribed by somebody not directly or personally concerned without asking the denominated group itself. Moreover, the highly political decision in the respective naming disputes must always be left to those personally most concerned with the decision, i.e. those persons to whom the anthroponyms refer, whether they are heteronyms or autonyms.

Arguing for and against discrimination

The answer to the question of how racist, ethnicist, nationalist and sexist preju-dices come into one's head and, once 'implanted', how they can again be put out of one's mind, is a very difficult and complex one (see chapter 1). From a linguistic or rhetorical perspective, a partial answer to this question will have to focus on persuasion.

Persuasion, the means of intentionally influencing a person so that she or he adopts, fixes or changes her or his ways of perception, attitudes to and views on persons, objects and ideas, and dispositions to behave or act in a specific way, is double-edged in nature. Unlike English, in languages like German this difference is explicitly lexicalised in the lexematic distinction between the verb '*überzeugen*' and the verb '*überreden*' (see Kopperschmidt 1989: 116–21). Both verbs can be translated into English by 'persuade'. In addition, '*überzeugen*' can be translated by 'convince', while there is no separate and distinct lexical item for '*überreden*'.

'*Überzeugen*' is designated to mean the practice of bringing about a rational, more or less 'universalisable' – 'universalisable' in the Perelmanian sense of 'under such conditions and proceduralised such that anyone should agree' – consent under conditions of widely equal opportunities and widely symmetrical, power-free communication. The speakers' and hearers' or readers' ability of rational and logical judgement and conclusion remain the final criteria in the intersubjective achievement of an agreement on a controversial point in question. This conceptualisation aligns with the Habermasian concepts of 'ideal communication' and 'ideal speech situation' that are to be understood as a critical, though mostly counterfactual and partly utopian, models to which societies and speech communities should try to approximate as much as possible.

'*Überreden*' denotes the reaching of a 'particular', that is to say, restricted consent under conditions of suspended rationality. Here, forms of non-argumentative compulsion (emotionalisation, suggestion, demagogy, propaganda, brainwashing, threatening and so on) force or compel to assent and approval by repressing the ability of rational and logical judgement and conclusion.

The distinction between argumentation ready for rational negotiation, i.e. attempts to convince ('*überzeugen*'), and its strategical perversion, i.e. manipulative attempts to persuade ('*überreden*'), is, first of all, an abstract and theoretical one, for one important criterion of distinction is manipulative intentionality, which is at best recognisable indirectly, as it is scarcely communicated explicitly and since nobody can look directly into the human head (see Dieckmann 1975: 37). In concrete cases, it is not always practicable neatly to differentiate the two forms of persuasion from each other.

However, there are rules for rational disputes and constructive arguing that allow for characterising and discerning reasonableness in critical discussions (see the pragma-dialectical approach of van Eeemeren and Grootendorst 1992 and 1994: 21; see also Kienpointner 1996: 26 ff.):

• *Rule 1* (freedom to argue): parties must not prevent each other from advancing or casting doubt on standpoints.
• *Rule 2* (obligation to give reasons): whoever advances a standpoint is obliged to defend it if asked to do so.
• *Rule 3* (correct reference to previous discourse by the antagonist): an attack on a standpoint must relate to the standpoint that has actually been advanced by the protagonist.
• *Rule 4* (obligation to 'matter-of-factness'): a standpoint may be defended only by advancing argumentation relating to that standpoint.

- *Rule 5* (correct reference to implicit premises): a person can be held to the premises she or he leaves implicit. Conversely, antagonists must not be attacked on premises that cannot be inferred from their utterances.
- *Rule 6* (respect of shared starting points): a standpoint must be regarded as conclusively defended if the defence takes place by means of arguments belonging to the common starting point. A premise must not falsely be taken as a common starting point, and, conversely, a shared premise must not be rejected.
- *Rule 7* (use of plausible arguments and schemes of argumentation): a standpoint must be regarded as conclusively defended if the defence takes place by means of arguments in which a commonly accepted scheme of argumentation is correctly applied. A standpoint must not be considered to be conclusively defended if the defence does not take place by means of schemes of argumentation which are plausible and correctly applied.
- *Rule 8* (logical validity): the arguments used in a discursive text must be valid or capable of being validated by the explicitisation of one or more unexpressed premises.
- *Rule 9* (acceptance of the discussion's results): a failed defence must result in the protagonist withdrawing her or his standpoint, and a successful defence in the antagonist withdrawing her or his doubt about the standpoint.
- *Rule 10* (clarity of expression and correct interpretation): formulations must be neither puzzlingly vague nor confusingly ambiguous, and must be interpreted as accurately as possible.

In our view, these ten rules for rational arguing should form the basis of a discourse ethics on which a political model of discursive, deliberative democracy (see chapters 5 and 6) can be grounded and against the background of which one is capable of controlling the discursive political exchange and of identifying and criticising a political rhetoric beyond a constructive discussion in which the participants aim at obtaining an intersubjective consent on a controversial point.

If one wants to analyse the persuasive, manipulative, discursive legitimation of racist, ethnicist, nationalist, sexist and other forms of discrimination and the pseudo-argumentative backing and strengthening of negative, discriminatory prejudices, one encounters many violations of these ten rules. In rhetoric and argumentation theory, these violations are called 'fallacies' (among many others see Kienpointner 1996, van Eemeren, Grootendorst and Kruiger 1987: 78–94, van Eemeren and Grootendorst 1992, Lamham 1991: 77ff., Ulrich 1992).

There is a series of 'pragmatic fallacies' serving the justification of discrimination. The *argumentum ad baculum* consists in 'threatening with the stick' (Latin '*baculum*'), in verbally threatening to use force against the antagonist, in verbally trying to intimidate or to frighten by appealing to physical or other forms of force, violence and fear instead of using plausible and relevant arguments. Antagonists are threatened with exposure to negative sanctionings if they do not give up or adopt a specific standpoint or if they use a specific argument. In such cases, the threat is clearly not in the antagonists' own interests. This fallacy violates rule 1 and rule 4 (for this fallacy see also Hooke 1991). An example would be: 'Anyone who does not agree with our claims for restricting immigration policy can forget about getting elected next time'.

The *argumentum ad hominem* is a verbal attack on the antagonist's personality and character (of her or his credibility, integrity, honesty, expertise, competence and so on) instead of argumentatively trying to refute the antagonist's arguments. As this *argumentum ad* is not concerned with the 'facts' of the matter in question, but with attacking (alleged) concealed motives of those who advance an argument, it violates rule 4. We will illustrate this fallacy in the next section on p. 85 with an example.

The *argumentum ad misericordiam* consists of unjustifiably appealing for compassion and empathy in cases where a specific situation of serious difficulties, crisis or plight intended to evoke compassion and to win an antagonist over to one's side is faked or pretended. In such cases, the appeal for compassion is intended to replace relevant arguments This fallacy violates rule 4. It can be found in examples like 'The voters perfectly know that we, the Austrian Freedom Party, are the real victims of the policy of exclusion'. (This is also an example for a *trajectio in alium*, a victim-victimiser reversal.)

The *argumentum ad populum* or *pathetic fallacy* encompasses more or less populist appeals to 'masses' of people, to 'mobs' or 'snobs'. It consists of the appeal to the prejudiced emotions, opinions and convictions of a specific social group or to the *vox populi* instead of relevant arguments. This fallacy also violates rule 4. We will encounter two examples for pathetic fallacy combined with the topos of numbers below on p. 79.

The *argumentum ad ignorantiam* is an appeal to ignorance. This *argumentum ad* means that a standpoint, argument or thesis is to be regarded as true if it has not been refuted, that is to say, if it has not been proven not to be the case. Conversely, this fallacy also means that from a failed defence one unjustifiably tries to conclude that the contrary standpoint, thesis or argument is true or proven. The appeal to ignorance violates rule 9. Nevertheless, one should not forget that the whole jurisdiction and administration of justice relies on a principle based on this 'argument': '*in dubio pro reo*', if the guilt of an accused person has not been proven, she or he has to be regarded as innocent (see van Eeemeren, Grootendorst and Kruiger 1987: 92).

The *argumentum ad verecundiam* is the misplaced appeal to deep respect and reverence (Latin *verecundia*) for authorities. This fallacy consists of backing one's own standpoint by means of reference to authorities considered to be or passed off as being competent, superior, sacrosanct, unimpeachable and so on. The appeal to an authority is always fallacious if the respective authority is not competent or qualified, if she or he is prejudiced or if she or he is quoted inaccurately. A special 'fallacy of authority' consists of presenting oneself as an authority or expert if one is not, that is to say, in falsely 'parading one's own qualities'. This fallacy violates rules 4 and 7. For an example of this fallacy, see below, i.e. the fallacy of ambiguity, equivocation, amphibole and clarity.

We have already mentioned the fallacy of 'hasty generalisation' or *secundum quid*, which is a generalisation on the basis of a quantitative sample that is not representative. This fallacy can either take the form of a *compositio* or of a *divisio*, the former consisting of replacing the whole by a part, the latter consisting of replacing a part by the whole. This fallacy violates the rules of logic as well as the rules 5 and 7.

The '*post hoc, ergo propter hoc*' fallacy (Latin for 'after this, therefore because of this', i.e. A before B, therefore B because of A) relies on mixing up a temporally chronological relationship with a causally consequential one. That means that this fallacy, violating rule 7, confusingly considers events occurring earlier in time as the causes of events happening later. One can find an example of such a fallacious reasoning in the populist and very often racist or ethnicist argumentation that the increase in unemployment rates within a specific nation-state is the consequence of the growing number of immigrants. This mono-causal '*post hoc*' fallacy, which is without any empirical proof, completely ignores all the complex economic relationships and relevant economic, political and social factors responsible for unemployment.

The *petitio principii*, also known as *begging the question* or as *circular argument/reasoning*, means that what is controversial and in question, and has thus to be proved, is presupposed as the starting point of the argumentation. The fact that in the argument it is assumed that what has to be proved has already been proved is linguistically often hidden by using varying formulations, i.e. paraphrases, for the same proposition in the premises and in the conclusion. This fallacy violates rule 6, as in the following example: 'Immigrants are a burden on the country as they overload the nationals with problems'.

The fallacy of *rigged questions* is committed if one manipulatively asks questions containing one or more presuppositions that are open to discussion, that presuppose an incorrect starting point or that falsely impute something to someone. This fallacy violates rule 6. It is found in utterances like 'When will the Ministry of the Interior finally stop favouring the foreigners over us nationals?' when it is clear that foreigners are not privileged over citizens. This question contains the presupposition that the Ministry of the Interior has been favouring the foreigners over the nationals.

The fallacy of *ignoratio elenchi*, of 'ignoring the counter-proof or counter-argument', consists of discussing or proving a thesis or standpoint that is not the thesis or standpoint in question, but a totally different and irrelevant one that is ascribed to the antagonist and does not matter in the actual 'discourse' (in the sense of 'discussion'). This evasive fallacy is widely used by politicians. It violates rule 3 and 4 (see also p. 104).

The *straw man fallacy* amounts to 'twisting somebody's words', that is to say, to presenting a distorted picture of the antagonist's standpoint in order to be able to refute the standpoint or argument more easily and to make it less tenable. This biasing fallacy violates rule 3 and, in the case of intentionally misinterpreting the premises, rule 5. A special straw man fallacy is the denying of a premise not verbalised or not in question. For an example see pp. 194–5.

The *fallacies of ambiguity, equivocation, amphibole* or *clarity* (the Aristotelian '*fallacies in dictione* ') consist of surreptitiously changing the interpretation of an ambiguous utterance or of intentionally playing with ambiguous, polysemic meanings for the purpose of weakening the antagonist's arguments and standpoint, and for strengthening one's own arguments and standpoint. These fallacies mean misinterpreting words, phrases or sentences literally, which were intended in their figurative sense, or, conversely, taking a word, phrase or sentence in its figurative meaning while it was intended in its literal meaning by the antagonist. They also mean neglecting mitigating and restrictive modifications of utterances in order to be able to impute an exaggerated standpoint to the antagonist (as one can see, these fallacies may overlap with the straw man fallacy). They also mean playing with syntactic or grammatical ambiguity (amphibole), by accent (the fallacy of accent consists of shifting the meaning by means of shifting the stress and emphasis within the sentence), composition and division (for the fallacies of composition and division see the fallacy of 'hasty generalisation'). Some of these fallacies rely on moving out a fragmented piece of discourse from its original context and, in doing so, of falsely reinterpreting it. And some of them consist of deviating from the subject in question by intentionally misunderstanding it. These fallacies violate rule 10. They may, as in the example of the intentional misinterpretation of the concept of 'Christian charity' by the leader of the Austrian Freedom Party, Jörg Haider, be based on the a topos of definition (see also chapter 4, pp.194–5).

There are many other fallacies we cannot discuss in this short overview that seeks to focus on the most important fallacious argumentation schemes that are persuasively employed in the discursive legitimation of racist, ethnicist, nationalist and other forms of discrimination.

There is the *argumentum at consequentiam*, 'in which unfavourable light is cast on a thesis by pointing out its possible consequences, without the rightness of the thesis itself being disputed' (van Eemeren, Grootendorst and Kruiger 1987: 30). There is the *non sequitur* that violates rule 7 and consists of argumentatively tying arguments to a conclusion that would *per se* be correct but where the connection is false, for the conclusion does not follow from the arguments. There is the *trajectio in alium*, strategically employed in rationalisations, in the discursive construction of scapegoats, in victim-victimiser reversals and so on, consisting of putting the responsibility, guilt or blame on somebody else and, thus, also violating rule 7. Finally, there are many formal, logical fallacies violating rule 8: that is to say, the rules of logical conclusion, of syllogism, for example 'affirming the consequent', 'denying the antecedent', 'the fallacy of false dilemma', and so on. We cannot discuss them here and simply refer the reader to Kienpointner (1996: 57–63).

Apart from fallacies, the different forms of social exclusion and discrimination can also be discussed by means of *topoi*, both arguing for and against racism, ethnicism and nationalism.

Within argumentation theory, '*topoi* ' or '*loci* ' can be described as parts of argumentation that belong to the obligatory, either explicit or inferable, premises. They are the content-related warrants or 'conclusion rules' that connect the argument or arguments with the conclusion, the claim. As such, they justify the transition from the argument or arguments to the conclusion (Kienpointner 1992: 194).

As already said, discourse analysts should always keep in mind that the lines between more or less plausible argumentation and fallacies (*'argumenta ad* x') cannot be drawn clearly in any case, especially where prejudiced predications are part of the argumentation schemes.

The analysis of typical content-related argument schemes used in argumentation for and against discrimination (see, for example, Kindt 1992, Kienpointner 1992, Kienpointner 1996, Kienpointner and Kindt 1997, Kopperschmidt 1989, Wengeler 1997, Reeves 1989, Woods 1992) can be done against the background of the following, though incomplete and not always disjunctive, list of topoi. Some of the examples are taken from the written 'Anti-Foreigner Petition' and from the petition campaign that we will analyse in greater detail in chapter 4 (most of the category labels are adopted from Wengeler 1997).

The *topos of advantage* or *usefulness* can be paraphrased through the following conditional: if an action under a specific relevant point of view will be useful, then one should perform it (e.g. usefulness of *'guest workers'* for a national economy). To this topos belong different subtypes, for example the topos of *'pro bono publico'*, (to the advantage of all), the topos of *'pro bono nobis'* (to the advantage of 'us'), and the topos of *'pro bono eorum'* (to the advantage of 'them').

Let us mention just one example of the topos of *'pro bono publico'*. In a decision of the Viennese municipal authorities ('Amtsbescheid der Magistratsabteilung 62'), a refusal of the residence permit is argued as follows (see also chapter 5, p. 219, p. 226):

> Because of the private and family situation of the claimant, the refusal of the application at issue represents quite an intrusion into her private and family life. The public interest, which is against the residence permit, is, however, to be valued more strongly than the contrasting private and familiar interests of the claimant. Thus, it had to be decided according to the judgement.[11]

For another example of this topos, see the explanation of point 12 of the 'Anti-Foreigner Petition' in chapter 4, p. 158.

Like the *topos of advantage* or *usefulness*, the *topos of uselessness/disadvantage* is also a specific causal argumentation scheme, but in contrast to the former, the latter relies on the conditional: If one can anticipate that the prognosticated consequences of a decision will not occur or if other political actions are more likely to lead to the declared aim, the decision has to be rejected. If existing rulings do not help to reach the declared aims, they have to be changed. This topos was employed in Austria in 1992, when the *'Verbotsgesetz'* – the law against revitalising the National Socialist ideology and practices (*'Wiederbetätigung'*) and against the dissemination of the so-called '*Auschwitzlüge*' was amended. The 'Auschwitz lie' consists in the dissemination of the falsehood that it is a lie that there were gas chambers in the concentration camps and that it is a lie that whithin the gas chambers so many Jews, Romany and Sinti, homosexuals, politically persecuted persons, differently abled persons and so-called antisocial persons were murdered by gassing. The '*Verbotsgesetz*' was amended inasmuch as the very high penalties were lowered in order to make an accusation and a verdict of guilty more probable. Before 1992, many judges were deterred by the high penalties and, thus, avoided sentencing the defendants who, consequently, were not called to account for their delicts at all.

The *topos of definition* or *topos of name-interpretation* or *locus a nominis interpretatione* can be traced back to the following conclusion rule: if an action, a thing or a person (group of persons) is named/designated (as) X, the action, thing or person (group of persons) carries or should carry the qualities/traits/attributes contained in the (literal) meaning of X.

This topos is employed if immigrant workers in Austria or Germany are euphemistically called '*Gastarbeiter*' ('guest workers'). The term implies that, because they are 'only guests', they will or they have to return to the countries they came from. Against this specific topos of definition, sometimes another (relying on the same 'econonym', 'actionym' and 'professionym') is mobilised: in such cases it is said that if somebody is a 'guest', she or he has to be treated hospitably like a guest.

The example of 'guest worker', but also of the oxymoronic econo-politonym 'economic refugee' and of naturalising metaphors like 'flood of immigrants', brings us to the question of the relationship between referential strategies and argumentation strategies. We already observed that there can be a close relationship between reference and predication (see p. 46 and pp. 54–5). As the three examples just mentioned clearly show, reference and argumentation can also be neatly associated. The 'guest worker' may contain at least the two contradictory conclusion rules paraphrased above. The naturalising reference 'flood of immigrants' implicitly carries at least two conclusion rules. If something is a flood, it is dangerous and threatening. If something is dangerous and threatening, one should do something against it (the topos of danger or threat, and this is an example of it, will be discussed as the next topos). The conclusion goes as follows: one should prevent the flood from inundating the endangered area. To be precise: one should take measures in order to prevent the immigrants from becoming too many. The phrase 'economic refugee' finally contains the conclusion rules: if somebody is a refugee, she or he leaves her or his country for reasons of persecution. If somebody abandons her or his country for economic reasons, she or he is not a victim of persecution. If somebody is not persecuted, she or he is not a real refugee. If somebody is not a real refugee, she or he should not enjoy the rights of a refugee (in simple terms: she or he should not be taken in and granted asylum).

One can find another topos of definition if one looks back about two-and-a-half decades in the immigration-political history of Austria. Then, in 1972, the following question was employed as a *locus a nominis interpretatione* in an anti-discrimination campaign (named '*Aktion Mitmensch*'): '*I haaß Kolaric, du haaßt Kolaric, warum sogn's zu dir Tschusch?*' ('My name is Kolaric, your name is Kolaric, why do they call you Tschusch?') Here, the topos relies on the multiethnic character of the Austrian population and on the fact that many native Austrians – in this example the person (a child) who asks the question – have Slavic names like 'Kolaric' (which indicates that their genitors, grandparents or ancestors were immigrants). The person asked is a so-called 'guest worker'. '*Tschusch* ' is an Austrian depreciatory insult/name-calling designating foreigners from south-eastern Europe and from the near East. The implicit argument scheme is based on the identity of names of 'Austrians' and 'foreigners' ('Kolaric'). As many of those people who consider themselves to be 'real' Austrians have the same surnames as many so-called 'guest workers' – a fact which testifies that their ancestors were immigrants who were assimilated – these Austrians are not to name-call alien workers: that is to say, are not to discriminate against 'foreigners'. (Another example of a topos of definition and, simultaneously, of a fallacy of ambiguity is the idiosyncratic interpretation of 'Christian charity' by Haider that we will discuss in chapter 4, pp 194–6).

The *topos of danger* or *topos of threat* is based on the following conditionals: if a political action or decision bears specific dangerous, threatening consequences, one should not perform or do it. Or formulated differently: if there are specific dangers and threats, one should do something against them. There are many subtypes of this argument scheme. Here we mention only one of them, namely the '*topos of threat of racism*', which goes as follows: if too many immigrants or refugees enter the country, the native population will not be able to cope with the situation and will become hostile to foreigners. This argument scheme can lead to a victim-victimiser reversal. It was employed by the Austrian government after the Second World War to argue antisemitically for the prevention of remigration and 'reparation' of Austrian Jews driven out of their country (see Knight 1988). Nowadays, it is sometimes backed by the sociobiological assumption of a natural, innate animal and human instinct of territorial defence.

A piece of text in which several dangers are simultaneously and stereotypically mentioned in the form of imaginary, pseudo-argumentative examples can be found in the '*Bezirksjournal Währing* ' (No. 10, 1992). This text, in which the claim of the argumentation is only implied, was published during the period of the 'Anti-Foreigner Petition' campaign (see chapter 4). The author, the FPÖ District Council Member Robert Egghart, evokes the prejudiced dangers of insecurity, of criminality, of aggressivity, of threatening the biological substance of the national people ('*Überfremdung*'/'*Umvolkung* ') and of 'sexual threat':

Public parks – maintained through district budgets – are constantly being destroyed and completely taken over by foreigners. Night-time tram travel is becoming a security risk. Our women, chic and fashionably dressed, are being harassed by sex scoundrels that are clearly classifiable. The over-foreignerisation [*Überfremdung*] has already reached an unbearable level and is leading to a growing threat to all age groups in our district.[12]

As one can easily see from this example, the topos of threat is not always distinguishable from the fallacy of *argumentum ad baculum* (in a wider sense) and from the *argumentum ad populum*. However, this populist text is in any case fallacious, since it is based on a number of prejudices against 'foreigners'.

The *topos of humanitarianism* can be paraphrased by the following conditional: if a political action or decision does or does not conform with human rights or humanitarian convictions and values, one should or should not perform or make it. This topos can be employed in every situation where one argues against unequal treatment and discrimination and for the recognition of 'racialised', ethnic, religious, gendered or other differences.

It is closely connected with the *topos of justice* that is based on the principle and claim of 'equal rights for all'. As a conditional phrase, it means that if persons/actions/situations are equal in specific respects, they should be treated/ dealt with in the same way. For example: as far as social security is concerned, workers should be treated equally, that is to say, irrespective of their citizenship, as they make the same social security payment contributions.

A third argumentation scheme closely related to the two topoi just mentioned is the *topos of responsibility*. It can be summarised by the conditional formula: because a state or a group of persons is responsible for the emergence of specific problems, it or they should act in order to find solutions of these problems. Although this topos is very often employed to argue against discrimination or for 'compensation' or 'reparations' for a committed crime (e.g. a Nazi crime), it can also serve the opposite aim – for example, in cases where a government is held responsible for unemployment and required to reduce the quota of immigrants as they are falsely considered to be the cause of unemployment.

The *topos of burdening* or *weighing down* is to be regarded as a specific causal topos (a topos of consequence) and can be reduced to the following conditional: if a person, an institution or a 'country' is burdened by specific problems, one should act in order to diminish these burdens. Within this context, one can find the metaphorical phrase *'das Boot ist voll'*, 'the boat is full/overcrowded'. Points 2, 6 and 7 of the 'Anti-Foreigner Petition' also contain this topos (see chapter 4).

The *topos of finances* can be characterised by the following conclusion rule: if a specific situation or action costs too much money or causes a loss of revenue, one should perform actions that diminish the costs or help to avoid the loss. This topos, which is also a specific causal topos (topos of consequence), comes close to the 'topos of burdening'. It was employed implicitly by the former head of Upper Austria, Josef Ratzenböck, when he argued against the accommodation of Romanian refugees in the community of Franking (see the Austrian newspaper *Standard* from 10 March 1990): 'Here, we are dealing with people whose origin one can explicitly identify by looking at them, and thus, one is afraid of losses within the framework of tourism'.[13] Though Ratzenböck does not employ an explicit biological/genetic concept of 'race', he implies such a concept by referring to external, perceptible traits, which he connects with descent and which, thus, are somatic, phenotypic and cannot be taken off like clothes. In this example, the 'topos of finances' focuses on allegedly negative socioeconomic consequences.

The *topos of reality* is rather a tautological argumentation scheme that can be paraphrased as follows: because reality is as it is, a specific action/decision should be performed/made. A general example would be: social, economic and political realities have changed and the Asylum Act does not fit anymore. Therefore, the law must also be changed.

The *topos of numbers* may be subsumed under the conclusion rule: if the numbers prove a specific topos, a specific action should be performed/not be carried out. This topos can become fallacious if it is related to incorrectly presumed majorities that are not verified empirically. To mention two examples that combine the topos of numbers with an *argumentum ad populum*: in an article entitled ' "Cute" and other LIF-ideas' (*' "Putzige" und andere LIF-Vorstellungen'*) and published in the local socialist periodical *SPÖ Wien Telegramm – Magazin der Wiener Sozialdemokraten* No. 10/96, the Viennese socialists refute the LIF's (i.e. *'Liberales Forum'*, meaning 'Liberal Forum', the name of the Austrian liberal-democratic party that split off from the right-wing Austrian Freedom Party just after the 'Anti-Foreigner Petition', M.R and R.W.) proposal of awarding the right to vote (for the Viennese State Parliament) to all foreigners who have a permanent residence permit: 'The LIF demands a right to vote for all foreigners who are in possession of a permanent residence permit – that is to say a foreigner franchise with which the majority of the population would probably not agree'.[14] Very similarly, the topos of numbers is combined with the same *argumentum ad populum* by the socialist mayor of Vienna, Michael Häupl, in a second example. In a letter addressed to a student who asked Häupl to explain the vague assertion just quoted, he writes tautologically: 'The reason for the fact that there is no general right to vote for foreigners in these parts is that an extraordinarily large majority of the Austrians are against it'.[15]

The *topos of law* or *topos of right* can be condensed in the conditional: if a law or an otherwise codified norm prescribes or forbids a specific politico-adminis-trative action, the action has to be performed or omitted. The use of this topos is institutionalised in politico-administrative genres like rejections of applications for residence permits: 'The application of the 1st of July 1995 by [... = name of the claimant] for a residence permit in accordance with §1 section 1 and §6 section 1 [...] of the residence law is rejected with regard to §3 section 5 of the residence law'.[16] This topos can be considered to be a specific form of the topos of authority. As such, it is not always easy to delimit it from the *argumentum ad verecundiam*.

The *topos of authority* is based on the conclusion rule: X is right or X has to be done or X has to be omitted because A (= an authority) says that it is right or that is has to be done or that it has to be omitted. Of course, this topos is not easily distinguishable from the fallacy called *argumentum ad verecundiam*. To mention just one example: during the Austrian asylum debate in April 1991, the FPÖ representative Alois Huber argued against 'the mixture of races' (see *Standard*, 6/7 April 1991) by appealing to religious authorities: 'I am opposed to this type of mixture. If the Creator had wanted a single race, he would have created only one race. However there are several races of peoples, and the Lord must have meant something by that'.[17] In this example, Huber holds a biologising concept of race, which he associates with the biblical story of the Creation. By reference to the Creation, Huber tries to justify the racist banning of 'racial mixing', and this banning serves as an argument against immigration for Huber.

The *topos of history* can be described as follows: because history teaches that specific actions have specific consequences, one should perform or omit a specific action in a specific situation (allegedly) comparable with the historical example referred to. A specific subtype of this argumentation scheme is the already Ciceronian topos of *historia magistra vitae*, of 'history teaching lessons' (see Wodak *et al.* 1998: 205–7). This argumentation scheme focuses on a change situated in the past: strictly speaking, on supposedly having learned from history. As such, the topos can be employed as a means of playing down and trivialising terrible and horrendous crimes committed in the past, for the focus of attention is primarily self-referential and concerned with the change ('We have learned from the past, thus, we are now different from then, when we committed the crimes'). This specific topos backgrounds the victims afflicted by the wrongful acts. Topoi of history are sometimes also used to warn of a repetition of the past, the historical analogies being more or less adequate. To compare the leader of the Austrian Freedom Party, Jörg Haider, simply and generally with Hitler, is very often an undifferentiated and counter-productive hyperbole, which does not serve the promotion of anti-discrimination.

The *topos of culture* is based on the following argumentation scheme: because the culture of a specific group of people is as it is, specific problems arise in specific situations. This topos is employed by Haider in combination with the topos of danger in his appeal in the *Neue Freie Zeitung* of 16 December 1992: 'The greatest damage that one can do to a people is to put its identity, its cultural heritage, and the opportunities of its youth negligently at stake. That's why we have introduced the 'Austria First' Petition. In order to guarantee the Austrians their right to a fatherland'.[18] As we will see in chapter 4, point 6 of the petition also contains this type of topos.

To come to the last topos we want to mention in this section, the *topos of abuse* – extensively employed in the petition campaign – can be paraphrased by the following conclusion rule: if a right or an offer for help is abused, the right should be changed or the help should be withdrawn or measures against the abuse should be taken. Rightist politicians fall back upon this topos when they argue for restricting asylum policy by means of reference to an alleged abuse of the asylum law. The topos of abuse is also employed when a change to the social security law is demanded by politicians who are hostile to foreigners and it is attempted to account for this claim by the accusation that aliens exploit the welfare system or social security system of the state in which they are or have been working. Point 10 of the petition and several passages of its 'explanation' rely on this topos (see chapter 4).

Perspectivation and framing, mitigation and intensification

Up to now we have been concerned with three strategic aspects of self-presentation and other-presentation, i.e. with referential strategies, predicational strategies and – non-fallacious as well as fallacious – argumentation strategies. They all play an important role in the discursive discrimination of persons and – at least also partly – in discursively proceeding against social discrimination and exclusion. Apart from these three types of strategies, discourse analysts may also, on the one hand, focus on the perspectivation, framing and discourse representation, and, on the other, on intensifying as well as mitigation strategies. By means of application of the former, speakers express their involvement in discourse and position their point of view in the discursive flux: for example, in the reporting, description, narration and quotation of discriminatory events or utterances and, not least, in the discursive practice of discrimination itself. The latter are applied to qualify and modify the epistemic status of a proposition, the degree of certainty, and to modify the speakers' or writers' expressiveness as well as the persuasive impact on the hearers and readers. They either intensify or mitigate the illocutionary force of racist, antisemitic, nationalist or ethnicist utterances.

We will consider briefly the most frequent of these strategies, as there already exists a substantial amount of linguistic work about involvement, detachment, frame/framing, mitigation and intensification (see, for example, Goffman 1974, Goffman 1981, Gumperz 1982, Chafe 1982, Quirk, Greenbaum, Leech and Svartvik 1985, Tannen 1989, Schiffrin 1994, Langner 1994, Georgakopoulou and Goutsos 1997, Willems 1997, Wodak *et al.* 1997), and as the respective strategies are, in contrast to the three sorts of strategic manoeuvres mentioned above, much more detached from concrete prejudiced contents or topics. These two sorts of strategies can be applied in every discourse and are not a peculiarity of discourses about migration, multiculturalism, 'foreigners', racism, nationalism, ethnicism and so on.

Many of the involvement and detachment strategies are related to the three Goffmanian concepts of 'participation framework', 'frame' and 'footing' (see Goffman 1974: 143–75 and 531–601, Goffman 1981, Schiffrin 1994: 102–5 and Knoblauch 1994: 31).

The concept of '*participation framework*' is intended to mean a set of relationships between individuals present within the perceptual range of specific utterances and utterances themselves. Goffman distinguishes between four forms of relationship or 'participation status', viz. between 'animator', 'author', 'figure', and 'principal'. These four statuses can meet in one and the same person, but they can also fall upon four different people. However: the animator is the person who produces, voices an utterance or fragment of talk, the author is the person who originates, conceives or creates the utterance or talk, a figure is a person portrayed through the utterance or talk, and the principal is the person who is responsible for the utterance or talk and committed to what is said. The melting of the four statuses into one person can be the case in a narrative, if the narrator of the story is the author of it as well as the principal, who is committed to the contents of the narrative, and the animator who verbally tells the story in which the narrator finally is also the main protagonist (figure) who may be positively self-presented.

'*Frames*' are conceptualised as organisational and interactional principles by which situations are defined and sustained as experiences (Goffman 1974). A 'key' is a system of conventions which transforms a specific activity within a specific frame into another activity that imitates the first activity, but which is perceived by the participants as something else (Goffman 1974: 53). Goffman apostrophises the respective processes of systematic transformation as 'modulations'. Among others, Goffman distinguishes between five main keys, viz. pretending, contest, ceremony, special version and putting into another context. Accordingly, one can differentiate different frames, for example, (a) frames of deception, playing, joking, dreaming, (b) frames of contest and fight, (c) frames of celebration (matrimony, funeral, and so on), (d) frames of testing or rehearsal, demonstration or performance, (e) frames of participatory observation, and so on.

'*Footing*', finally, is the way in which writers or speakers arrange themselves and their relationships to others. To put it in Goffman's terms: 'Footing' relates to 'the alignments we take up to ourselves and the others present as expressed in the way we manage the production or reception of an utterance' (Goffman 1981: 128). In other words, 'footing' means the speakers' or writers' discursive establishment of the self as a social entity and the discursive transformation of the self.

As we have already said, footing and framing are closely connected with the speakers' or writers' involvement and distance. *Strategies of involvement* (see Tannen 1989: 9–35) aim both at expressing the speakers' inner states, attitudes and feelings or degrees of emotional interest and engagement and at emotionally and cognitively engaging the hearers in the discourse. These strategies are opposed to *strategies of detachment*, which are realised by discursive means for encoding distance (see Georgakopoulou and Goutsos 1997: 134–9).

To begin with the latter: detachment can be expressed by means of complex, hypotactic syntax such as relative and complement clauses, or sequences of prepositional phrases, or the abstractive passive voice, nominalisations and metonymisations instead of 'vivid' metaphors, or distancing personal, local and temporal deictics and forms of address and salutation, or of indirect speech, and so on (see Georgakopoulou and Goutsos 1997: 134).

Involvement becomes manifest, first of all, in the discoursal organisation of turn-taking: that is to say, in interruptions and overlapping talk. Furthermore, involvement, which very often – but not always – goes hand in hand with intensification, can be expressed and achieved by various linguistic means: for example, by linguistic markers of emphasis and intensification. There are sound markers of involvement operating with all possible sound features that are relevant in a concrete single language to express emphasis, i.e. with melodical parameters (pitch and pitch movement, tone colour), dynamic parameters (stress and modulation of stress, volume and modulation of volume), temporal parameters (tempo, change of tempo, lengthening and shortening, pauses) and articulatory parameters (clarity, change of clarity, legato, staccato) (see Slembek 1983). Apart from expressive phonology, involvement is also verbalised by repetition at all textual or discursive 'levels', for example, by repetitions of phonemes, morphemes, words, collocations of words, phrases and even longer sequences of discourse. In addition, it is non-verbally externalised by gestures and facial expression, and verbally expressed by intensity markers such as emphasising particles ('really', 'very', 'absolutely', 'only'), amplifying particles ('very', 'too', 'absolutely') and emphasising as well as amplifying morphemes (for example, 'super-' and 'mega-'), exaggerating quantifiers and intensifying verbs (not least modal verbs) and verb phrases, adjectives and adverbs that encode the speakers' emotions, feelings, moods and general dispositions (see also Quirk, Greenbaum, Leech and Svartvik 1985). Superlative and primary as well as secondary interjections (see Reisigl 1999a, Sornig 1986, Sornig 1989) intensify and express involvement, as do ellipses, rhetorical figures (especially tropes like the metaphor, irony and hyperbole), meta-communicative parts of utterances (see Langner 1994: 58) and fictitious scenarios.

One way of expressing involvement – as well as detachment – is discourse representation. One can represent, for example, racist, nationalist or ethnicist discourse by means of direct quotation, indirect quotation and free indirect speech. As already noted, indirect speech is, for the most part, an indicator of distance. In comparison, direct speech and free indirect speech often express the speakers' and evoke the hearers' involvement. As far as direct speech is concerned, 'constructed dialogue' (see Tannen 1989: 98–133) and the 'voicing' or animation of voices of constructed or represented figures are particularly outstanding means of dramatisation and authentication designed to express involvement and to involve by enlivening and creating a sense of concreteness. 'Constructed dialogue refers to the representation of characters' speech as direct quotation rather than as a report (indirect speech) or as a dialogue with other characters or with oneself (direct thought representation)' (Georgakopoulou and Goutsos 1997: 136).

Involvement and detachment are highly dependent on the discourse genre and the field of social action with which the genre is associated. Narratives and conversations in particular can have a high degree of involvement, intensifiers being generously superimposed onto the basic narrative syntax.

Detachment can be, though not necessarily, associated with the opposite of intensification, that is to say, with *mitigating*, particularly if mitigation is an expression of prudence and deliberation.

The analysis of mitigation strategies (see Langner 1994, Wodak *et al.* 1997: 293–4) can combine the local analysis of mood/speech act structure and modality with the analysis of the perspective, of the linguistic representation of social actors as well as with the analysis of presuppositions and implications. This is shown by the three tables in figure 2.6, which we adopt from Wodak et al. (1997: 293–4).

Macro-mitigation

(macro-strategies: mitigation in the matrix clause/sentence or in parenthesis)

Categories	Forms/Examples of realisation
• Forms indicating degrees of reservation: – Addressee-oriented	– If you don't mind.../unless I have misunderstood you.../unless I heard it incorrectly
– Speaker-oriented Related to the importance/relevance of the following/previous part of discourse/text or related to the conversational organisation	– I'm not an expert, but... – I have just some additional remarks...
• Modal verbs + verbs of saying	I would like to tell you something...
• Verbs of feeling (verba sentiendi) and verbs of thinking (verba cogitandi)	I think, we can do it over again... I guess, I suppose, I reckon, I gather (used parenthetically)
• Anonymisation by means of impersonalising constructions	It seems quite clear that... (mitigation also by 'seem' and 'quite') It appears that... (mitigation also by 'appear')
• Stereotypical conjunctive	I would like to say...

Indirect micro-mitigation

(micro-strategies: competition between the basic illocution and the realised illocution, ordered according to the strength of indirectness)

Categories	Forms/Examples of realisation

• Question instead of assertion
  Basic: question/realised: directive
  (Especially together with negations)
	Shouldn't we go further?
	Can you shut the window, Robert?

• Assertion with 'we'/'one'/'it' instead of directive with 'you'	We have to consider recent developments in... It will be necessary to consider...
• Assertion 'we'/'one'/'it' instead of assertion with 'I'	We proposed the new strategy yesterday... One cannot carry on as usual after this...
• Particles and adverbs in questions and directives	Surely you are not serious? Would you kindly fasten your seatbelts?

Direct micro-mitigation

(micro-strategies)

Categories	Forms/Examples of realisation
• Vague expressions	There may be some points you didn't mention before.
• Tag questions	It was because of the tension, wasn't it?
• Particles and adverbs	fairly, pretty, quite, rather, somewhat, supposedly, perhaps, theoretically, technically, strictly speaking, just, possibly, probably, likely,...
• Subjunctive	Such a move might anger much of black Africa/it would be endangering relations to black Africa
• Negation/litotes	not unlikely, not unhappy, not unreasonable,... The relationship here is not unproblematic.
• Hesitations, false starts, self-corrections, repetitions	well - - -/yes uhm they don't want ah to adapt themselves

Figure 2.6 Mitigation strategies

All these strategies can be employed in mitigating discriminatory (racist, antisemitic, nationalist and ethnicist) utterances, but also in mitigating the critique of racism, antisemitism, nationalism, ethnicism and so on. It is clearly not possible to illustrate these as well as the above listed intensification/ involvement and detachment strategies example by example. At this point, therefore, we can only refer the reader to the following three chapters, where we will illustrate and discuss these strategies selectively, from case to case. Especially in chapter 3, when we exemplify and analyse the explicitness and implicitness of antisemitic utterances, the readers will have the occasion to become acquainted with lingustic strategies of mitigation. However, to conclude the present chapter, we will briefly illustrate the discourse-historical approach with an example of political discourse.

'Even black Africans': a short discourse-historical analysis

The following example is taken from an interview with Jörg Haider, the leader of the Austrian Freedom Party (FPÖ). The interview was printed in the Austrian weekly *profil* on 24 February 1997, on page 19. The topic was a directive (*Weisung*) issued on 26 November 1996 by the FPÖ politician Karl-Heinz Grasser, at that time deputy head of the government of the Province of Carinthia in Austria and also the highest official (*Landesrat*) in the building and tourist industries in Carinthia. In his directive, Grasser instructed his consultant (*Referenten*) for roadwork to include a regulation in the tender invitations for public building projects that such projects were exclusively to be carried out by indigenous (*heimisch*) workers or by workers from states of the European Union. As a consequence, an intensive public discussion arose, and there was strong protest against Grasser's proposal of institutionalising such an 'exclusionary practice'. Finally, Grasser revoked the directive. During the discussion, Jörg Haider was interviewed about the 'Grasser affair'. The journalist from *profil*, Klaus Dutzler, asked Haider what he, as leader of the FPÖ, was going to recommend to Grasser, his fellow party member and protégé at that time:

PROFIL: You will not recommend to Karl-Heinz Grasser that he give in?

HAIDER: We never thought differently and will continue to do so. The indigna-
tion, of course, just comes from the side of those like the Carinthian guild
master for construction, a socialist, who makes money out of cheap labour
from Slovenia and Croatia. And if, today, one goes by one of Hans Peter
Haselsteiner's 'Illbau' building sites, and there, the foreigners, even down
to black Africans, cut and carry bricks, then the Austrian construction
worker really thinks something. Then one must understand, if there are
emotions.[19]

Haider's answer is remarkable in respect of the employed referential strategies, the negative other-presentation by the attributions and predications

directed against the different groups of 'them', and the enthymemic argumentation serving the justification of 'emotions' against 'the foreigners even down to
black Africans'.

The social actors mentioned by the journalist are 'Jörg Haider', social-
deictically addressed as '*Sie*' (the German formal term of address), and 'Karl-
Heinz Grasser'. The social actors mentioned by Haider are – in chronological
order of their sequential appearance – 'we', 'the socialist Carinthian guild
master for construction', 'the cheap labour from Slovenia and Croatia', 'the
building contractor (and politician of the Austrian party *Liberales Forum*) Hans
Peter Haselsteiner', 'the foreigners', 'black Africans' and 'the Austrian
construction worker'.

There are at least three strategic moves in this short transcript from the
interview.

The first one is the political self-presentation of the FPÖ as a party which
holds firm positions and acts publicly in unison. In this way Haider woos the
voters' favour. According to the question asked by the journalist, one would
expect an answer with a transitivity structure in which Haider (as a sayer)
would recommend (a verbal or/and mental process in Halliday's (1994) terms)
to Grasser (the receiver or target) that he do something (a proposal). Haider
does not meet this expectation. He refuses to present himself explicitly as a
leader advising his fellow party member in public (and thereby threatening
Grasser's reputation and that of the party) and instead takes refuge in a referentially ambiguous 'we' (rather than using the expected 'I'), which helps to evade
the exclusive referential focus both on Grasser and on himself. The ambivalent
'we' allows different, although not mutually exclusive, interpretations. On the
one hand, it can be understood as 'party-we' that is intended to demonstrate a
closed, unanimous, fixed position of the whole party on the issue in question.
The temporal deixis by past and future tense backs this conjecture. If one
knows the history of the FPÖ and the fact that Haider has been an authoritarian
party leader since he came into power in 1986, on the other hand, one is led to
interpret the 'we' as a sort of plural of majesty that is employed regulatively to
prescribe how the party members of the FPÖ are required to think at the
moment and in future.

However, after having introduced this ambiguous 'we', which, in addition
to having the two functions mentioned above, invites potential FPÖ voters to
acclaim or join Haider's position, Haider then sets out to present the critics of
the directive negatively. This is the second strategic move. Haider deliberately
chooses two prominent critics (who are also political adversaries) as *partes pro
toto* in the groups of critics. He debases the socialist Carinthian guild master
(whom he does not identify by proper name) by depicting him as an unsocial,
capitalist socialist who exploits 'the cheap labour (*Arbeitskräfte*) from Slovenia
and Croatia' (here, one may take note of Haider's impersonal and abstract
reference to human beings as a cheap labour). This image of the unsocial
capitalist who egoistically wants to profit from wage dumping is also inferentially
passed on to the second political opponent mentioned by Haider. We can assume

that the reader knows from the Austrian political context that the building contractor, Hans Peter Haselsteiner, is a politician. Viewed from an argumentation analytical perspective, Haider argues here at one and the same time *secundum quid*, i.e. taking a part (as = two critics) for the whole (as = for all critics of Grasser's directive), and *ad hominem* (i.e., he employs a fallacy of relevance, see Lanham 1991: 779), and he disparages the character of the critics in order to call into question the credibility of all critics – instead of attacking their arguments.

Haider's third strategic move is partly embedded in the negative presentation of Hans Peter Haselsteiner. It is realised as an imaginary scenario (with the character of an argumentative example) and aims to justify the 'emotions' of hostility towards foreigners. This move relies on the shift of responsibility, in rhetorical terms, on a *trajectio in alium* that places the blames on Haselsteiner and the socialist Carinthian guild master, instead of on those who have racist 'emotions' and Haider himself (for instigating populism).

Haider's third move contains a blatant racist utterance. Here, the party leader discursively constructs a discriminatory hierarchy of 'foreigners' around the phenotypic feature of skin colour – strictly speaking, around the visible 'deviation' (black) of a specific group of 'foreigners' (i.e. black Africans) from the 'average white Austrian'. Most probably it is no accident that Haider refers to 'black Africans' – that is to say, that he explicitly uses the word 'black'. In the context given, the attribute 'black' has an intensifying function. It helps Haider (who, though he explicitly denies it later on in the interview, wants to emotionalise) to carry his *black-and-white portrayal* to extremes in a literal sense as well. The racist intensification 'even down to black Africans' implies that in Austria, black African workers, because of their most visible 'otherness', are 'an even worse evil' than other 'foreigners', and therefore functions as argumentative 'backing'. Haider seems to intend to construct the greatest possible visual difference between Austrians and 'foreigners'. His utterance can thus be seen as an example of 'differentialist racism' in its literal sense. The outgroups of 'the foreigners, even down to black Africans' (the definite article is characteristic for stereotypical discourse) employed as construction workers are opposed to the ingroup of construction workers. Haider apostrophises the latter synecdochically as 'the Austrian construction worker'. As their self-appointed spokesman, he asks for understanding for the Austrian workers' 'emotions' in the face of the 'foreign, and even black African workers'. At this point, Haider does not argue why 'one' should understand the 'emotions'. He simply relies on the discriminatory prejudice (functioning as an inferable 'warrant' in this enthymemic argumentation) that 'foreigners' take away working places from 'ingroup members'. Furthermore, he relies on the unspoken postulate that 'Austrians', in comparison with 'foreigners', should be privileged with respect to employment.

However, it is not just Haider's argumentation that is truncated, incomplete and vague. In particular, the naming of the prejudicial (mental, attitudinal), verbal and actional hostilities to 'foreigners' is extremely evasive and euphemistic in Haider's utterance. In this regard, Haider exclusively identifies and names mental and emotional processes: with respect to 'foreigners' (including black Africans), 'the Austrian construction worker' is clearly thinking of something – the German particle *schon* ('really') serves here as an inference triggering device that suggests comprehensibility. And in his last sentence, Haider lays down a very euphemistic concluding overall claim with an instigatory potential: 'one' is obligated ('must') to be understanding if there are emotions. In other words, the 'emotions', and whatever the reader of Haider's interview connects with this nonspecific cover-term that opens the way to a vast variety of associations, are totally justifiable.

Notes

1 In the German original, Horkheimer, quoted by O'Neill (1979: 273), writes: 'Aus der kritischen Theorie Konsequenzen für politisches Handeln zu ziehen, ist die Sehnsucht derer, die es ernst meinen, jedoch besteht kein allgemeines Rezept, es sei denn die Notwendigkeit der Einsicht in die eigene Verantwortung'.

2 The German original reads as follows: 'In einem weiteren, Lebensformen, Mentalitäten und Selbstverständnis einschließendem Sinne aber sind die meisten längst so etwas wie einheimische Ausländer, ausländische Inländer, Bindestrich-Deutsche (in reference to Germany), Paß-Ausländer oder Deutsche mit einem fremden Paß. Begriffe "greifen" nur, wenn sie ihrem Gegenstand entsprechen. Deswegen entlarven paradoxe Begriffe eine paradoxe Situation – in diesem Falle eine Einwanderungssituation ohne Einwanderungsland' (Bade 1994: 10).

3 The original version is: 'Die Herkunft der Ausländer in Österreich weicht stark von der anderer europäischer Länder ab. In der Schweiz kommen etwa 70% der Ausländer aus der EG, in Schweden etwa die Hälfte aus dem europäischen Wirtschaftsraum. Im Gegensatz dazu stammt der Großteil der Ausländer in der BRD, aber auch in Österreich, aus Gebieten außerhalb des europäischen Wirtschaftsraumes. (Begründung, 2)'.

4 The German version goes as follows: 'Wir [= the Jews] haben auch Verbrecher. Wenn Herr Müller ein Verbrecher ist, heißt es, Herr Müller ist ein Verbrecher. Aber wenn Moses Gercek ein Verbrecher ist, sagt man: "Die Juden sind Verbrecher".' (Heenen-Wolff 1994: 26 f.).

5 Verbatim in German: 'Jeder Buschneger hat in Zukunft die Möglichkeit, seine Kollegen in Österreich zu behandeln' (see *Der Standard*, 13 October 1998: 7).

6 The original reads as follows: '*Headline*: Zwei Afrikaner in Haft. 6000mal Rauschgift verscherbelt. *Lead*: Einen "Rekord" stellten zwei Dealer aus Afrika auf: Das Duo verscherbelte in nur viereinhalb Monaten mehr als 6000mal Kokain und Heroin an Süchtige in Wien! Noch Stunden, bevor sie gefaßt wurden, hatten sie ihren "Wochengewinn" von 150.000 Schilling nach Senegal überwiesen. *Text*: Als "Büro" diente den Männern – täglich exakt von 17 bis 19 Uhr – entweder der Döblinger Steg oder die Friedensbrücke in Wien. Zwei süchtige Wiener standen Schmiere, gaben sofort Zeichen, wenn sich Polizisten näherten. Laut Ermittlungen hatten die Afrikaner – in der Szene waren sie als "Jimmy" und "Ali" bekannt – pro Tag 40 bis 50 Kunden. Und das rund 120 Tage lang. Bei der Einvernahme wollten die beiden, die gefälschte Ausweise bei sich hatten, von nichts wissen. Nicht einmal die eigenen Namen fielen ihnen ein. Nur einmal sah "Ali" plötzlich auf einen Aktenordner, las den Firmennamen und sagte: "Ich heiße «Bene» ...". Ein Komplice namens "Rene" ist noch flüchtig'.

7 The Austrian German transcript goes as follows: 'Es san ganz grund/diese grundlegendn – öh Mentalitätn und aus den untaschiedlichn Lebnsformen i ma:n des – lieg schon – öh allein darin daß vielleicht da Südlända – bedingt durch die dort herrschende Hitze ebm mehr unta togs – öh Siesta mocht und herumliegt und eignlich

am Obnd erst munta wird. nein? des san natürlich Gegensätze die: – automatisch bei uns zum Konflikt führn'.

8 The original version is: 'Da war der Außenminister und noch so ein Bloßfüßiger, und wir warten, bis die Baraber hereinkommen und die Kamera hereintragen ...'.

9 In German: 'Der ist dort gesessen wie ein Kümmeltürk, mit seinem Bart, und hat stundenlang nicht geredet'.

10 The German version reads as follows: 'Wenn ich das so sage: Zigeuner. Wir sind unter diesem Namen verfolgt worden, und ich finde, daß man den Namen, unter dem man verfolgt wurde, tragen sollte. Sinti wollte man uns nennen, aber das ist etwas, was uns persönlich angeht. Sinti, das ist mein Sittengesetz. Aber nach Dachau verlangte man, daß man "Zigeuner" – weil es ein Schimpfwort ist und von der Landfahrerstelle noch immer nicht rausgestrichen ist – nicht mehr gebraucht und das Wort "Sinti" sagt. Aber wenn man seit dem 16. Jahrhundert vogelfrei war und verfolgt ist unter diesem Namen, dann bin ich sehr stolz, daß ich ein Zigeunerle bin. Und ich bleib auch bei dem Wort Zigeunerle. Es sind Tausende von uns unter diesem Wort verfolgt und vergast worden. Man sollte diesem Wort richtig Achtung entgegenbringen' (Ebbinghaus 1994: 377).

11 Verbatim originally: 'Aufgrund der privaten und familiären Situation der antrag-stellenden Partei stellt die Abweisung des gegenständlichen Antrags durchaus einen Eingriff in ihr Privat- und Familienleben dar. Das öffentliche Interesse, welches gegen die Erteilung einer Aufenthaltsbewilligung spricht, ist aber höher zu veranschlagen als die gegenläufigen privaten und familiären Interessen der antragstellenden Partei. Es war daher spruchgemäß zu entscheiden'.

12 The German version goes as follows: 'Parkanlagen – erhalten aus dem Bezirksbudget – dauernd demoliert und von Ausländern regelrecht besetzt. Die nächtliche Straßenbahn wird zum Sicherheitsrisiko. Unsere Frauen, chic und modisch gekleidet, werden von eindeutig zuordenbaren Sexstrolchen angepöbelt. Die Überfremdung hat bereits ein unzumutbares Maß erreicht und führt zu einer wachsenden Bedrohung aller Altersgruppen in unserem Bezirk'.

13 In German: 'Es handelt sich hier um Leute aus Ländern, denen man die Abstammung eindeutig ansieht, und man fürchtet dadurch Rückgänge im Rahmen des Fremdenverkehrs'.

14 The original text is: 'Das LIF will ein Wahlrecht für alle Ausländer, die im Besitz einer unbefristeten Aufenthaltsgenehmigung sind – also ein Ausländerwahlrecht, das bei der Mehrheit der Bevölkerung wohl keine mehrheitliche Zustimmung fände'.

15 In the German version one reads: 'Ein generelles Wahlrecht für Ausländer gibt es deshalb hierzulande nicht, weil eine außerordentlich große Mehrheit der Österreicher-innen und Österreicher dagegen ist'.

16 The German text is: 'Der Antrag vom 1. 7. 1995 der [..., = name of the applicant] auf Erteilung einer Bewilligung gemäß §§ 1 Abs. 1 und 6 Abs. 1 Aufenthaltsgesetz, BGBl. Nr. 466/1992, i.d.F. BGBl. Nr. 351/95 wird im Hinblick auf § 3 Abs. 5 AufG. abgewiesen'.

17 Verbatim in German: 'Ich bin ein Gegner einer diesbezüglichen Vermischung. Wenn der Schöpfer eine einzige Rasse gewollt hätte, hätte er auch nur eine einzige Rasse gemacht. So aber gibt es mehrere Volksrassen, und da wird sich der Herrgott etwas dabei gedacht haben'.

18 The original text goes as follows: 'Der ärgste Schaden, den man einem Volk zufügen kann, ist es, seine Identität, sein kulturelles Erbe, die Chancen seiner Jugend fahrlässig aufs Spiel zu setzen. Darum haben wir das Volksbegehren "Österreich zuerst" eingeleitet. Um den Österreichern ihr Recht auf Heimat zu sichern'.

19 The excerpt in the original German is as follows:
profil: Sie werden Karl-Heinz Grasser nicht empfehlen nachzugeben?
Haider: Wir haben zu keiner Zeit anders gedacht und werden das weiter tun. Die Empörung kommt ohnehin nur aus der Richtung jener wie dem Kärntner Bau-

Innungsmeister, einem Sozialisten, der sein Geschäft mit Billigarbeitskräften aus Slowenien und Kroatien macht. Und wenn man heute in Kärnten an einer Illbau-Baustelle von Hans Peter Haselsteiner vorbeigeht und dort die Ausländer bis hin zu Schwarzafrikanern Ziegel schneiden und tragen, dann denkt sich der österreichische Bauarbeiter schon etwas. Da muß man verstehen, wenn es Emotionen gibt.

Please note that the linguistic analysis of this piece of text, as well as of all other German examples within the present book, is always based on the original German data and not on their translation into English.

3 The coding of a taboo

Antisemitic everyday discourse in postwar Austria

We are now in a position to understand the antisemite. He is a man who is afraid. Not of the Jews, to be sure, but of himself, of his own consciousness, of his liberty, of his instincts, of his responsibilities, of solitariness, of change, of society, and of the world – of everything except the Jews.

(Sartre, 1994[1954]: 35)

Comment expliquez-vous que la presse internationale ait été aussi largement critique envers vous? [...] Mais parce qu'elle est dominée *par le Congrès juif mondial, c'est bien connu!*

(Kurt Waldheim in an interview with Claire Trean,
Le Monde, 3 May 1986: 4)

It would be ridiculous to deny that the racist Nazi propaganda found a certain echo among some Austrians; but once they saw the means by which this anti-semitism was translated into action, they were cured. One can confidently assert that compassion for the persecuted Jews has obliterated antisemitism in Austria. I do not believe that this question will ever again have the slightest significance [for Austria].

(Leopold Figl, the first elected Federal Chancellor of the
Second Austrian Republic, Shanghai Echo,
cited in *Der Neue Weg*, No. 10, June 1947: 11)[1]

Unfortunately, these words of Figl, one of the 'founding fathers' of the Second Austrian Republic, have proven to be untrue in at least two senses. Apart from the fact that they play down the extent of antisemitic acclamation by Austrians during the Nazi period by mitigating quantifiers like 'some' and adjectives like 'certain' (see chapter 2, p. 84) – these words have been falsified by the fact that even after 'Auschwitz', after 1945, antisemitism in various discursive forms continued to be virulent in Austria, in all public and private domains and political spheres (see Knight 1988, Mitten 1992, 1997, Mitten and Wodak 1993, Wodak *et al.* 1990, Wodak 1990a, 1990b, 1991a, 1996a, 1997a, 1997b, Pelinka and Mayr 1998). But, in contrast to the First Austrian Republic that lasted from 1918 to 1934, when antisemitic utterances were explicit and permitted in all political parties, the situation in postwar Austria was different. Antisemitism was officially taboo, but paradoxically still visible. A coded discourse of antisemitism evolved, specifically in the public domains where the traditional antisemitic content and stereotypes (like the stereotype of the Jewish world conspiracy, see chapter 2, p. 56) could be uttered in new and subtle discursive ways. On the other hand, in private conversations, even in political meetings, the antisemitic discourse was and is still very open and explicit. Thus, we can observe a context-dependence of the form of antisemitism. While much of the content has stayed the same, some new variations have been created, like the stereotype of the 'rich Jew who could emigrate anyway and did not suffer'.

The most important aspect of postwar Austrian history has been the establishment of the myth of having been the first victim of the Hitlerite regime, and thus not being guilty for anything that happened during the Third Reich. The 'Moscow declaration', issued by the foreign ministers of the US, Great Britain and the Soviet Union in October 1943, included both the statement that Austria 'was the first victim of Hitler's typical policy of aggression' and that Austria has to take responsibility for having fought on the German side. After 1945, the incriminating part of the declaration was backgrounded and the victimising part of the declaration was one-sidedly employed for a fallacious, heteronomising *argumentum ad verecundiam* (the misplaced appeal to authorities) by means of which the Austrian National-Socialists should be exculpated. Thus, the extermination of the Jews was projected as being the guilt of the Germans and not seen as an Austrian problem. This led to silence, to a taboo on the Austrian past, and if anybody dared touch these issues – as happened during the 'Waldheim Affair' in the 1980s – legitimating and justifying strategies emerged and almost any involvement was denied. Very different argumentation strategies characterise these discourses, which we will elaborate in this chapter.

The German situation was very different (Stern 1993, Bergmann and Erb 1990, Bergmann, Erb and Lichtblau 1995). In Germany, which was occupied by the Allied forces (as was Austria until 1955), guilt was acknowledged and the past could not be denied. As Frank Stern has analysed in detail, antisemitism turned into philosemitism, whereby suddenly almost everything a Jew allegedly did or was would be evaluated positively, the negative stereotypes turning into positive stereotypes. Stern describes this attitude as the 'philosemitic habitus' of the Germans.

At the 'zero hour' in 1945, the Second Austrian Republic's main concern was whether and how Austria's ruling elite could ideologically, constitutionally, and politically do justice to the various demands it was faced with, demands that frequently arose out of opposing values (see Mitten 1997). The result was the discursive construction of a self-image in which the 'Jewish question' was not so much denied as concealed. Several critical studies (Knight 1988, Rathkolb 1988, Wagnleitner 1984, Pelinka and Mayr 1998) tend to attribute this lack of public debate and deliberation (in comparison to Germany) about the 'Jewish question' to bare cynicism or the remains of antisemitic hostility on the part of the ruling politicians. However, when one considers the contradictory conditions – the occupation, the still existing reservoir of antisemitic prejudices from the First Austrian Republic and the commitment to becoming a 'Western democracy' – within which a new 'Austrian identity', a new 'collective memory' or a 'public memory' was to be constituted, one could hardly have been surprised by the outcome: the 'Jewish question' ended up by taking a subordinate place in Austria's official 'public memory' about the Nazi period (see Mitten 1999).

Ultimately, the new, exculpating, self-victimising 'identity policy', as described in detail by Richard Mitten (1997), led to the creation of a new community of 'victims', where the Jews occupied an insignificant place. In other words, they were just victims like everyone else, the Austrian Nazi policy concerning the Jews was trivialised, minimised or concealed, and the question of an – at least – symbolic material 'compensation' or of 'reparations' (*Wiedergutmachung*) was protracted for roughly four decades. In the eyes of the political elite who constructed the new national identity, new values and myths, the 'silence' about the Jews was as much a sign of moral conviction as it was of moral deficit.

This silence was first broken through the 'Waldheim Affair' in 1986 and the commemorative year 1988 (Wodak *et al.* 1990, 1994). Since the beginning of the 1990s, Austrian politicians have been debating the question of Austrian responsibility (cf. Wodak *et al.* 1998 and Wodak *et al.* 1999), and, more recently, the exhibit about the crimes of the *Wehrmacht* (Manoschek 1996) has further contributed to the lifting of the taboo.

In this chapter, we would like to summarise some aspects of the revival or persistence of Austrian antisemitism since 1945. The research from which these results derive was undertaken at the Department of Applied Linguistics at the University of Vienna, in several interdisciplinary projects (involving linguists, historians, psychologists and political scientists) in recent years (see especially Wodak *et al.* 1990, but also Wodak *et al.* 1994 and Wodak *et al.* 1999).

In these investigations, the discursive (including referential, argumentation and mitigation) strategies and linguistic realisations of antisemitic prejudices were explored and made explicit, taking the concept of 'syncretic antisemitism' (see Mitten 1992 and chapter 1, p. 6 and p. 10, as well as chapter 2, p. 56) as a point of departure, which is based on the assumption that the boundaries between a racist, ethnicist, economist or religious antisemitism are fluid, and that antisemitic stereotypes are (re-)produced and functionalised differently depending on the sociopolitical situation and interactional context. The data which were analysed come from the media (TV, news broadcasts, newspapers and journals) on the one hand, and speeches of politicians or everyday conversations on the street on the other. Where necessary and available, data from opinion polls were integrated and analysed critically (Mitten 1994b, Wodak 1997a).

In our selective summary, we elaborate on some points of Austrian history as background for recent political developments, focusing on the 'Waldheim Affair'. Our understanding of 'discursively coded antisemitism' will be illustrated with a number of examples from this political discussion.

The political and historical Austrian context and the 'Waldheim Affair'

Postwar antisemitism in Austria

The German-Jewish author Henryk Broder, in his book *'Der ewige Antisemit'* (1986) – as one can easily guess, the title of this book is an inverted analogical allusion to the prejudice of 'the eternal Jew', 'the eternally restless, homeless migrant' (see the third antisemitic prejudice in chapter 2: 'Jews are restless, homeless and eternal migrants') – has repeated the halting phrase attributed to Zvi Rix, that the Germans will never forgive the Jews for Auschwitz. Surveying the past decades in Austria, it seems as though Broder's cynical phrase ironically describing the Germans' rationalising projection that aims at putting the guilt on the victims, could apply equally to Austria. Many of the qualms one might have had earlier were overcome in the 1986 presidential election campaign of Kurt Waldheim. Then, particularly in private discourse contexts, few Austrians with antisemitic convictions felt constrained in their utterances, and anti-Jewish prejudices found various verbal outlets of a more or less explicit kind.

Bernd Marin, a sociologist, has characterised the postwar Austrian situation as 'antisemitism without Jews and without antisemites' (Marin 1983). He assumed that antisemitism was constantly used as a political tool, that it was functionalised, but that almost nobody could dare to call him- or herself antisemitic after the Holocaust. This widely holds true, although politicians like Oskar Helmer, a socialist and the first Austrian minister of the interior of the Second Republic, as well as Leopold Kunschak, the first leader of the Christian Austrian People's Party ÖVP, even after 1945 made no great secret of their antisemitic attitudes.

Antisemitism was present in Austria immediately after 1945, before 1938, during the Second World War, and is still present today. Throughout the past 55 years, statistical surveys, opinion polls and content analysis have developed different standardised quantitative research and survey procedures for identifying and measuring antisemitic prejudices. Of course, these procedures are always dependent on the design of the studies, the intentions of the researchers, the questions asked and on the samples themselves (e.g. Weiss 1987, Kienzl and Gehmacher 1987 and Gottschlich 1987). One of the polls (Kienzl 1987) showed that 7 per cent of the Austrian population are radical antisemites: nobody, however, has clearly defined what a radical or less radical antisemite might be. All the quantitative studies which rely on standarised questionnaires or on content analysis work with relatively fixed, preshaped categories of coding and analysis. They obviously have to neglect a whole range of possible – explicit and implicit – prejudices and their linguistic manifestation. Of course, many informants give biased answers or do not answer at all. In Kienzl's and Gehmacher's study (1987) which presented this 'famous' 7 per cent, there were 40 per cent non-answers.

This research deficiency is a strong argument for promoting a linguistic, discourse-analytical approach to antisemitism. Unfortunately, up to now, only very few have attempted to analyse the nature of anti-Jewish prejudice after the mass-exterminations from a linguistic perspective that, *inter alia*, takes into consideration 'authentic' communicative data from different interactional settings, including everyday conversations. A linguistic analysis, however, would allow us particularly to detect, diagnose and interpret precisely the more subtle, hidden and latent forms of antisemitic prejudices.

The persistence of antisemitic attitudes in the above-mentioned opinion polls is ascribed to a small group of right-wing radicals. The number of such (radical) antisemites could thus be carefully delimited, and their numbers be shown to be falling. 'Antisemitism' is also frequently identified with a purely racist variety of anti-Jewish prejudice, which is equated with Nazism or with the Nazi extermination of the Jews, thereby effectively excluding or minimising other antisemitic trends in Austria, such as the Christian or the Christian-Social traditions.

If one looks at the history of the political parties in the First Austrian Republic, for example, it is clear that the line dividing the different currents of antisemitism was indistinct. There has remained a reservoir of antisemitic prejudice on which, appropriately packaged, one could (and can) draw as occasion required. Since 1945, moreover, new motives for antisemitism have arisen. What Broder said about the Germans is certainly applicable to the Austrians as well: they will never forgive the Jews for Auschwitz. The collapse of the Third Reich forced many, in Austria as in Germany, to be confronted with the extent of the Nazi crimes. Doubts, guilt feelings and the need to justify or rationalise one's behaviour encouraged the development of strategies for 'dealing with the past': playing down the actions and events themselves, denying knowledge of them, transforming the victims into the causes of present woes. Moreover, since the Moscow Declaration in 1943 (see above, p. 92) was interpreted as offering Allied support for Austria's claim to have been 'collectively' the first 'victim' of Hitlerite aggression, such reversals could draw upon an especially potent form of legitimation.

The putative victim status also made it possible to deny any responsibility which went beyond individual crimes. The newly constructed Austrian identity could produce a stronger feeling of nationalism, which in turn reinforced a specific definition of insiders and outsiders and delimitation of 'us' from 'them'.

Since 1945 in Austria, there have been intermittent scandals involving antisemitic prejudice. In 1967, for example, the openly antisemitic outpourings of Thaddeus Borodajkiewicz, economics professor in Vienna, led to protests both from his opponents and his supporters. At one of these protests, a Borodajkiewicz opponent was killed by the economics professor's neo-Nazi supporters. This occasioned a bipartisan demonstration against political violence, but no corresponding campaign against his views. Borodajkiewicz himself was forced into early retirement (see Welzig 1985). In the 1970 electoral campaign before the elections for the Austrian national assembly, posters of the candidate of the Austrian People's Party for chancellor, Josef Klaus, emphasised that he, unlike his opponent Bruno Kreisky, whose Jewish origins were well known, was 'a genuine Austrian' (see Wodak and de Cillia 1988).

Between 1945 to 1949, former members of what were termed 'more incriminated' Nazi organisations were disenfranchised as a part of the de-Nazification policy. In the 1949 elections, the '*Verband der Unabhängigen*', the Union of Independents, which reorganised the Pan-German, 'nationally inclined' voters, captured twenty seats in parliament. The Austrian Freedom Party (FPÖ) was formed in 1954 out of the Union of Independents (see chapter 4, p. 151). Friedrich Peter was chairman of the FPÖ in 1975 when Simon Wiesenthal published incriminating material about him. The documentary material ostensibly linked the leader of the Freedom Party to massacres carried out by the SS-unit to which he had belonged. This was the occasion for a spate of public invective against Wiesenthal led by Bruno Kreisky. Kreisky insinuated, for example, that Wiesenthal had been a Gestapo informer. Moreover, another Kreisky comment, in an interview with a foreign journalist ('if the Jews are a people, they are a lousy (*mies*) people'), could in this context only serve to provide Jewish 'cover' for hostilities against Wiesenthal by those less schooled in the complexities of Kreisky's views. Kreisky's own conception of nationhood, among others, derived from the Austrian socialist theorist Otto Bauer. Bauer's criterion for a nation was that it be a 'community of fate' ('*Schicksalsgemeinschaft*'). Neither Bauer, who died in 1938, nor Kreisky, who died in 1990, would concede that the Jews are a nation. This in itself is a legitimate position to defend, and Kreisky's pejorative and contemptuous aside probably referred to the difficulty of the Jews conforming to his (unspecified) criteria of nationhood. This, however, in no way mitigates the charge of irresponsibility, and, in the context, would easily be seen as pandering to the anti-Wiesenthal hostilities of the FPÖ voters (for more background information on this 'affair' see van Amerongen 1977; Wodak *et al.* 1990).

Against the wave of antisemitic hostilities unleashed by the events of 1986, these two prior scandals appear as minor affairs, as we will show in the following sections of this chapter. Under the perspective of referential strategies (see chapter 2, pp. 45–69), the public discourse switched in 1986 – during the 'Waldheim Affair' – noticeably into a sharp 'us' and 'them' pattern. 'We', the ingroups, in this discourse were: 'Austria' (note the metonymic-synecdochic *totum pro parte*), 'Waldheim' (often taken as a *pars pro toto* for all 'respectable' Austrians), 'the People's Party', 'the *Wehrmachtgeneration*' (note the militarising metonymic gerontonym), 'all the people who wanted to stop thinking about the past', 'who were interested in the future', etc. The 'others', the outgroups, were, apart from the Jews, leftists (note the directional metaphor and politonym), those Austrians 'who foul their own nest', in German *Nestbeschmutzer* (note the defamatory nationalist naturalising metaphor), and *das Ausland*. This macro-toponymic metonymical collective singular describing everything outside the state borders of Austria could mean 'the international press' (note the utterance autonomyzing metonymy) and, lastly, 'the powerful Jews on the US East-Coast' (see Mitten 1992). In between these two poles of referential dichotomisation were 'the Jewish fellow citizens', the beloved '*jüdischen Mitbürger*'. This sociative relationym identifies the group of Jews in terms of being co-citizens of another group of persons who are presupposed to be the referential centre or starting point. Thus, in contrast to the seemingly integrating function, this relationymic referring form very often has an exclusionary, albeit mitigated, and segregating effect (this observation holds true for the 'foreign fellow citizens' as well, who, in contrast to the literal suggestion in the politonym 'citizen', are not 'citizens' at all (see chapter 2, p. 61). Austrian Jews – they are the good Jews whose behaviour is contrasted to those 'outside' – are allowed to live in peace as (half-heartedly) tolerated '*Mitbürger*', so long as they behave themselves.

In the discourse about Waldheim's Nazi past, the exclusionary boundaries of the 'us' group have shifted constantly. Nonetheless, in the context of the disclosures about the president's wartime past, the constant allusion to the 'us' group facilitated the constitution of a *Feindbild Jude*, of an image of 'the Jew as enemy' – which in turn reinforced existing prejudices. Certain taboos did exist up to 1986: not to make explicit, manifest antisemitic remarks on TV or the radio, for example. Even these taboos were broken in 1986, as the data analysed below will show.

Summarising the development and continuation of antisemitic hostilities in Austria, one can observe that the linguistic forms of expression of antisemitism in postwar Austria are quite different, either manifest or latent, explicit or implicit. But each and every one appears to be part of a strategy of justification (or varieties of justification and defence). Antisemitism in postwar Austria must be viewed chiefly in relation to the way in which alleged or real guilt, with alleged or actual accusations, is dealt with. One can observe that antisemitic prejudice in Austria is not exhausted by merely repeating the clichés of the nineteenth and early twentieth centuries. There are also new additional material roots and motives for antisemitism, and several new topoi were added since 1945. The fear of revenge, although an old motive, has acquired a new urgency as a result of the actual guilt of many and feelings of guilt of others because of the Holocaust. Closely related is the fear that the Jews will reclaim their property which was 'aryanised – that is to say, stolen. The Austrians' postwar identity is grounded on the formulation of the 1943 'Moscow Declaration', according to which Austria was the first victim of Nazi expansionism. The incriminating part of the declaration speaks of Austrian responsibility for Nazi crimes. 'Digging up the past' counts now as a threat to this image, all the more so when it recalls events which are not easily denied.

The revelation of Waldheim's past

The 'Waldheim Affair' is the condensing term conventionally applied to the controversy surrounding the disclosure of the previously unknown past of Kurt Waldheim, former secretary-general of the United Nations, which arose during his campaign for the Austrian presidency in 1986. The affair not only focused international attention on Waldheim personally, but also raised broader questions relating to the history of antisemitism in Austria (Mitten 1992). Employing a coded idiom more appropriate to 'post-Auschwitz' political debate, 'the

Waldheim camp' – the Christian democratic Austrian People's Party (ÖVP), which had nominated him – helped construct a hostile image of Jews ('*Feindbild* '), which served both to deflect criticism of Waldheim's credibility and to explain the international 'campaign' against him. The central assumption of this '*Feindbild* ' was that Waldheim (synecdochisingly equated with 'Austria') was under attack by an international Jewish conspiracy, the '*Ausland* '.

The relatively uneventful early phase of the election campaign ended abruptly in March 1986, when the Austrian weekly *profil* published documents revealing details of Waldheim's unknown past during the Second World War. *Profil's* disclosures were followed on 4 March by nearly identical revelations by the World Jewish Congress (WJC) and the *New York Times* (*NYT*). Waldheim had always denied any affiliation of any kind with the Nazis and had claimed in his memoirs that his military service ended in the winter 1941–2, with his being wounded on the Eastern front. The evidence made public by *profil*, the World Jewish Congress and the *New York Times* suggested the contrary: Waldheim had been a member of the Nazi Student Union, and he had also belonged to a mounted riding unit of the *Sturmabteilung*, or SA, while attending the Consular Academy in Vienna between 1937 and 1939. Other documents revealed that Waldheim had served in the Balkans, after March 1942, in the Army Group E, commanded by Alexander Löhr. This army group was known for its involvement in the deportation of Jews from Greece and for the savagery of its military operations against Yugoslav partisans.

For his part, Waldheim first denied any membership of any Nazi organisation and claimed to have known nothing about the deportation of Jews of Thessalonica. The general strategy of 'the Waldheim camp' was to brand any disclosures as a 'defamation campaign', an international conspiracy by 'the foreign press' and 'the Jews' ('*im Ausland* '). In addition, he stated that he had simply forgotten to mention such minor events in his life because his injury had been the major *caesura*. In the course of the election campaign, the World Jewish Congress became the major object of abuse, and the abundant political invective by politicians of the ÖVP against it helped promote and legitimise antisemitic prejudice in public discourse to an extent unseen since 1945. Waldheim also attempted to identify his own 'fate' with that of his generation and country by claiming that he, like thousands of other Austrians, had merely done his 'duty' ('*er habe nur seine Pflicht erfüllt* ') under Nazi Germany. This euphemistic, relativisising positive presentational argumentation topos relies on – at least – two conclusion rules: if somebody does his or her duty, he or she is a conscientious, responsible person. If somebody is a conscientious, responsible person, he or she cannot be blamed for his or her deeds. Waldheim's self-exculpating argumentation struck a positive responsive note among many Austrian voters of his generation, but also of the younger generations, the children of the *Wehrmacht* soldiers. Waldheim finally won the second round of the election on 6 June 1986, with 53.9 per cent of the votes.

Contrary to Waldheim's expectations, however, interest in the unanswered questions about his past did not disappear after the election (see Wodak *et al.*

1994). Waldheim received no official invitation from any country in Western Europe, and some official visitors even avoided travelling to Vienna, because they did not want to call on him. In April 1987, the US Department of Justice announced that it was placing Waldheim on a watch list, further reinforcing his pariah status (see Mitten 1992 for more details). More broadly conceived, the 'Waldheim Affair' symbolises the postwar unwillingness or inability to adequately confront the implications of Nazi abomination.

In the following, we will first characterise the discourse about the 'Waldheim Affair' as a whole. Then, we will describe antisemitic language use in Austria during the affair, illustrating it with 'authentic' data from the discourse. Finally, we will focus on two selected, but significant examples: one is taken from the official political domain, while the other represents the everyday antisemitism as recorded on the streets in Vienna 1987.

The discourse about the 'Waldheim Affair'

The relationships between the fields of action, genres and discourse topics and the discourse-historical frame of investigation

As a whole, the discourse about the 'Waldheim Affair' 'spread' to different fields of political action, involving many different discourse genres and many different discourse topics. Figure 3.1 portrays diagrammatically the whole discourse and the most relevant relationships between fields of action, genres and discourse topics in simplified terms.

In order to be able to study the discourse about the 'Waldheim Affair', the context was unravelled into various dimensions (some of which are illustrated by this diagrammatical overview), and the research team, consisting of six researchers from three different fields (linguistics, psychology and history), decided in favour of a triangulatory approach, which made it possible to focus on the many different genres that were situated in the different political fields of action. Obviously, these different fields had an impact on the analytical methods used and the interpretation of the data. Ultimately, the team developed its own categories that led to the 'discourse-historical' approach (see Wodak *et al.* 1990. For further elaboration of this approach see chapter 2).

To summarise briefly: on the one hand, the linguistic manifestations of prejudice in this specific discourse, embedded in their linguistic and political context (e.g. newspaper reports or news in Austria), were analysed. On the other hand, the media reports were critically contrasted with other facts and context-phenomena (the reporting in the United States, which was also biased in certain aspects). Thus, we compared one report with the reports on the report, and with historical knowledge. In other words, we did not rely on the 'meta-data' alone; but collated 'Waldheim's story' with the historical documentation of the *Wehrmacht* atrocities in the Balkans and the deportation of Jews from Greece. In this way, we were able to detect and depict the distortion

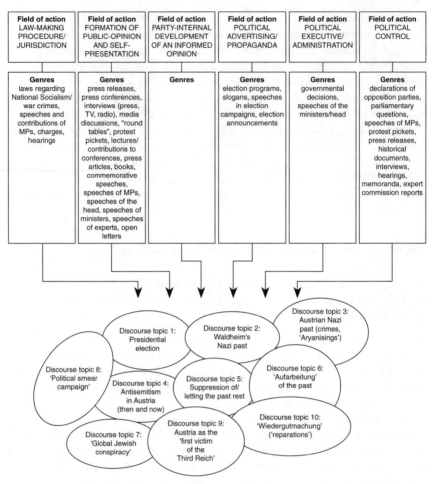

Figure 3.1 The discourse about the 'Waldheim Affair'

of documented 'facts' and 'realities'. Our comparison of the *New York Times* with the reports in the Austrian press and statements of politicians proved that this distortion was systematic (see also Mitten 1992 and Gruber 1991 for more details on the press and the media).

The analysed data comprise both written texts and oral utterances. Three newspapers were read systematically, every day, during the four months of the presidential election campaign (from March to June 1986), and then at regular intervals after June 1986 (*Die Presse, Neue Kronen Zeitung, New York Times*). Day-to-day radio and TV news, interviews, TV discussions, hearings, larger news documentary series (about fifty hours of video) were systematically tape-recorded and partly transcribed. Discussions in diverse institutional settings and parts of the '*Mahnwache*', the vigil commemorating Austrian resistance in

June 1987 on Stephansplatz in Vienna, were also recorded and partly transcribed (e.g. Wodak 1990a, 1990b, 1990c and 1991b).

The memorial vigil, the '*Mahnwache*', took place for twenty-four hours continuously, one year after the election of Kurt Waldheim as Austrian president. It was an expression of political protest and the wish to contribute critically to the formation of public opinion on the side of a nascent democratic civil society in Austria. It aimed at sensitising the Austrian public, and especially the passers-by, to the negative, up-to-then widely repressed aspects of the Austrian past. The research team taped some of the spontaneous, semi-public discussions, which developed in the informal setting on the square in the center of Vienna. The controversial discussions showed a high degree of emotionality, which the readers can see for themselves in the translated transcripts in later sections of the present chapter (the originals can be found in Wodak 1990c).

All in all, very different degrees of formality and very different interactional settings were taken into account in the analysis of the discourse about the 'Waldheim Affair'. The team prepared an exhibition with some of the collected and analysed material (see Wodak and de Cillia 1988). This exhibition was presented in March 1988, on the occasion of the Austrian '*Gedenkjahr* 1988', the year in which the fiftieth anniversary of Austria's occupation by the 'Third Reich' was commemorated. The research team even filmed the discussions which occurred when people visited the exhibition.

The analysis of the linguistic manifestations of antisemitic prejudices, which we will present below, needs to be prefaced by specifying the purpose of the analysis, which did not merely consist of discovering the 'language of antisemitism' and describing it. The situation was not as simple as this, for there is not a totally characteristic, identifiable language of prejudice. If there were, it would be easy to recognise and rhetorically would not be so manipulative and persuasive. What had to be investigated were the very different explicit and implicit rhetorical means by which antisemitic prejudices are expressed or reproduced. Each genre that we analysed required slightly different methods of analysis. But although the specific methods employed depended on the genre, all data from the discourse about the 'Waldheim Affair' were analysed on three dimensions: the antisemitic content expressed, the discursive strategies applied, and the linguistic realisations utilised at several levels of language. Among the common features found in almost all the data, there were specific antisemitic prejudices (see below, pp. 103–4 and also chapter 2, p. 56) that were linguistically presented in a 'black-and-white depiction' and that, as far as the fallacious argumentation structure is concerned, were grounded on the transformation of the victims into the perpetrators (*trajectio in alium*). One of the central interests of this study was the use of mitigating strategies – that is to say, the different degrees of directness and explicitness of the antisemitic utterances and the question whether the illocutionary force of antisemitic statements is toned down or not (see below, 'pp. 104–5 and chapter 2, pp. 81–5).

The analysis was almost exclusively qualitative, though in one respect there was an attempt to quantify. As already mentioned, two large Austrian newspapers, *Die Presse* and the *Neue Kronen Zeitung*, appearing daily during the election campaign, were diacronically analysed for quite a long period. The first is a paper with pretensions to serious journalism. Its editorial line represents broadly the views of the industrial wing of the Christian conservative Austrian People's Party. The tabloid *Neue Kronen Zeitung*, on the other hand, which in relative terms is the most popular newspaper in the Western world, aspires to (and certainly attains) much lower journalistic standards. The analysis of these two newspapers showed that the manifestation of antisemitic prejudices not only depended on the political and ideological orientation and affiliation, or on the editorial policy of the newspapers, but also on the respective subgenre (column, commentary or report) in which the 'Waldheim Affair' was a subject, and on external factors such as the readership and, for example, events such as the holding of press conferences in New York on the World Jewish Congress. The results suggest that the *Kronen Zeitung* helped concretise and, in some cases, constitute implicit or inchoate antisemitic prejudices, while *Die Presse* could refer to a stable reservoir of pre-existing prejudice. With few exceptions, anti-semitic prejudice in *Die Presse* was realised through allusions rather than explicit stereotypical utterances. These two different forms may be termed 'antisemitism for beginners' and 'antisemitism for advanced users'.

What do we mean by 'antisemitic language use'?

We characterise 'antisemitic language use' as hostile or antagonistic linguistic behaviour towards Jews (see also Bauer 1988, Wistrich 1991, Levy 1991). Often enough, this is very clear: 'Kill Jews!' smeared on the monument dedicated to Sigmund Freud is openly antisemitic, an appeal for action in the imperative. A Jewish joke, on the other hand, can have various meanings, depending on the setting, the listeners and speakers and the function of the utterance.

Two other points should be emphasised here. Firstly, the context of an utterance is indispensable in determining whether a statement (for example a joke) is antisemitic or not. Secondly, antisemitic language behaviour covers a wide range of speech acts, from explicit remarks or calls to action, to mere allusions. In addition, antisemitic language use covers various unities or aspects of language: from text or discourse to the individual word, or even to sounds (for example, the Yiddish intonation of certain words or phrases), from reference, predication and argumentation to the perspectivation and involvement, as well as the intensification or mitigation (see chapter 2).

Antisemitic content can be expressed in a manifest or latent way depending on the setting (public, semi-public, semi-private, private), the formality of the situation, the persons gathered, the topic discussed and the presence or absence of Jews. Although certain contents depend on the communicative function of the utterance, one can find all traditional antisemitic contents, except those dealing with sexuality (see 'Everyday discourse: Conversations on the street' below), in the data taken from the Austrian discourse about the 'Waldheim Affair'. This once again corroborates our key assumption of a 'syncretic antisemitism': the various roots (racist, Christian, economist, political etc.) of antisemitism become blurred; wherever it is thought necessary and effective, certain prejudices are recycled and functionalised, without explicitly focusing on their traditional development or use.

The content of antisemitic discourse

What then are the most important clichés and content of prejudices attached to Jews? We will list only five that occurred with especially high frequency in 1986 (for other prejudices, see chapter 2). We do not, however, deal in detail with the historical underpinnings, but refer to the literature as a source for the unusual features and uniqueness of the 'antisemitic syndrome' (see Wodak *et al.* 1990, Mitten 1997, Gilman and Katz 1991, Brown 1994 for details).

The first two prejudices we will mention here are both rooted in Christian antisemitism. According to the first prejudice, Jews are regarded as the murderers of Christ, as traitors. The biblical character of 'Judas' is taken as 'proof' of the unreliability and lack of credibility of the Jews. Christian antisemitism was found especially in the mass media in 1986 (in the public press and also in the semi-public realm). This prejudice has the longest and most consistent history in Austria, being deeply embedded in the 'collective experience'.

The second prejudice, the stereotype of the 'dishonest' or 'dishonourable Jew', the 'tricky', 'business-minded', 'fraudulent Jew', also has its origins in Christian antisemitism – strictly speaking, in the biblical story about Judas's betrayal of Christ. In addition, this view is also based on economist stereotypes: in the Middle Ages, Jews were responsible for lending money – they were not allowed to pursue many other occupations. This negative cliché was used repeatedly in reference to the World Jewish Congress in the course of the 'Waldheim debate'.

The third frequently found prejudice in the discourse about the 'Waldheim Affair' is that of the alleged 'Jewish conspiracy': the Jews in the world are considered to dominate or control the international press, the banks, the political power and the capital, and they are assumed to be planning a world conspiracy, e.g. the 'campaign' against Waldheim or Austria.

The fourth prejudice consists of the conviction that Jews are privileged. Persisting since the beginning of the postwar debate about 'compensating' Jewish Nazi victims (*'Wiedergutmachung'*), this new prejudice holds that a large number of Jews emigrated, especially the many rich ones. They had no reason to complain. 'Emigration' – this euphemism very often linguistically disguises the fact of coercive expulsion – is not anything terrible, and those who were not in concentration camps had nothing to complain about anyway.

Hand in hand with this prejudice, a fifth one is promulgated that consists of the accusation that Jews are irreconcilable and always thirsting for vengeance. This prejudiced attribution was employed in the discourse about the 'Waldheim Affair'; it reached its peak of frequency, however, in the discourse about 'reparations' for Jewish Nazi victims that has been ongoing since the early 1990s in Austria.

All of these deprecatory, anti-Jewish or 'antisemitic' prejudices were adjusted to the specific historical and sociopolitical situation at the time when the debate about the 'Waldheim Affair' was going on in the Austrian public, and, consequently, varied greatly in the extent of menace and hostility. Through different predication and mitigation strategies as well as the respective linguistic means, these prejudices were discursively realised in ways that included more or less explicit or vague attributions and comparisons, or more or less implicit allusions/insinuations, evocations and presuppositions/implications.

A heuristic 'hierarchy in explicitness' in anti-Jewish (antisemitic) language use

The different forms and degrees of directness and boldness of antisemitic language use can be differentiated depending on political context, interactional setting and speaker. In analysing the material, four hierarchical stages of antisemitic statements, which correspond to different individual argumentation strategies of justification, can be identified. Antisemitism subsumed under stage 1 could be heard or read in almost every context from which the analysed discursive data about the 'Waldheim Affair' were taken. While the frequency of the respective form of antisemitism decreases from stage 1 to stage 4, the form itself becomes more and more extreme and explicit.

Stage 1: Here, antisemitism and the negative uniqueness of Auschwitz are trivialised and relativised. The discriminatory form of antisemitism is played down by evasively emphasising negative sameness and negative common features (in terms of argumentation theory: by committing the fallacy of 'hasty generalisation' with respect to the specific conditions and excesses of antisemitic discrimination), by casting doubt on the veracity of certain well-documented historical facts (e.g. by employing a fallacious *argumentum ad ignorantiam* that pretends that certain crimes are not proven or that one did not oneself know anything about these crimes), and by trying to balance one thing against another: for example, the Nazi crimes against the crimes committed under the rule of Stalin (e.g. by applying the fallacy of *'ignoratio elenchi '* – that is to say, by introducing a point that is completely irrelevant in the actual discussion) (see chapter 2, p 73, but also Wodak *et al.* 1999: 36). This form of antisemitism, during the discourse about the 'Waldheim Affair', even occurs in totally formal and official contexts, such as the mass media, news broadcasts and informative programs.

At *stage 2*, antisemites argue that antisemitism is the Jews' own fault. Here, the blame and responsibility for the Nazi crimes are put on the victims themselves. From an argumentation theoretical point of view, the linguistic realisation of this form of an antisemitic victim-perpetrator-reversal can, in general, be described as the application of an *argumentum ad consequentiam* or *trajectio in alium* (see chapter 2 , p. 74). The respective statements are packaged differently, as direct accusations or insinuations, as topoi of threat (see chapter 2, pp. 77–8), *argumenta ad baculum* or *argumenta ad hominem* (see chapter 2, p. 71–2) and occur in many contexts, especially in semi-public ones, i.e. in interviews or in TV discussions, just as in the memorial vigil (see below).

At *stage 3*, the other traditional antisemitic prejudices appear, either the explicit form of 'hasty generalisations', linguistically often realised with the help of generalising or particularising synecdoches, or in implicit forms, linguistically often conveyed via stories that contain fallacious examples and allusions. Greed, dishonesty and vindictiveness constitute the content of prejudices appearing in this context, not least in the linguistic form of fallacious *argumenta ad hominem*. The prejudice of a Jewish world conspiracy is also linguistically reproduced within this context, which is primarily formed by more informal situations and especially protected (well-known) figures. Within this stage of the discursive manifestation of antisemitism, the chief purpose is to justify the hostility against Jews by systematic distortion and the creation of an enemy image, a Jewish scapegoat.

Stage 4, finally, is constituted by direct and open abuse of Jews. Such insulting labels like the derogatory metaphors 'swine' and 'cut-throat' appear only in anonymous spheres; in the memorial vigil, for example, or in complaint calls to the state-run radio station (ORF). In this case, there are very severe restrictive taboos when the speakers in public do not remain anonymous.

The selective illustration of some categories of analysis

As explained in chapter 2 (pp. 54–5), predication strategies are employed to ascribe certain characteristics and traits – either positive or negative ones – to people and groups of people. In combination with specific referential strategies, they are discursively utilised to construct a dichotomous world of 'insiders' and 'outsiders', of 'them' and 'us', and, strictly speaking, to make positive or negative judgements on the imagined or represented social actors. Predicational strategies partly overlap with referential strategies and can be part of argumentation strategies. Predications can assume the character of abuse, according to the context and explicitness of the four hierarchical levels. Let us quote a few examples of predications from the discourse about the 'Waldheim Affair':

> '...that whippersnapper General Secretary Singer ...
> the private club with the bombastic name World Jewish Congress ...
> the wheeling and dealing of the first president of the club, N. Goldmann,
> with the Arabs, the arch enemy of the Jewish state ...'.
> (*Neue Kronen Zeitung*, 'Staberl', 2 April 1986: 8)[2]

The first predication is realised in German as the metaphorical (animalising) attributive adjective '*grünschnäblig* '. This adjective would literally be translated into English as 'like a green beak', meaning 'whippersnapper-like', 'greenhorn-like'. The 'beak' stands for the 'mouth' of Singer and symbolises both metonymically and metaphorically the words that are said or written by Singer with respect to the 'Waldheim Affair'. The colour term 'green' metaphorically qualifies Singer's utterances as 'immature'. As one can see – and this illustrates once more our thesis that predication and argumentation can overlap – the simple one-word-predication is utilised by the author of the article for an *argumentum ad hominem* that aims at delegitimising Singer by characterising him as incompetent. The second example contains two predications: the first one has the form of a noun phrase ('the private club'), the second one of a prepositional phrase ('with the bombastic name'). The collectivised 'social actor', which is the subject of the author's antisemitic attacks, i.e. 'the Jewish World Congress', syntactically only appears backgrounded as the second part of the juxtaposition contained in the prepositional phrase. Rhetorically, the entire double-form of predication (consisting of two predications) may be described as a condescending periphrasis which, again, has the quality of an implicit delegitimising argumentation. By the two predications, *Staberl*, the author, tries to deny the international Jewish organisation the claim of representing or being a voice for Jews at an international level. The third predication taken from the same press article, finally, is the most antisemitic one. In the form of a very expanded noun phrase that contains the central social actor ('N. Goldmann') and object of antisemitic attack as a genitive attribute, it insinuates the prejudice of the 'tricky, spineless Jew' who, if it is only opportune, even makes a deal with his arch enemy.

An excerpt quoted from a press conference of the Jewish *Gemeinde* (community) in Vienna on 18 June 1986 is given below. It represents a collage of statements by spokespersons of the Austrian People's Party and serves as an example of the techniques of explicit antisemitic predication of negative, derogatory traits, e.g. of dishonesty, mendacity, untrustworthiness, primitivity, inclination to criminality, spitefulness and egocentric megalomania (the entire interview illustrates numerous strategies of justification; see Wodak *et al.* 1990: 19–30 and 352–5):

> Untrustworthy and dishonourable methods ... Dishonourable members of the World Jewish Congress ... Untrustworthy – dishonourable and full of hate ... Lies ... deception and breaking promises ... having no culture and simplistic and unfounded hate ... The crying of the puppets of the World Jewish Congress motivated by hate and the need for admiration ... Assassins ... Mafia of slanderers ... The epitome of baseness ... Bribed witnesses ... Methods of the mafia ... Astoundingly stupid ... Dirty self-aggrandisement campaigns... The habitual slanderer Singer.

Antisemitic predications are linguistically not always realised as overt and explicit. They sometimes assume the form of allusions. Allusions themselves become linguistically manifest in very different ways of intertextual or inter-discursive tying: for example, by means of citations, formal text construction, style and word choice. All forms of allusion, however, share the feature that the connection between two contents is established implicitly rather than explicitly (very often, the allusion is characterised by elements of linguistic vagueness), and assumes previous knowledge on the part of the audience. Consequently, the responsibility for the interpretation is shifted to the hearers or readers, who are believed to know the background of the insinuation: for example, of the allusion made by negative predications like '*ehrlose Gesellen*' ('dishonourable lots').

This allusive predication was uttered during the debate about Waldheim's past in reference to the World Jewish Congress by the ÖVP politician Michael Graff (on 25 April 1986). '*Ehrlose Gesellen*' was used as a label for Jews in the documents and regulations of fraternities at the end of the nineteenth century in Austria, meaning that they were not allowed to join these fraternities and also not thought dignified enough to take part in a duel.

Although the differentiation is not strictly mutually exclusive, one can – at least analytically – distinguish between 'formal allusions', 'semantic allusions by quotation', 'allusions with the help of typical lexemes' and 'allusions with the help of atypical lexemes' (for this distinction see Gruber 1991: 183–91).

Formal allusions consist of the utilisation of the implicative potential of a specific stylistic register and its formal linguistic characteristics, that is to say, of a manner of speaking or writing within a particular social domain, that reminds one of a specific genre which is located within a specific field of social action. This category of allusion is also called 'evocation' (see Januschek 1992: 48–55). An example of this is: 'those who, with hate, sow new hate and thereby accept – maybe even hope for – a harvest that can only be additional hate ...'. (*Die Presse*, Th. Chorherr, 5/6 April 1986: 1).[3] These lines exploit the readers' specific knowledge of the biblical, Old Testament metaphorising proverb 'sow the wind and reap the whirlwind' (Hosea, 8,7; in German: '*Wer Wind sät, wird Sturm ernten* '). This menacing oxymoronic allegory that combines a meteorological with an agricultural metaphor means that those who attack somebody violently will be counterattacked even more violently still. The threatening topos of consequence expressed in this biblical saying is transformed in the article in *Die Presse* into an implicit *argumentum ad baculum* and *argumentum ad verecundiam* that tries to rely on the authority of the bible, thus aiming at rationalising and justifying the hostility against Jews.

Semantic allusions by quotation are based on the utilisation of quotes which contain specific taboo expressions or phrases with a strong connotative potential that suffices for conveying a prejudiced content (see Gruber 1991: 185). Through this form of allusion, the speaker or author has the possibility of distancing her- or himself from the content of the quoted utterance by applying strategies of detachment and mitigation – for example, by framing the quote as direct or indirect speech and (seemingly) critically commenting on the meaning of the quote in the matrix sentence that includes the 'verb of saying' (see chapter 2, p. 84). However, the very citation of the taboo lexical items or phrases can have the effect that the strong connotations gather momentum in the mind of hardened hearers or readers and drown the seemingly critical remarks that frame the quotations. The form of discourse representation and perspectivation (see chapter 2, pp. 81–3) can support the unhindered 'unfolding' of the connotations that contain the prejudices. This is the case in the following example, in which the columnist 'Staberl' reports on the prejudice about the 'Jewish conspiracy'. The journalist frames the antisemitic utterance 'The Jews – our misfortune' by quotation marks, but omits to frame it also by a matrix sentence that contains a verb of saying and comments on the utterance critically:

One of the most ridiculous clichés from the poison-and-filth kitchen of Goebbel's propaganda ministry ... was the myth of the disastrous effects of 'World Jewry'. The Jews ... supposedly united in an insidious conspiracy against the ... Germanic super-race. 'The Jews – our misfortune'.

(*Neue Kronen Zeitung*, 'Staberl', 27 March 1986: 8)[4]

Allusions of the third type are 'allusions with the help of typical lexemes'. They are realised by the selection of specific lexemes that, in the case of anti-semitism, are designated to characterise Jews and that are associated with 'typical' traditional prejudiced content (see Gruber 1991: 190). In the following example, the prejudice of 'the business-minded Jew' is alluded to and perfidiously associated with the topic of 'compensation policy':

... and they [= the Jews, R.W. and M.R.] all were back again! Came, one or two stayed, the dentist and others, they/th-/they got their things straightened out again, (and) compensation, right, and/and because of the injustice and so on! And then they left again!

(Memorial Vigil, June 1987, see below p. 120)[5]

In contrast to this type of allusions, 'allusions with the help of atypical lexemes' make an intentional, but surprising, atypical use of lexemes that are 'normally' associated with a specific group of people. These lexemes are recontextualised and related with another group of persons. Thus, specific connotative aspects are transferred from the one group to the other. In this way, a sort of assimilation of the two groups is brought about, as in the following example: 'Attacks from a side that thinks it is untouchable, but which has always made itself a willing tool for a handful of stick-in-the-muds, who never pass up an opportunity to make a profit from a dark past'. (*Die Presse*, Leiten-berger, 25 March 1986).[6] 'Stick-in-the muds' (in its German translation '*Ewiggestrige* ') is a term normally used for old (dyed-in-the-wool) Nazis and for persons who are considered to still live in the past. This second meaning and the general association with a 'dark past' makes it possible also to refer to non-Nazis with this term without totally violating the word's usage rules. However, by means of this usage the journalist carries out an implicit equation of Nazis and Jews.

Such implicit equations qua allusion as well as other *equations* and *fallacious generalisations* of statements about persons, groups or experiences (which can be either self-made or narrated by others and as such adopted) serve to present the group of 'others' negatively and to establish prejudices about them. In many cases, synecdoches (both in the form of a person or some persons standing for a whole group and, conversely, in the form of a whole standing for a part) and metonymies (especially those of the type 'country standing for the population of the country', which, in most cases, simultaneously also function as a *totum pro parte*) are linguistically employed for hasty generalisations (see also chapter 2, p. 73). In the 1986 presidential election campaign, we find several equations, some of which reveal antisemitic sentiments (e.g. 'Singer/Bronfman = WJC = Israel = Jews'; this equation contains several *partes pro toto* and metonymies), some of which are the expression of Austrian nationalism (e.g. 'Waldheim = all Austrians = Austria'; this is a *pars pro toto* or/and metonymy), and some of which serve as relativisation of the Austrian Nazi crimes (e.g. 'Hitler = Stalin', these are two equated *partes pro totibus*). Such equations are – in contrast to equations which appear in the counter argumentation directed against antisemitic prejudices (e.g. '*Wehrmacht* = Nazis', 'Austrians = Nazis') – especially pertinent for the justification and trivialisation of Austrian National-Socialism. A trivialising equation also occurs in the following remark from the 1987 memorial vigil: 'The guilty ones have already been hanged!'.[7] Equating the execution of war criminals with 'all the guilty ones' from the Nazi era – in rhetorical terms, synecdochisingly taking the 'hanged ones' for 'all the guilty ones' – functions to shift the blame.

'Generalisations' are the transferring of isolated – often just narrated – situations of experiences with individuals to a whole group. They can even be 'across-the-board statements': 'They take all the jobs; we've only got more Jews' (1987 Memorial Vigil; cf. Wodak, 1989, 1990c).

Comparisons and analogies are rhetorical techniques employed for equating predication and argumentation strategies. Making explicit and implicit *comparisons*, or drawing *analogies* between actual events and fictitious ones, often fulfils a persuasive function similar to the invention of unreal scenarios that are designated to function as an 'illustrative example' in an argumentation. They serve additionally to minimise or exaggerate. The following speaker reproduces the prejudice of 'the unforgiving and vindictive Jews'. He insinuates that the Jews always start from the beginning, i.e. with remembering the Nazi crimes of which they were the victims, and considers this to be the same as 'if I said to someone who's a friend of mine, you're an idiot, right? He accepts it. Then he doesn't say to me twenty years later, you said twenty years ago that I'm an idiot!' (Memorial Vigil, June 1987).[8] With this analogy, the speaker relativises the Nazi crimes by comparing and equating them with a simple insulting anthroponym that denotes a mental deficiency (see chapter 2, figure 2.5). Moreover, it minimises the antisemitic Nazi crimes by presupposing that 'the Jews' were once friends of the speaker and the speaker's ingroup and they only became opponents because they could not tolerate a rather harmless slur.

Minimisations, as a part of mitigating strategies, often appear in the form of *euphemism* – that is to say, of pleasant replacements for unpleasant words with a negative denotative and/or connotative meaning. As already mentioned, the terms 'emigration' or 'emigration of the Jews' are used instead of 'expulsion'. Further, 'the recent emergence of antisemitic discussions' is employed instead of 'the revival of antisemitism' and the 'Holocaust' (originally meaning 'sacrifice consumed by fire', coming from Greek '*holokaustos*', meaning 'burnt whole'), instead of 'gassing' or 'extermination of Jews'. Nazi expressions can also serve to mitigate, strictly speaking, to obscure and minimise, since such functions are inherent in their literal meaning: 'Aryanisation' linguistically disguises the systematic robbery and theft of Jewish property; 'Crystal Glass Night' is used as a synecdochic metaphor to refer to the 'November Pogrom'; 'Jewish matters' abstractly stands for 'separatist treatment' of the Jews during the Nazi era, and 'separatist treatment' is, of course, a euphemism as well (see Brackman and Birkenhauer 1988: 174).

Another example which illustrates a minimisation of events by the application of mitigation strategies is found in the comment and view regarding Waldheim's past expressed by Austria's previous Federal President Kirchschläger (22 April 1986), in which he used euphemisms such as 'with regard to the fate of the Jews' instead of 'murder and expulsion', or that of 'the deportation of hundreds of thousands of Jews from Thessalonica', or 'throughout our history, antisemitic sentiments have brought neither benefits nor blessings. Moreover, they are extremely inhuman'.[9] All the three utterances by Kirchschläger have in common that they hide the responsible perpetrators who persecuted, expelled and murdered the Jews. The first euphemism shifts the blame to fate, destiny, i.e. to a deterministic power beyond human control. The second euphemism reduces the Nazi crimes against the Jews from Thessalonica to 'deportation', to the act of forcing the Jews to leave the place. The third euphemistic utterance by Kirchschläger, finally, draws a cost-benefit calculation into an issue such as antisemitism, and refers to antisemitism with its resulting extermination of millions of Jews in purely 'mentalising' terms of 'antisemitic sentiments'.

As explained in chapter 2, the linguistic presentation of groups and their activities, especially concerning the questions of guilt or innocence, can be carried out by referentially *identifying* and *naming individuals through proper names or anthroponyms* (for example by criminonyms) as well as by *backgrounding* or *oppressing* them, thus maintaining their anonymity, whichever is best suited for the authors' purposes. In the case of maintaining anonymity, persons often are only vaguely or abstractly (e.g. metonymically or metaphorically) referred to and named. Deictics or 'personal pronouns' with unclear referents, passive constructions or the complete omission of an agent can also be used for this purpose. The impersonal third-person point of view also can serve a similar purpose. This allows for the free expression of opinions normally regarded as 'taboo' in reference to the 'enemy group' (the addressees are not mentioned and the authors can thus shift the responsibility). In this way, attacks on the 'us-group' (e.g. Waldheim and Austria) can also be mystified and be made to seem menacing:

> In fact, almost everything that's been 'uncovered' to date, is steeped in half-truths, and with clear or subliminal misrepresentations, ... It may be that someone is unable to control the spirits that he's called up from the dead, but the game can be totally different too.
>
> (*Die Presse*, 6 March 1986: 1)[10]

Those, therefore, who make accusations and whose methods are to be denounced remain in obscurity. Either the passive is used to avoid naming an active subject or the anonymous indefinite pronoun 'someone' is employed to refer to an unspecified person, who is then also referred to by the male third-person anaphora 'he'. The identity of the subject appears to be open to inter-pretation, but it is clearly pre-determined by means of the cotext and context.

The situation is reversed in the case of *synecdochising personalisation*, whereby the responsibility of groups of individuals is reduced to the responsibility of one or few persons who replace 'the whole as a part' (e.g. 'that Mr. Singer and Bronfman' instead of 'World Jewish Congress', or 'Hitler' instead of 'National-Socialists' or 'Nazis').

As far as the perspectivation, framing and discourse representation strategies are concerned, which help to express the speakers' involvement or distance and to position their point of view with respect to antisemitic discrimination and the question of guilt, quotes (either in direct speech, indirect speech or free indirect speech), the genre of narratives as well as the discursive construction of unreal scenarios are discursive phenomena that are often encountered.

Quotes are a recurring part of antisemitic argumentation which very often serve as topoi of authority or as fallacious *argumenta ad verecundiam*. It is precisely this form of argumentation that aims at appearing to be especially 'objective', rational and based on the authority of respectable personalities or institutions. Apart from that, quotes often fulfil the function of expressing antisemitic assertions without the speaker or writer having to take responsibility for the statements. That is to say: they enable the speaker apparently to detach her- or himself from antisemitic prejudices by simultaneously reproducing them. This is especially true of quotes by generally recognised authorities and, in the case of antisemitic argumentation, of those by Jews, whose words are employed to support the argumentation ('the token Jew', for example Bruno Kreisky and Simon Wiesenthal).

In addition to being used to shift responsibility and to back an argument, quotes can also be employed for insinuations and for expressing harsh anti-semitism. What is decisive here is the special way in which the comments of a third person are reported; which has been especially investigated with regard to reporting in the media.

The term *'discourse representation '* was introduced for the analysis of this basic aspect of reporting (cf. Hak 1987). In the course of a report about a 'speech event', not only is the actual text given, but the situation in which the quote in question occurred is almost always provided as well. Views and characterisations regarding the speaker are also made by comments or evaluative descriptions framing the represented discourse: 'The Israeli Secretary of State, Ytzhak Shamir, appears to be losing his mind: yesterday in Jerusalem he appealed to the leaders of all the countries in the world to join the fight against Kurt Waldheim' (*Neue Kronen Zeitung*, 28 May 1986: 2).[11] In this case, something Shamir said is used as an occasion for making a comment on the speaker's mental condition. The utterance itself is reported only in an extremely brief, indirect summary and serves mainly as the point of departure for further assessments.

Often prejudices are packaged in *narratives* about individual Jews. These narratives have the task of 'verifying' prejudices with examples, i.e. of ration-alising. Most often they are unreliable stories from a second source which relate supposedly bad experiences others have allegedly had with Jews. The following is a story told during the memorial vigil and is probably intended to illustrate 'the dishonesty and craftiness of Jews':

> Let me tell you a story, a story that wa/that (I) still remember from my grandfather; my grandfather was very, very poor, they were farmers. They had to fight for their existence back then. What has/there (was) a Jew who came along, brought him geese, young geese. 'You don't have to pay for right away, pay in half a year'. What was the deal? In half a year he couldn't pay, the Jew took the fattened geese without paying, where he had given the feed! ((shouting)) That's ((screaming)) the other side of it, and no one talks about that!
>
> (Memorial Vigil, June 1987)[12]

It is precisely this strategy of packaging prejudices in stories which is also dealt with in other studies of the connection between 'language and prejudice' (cf. van Dijk 1984, van Dijk 1987, Quasthoff 1980, Quasthoff 1998, Mitten and Wodak 1993, Wodak and Matouschek 1993). The data taken from the discourse about the 'Waldheim Affair' show that the antisemitic convictions of a speaker can lead to a content beyond the topic of the 'Waldheim Affair' and to other stories and topoi, and even to other forms of social discrimination, such as hostility towards foreigners – for example towards the so-called 'guest workers'. Stories about allegedly 'bad Jews' can be employed for purposes of justification, provocation and 'empirical illustration and proof'. The few stories about 'good Jews', however, are marked as exceptions and are never generalised.

In the case of *unreal scenarios*, the speaker or writer describes an invented, non-existent scenario which is intended persuasively to render his or her arguments irrefutable. The argumentative purpose of unreal scenarios is to portray the speaker's point of view as the only one possible, and to induce the hearers or readers to identify with the speaker's or writer's 'we-group':

> Listen, one could say so much! I could/I first told you about our general, who was ripped apart, you know? Just like the Magdeburger Halbkugel. Now, I ask you: You are/if you had been a prisoner of war like us down there, okay. The way it happened to us, and they were beyond human rights law. They weren't recognised at all then, not by any power, those guys were bandits and snipers. But if you had the choice now, that no other alternative, that you have to die, have to. And you have the choice: to be ripped apart like our general, or in a gas chamber? What would you do?
>
> (Memorial Vigil, June 1986)[13]

Here, the speaker constructs an unreal alternative from which the interlocutor is supposed to choose, implying that the gas chamber would be the lesser of two evils. In this way, extermination of Jews in concentration camps is euphemised and apparently 'better', than the death of the general in the unreal scenario described by the speaker.

A segment of the semi-official written discourse

In what is left of this chapter, we will selectively illustrate the different realisation and functionalisation of antisemitism in the discourse about the 'Waldheim Affair', depending on the discursive genres that are situated in different fields of political action. Examples of the different stages of explicitness can be found in the passages from the analysed data quoted below. As all examples relate to the discourse about the 'Waldheim Affair', 'recontextualisation' and intertextual as well as intradiscursive relationships are especially noticeable, since specific antisemitic prejudices are realised in different ways in the different genres.

In this chapter, it is our objective to support an understanding of discourse strategies used for political ends during the Austrian presidential election campaign in 1986 and to demonstrate the impact of political discourse in the private sphere. In the example used in this section, we cover the written genre of a semi-official open letter, whereas in the next section, we focus on anonymous tape-recorded conversations on the streets during a vigil that took place one year after the campaign.

In advance of the two sections, we wish to emphasise that our main interest lies in the antisemitic content expressed as well as in the most frequent presentational strategies. We dispense with minute discourse analyses at all linguistic levels in all of the following examples of this chapter, and restrict ourselves to a single detailed linguistic analyses of a few events at the vigil, since elaborate and extensive analyses of all the examples is beyond the scope and purpose of the present book. In this book in general, and in this chapter in particular, our goal is rather different: it is not linguistic description per se that we are interested in. Rather, we aim to analyse how racist or antisemitic prejudices are expressed at a specific historical time in different genres and with differing degrees of linguistic explicitness. Thus, the detailed linguistic analysis – which at best is only partly feasible and practicable for non-linguists – is subordinate to this aim, and will only be carried out if it allows for a better detection of the coded discriminatory language. In this way, we attempt to achieve a balance between a scholarly, linguistically precise analysis and an analysis that is relevant for social sciences and also helps non-linguists to diagnose and criticise discursive discriminatory practices.

Our written example is the so-called 'Hödl letter' (see Mitten and Wodak 1993). One of the questions most intensely debated in 1986 and 1987 was the recommendation of the US Justice Department's Office of Special Investigations that Waldheim's name be placed on the US government's so-called 'watch list' of undesirable aliens, a move that would effectively bar him from entering the United States. After an initial deferral of the decision in 1986, then Attorney General Edwin Meese did eventually place Waldheim on the list in April 1987. The World Jewish Congress, whose president was Edgar Bronfman, had been a strong advocate of such a measure since March 1986. Carl Hödl, at that time deputy mayor of Linz and an enthusiastic supporter of Waldheim, wrote an open letter to Bronfman on 12 May 1987, which is full of religious anti-Jewish allusions. We reproduce below the sections of the letter that are relevant to our point:

> It is difficult for an Austrian not to employ a polite phrase in the salutation. In your case, my tongue would indeed balk. As an Austrian, a Christian and a trained lawyer, I must protest against your biased, unqualified and most infernal attacks on our President and thus on us Austrians.
> [...]
> You, my dear Mr. Bronfman, probably lived in a safe country during the Second World War, or perhaps had then just outgrown your diapers [nappies]. Otherwise you would remember that millions of innocent civilians were senseless victims of bombings, especially in the German city of Dresden.
> [...]
> Thus your allegations are to be judged like those of your co-religionists 2000 years ago. These allowed Jesus Christ to be condemned to death in a sham trial, because he did not conform to the thinking of the masters of Jerusalem. And I should like to make another comparison. Just as it was then left to a Roman to pronounce the judgement, so now you were able to find the 'culprit' in the American Department of Justice, which is [now] to place Dr. Waldheim on the Watch List.
> [...]
> I only hope that the members of your association will call you to account [for your actions, 'which have damaged Jews in Austria, Germany, Hungary and God knows where else']. An eye for an eye, a tooth for a tooth, is not our European conception. I leave it to you and your ilk to advocate this talmudic tendency in the wider world. I can merely take note of this, but with the deepest horror and shock.

In the first paragraph quoted from the letter, Hödl establishes an Austrian, Christian ingroup with himself, as a lawyer, being a member of this group, and opposes Bronfman to this ingroup. The religious and national dissociation serves as the basis for all of his anti-Jewish remarks. Hödl begins the paragraph with essentially attributing politeness as a national character trait to the Austrians and to himself as an Austrian. Then, he self-identifies himself by relating a nationym, a religionym and a professionym to the first-person-deictic 'I' through an explicit equating comparison ('as'). After having linguistically constructed the ingroup of the Austrians, Christians and lawyers, he attacks his addressee Edgar Bronfman, the president of the World Jewish Congress, by accusing him of aggression against Waldheim. As a nationalist, Hödl takes Waldheim as a living *pars pro toto* for all Austrians. Hödl debases the critique of the Austrian president (and, thus, of all Austrains) by Bronfman in a triple qualification as 'untrue', 'incompetent' and 'most hellish'. The use of 'infernal' itself intimates the religious ambiance: Bronfman is associated with hell and the devil.

In the second paragraph, another, albeit indirect, religious motif may be inferred from Hödl's attempt quoted above to criticise Bronfman for having survived the war: apart from implying that his avoiding the fate of the Jews in Europe somehow morally disqualifies any statement he might make against Waldheim, the *non-sequitur* introduced by Hödl, contrasting Bronfman's ostensible secure living environment with the civilian victims of Dresden, also seems designed to underline Bronfman's lack of proper 'Christian' virtues like charity and to victimise the Germans. Presumably uncertain as to Bronfman's age, Hödl complements this argumentation with one invalidating the postwar generation's right to pass any verdict over the Nazi past. In terms of fallacious argumentation, this is an *argumentum ad hominem* that aims at delegitimising Bronfman, at undermining his authority as a critic of Waldheim.

In the third and fourth paragraphs, on a more explicitly religious note, Hödl – with two explicit biblical comparisons (which also function as *argumenta ad verecundiam* that are intended to back Hödl's antisemitic prejudices) – recalls the traditional story of Christian salvation as an allegory explaining Bronfman's actions in the 1980s, with Waldheim as Jesus Christ, Edwin Meese as Pontius Pilate, and the World Jewish Congress, like their forebears thirsting for vengeance, urging his crucifixion. By the second comparison in the third paragraph, Hödl reproduces the prejudice that Bronfman, as a representative of 'the Jews', is underhanded and cowardly and, thus, hands over the execution of and responsibility for the concrete political measures against Waldheim to the American Department of Justice.

In its current epistolary form, of course, Hödl's biblical morality play required an assumption of Jewish power which is far more contemporary, and which only makes sense as part of the prejudice of the Jewish world conspiracy to 'get' Waldheim and Austria. In the last paragraph, this prejudice is associated with the prejudice of 'the Jews thirsting for vengeance'. Hödl connects the two prejudices with the help of an allusion to the Old Testament principle of justice condensed into the formula 'an eye for an eye and a tooth for a tooth'. The allusion is again designed to back Hödl's antisemitic convictions as an *argumentum ad verecundiam*. In this last paragraph, Hödl shifts the referential borders between the two groups opposed to each other. With respect to his outgroup, Hödl has already implicitly moved to a worldwide extension by reproducing the prejudice of a Jewish world conspiracy. With respect to the ingroup, Hödl only now moves from a national Austrian level to a supranational, i.e. a European level. With this, he attempts to construct linguistically an exclusive opposition between 'the Europeans' and 'the Jews'. This opposition is, however, implicitly undermined by Hödl's topos of disadvantage (see also chapter 2, pp. 75 f.), which is quoted within brackets and which lists different groups of Jews living in different European states. The topos of disadvantage may be explicated by the conditional: 'if the Jewish attacks against Waldheim damage the Jews in Austria, Germany, Hungary and God knows where else, these attacks should be stopped'. The 'damage' Hödl is writing about may itself be revealed as an implicit 'topos of threat of antisemitism' (see chapter 2, p. 77) that can be paraphrased as follows: 'if you attack Waldheim and Austria, you have to accept an increase of antisemitism'.

All of the antisemitic stereotypes expressed by Hödl in his letter to Edgar Bronfman (i.e. the prejudices that 'the Jews' are 'murderers of Jesus', that there is a 'Jewish world conspiracy', that 'the Jews are false, underhanded and coward-ly' and that 'they are irreconcilable and thirsting for vengeance') seem to be multi-motivated by strong religious resentment as well as by nationalist or ethnicist hostility and by a rationalising projecting 'anti-super-ego-antisemitism' (see chapter 1, pp. 12–13). Hödl's letter, thus, provides a good example for our concept of 'syncretic antisemitism'. It seems far better to describe these anti-semitic prejudices in terms of syncretism and to point to their different origins and discursive functions, than to view them either as monocausally determined and as an exception granted for an 'historically special case of racism' or as 'ethnicism'. Although there is no doubt that the religious dimension of Hödl's antisemitism is outrageous, our multiple perspective on antisemitism seems to be the most adequate one, all the more so since the question of what criteria determine who is a Jew is a extremely complicated one (see, for example, Beck-Gernsheim 1999: 53–69, 146–64 and 233–70). In figure 2.5 (chapter 2), for the sake of simplicity we listed the anthroponym 'Jew' simply among the religionyms. The Nazis tended to regard 'the Jews' as a 'race', even though Hitler himself did not consider the Jews to be a 'biological race', but a 'race of the mind': in German, a '*Rasse des Geistes* '. However, at least in part and in some respects, the National-Socialists took the personal name 'the Jews' as a 'racionym'. It is not only the assumption of a 'Jewish race' that is untenable. The religious criterion is also problematic, since it is irrelevant for all those who consider themselves to be Jews without being religious at all. And the 'story' is even more complicated: apart from employing the anthroponym as a religionym or 'racionym', 'the Jews' have also been considered, or considered themselves, to be an ethnicity, a 'people' or a 'nation'. Each of these self- and other-characterisations is controversial and historically as well as politically dependent. There is no consent in these questions of 'collective' Jewish identifi-cation, except perhaps of the wide agreement that the singular experience of Auschwitz is actually one of the strongest identity-founding moments that unifies Jews into a sort of 'community of fate' ('*Schicksalsgemeinschaft* '). But even in this respect the question is open whether future generations will equally base their 'collective identity' as Jews on the recollection of this uniquely terrible experience.

Everyday discourse: conversations on the street

June 1987. Vienna. St Stephen's Square, the centre of the city. People stand gesticulating in clusters; approaching, one hears excited shouts, talk and discussions. What's going on? A memorial vigil is being held there, twenty-four hours a day, around the clock, for an entire month, with posters, commemora-ting the victims of World War Two. The vigil is organised by various groups, leftist organisations, students, pensioners, Resistance fighters, and the Green

Party. But why such excitement? And such emotions? Almost to the point of violence and fights? The whole event often seems to be on the verge of coming apart.

On this Viennese square, rich in tradition, people gathered and were angry that the past was not being allowed to rest. The reason for this gathering was again the 'Waldheim Affair', which threatened the Austrian '*Lebenslüge*' (sham existence): namely, that Austria was Hitlerian Germany's first victim. And attack is always – according to an old saying – the best form of defence. Not wanting to be reminded of these things, one felt attacked, offering justifications at any cost: by those holding the vigil, by the press, by the '*Nestbeschmutzer*' (those who foul the nest), by the Jews, and other countries in general.

If one listens to the conversations, one notices that they concern Waldheim, Austria's past, the Nazis, 'reparations', Christianity, and other current topics. It is precisely these topics that generate the emotions; old prejudices and *Feindbilder* (images of the enemy) long considered dead emerge from the deep. At first, the holders of the vigil remain silent; but over time they feel provoked and join in the discussions.

In the following sections, excerpts from these conversations, which were tape-recorded and transcribed, illustrate the antisemitic ferocity with which such discussions took place. Furthermore, it remains open to speculation what the conditions were that prevented a total dissolution of the vigil, and that really prevented physical violence from breaking out. Here we aim to illustrate the linguistic realisations of the most frequent antisemitic prejudices by the different discursive strategies we identified in chapter 2, especially focusing on argumentation (both on fallacies and topoi).

The '*Magdeburger Halbkugel*' (hemisphere)

In the following transcription, 'F' stands for 'female' and 'M' stands for 'male'. Acoustic data that are impossible to make out are represented as '(xxx)'. In cases where the transcriber is not absolutely sure about her or his understanding and decoding of the acoustic material, the presumptive spoken words are put within simple round brackets. The oblique '/' symbolises a syntactic rupture or a word rupture. The length of pauses is indicated by one, two or three short dashes. Commentaries on 'non-verbal' features of communication like laughing are framed by double round parenthesis.

F: It's/the fact is, the others are the stronger ones, and not there. From this action, it's very/I think it's really useful so that/especially people who just don't (xxx) us/right? who are now convinced that Austria is a Nazi country, that they then see that not all Austrians are Nazis!/That is, that a majority of Austrians (aren't Nazis)

M1: Excuse me for interrupting! What kind of a vigil is this supposed to be, what resistance is it for?

M2: Well, for the Austrian Resistance group (who) for oh/uh/five stands for/ for the fifth letter in the alphabet, that means Austria. That was the code for Austrian Resistance fighters, (and) they, I don't know, you can probably say more about it. Explain to this man the/what kind of (a) vigil this is.

M1: What do they mean by 'Resistance'?

M3: The Resistance that was in Austria.

M1: Even back then? Yeah, it was.

M2: Against the Nazis, yeah.

M1: Against National-Socialism?

M2: Yes. Yeah, yeah. Of course, yes.

M1: And what do you want to be now, for it or for/against, or what?

M2: No, it's only, it's supposed to be a vigil so that one/doesn't forget something like that because, uh, forgetting is just very, very

M1: Yeah, and I won't forget the assassination in Sarajevo either! I'm a German!

M2: Yeah, that.

Mx: Yeah.

M1: I won't forget the assassination! Austria caused that, and we/we paid in blood. And? But that's history. I'm no bad guy! (But now you're beginning)

M2: Yeah, and so what's your point?/or how/

M1: What my point is?

M2: Yeah.

M1: Nineteen-forty-five! That's over forty years ago! There are a lot of things one shouldn't forget, but at some point one should slowly start, and look ahead for once, not always back to the past! Don't always point a finger at the bad Germans!

M2: Mhmmm. No no/no, that:

M1: The worst genocide ever, and in no way do I want to justify that! That's/ what happened is, is unforgivable! But no one ever says anything about America, that there are hardly any Indians anymore.

M2: Yeah, that's/that's no doubt true, too, but. There's still a diff-/I mean it's

M1: Exactly! That's three/two or three hundred years ago!

M2: Mhm, mhm.

M1: And here it's only been forty years!

M2: It's all his- /

M1: Exactly!

M2: Yeah, that's right! Exactly! ((laughs))

M1: And that's why you're starting with the Holocaust again. I can't stand that word anymore!

M2: No, I'm not starting with that! You can't/yeah, please.

M1: Not at all.

M2: That's

M1: Just once one should

M2: But.

M1: Y' know – Y'know what/

M2: But, uh. If you/if you/if you look at what's going on here in Vienna!

M1: Y'know/y'know what we suffer from?

M2: What?

M1: We suffer from the fact that people have forgotten Christianity.

M2: Right.

M1: Christianity is built on.

M2: Without a doubt!

M1: It's built on love, but not on hate!

M2: Yeah, right! Right!

M1: Exactly.

M2: Right, I agree with you completely!

M1: No, but it seems/Yeah, exactly. But you don't seem to remember any of that anymore.

M2: Of course/

M1: At lea/at least the people here are standing in front of a cathedral, go in once in a while, take a look at it.

M2: Yeah. The symbol zero five is engraved in the cathedral.

M1: But don't even know/and don't even know/and don't even know/and don't even know what it's all about!

M2: Yeah, that's true, too!

M4: Listen, one could say so much. I could/I first told you about our general, who was ripped apart, you know?

M2: Yeah, mhm.

M4: Just like the Magdeburger Halbkugel.

M2: Yeah.

M4: Now I ask you: You are/if you had been a prisoner of war like us down there, okay. The way it happened to us.

M2: Mhm, mhm.

M4: And they were beyond human rights law.

M2: Mhm.

M4: They weren't even recognised at all then, not by any power, those guys were bandits and snipers.

M2: Yeah.

M4: But if you had the choice now, that no other alternative, that you have to die, have to!

M2: Yeah – mhm – yeah.

M4: And you have the choice: to be ripped apart like our general, or in a gas chamber?

M2: Yeah, mhm, mhm.

M4: What would you do?

M2: Yeah.

M4: That's demagoguery, isn't it? Yeah

M2: ((laughs)) Probably/Yeah, that's really terrible demagoguery!

M4: Yeah, Yeah.

M2: Probably in the gas chamber of course.

M4: There, you see! Yeah. But they talk about/well okay, I'm talking

M2: No, but that's really a very strange comparison!

M4: Why don't you let the others have their say!?/the other guy have his say!?

M2: Well. It (also) wasn't four point, or fi/five to six million Germans who were uh quartered or by/by/by/by horses. And. But just because they are Germans, or just because they're Catholics, or something like that. So, that's still a fine difference. Between.

M4: Yeah, and what/what/okay how many (Jews) do you think were killed?

M2: Yeah, it. Yeah, five million I think, or five to six or so, yeah.

M4: Yeah. I was, before I went to college, in a private school, and we had a lot of Jewish professors there. And at some point there was uh, there was talk about – that was still a long time before, we didn't have (xxx) yet /, and so we asked him, how big the Jewish population is. And the professor says, he says: 'Well, it's estimated to be about fourteen million', okay. And of that, about half live abroad. In North America, in Canada, in Central Am/and so on/and the other half is spread around. And then there was talk about it again with another one, independent of --- He said the same thing! --- Now I ask myself, were seven million gone from their homes, if so, there are, I don't know, well where we're from in the/ my home town, there were Jewish families. Sure, it was aw-/terrible, they were expelled, they had to go, and so on, and so on, and so on, right? Except for the doctor who made a house call at three in the morning when I was a child, (and) they all were back again! Came, one or two stayed, the dentist and others, they/th-/they got their things straightened out again, (and) compensation, right, and/and because of the injustice and so on! And then they left again! That's a representative sample! Don't you think?

M2: No.

M4: Well/Yeah.

M5: My grandparents were ga-/gassed

M4: Excuse me?

M5: My grandparents were gassed.

M4: Sure, I believe/I'm not argu/denying that! But to say six million! That's just a, a/that's just an impossibility.[14]

The course of the argument

The conversation begins with several opinions about the function and importance of the vigil as a form of political protest and resistance: F (a women) appreciates that that – because of the vigil – other countries take note that Austria is not just a 'Nazi country'. M1 (male 1), a German (as he identifies himself), asks what the point of the vigil is. M2 (male 2) explains its purpose of commemorating the Austrian Resistance to National-Socialism. M1 seems to interpret M2's emphasis on the importance of recollecting the Austrian Resistance against the Nazis as an attempt by the Austrians to distinguish themselves from the

Germans with respect to the past, and as an accusation against the German Nazis of having 'occupied' Austria. M1 does not stress that in 1938, the German Nazis were welcomed in Austria by the majority of Austrians. He tries to square or balance one thing against another and sets the Austrian responsibility for World War One – symbolised by the assassination in Sarajevo, which, according to the speaker, was provoked by 'Austria' (please note the metonymic reference) – against the Third Reich's 'annexation' of Austria. M2 wants to know from M1 what he intended to communicate by this statement, and invites him with a metalinguistic question to specify. M1 does not really explicate his attempt to offset the 'occupation' in 1938 against the Austrian role in causing World War One, but argues with the help of a sort of 'topos of limitation period' and of the visual metaphor 'look ahead, not back' that 'one' (please note the impersonal reference) should be concerned with future matters instead of past matters, and not 'always point a finger at the bad Germans'.

After having expressed this demand, M1 makes use of a rhetorical appellative figure, namely a procataleptic concession (*concessio*), which seemingly concedes to the interlocutors that the antisemitic Nazi genocide was the worst one in the whole of history and that he by no means wants to justify it. Then, however, he continues with his attempts to balance one thing against another and refers, as a counterexample to the extermination of the Jews, to the responsibility of America (please note the metonymic reference) for the eradication of 'the Indians'. M2 begins to question this equating historical comparison and tries to explain some of the differences, but M1 interrupts M2 and admits that the American genocide of 'the Indians' was committed two or three centuries ago, whereas the National-Socialist genocide of the Jews was committed forty years ago. After this, M1 begins a turn by saying 'it's all his-/'. It is not clear what M1 exactly intends to say in this interrupted utterance, but M2 seems to know and affirmatively agrees with M1, who emphatically confirms the affirmation of M1. We assume – and this conjecture is backed by the content of M1's subsequent turn – that M1 interprets M2's utterance as a specific 'topos of history' that is designated to historicise, to declare the present consideration of the historical period of National-Socialism, the Nazi crimes and the Nazi victims as something obsolete. We also assume that this interpretation does not correspond to M2's intended meaning. Both the emphatic twofold affirmation and M2's laughter seem to be indicators of M2 being conscious of M1's misunderstanding. It is also possible that the laughter signals that M2's utterance is to be interpreted as ironic.

However, after this short, unclear, amphibolic verbal exchange, M1 very clearly takes a position against 'dealing with the past': 'And that's why you're starting with the Holocaust again. I can't stand that word anymore!' After several brief and rapid exchanges between the two speakers, there is an immediate break in the discursive coherence. M1, the speaker who dominates this part of the conversation, introduces a topical shift with an appellative rhetorical question that he asks four times to get the attention of M2. M1 has recourse to Christianity, which he characterises as being grounded on love, and not hate. The meaning of this assertion can be polyphonic: one possible interpretation is that M1 wants to insinuate that the vigil is unnecessary or damaging because it stirs up hate. Ultimately, such an interpretation leads to the assumption that M1 turns the victim-victimiser relationship around: the ones causing the 'commotion' are considered to be responsible for the new anti-semitism. Another interpretation, which does not contradict the first 'reading', could be that M1, by arguing that love is better than hate, alludes to and impli-citly reproduces the antisemitic prejudice that 'the Jews – who are associated with the vigil – are religiously different from the Christians in that they are guilty of hatred, are irreconcilable and always thirsting for vengeance'.

However, with such types of argumentation, recontextualisation becomes clear, as does interdiscursivity or intertextuality: similar arguments were also used in public or semi-public discourse (see above); here they reappear, packaged differently. It is difficult to determine whether the relationship of borrowing or adoption is one from (semi-)public into (semi-)private or from (semi-)private into (semi-)public, or one from 'top' (meaning leading opinion-makers who act in public) to 'bottom' (meaning 'the person in the street') or 'bottom-up', but we assume there to be a dialectical relationship between private and public discourses.

Narrative 1: The 'Halbkugel'

M4 (male 4) gets involved at this point and tells the first narrative of the transcript excerpt. We already quoted this passage earlier as an example of an unreal scenario. This narrative serves several discursive, and especially argumentational, purposes: it adds personal experience, furthers the accusation, trivialises the extermination of Jews by balancing one thing against another, thus implying that the gas chamber would have been the lesser of two evils, and finally pushes its recipient into a corner.

The strategy which M4 uses consistently, from the moment he enters the discussion, is to present himself as a witness of the times who personally obser-ved certain exemplary events and as a result of these experiences arrived at particular conclusions. This is also the order in which he proceeds in the conversation: first he tells the narratives in which events are described so that the listener should himself come to his (M4's) conclusions. Only at the end, as a sort of 'moral of the story', does M4 express his opinions explicitly.

With his opening gambit M4 blocks the previous conversation and at the same time indicates that 'one' would have a lot to say. The impersonal reference by German '*man*' implies that the speaker tends towards speaking from a per-spective that is not just his personal one, but that he assumes a more general, intersubjective view that reaches far beyond his subjective standpoint. M4 ties his contribution to the 'pre-discourse' by explicitly referring 'back' to a story he previously told to M2, and begins to establish a hypothetical scenario: His interlocutor (M2) – who is apparently too young to have lived at that time – is taken prisoner of war by 'bandits and snipers', 'the way it happened to us'. In this way, the interlocutor is supposedly drawn into the 'we'-group of M4 (i.e. the '*Wehrmacht*' generation) and is asked to put himself into M4's shoes. M4 apparently identifies himself with a troop that was stationed in the Balkans during World War Two. It is already clear at this point that he accepts the ideology prevailing at the time in that he adopts the phrase 'bandits and snipers' to refer to partisans.

As a next step, M4 makes clear to his younger interlocutor that he has to die a merciless death (since he is a victim of the bandits and snipers). His only choice is between two ways – and only two – of dying: 'to be ripped apart like our general, or in a gas chamber'. M4 is quite conscious of the point of this strategy: demagoguery. By saying it himself, M4 displays the fact that he is well aware of existing norms and that he is quite intentionally breaking them.

M4's discussion partner – even if apparently feeling uncertain – falls for this demagogic trick and gives exactly the answer that M4 expects. The fallacious presupposition in this topos of comparison exists in that the premises of the two means of death in this fictional story are put on equal footing, as though prisoners of war were always either gassed or torn in two. In this way, the Nazi extermination machinery is put on the same level as regular wartime events (assuming that this story actually happened).

M2 falls for the story, names the gas chamber as his preferred alternative, but at the same time observes that it is a rather 'strange comparison'. In this way, however, M2 has essentially accepted the story and the attempt to balance one thing against another or, strictly speaking, the attempt to relativise one evil with an allegedly even worse evil. Thus, although trying to counter-argue, in some respect he becomes involved in the same level as M4.

M2 takes it further, however: six million (prisoners of war) were not ripped apart nor were they singled out on account of their religion or nationality: 'Well. It (also) wasn't four point, or fi/five to six million Germans who were uh quartered or by/by/by/by horses. And. But just because they are Germans, or just because they're Catholics, or something like that. So, that's still a fine difference'.

Narrative 2: The Jewish population in the world

At this point, M4 asks M2 – with feigned naïvety? – how many Jews were killed. This question is rhetorical, for the answer was already implied in the objection by his opponent, who nevertheless answers the question by saying: 'Yeah, five million I think, or five to six or so, yeah'. M4's question serves as a pretext for the story that follows, in which M4 answers his own question, suggesting that he learned from Jewish authorities and from personal experience – based on the observation that Jewish families in his village apparently survived relatively unscathed – that there could not have been six million Jews in Europe at the time.

In terms of argumentation theory, the second narrative serves as a specific, relativising topos of numbers (see also chapter 2, p. 79) that may be subsumed under the conclusion rule: if it can be proved that the number of Jews murdered by the Nazis is not as high as it is generally maintained, the National-Socialist crimes cannot have been as bad and as terrible as generally contended. M4 tries to prove this topos by two fallacies, and accordingly, the narrative can be divided into two parts, the first one serving as an *argumentum ad verecundiam*, the second one as an illustrative example (*exemplum*) that is employed for an incorrect 'pseudo-empirical' generalisation.

At the beginning of the first part of the narrative, M4 presents himself as someone who had been a student of Jewish professors, apparently before the Nazi period, before the planned extermination of the Jews, which he does not mention in so many words. The main portion of this first narrative consists of a quotation: what one of his Jewish professors said about the size and distribution of the Jewish population around the world. M4 attempts to support the truth of this statement by representing himself as an honest witness, who heard the information with his own ears, not from just anyone, but from a Jewish professor. In other words, M4 can cite an authority, using an *argumentum ad verecundiam*. The third form of support comes from a further Jewish professor, who, independently of the first, supposedly said the same thing. The summary of the professorial calculations establishes the 'moral' or the point of the first narrative: there were not seven million Jews living in Europe to begin with. Consequently, M4 asks himself 'a question'. He does not say which one, although one can easily infer that after the performative prefix 'I ask myself', which indicates the illocutionary force of the incomplete interrogative speech act, M4 would have asked 'How is it possible in view of the numbers mentioned that six million Jews were murdered?'.

The second part of the story follows. In extracts, we have already quoted this section above, when we analysed it incompletely as an example of an 'allusion with the help of typical lexemes', which alludes to the prejudice of 'the business-minded Jew' and associates this prejudice with the topic of 'compensation policy'. M4 states that in his home town there were Jewish families. First, in the form of a procataleptic rhetorical *concessio*, M4 assures his listener that he finds it terrible that the Jews were expelled, a half-hearted concession to the dominant democratic norms that serves the positive self-representation (please note the euphemistic omission and replacement of the other, more serious Nazi crimes by the semantically almost empty 'and so on', which M4 reels off three times). After this, M4 describes the behaviour of these Jews, ostensibly after the war, although he does not say this explicitly. Whether a strategy, or a form of taboo, nothing is said about the time period between the Jews' expulsion and their return (i.e., what happened during this time). 'They were all back again!' exclaims M4 in an indignant tone of voice. There was only one exception – the all-important exception that upholds the prejudices. And this Jew who didn't 'come back' was twice the exception: he was 'the good Jew', whose selfless behaviour as M4's childhood doctor is described in considerable detail. Of those who returned, two remained, 'the others' left again after they organised their things and collected 'compensation'.

As explained above, here, M4 alludes to the prejudice relating to 'the business-minded Jew' and connects it with the topic of 'compensation policy'. The main purpose of the narration of this allegedly personal experience, however, is to give an illustrative example that backs the fallacious 'pseudo-empirical' generalisation of a specific episode. And indeed, in closing, M4 observes: 'That's a representative sample!'.

The 'representative sample' can stand for several things: the fact that because the 'good Jews' did not survive, only the bad ones remain; that only one didn't 'come back' (the exception); that 'all the others' did return. This fallacious argumentation so concerned with providing a semblance of 'objectivity' suffers from noticeable vagueness and generalisations: 'all'. How many does 'all' constitute? This is as remarkably absent in M4's story, as is the number of those who 'left again'.

In the last part of the transcript excerpt, a listener (M5) objects with 'my grandparents were gassed' to dispute the representativeness of M4's 'evidence'. M4 seems to be slightly irritated by M5's objection, which shifts the perspective to the victims and their descendants by giving insight into the personal involvement of the speaker in the experience of the murdering of his grandparents by the Nazis. M4 first hesitates and searches for the right word. Then, he affirms that he does not deny that M5's grandparents were gassed. Immediately after that, however, he explicitly and emphatically summarises the conclusion of his fallacious 'topos of numbers': 'but to say six million! That's just a, a/that's just an impossibility!'.

In this case, then, we find a perfect example of the trivialisation and even denial of Jewish extermination, an 'Auschwitz lie' of the sort one finds only in extreme right-wing circles or in anonymous conversations. This transcript offers a 'good' instance for the weaving together of the Nazi era with antisemitism and the degree to which dealing with the Nazi period influences and determines the shape of discussions about Jews and antisemitism (cf. Wodak *et al.* 1994, 1999). The 'German' feels attacked, seems to live under duress to refute the presumption of a 'collective guilt', and tries to justify himself and 'the Germans' with a squaring strategy. The 'Austrian' attempts, on the basis of an unreal, squaring scenario, a topos of numbers, an *argumentum ad verecundiam* and a fallacious generalisation to minimise the horrible extent of the Nazi crimes, to prove the impossibility of the whole extension that is historically documented. The narratives are oral realisations and argumentative means of justification that back or allude to antisemitic prejudices. They function as alleged 'typical' examples, drawn from alleged 'personal experience' that 'vividly', but nevertheless fallaciously, support the 'Auschwitz lie'.

'Nothing but Jews'

The following short transcribed excerpt of a conversation during the vigil illustrates the argumentative utilisation of the topos of ignorance (see Wodak *et al.* 1999: 36 and 160–1) for the exculpation of 'the average Austrians in the street' who lived in the period of National-Socialism and supposedly did not know anything about the industrialised genocide of the Jews committed by the Nazis:

M1:   Around Czerny Square there (was) nothing but Jews. You don't have to tell me anything! You know (what). The streets around Czerny Square! There was one (house) after another (with Jews)!

M2:   Then one also saw (xxx) the way they disappeared one after another!

M1:   Right (look) and I was young at the time. I know only what I heard, and that was.

M?:   In Sperlgasse everyone could see it for themselves.

M1:   Nobody said: 'We're going to Dachau now!'. It was: 'Why aren't they here anymore? They emigrated, they have relatives abroad'. No-one said: 'We're going to Mauthausen or to Dachau'. I'm not trying to deny that one heard about this later! How how it (xxx)

M3:   Yeah, come on, stop it!

M2:   Yeah, but. No, I went to high school in the second district, and we looked out on to where they deported them, the way the people (in the small Sperlgasse) on to the trucks – onto the uh, uh

M1:   The way they loaded them on to the trucks, the way the women came (in pairs), the way the women with the bundles (xxx) uh everyone could take a bag with them.

Voices mixed together:

> Not everyone could be a Resistance fighter. The claim that 'no one could have known' – that's nonsense! The guy never said anything about America: and all of a sudden he's going to America! We have to face the facts today and not act like it never
> [...]

M3:   (No one knew about that in Austria). (You can say) Bronfmann knows because he wasn't there at the time![15]

Here, three men come into considerable conflict: where did the Jews 'disappear to'? This question summarises the self-exculpating taken-back-to-the-Nazi-period perspective of M1 in this piece of transcript. The euphemistic verb of disappearing, in blurring any trace of the Nazi perpetrators, helps M1 to establish linguistically the topos of ignorance (which should not be confused with the '*argumentum ad ignorantiam*' that we explained in chapter 2) that dominates this part of the conversation and can be rephrased as follows: if somebody did not know anything about the Nazi crimes, the systematic extermination of Jews by the Nazis and the existence of concentration camps, he or she has not participated in committing these crimes and cannot be held responsible for them, nor for not having made attempts to prevent the perpetrators from committing these crimes.

In this extract, M1 introduces the fact that there were once (nothing but) Jews in the second Viennese district. This observation is not disputed. After

M1's first turn, a male speaker, whose voice cannot exactly be identified, makes mention of the fact that 'one' (please note the generalising perspective) has seen how the Jews slowly 'disappeared' from this district. Now, M1 feels called upon to reject any suspicion of himself and to state that, then, he was a child and that he knows only what he heard, implying that he saw 'nothing'. As we can see from M1's last turn of this extract, this assertion is not upheld, since, together with M2, M1 describes the deportation of Jews, and especially of Jewish women, from the perspective of an eye witness. However, after M1's dismissive second turn, M2 emphasises that, in Sperlgasse, everybody could see 'it' well, not yet specifying what 'it' is intended to refer to. At this time, M1 in his exculpating argumentation brings in the victims, the deported Jews, and backs his topos of ignorance by a victim-victimiser reversal, utilising direct speech as a means of involvement that underlines the character of the personal-experience perspective: 'Nobody said: "We're going to Dachau now!" It was: "Why aren't they here anymore?" ' In this way, the Jews are presented as guilty of not having revealed their destination. Because they did not do so, no one knew what was really going on. Instead, one looked around in amazement and noticed that they were all gone. Saw nothing, heard nothing, knew nothing. And a further speculation follows immediately: 'They emigrated, they have relatives abroad'. No-one said: 'We're going to Mauthausen or to Dachau'. Two prejudices are wrapped up here: on the one hand, it is insinuated that most Jews managed to emigrate to America; on the other hand, the prejudice that 'the Jews are themselves responsible for their own misfortune' is reproduced by turning around the victim-victimiser relationship again: the Jews are accused of failing to tell people where they were really going. This topos of ignorance is only mitigated by M1's concession that 'one' learned 'this' later, after 1945. Apropos 'this': the systematically organised genocide is only vaguely, and primarily metaphorically and metonymically, referred to in this piece of conversation. It is disguised by the 'travelling to Dachau and Mauthausen', a combination of a symbolic moving metaphor and a metonymy that consists of replacing the actions or events by the name of the place where the actions are performed or where the event takes place. The Nazi perpetrators, up to this point of the conversation, are completely suppressed.

The first linguistic trace of the perpetrators appears in the subsequent turn by M2, who speaks for the second time in this excerpt, right after M3's demand to 'stop it' addressed to M1. M2, in contrast, tells what he really saw – that is, the deportation of the Jews, the way 'they' loaded them onto the trucks. Although 'they' are not identified more closely, 'they' are at least mentioned as actors who commit the deportation. All of a sudden and in contradiction to his earlier declaration, M1 now also seems to remember that he saw how 'they' loaded women with bundles and in pairs on to the trucks.

At this point, emotionality increases; these sorts of eyewitness reports are apparently not well liked. One hears comments like 'Not everyone could be a Resistance fighter' – a statement that implicitly argues on the basis of the exculpating topos of external constraints, which heteronomises the responsibility and shifts it to external 'forces' (see Wodak *et al.* 1999: 36 and 88). But one hears also critical objections like 'The claim that "no one could have known" – that's nonsense!'.

The closing point, however, is: 'No one knew about that in Austria. (You can say) Bronfmann knows because he wasn't there at the time!' With this comment, the topos of ignorance is employed once more, and the distortion is expanded: those who were there at the time knew nothing, and at the same time, a prominent Jew – who, as it happened, was not there at the time, is from a postwar generation, and lives in the United States – is accused of stirring unrest. This is a delegitimising form of argumentation that was repeatedly recontextualised and that one could very often hear and read during the ongoing discourse about the 'Waldheim Affair' in many different forms, genres and fields of political action. Who, then, should be allowed to say anything, and to criticise the Austrian Nazi crimes? Those who were actually there and choose not to keep silent seemed and still seem not to be listened to: these are people many Austrians would still most like to silence. A sticky topic, the past. 'The Jews are guilty', because they didn't even tell people where they were going, because they survived, or because they don't keep silent.

War criminals?

The next example taken from the vigil illustrates how nationalist synec-dochisation and generalisation works and manifests itself in everyday discourse about the controversial 'collective' past. That is to say, this transcript shows how the nationalist principle 'one for all and all for one' became virulent during the 'Waldheim Affair', how the Austrian president was willingly accepted as a living *pars pro toto* by his voters and supporters, and how, consequently, they identified themselves as a 'whole' with the 'part' and were ready to defend this part against all attacks. Apart from that, it shows also a second inclusionary relationship and synecdochising expansion, namely one that concerns the realm of the military. This second fallacious generalisation can be condensed into the conditional: if somebody says that Waldheim was a war criminal, he or she says that everyone who was a soldier was a war criminal. In others words: if somebody insults Waldheim by this accusation, he or she insults everyone who was a soldier by this reproach:

M1: Who's being insulted? Then. Yeah. By whom? How and how? How?

M2: That goes from WE! I feel insulted. Because of this whole propaganda against the President. Excuse me?

M1: Concretely now! So, are you the President? Are you the President? Tell me, who's insulting you?

M2: The Presi-/The President was elected by 54 per cent of the population. Voted for by the electorate.

M3: No, not the population, by the way. At the same time, yeah.

M2: Sinowatz explained that we have to acknowledge that. And a certain Dr Kirchschläger, who was President before, said I have the Waldheim files/ lawyer/judge. I studied the Waldheim files and found no improprieties. Kirchschläger did/I'm also insulting Dr. Kirchschläger with all the commotion that's going on now.

M3: Yeah – yeah – I know. I heard about it. Yeah, yeah, I heard about it, yeah. Yeah, yeah.

M2: Unbelievable (shouting) this bloody mess that's come about now because of this whole thing.

Mx: (It's)

M4: Outrageous. Yeah. And Bronfmann and Singer didn't say that it won't be a picnic for Waldheim when he becomes President, but that it won't be a picnic for Austria!

M3: Austria, yeah.

M4: And those are all, that's you and me.

M2: yeah – yeah ((quietly)), yeah, yeah.

M4: And/and everyone! Even the ones who didn't elect him, who (voted for) the other one, the (xxx)

M2: Yes! Yes! Yeesss! That's what I/that's what I wanted to say, too!

M4: Yeah, yeah, yeah.

M2: Those who/those who pull Kirchschläger into the mess because he says there's no evidence.

M4: That's just unbelievable! To put up with something like that, well, well, yeah.

M2: The thing now with Partik again, too!

M4: Yeah, yeah.

M2: With a passport they send him and then tell him when he gets here that it's not valid!

M5: Yeah ((laughs)).

M2: That's really ((laughing)) stupid. That's really stupid!

M5: ((laughs quietly)) Yeah, right! Exactly!

M6: No, because he's got so many friends here!

M5: I mean, because they welcome him here, right!

M2: But what uh/uh

M7: No, they insult everyone who was a soldier when they say that's a war criminal! He/he had to protect the troops against attacks by the partisans. They weren't soldiers. What would you do, you're a soldier, already retreating, and they're shooting out of the windows and bushes ((shouting)) CIVILIANS! Civilians!

M1: Gee, I don't know. I heard a different version!

M7: Of course, he has to protect his troops! And today he's a war criminal! That's just unbelievable! Something like that, isn't it! Yeah, we risked our skulls there/to/to the final day (xxx)

M1: Was a/so Hitler wasn't a war criminal, or what?

F: You can't compare Hitler with a soldier!

M1: No, of course not! I mean just be/because, uh. That means no-one was a war criminal!

M7: We/that you were at all able to/that you were able to hatch out, we/we (risked) in/in/(skulls).

M1: There weren't any at all! There probably weren't any war criminals at all then, right?[16]

As this transcript illustrates, the critique and accusation of political and generation representatives can be 'contagious' if nationalism functions as transmitter or catalyst. M2 feels personally attacked by the attacks on Waldheim: that is, he identifies completely, setting up the synecdochising, generalising equation 'Waldheim = we (including the speaker = I)'. M1, by ironically asking whether M2 was the president, attempts to convince M1 that he is taken in by a strawman fallacy (see chapter 2) and should not make such a generalising equation. Thereupon M2 tries to specify, and revises his generalisation, now equating Waldheim with 54 per cent of the Austrian voters. In order to support his equation, M2 adds a topos of authority, referring to a statement of a political opponent of Waldheim, the ex-chancellor Fred Sinowatz, who resigned on 9 June 1986, the day after Waldheim was elected president. This topos has the quality of an implicit *locus a minore*, an argumentation scheme that argues 'from the less', implying that if even a harsh political opponent pleads for the acceptance of Waldheim as a democratically elected president, the other Austrians should tolerate him too. M2 employs an additional topos of authority. This topos is designated to exonerate Waldheim. M2 argues: even the former Austrian president, Dr Rudolf Kirchschläger, as a lawyer, studied the files and came to the conclusion that there were no improprieties. This argument, the use of which can only be a consequence of media news reporting, is – at least in part – fallacious, since anyone who read or listened to Kirchschläger's statement closely, knew that it contained numerous ambivalent statements (cf. Gruber and Wodak 1987).

After having enriched the hasty generalisation, stating that by insulting Waldheim one also insults Kirchschläger, M3 takes a turn and with many repetitions emphatically confirms that he heard about Kirchschläger's statement. Now, the emotions begin to climb: 'Unbelievable this bloody mess!' *Iudeus ex machina!* In the next breath, M4, a supporter of M2, mentions Singer and Bronfman with their famous statement in the *profil* interview: 'It won't be a picnic for Austria'. This metaphorical, metonymic (the country is named instead of its inhabitants) and synecdochic statement (the whole replaces the part) was generally interpreted as a great threat and was met with violent reaction. M4 explicitly points to the referential inclusion of all Austrians in this prediction – in our tropological terms, to the generalising synecdoche within this metonymy: 'And those are all, that's you and me and/and everyone! Even the ones who didn't elect him, who (voted for) the other one'. M2 affirms M4's assertion and adds that he wanted to say the same. Then, M2 repeats that Kirchschläger's authority is being disparaged as well, and M4 continues that one could not stand for that.

After M2, having introduced the topic of Partik and his passport, more people involve themselves in the discussion, which is very agitated. After a few brief verbal exchanges, M7 brings up another synecdochising generalisation with respect to the realm of the military: 'they insult everyone who was a soldier when they say that's a war criminal!'.

This generalisation or equation, which must also be interpreted as a *non sequitur*, has at least two persuasive functions: First, it suggests that Waldheim was just a normal soldier. Second, it aims at exculpating these soldiers and at mobilising their opposition and that of the whole '*Wehrmacht* generation'.

M7 continues very emphatically to explain that Waldheim had to protect his troops against the attacks of the partisans, who were not soldiers but civilians. In order to give his argument more persuasive force, he applies an involvement strategy, addressing his interlocutors directly (in the second person singular) with a question and inviting them to take the perspective of a soldier in retreat who is threatened by civilian partisans shooting from windows and bushes. By this scenario, M7 wants to suggest that Waldheim and the soldiers merely tried to protect themselves against the partisans, and that killing them was therefore not a war crime. M1 casts doubt on this scenario and objects that he heard something different. Indignantly, M7 replies in the present tense, which makes the past become present and gives the statement a generic character: 'Of course he has to protect his troops. And today he's a war criminal!' Then, M7, becoming more and more involved, shifts from the third-person perspective to the first-person perspective and referentially establishes a 'we group' that refers to the 'soldier generation' which includes the speaker himself. What follows is an implicit topos of non-legitimation (see Wodak *et al.* 1999: 37) that aims at pointing out that the addressee has no right to criticise Waldheim and the 'soldier generation': 'we risked our skulls in order that you were able to hatch out'. The topos is rhetorically underpinned by the naturalising, or strictly speaking, animalising metaphor that literally would denote the 'chick's birth', its hatching out of the egg. The chick symbolises the young, inexperienced, ignorant person who should keep her or his big mouth shut.

M1's interim attempt at a counter move has failed. His question whether M7 thinks that Hitler was a war criminal or not is not answered by M7, but by a woman who criticises the comparison between Hitler and a soldier as inadequate. Although the woman performs a strawman fallacy (since M1 did not compare Hitler with a soldier), M1 does not point to this fallacious presumption (for example by explicitly stating that he did not compare a 'simple soldier' with Hitler), but retreats into a defensive position and tries to justify his question about Hitler by intimating that he took the worst of all Nazis as an example because it is said that nobody was a war criminal. Cynically and provocatively, M1 summarises the discussion and ironically concludes that, probably, there were no war criminals at all.

Within this group of discussants, it is apparently not clear to anyone that international discussion in the media concerned itself principally with the way in which the past was hypocritically dealt with: not primarily whether Waldheim was a war criminal. And this certainly cannot be on account of the Austrian press coverage. Instead, a complete distortion of the American press coverage had taken place, for the straight accusation that Waldheim was a war criminal arose neither at the World Jewish Congress nor in the *New York Times* (cf. Wodak *et al.* 1990, Mitten 1992). This conversation is alarming not only because of its intensity and the traces of incitement one can find in it, but because we see here the consequences of being poorly informed. Misinformation is quickly reduced to fallacious schemata of prejudice. The 'threat' posed by the Jewish World Congress is experienced as powerful and the nationalist identification of Waldheim with the Austrians and Austria is nearly complete, following the motto 'one for all, all for one' and 'right or wrong, my president'.

Fulfilling duties

The example we will analyse in this section is primarily intended to illustrate how the 'topos of fulfilling duties', the topos of the threat of antisemitism as well as the 'squaring' fallacy were employed in everyday argumentation during the discourse about Waldheim's past and the Nazi period.

F3:　We have to make sure that it doesn't happen again! But not that there. Yeah!

M:　In Austria we ha/In Austria we went through a de-Nazification, according to the rules! And this was discontinued because the Americans wanted it that way!

F3:　But not so as to incite people! Or?

M:　But I'm very much in favour that we show – also to other countries – that there was Resistance here, too. That's maybe what we've not mentioned enough.

F4:　Yes! The – the fact that there was Resistance here needs to be emphasised! We've really not emphasised that enough. We never mentioned that despite the fact that in 1938 so many shouted and screamed so loudly, others were stomped on in the ditches. They were never/was never talked about, those who had tears in their eyes and were murdered. We also have to talk about them, as well as those who later stood up against the Third Reich. BUT, if in the same context you say that he should resign after he's already been elected. I don't go along with that.

F2:　That's just politics, nothing else!

M:　(It's) an extension of the election campaign, isn't it?

F3:　That's why, when there's talk like that, that people get agitated on all sides, it doesn't make much sense! One should say, yeah, we regret that, but, we've regretted that for forty years now, we've worked our way up and those people are doing well, I mean also our fellow Jewish citizens I think can't complain, but now, I have to tell you, I think they're afraid of these events! Because if someone isn't antisemitic to begin with, he will be afterwards. Because the people get agitated! And I don't think that's good at all, don't you. (yeah) that we

M: I think. Forty years of reconstruction in Austria, I think, is proof that we've turned away, so to speak, from a past, which admittedly seduced, you could say, some of us.

F2: That's proof, yeah.

M: But the learning process in Austria has taken place, and it should take place in other countries, too! In Austria it's happened already! The discussion is basically useful, it's just that there should be something in it for all of us!

F2: Yes, of course, but I (have the impression), nothing will come out of it! Yeah, of course!

M: No, we can't avoid them anymore, the discussions!

M2: Yeah, but I think, uh – I think that it shouldn't be possible in Austria anymore for a presidential candidate to say, while campaigning, I fulfilled my duties in World War II!

F2: Well, don't you have any duties as an adult!

F2?: No! What! Oh, come on, that's quibbling!

F4: You know, I also have duties! No, I have to uh

M2: 'I only fulfilled my duty'. That's not possible in that context! You know.

F4: 'Fulfil my duty!'. When I'm at work I have to and I have to (xxx) my (child), too

F2: Yeah, exactly! We/we all have to fulfil our duties and in that case duty is such a crime! That word. Crime. No!

F4: The same with duty – today.

M: Older people have a different sense of duty! In today's/younger generation it's got something of a bad name, the word duty. That's why it's misunderstood.

F4: That's too bad. It would be good if more people had a sense of duty, people, wouldn't it.

F2: No.

M: But he actually wanted to say

F4: I have my duty in the office and you have the duty

F2: I mean – there's always quibbling with words

M: Okay, I didn't do it enthusiastically. That's how I/(You)

M2: But that's not what he said! But that's not what he said!

F2: Well, okay! But listen!

M: When someone is wounded, yeah? And there someone really wants to get married and here one's got something else to do, and he has to sit down there in an office and sign for the authenticity of the document. That's no ideal job! For sure!

F2: If someone stands behind what he writes/when he writes something/if one

M: I mean the Austrians weren't worth anything to the German army anyway, y'know.

F2:   My dear man, you have no idea/I think/it's more than clear

M2:   Why not? Why do you think that?

F2:   Well, because you didn't experience it!

F4:   You have to talk about it but, you don't have to/

F2:   Yeah, but it shouldn't be turned around then!

F4:   It shouldn't degenerate into spite! Shouldn't get turned around! Well, maybe you didn't hear it before.

F5:   No, of course it's not spiteful. What's spiteful (about it)?

F4:   But that everyone there/everyone is, everything's dumped onto one person. That's not right, that's not right! Is it?

F5:   Well, that our image has been tarnished.

F?:   Now, look here, this is a person.

F5:   A whole lot (to that) (he/one) can't be allowed. It happened once, but ((men's shouts))[17]

This transcript excerpt begins with F3 (female 3) directing a moral appeal to those standing around her: 'We have to make sure that it doesn't happen again!'. However, this concessive appeal is followed by the (in)famous 'but': 'But not to incite people'. At this time, F3 does not yet explicate what she exactly means by this statement. Only after her next contribution does it become clear that this procataleptic 'yes-but' figure is preparing a topos of threat of antisemitism that will function as a fallacious *trajectio im alium*, as a victim-victimiser-reversal.

After the first as well as after the second part of F3's 'yes-but' figure, M, an older man, each time takes the turn. He seems to be completely concerned about how to strategically present 'Austria' and the 'Austrians' positively to foreign countries. First, he stresses that there was a de-Nazification according to the rules in Austria, and that it was the wish of the Americans to stop it. Interestingly, he says literally 'we carried out a de-Nazification' (in German: '*wir ham...eine Entnazifizierung durchgeführt*'), thus representing himself as the member of a we-group that actively carried out these political measures, as acting participants. This part of M's contribution has at least two argumentation functions: apart from showing 'Austria' in a favourable light and backing F3's claim that 'it' must not happen again, it contains an 'assurance' against a relapse, since it shifts the responsibility for a potential repetition or the discovery that the de-Nazification was not as careful as it should have been. The responsibility is heteronomised by the contention that it was the Americans who wished the Austrians to stop de-Nazification. Second, M points to the significance of the Austrian anti-Nazi Resistance and the importance of telling other countries about it. F4 adds to this and says that even in 1938 many people were against (the Hitler regime). According to F4, this fact is just too little known. Here, F4 pursues a strategy of autonomisation that aims to delimit Austria from Germany with respect to the dark side of the Nazi past and implicitly to minimise the

Austrian contribution to the Nazi crimes. At this point the figure of Waldheim suddenly appears in this conversation: 'BUT, if in the same context you say that he should resign after he's already been elected. I don't go along with that'. 'In others words: on the one side, F4 strategically lays emphasis on the Austrian Resistance to National-Socialism; on the other side, he vehemently refuses the attacks against the elected president'.

After the two short contributions to the discussion by F2 and M, who denounce the critique of Waldheim and the demand for resignation as a political issue and a prolongation of the election campaign, F3 continues by employing the above-mentioned topos of threat of antisemitism. She argues that Jewish fellow citizens can be content with the Austrian 'working-through' of the Nazi past, but that they should be afraid, because it is specifically through 'these' agitations of the people that those who were not antisemitic adopt an antisemitic attitude. At this point, the older man (M) ties his turn to the contribution of the previous speaker by employing a sort of 'squaring' fallacy, or *non-sequitur*. M takes the forty-year-long process of rebuilding in Austria as proof of the claim that the Austrians have dealt with and turned away from a past, 'which, admittedly, seduced, you could say, some of us'. Please note the exonerating heteronomising personification, which transforms the past into an actor that leads a few susceptible people astray and into crime, and they are consequently victims, not perpetrators. In his attempt to 'neutralise' and relativise the past, M then emphasises the point that the learning process has 'happened' in Austria, but that it should now also start in 'other countries'. M holds that although the discussion per se is useful, everybody should get something out of it. F2 seemingly agrees, but then 'elliptically' expresses her impression that nothing comes of this debate. M replies that the discussion can no longer be avoided.

At this point, the discussion begins to evolve around the exculpating 'topos of fulfilling duty'. A second man, M2, joins in and maintains that it should no longer be possible that, in Austria, a candidate for the presidency says in the election campaign that he fulfilled his duty. We have already mentioned and described this euphemistic, relativising argumentation scheme earlier in this chapter, and here we refer to the two conclusion rules: if somebody fulfils her or his duty, she or he acts responsibly. If he or she acts responsibly, he or she cannot be blamed for his or her actions.

After M2's intervention, emotions rise. F2 asks M2: 'Well, don't you have any duties as an adult?' And she – or another woman who cannot exactly be identified – says that the discussion about the term 'duty' is just quibbling. Also F4 keeps on at M2 by stating that she too has a duty. M2 insists on his viewpoint and rejects the word 'duty' in reference to the Nazi period. The two women, for whom the expression 'fulfilling duty' has exclusively positive connotations, extend the term beyond this context and talk about duties at work and to one's children. Here, two points of view, two moral worlds collide with each other. People end up shouting past each other and engaging in a metalinguistic dispute. The older man (M) starts to throw his experience and age into the game, employing a delegitimising argument: since today's generation interprets the term 'duty' in another way, they just can't understand what Waldheim meant. According to him, Waldheim wanted to say: 'I didn't do it enthusiastically'. M2 objects: 'But he didn't say that'. M continues to find additional justification and excuses that we shall not analyse in detail here. Among other things, M sets out that, in addition, the Austrians meant nothing to the German army. The women present support the man, attempt to dispute M2's authority and competence with respect to the issue of the Nazi period, and again direct moral appeals to those standing around them: 'It shouldn't degenerate into spite', 'Everything's dumped onto one person. That's not right'. What exactly is being referred to is not clear. But finally, F5 gets to the point: 'that our image has been tarnished'. Again, the nationalist principle of synecdochising generalisation is applied, those who identify with Waldheim or the 'war generation' feel attacked and perceive themselves as being in the same boat. And the discussion ends in shouting.

'We are all innocent perpetrators'

In Austria, the 'Waldheim Affair' set off debates about the past which provided evidence that the conscious, self-critical working-through of the 'darkest' side of one's 'own' history has been repressively avoided for more than four decades – contrary to all the self-deceptive declarations that, until now actually, everything had been overcome, and learned. Still, the 'own' national, historically expanded ingroup are primarily perceived as victims, and the Jews as scapegoats still serve as a 'projection surface' on to which one's responsibility is repelled. People seem not to like having their sham existence taken from them. Justifications and rationalisations obscure one's view of the problematical past, and give way to aggression, which can be very clearly felt in these conversations recorded during the vigil. A final longer excerpt from the transcript, which again we will not analyse in detail (in the course of this chapter, we have already analysed a few short isolated passages of this conversation), shows in a tremendously intense verbal torrent many of the antisemitic prejudices that were reproduced in the discourse about the 'Waldheim Affair'. Apart from that, this extract also contains a formulation that condenses and summarises the Austrian 'living lie' in the form of an oxymoron: strictly speaking, of a paradoxical connection between a noun and an adjective (technically speaking: a *contradictio in adjecto*): 'We are all innocent perpetrators!'.

M2:   And who started the war, I ask you? Just say it, please!
M4:   And who killed thousands there? Yeah.
F: Of course/yeah. We're all innocent perpetrators! We're all ((yelling)) innocent perpetrators! Just a minute!
M2:   Just say who started the war!
M4:   There aren't any innocent perpetrators! No! There aren-/There aren't any innocent perpetrators!
F: The guilty ones were all hung anyway! We don't have any (xxx)

M4: Just a very small part!

M3: Who started the war? They always held down Germany.

F: Convicted! Well, then go and get your perpetrators, but just let the/leave new generations alone!

M5: Why do we always start all over again. If I said to someone who's a friend of mine you're an idiot, right. He accepts it. Then he doesn't say to me twenty years later, you said twenty years ago I'm an idiot! Why are we starting all over again now?

M?: Where's that/

M3: Because he lied! Say!

M6: (But if you) gas him, then that's something else, I think!

M5: Excuse me, please, okay, that was bad, that's unacceptable.

F? Oh, come on. What about it was a lie. Come on!

M5: That must be denied, that must be denied. But the question, the question why we always have to start all over again?

F?: Can you tell him a true story?

M5: Probably we'll still be talking about this in a hundred years/Wait a minute!

M4: I'll tell you, I'll tell you why.

M7: (we're missing)/the grieving! We're missing the words of regret!

M5: That's. That's. That's just not normal, ple-- /

M4: Everything always gets pushed away.

M5: It's/But I have to say one thing: I've always said, for me, a Jew is a Black, is an Arab, all of them are human beings. For me. But slowly I'm reaching the point.

M4: that

M?: (a) human being.

M5: Where I'm fed up with the Jews . Because they always go back to the beginning and start all over again with it!

M7: Wait a minute!

M5: That's not ridiculous!

M?: Yeah.

M4: What you're saying is ridiculous! Absolutely ridiculous! Yes!

M?: (I distinguish)

F?: Well, now. Just a minute! Just a minute.

M4: You're generalising. You can neither/You said before that you can't – the Jews.

F: Wait a minute. He's right. No.

M4: You can't – the Blacks, the English, the Russians, everywhere there're good ones and bad ones.

M5: All people

M4: There were people here/Wiesenthal and other Jews who/and just how much did the Jews do for Austrian culture!

M?: Right.

M5: And now/now. Yeah. Okay

M4: Yeah, and all of that is forgotten/one/

F7: Wait a minute!

M4: Vienna uh 1900/just wait/Unfortunately you talk (I'm terribly sorry)

F2: Can I – you?

M4: Like a neo-Nazi, right? Absolutely. Oh, yeah, oh, yeah. Absolutely!

M5: Yeah. No! no, no. No! I've/I've already told you: for me all people all the same.

M3: You can't.

M5: But/wait! Okay. Sorry. I can/I can for example.

M?: About the Jews (but then you can't be talking about the Jews!)

M4: Apparently (not after all). But some are more equal, eh?

Background:

Yeah, they're a chosen people, those Jews.

M5: Le- Let me tell you a story, a story, which wa/that (I) still remember from my grandfather; my grandfather was very, very poor, they were farmers.

M4: Yeah.

M5: They had to fight for their existence back then. What has/there (was) a Jew who came along; brought him geese, young geese. 'You don't have to pay for right away, pay in half a year'.

Fx: That's how they (worked).

M5: What was the deal? In half a year he couldn't pay, so the Jew took the fattened geese without paying, where he had given the fed! ((shouting))

M4: Yeah.

Fx: Yeah, yeah, yeah, yeah.

M4: That's ((screaming)) the other side of it, and no one talks about that!

Fx: Yeah, yeah, yeah.

M4: Yeah and/that's why we damn

M5: That's the way it looks. No! I'm not damning (anyone).

M4: You('re damning) a whole people?/What just listen! Just a minute! What do you think the Nazi armies did. I was in Yugoslavia, too, you know? Whole villages were destroyed.

M5: Yeahhhh! Yeah, I believe you/Miserable! Who's grieving about all the others that died in the war? Wh/Who's grieving about them? Why is it the Jews one should grieve about!

Fx: We've reached the point today where we were before the war!

M5: There were hundreds of thousands of others who died in the war! Why are we (xxx) (for them?)

Fx: I don't see any dirty Jews.

(Continuation of background conversation)

Fx: Why don't Jews go into industry?? Why don't they work as welders, locksmiths, in the mines? We don't need any advice, and we don't need any psychiatrists either! We're normal people! And they are pushing so far that we're back to where we were!

M?: Where?

Fx: People hate the Jews! It's true! They should also/get jobs! And not just/ they/they have all the positions, all (the) doctors, lawyers.

M?: Yeah, so.

Fx: And we just have more Jews!!! What are our sons doing? They don't get the positions, as doctors, as educated people!

(Continuation M5: Background conversation)

M2: I said that/(I said that we have to grieve for everyone). For everyone.

M5: Ridiculous! Ridiculous! But why does this keep coming up? Leave it (.) just leave it alone for once! Yeah, but we/we keep bringing it up again! There's so much (misery). There's so much misery in the world! The (xxx) arguments, there's so much misery in the world. No one grieves about that, why is it the Jews who grieved about. It's really too bad, no question about that!

M2: What is (xxx) grieve about the misery?

M5: Why do we bring up/(xxx) yeah, why don't we bring up other things.[18]

Within this piece of transcript, we find a whole range of more or less explicit antisemitic predications, reaching from 'Jews are irreconcilable and always thirsting for vengeance', 'Jews are business-minded, tricky and fraudulent', 'Jews are intellectuals that contributed a lot to the intellectual and cultural life in Austria' (a quite frequent philosemitic positive stigmatisation), 'Jews are super-fluous brainworkers who shy away from manual work and from getting themselves dirty' to 'Jews are to blame for the unemployment of our sons'.

The conversation extract reproduced above begins with two critical contributions by M2 and M4. M2 asks a quasi-rhetorical question about who started World War Two. He wants the previous speakers in favour of Waldheim (probably M1 or M3 or M5) to admit that it was the Germans who started the war, thus denying the lie peddled by the Nazis that Poland began it by attacking Germany. M4 asks another quasi-rhetorical question. He wants to know from M1, M3 or M5 who were those who killed thousands of people. At this point, a woman (F) becomes involved and twice admits – partly shouting – that 'we are innocent perpetrators'. It is interesting to note that F's assertion, which establishes an oxymoronic tension between guilt and exculpation, is uttered in the present tense (not the past), and from a first-person-plural perspective: that is to say, that the personal and temporal *origo* includes the speaker and is located in the speaker's now-time. This oxymoron, which seems not to have been pronounced ironically, perfectly characterises the great contradictions in which the majority of the Austrians became entangled after 1945, when dealing with their Nazi past. The fact that F chooses the present tense signals high involve-ment and identification, and the speaker-inclusive 'we' testifies the same. In addition, the present tense may be interpreted as being indicative that this oscillation between self-victimisation and a hesitant acceptance of personal responsibility today still determines the prevailing, hegemonic attitude towards the Austrian Nazi past. Taken literally, F's contention means that today, 'we' are still perpetrators (for example, antisemites) who consider 'ourselves' as innocent (for example – as in the case of the discourse about the 'Waldheim Affair', who rationalise their own present antisemitism by committing a victim-victimiser reversal). If one looks at F's next statement (which we will return to later), one must doubt whether F really intended to express this. Rather we can speculate that – in a certain respect – F's utterance has the character of a semantically polyphonic, unintentional quasi-Freudian parapraxis.

However, after F's second statement, M2 repeats that he wants to know from a previous speaker who started the war. Now, he is no longer asking a rhetorical question, but is expressing his demand in the imperative form (since he has so far received no answer). Still the answer is not given immediately after the question. First, M4 twice objects to F's second statement that innocent perpetrators do not exist. Now F takes the floor for the third time and states: 'The guilty ones were all hanged anyway'. We have already analysed this trivial-ising equation in the earlier section 'A heuristic "hierarchy in explicitness" in anti-Jewish language use'. It has the function of shifting the blame by equating 'the executed war criminals' with 'all the guilty ones from the Nazi era'. M4 replies to this trivialisation by employing a topos of numbers, arguing that only a small number of war criminals were executed. F seems to accept this correc-tion and answers by addressing M4 directly as someone who belongs to those who prosecute the Nazi perpetrators: 'Well, then go and get your perpetrators, but just let the/leave new generations alone!' As one can see, F's concession is associated with a demand. This demand was very frequently uttered during the 'Waldheim election campaign' and aimed at supporting the refusal to talk about the negative side of one's own history, according to the motto: 'Let the past rest!'.

Before F's fourth statement, M3 finally answers M2's question about the first war aggressor. M3 doesn't give a clear answer. Hesitatingly, he repeats M2's question. He then says: 'They always held down Germany'. Although the first aggressor is named in this sentence, it is not named as an acting partici-pant, an actor, but as a goal. The actor is 'they', standing for the victor states of World War One. By making 'them' actors and 'Germany' the goal, M2 insinuates that 'they' are responsible for the war.

After M3's appeal to 'leave the descendant generations in peace', a discussion begins about who is responsible for breaking the taboos, and bringing up the past. By a relativising and minimising fallacious equation that compares the insulting anthroponym 'idiot' with the Nazi crimes, M5 holds the Jews respon-sible and reproduces the prejudice of 'the unforgiving and vindictive Jews who always start from the beginning' (for a closer analysis of this passage see the earlier section 'The selective illustration of some categories of analysis'). M6 disputes this, and argues that gassing somebody cannot be compared with calling somebody an idiot. M5 concedes that the gassing of the Jews was bad and cannot be accepted, but then he repeats his question why 'one' should always start all over again. Both M4 and M7 answer this question by criticising the fact that everything (the listeners and readers can infer and complete: everything regarding the Austrian Nazi past) is repressed in Austria (M4), and that there is no activity of mourning and no word of regret (M7). This, by implication in the answers of M4 and M7, is the reason why one cannot stop dealing with the past.

M5 does not find it normal – we can infer: 'not to let the past rest' and 'always to start all over again'. Then he employs a seemingly concessive 'yes-but' figure by utilising a sort of topos of justice (see chapter 2, p. 78): strictly speaking, the topos of 'all human beings being equal'. This topos is integrated in a declaration, which serves as the 'yes' part of the 'yes-but' figure. Incidentally: the declaration contains three heterogeneous anthroponyms, apart from 'Jew' and Arab' there is also the racist discriminating anthroponym '*Neger*' (English: negro). The declaration has a mitigating function and rhetorically prepares the explicit communication that M5 begins to reject Jews as a whole ('*Judentum*'), because they always start 'it' over again. M4 and M7 protest, M4 finds M5's statement absolutely ridiculous and reproaches M5 with a generalisation. In disputing M5's generalisation, M4 himself employs the topos of 'all human beings being equal'. In his specification that there are good ones and bad ones everywhere, M4 also adopts the racist anthroponym '*Neger*'. In addition, M4's counter-argumentation also fails, in that M4 resorts to a common cliché of the 'permitted philosemitic discourse' – namely, to the stereotype that the Jews did so much for Austrian culture.

After this, M4 reproves M5 that he speaks like a neo-Nazi. M5 vehemently refutes this reproach and repeats his topos of 'all being equal'. Then he attempts to tell a story, but M4 also takes the floor and treats this topos, as M5 uses it, ironically by alluding to a dictum from Orwell's *Animal Farm*: 'But some are more equal'. M5 does not react to this *reductio ad absurdum* of his argumentation. He offers a typical antisemitic illustrative 'example' in the form of a story about a Jew dealing in livestock – an old theme – to support his prejudice of the 'dishonourable Jew' and 'Jewish trickery' that are held responsible for bad economic times (see the earlier section 'The selective illustration of some categories of analysis'). M5 concludes: 'That's the way it looks. No! I'm not damning (anyone)'.

As M4 reproaches M5 for damning a whole people and brings up the war crimes of the Nazis in his counter-argument, M5 responds evasively: instead of dealing with the content and the facts of the discussion, he commits a straw-man fallacy and tries to balance the Jewish Nazi victims against 'the others that died in the war', asking why 'one' should mourn for the Jews in view of 'hundreds of thousands of others who died in the war'.

At this point, the line of conversation breaks and the discussion shifts in another direction, full of other antisemitic prejudices. Fx directly and completely unexpectedly introduces the prejudices of the 'Jews as redundant brainworkers who shy away from manual work and from getting themselves dirty' as well as the prejudice that 'the Jews are to blame for the unemployment of our sons'. In addition to these two antisemitic fallacious predications, Fx employs the topos of threat of antisemitism: 'We're normal people! And they are pushing so far that we're back to where we were!'. This topos can also be interpreted as an implicit *argumentum ad baculum* that goes as follows: 'If the Jews continue this way, the same will happen to them as in the Nazi period'.

The discussion ends in a series of appeals, combined with an evasive straw-man fallacy: let the past finally rest, there are more important things in the world to be concerned about. Further discussion is thereby successfully prevented.

As we saw right at the end of the transcript, in this conversation, fragmenta-tion and the break in semantic coherence – in the form of unexpected topical shifts or transitions – are characteristic, and important. Whenever the arguments against M4 run out, the 'Jew' appears as placeholder, as final argument, as scapegoat, as '*Iudeus ex machina*'.

In view of all the examples analysed in the present chapter, one has the impression that antisemitic prejudices are almost universal in Austria. However, we wish to refrain from making such an undifferentiated, generic and unhis-torical statement here, since our empirical findings are taken from the very specific historical period in which the discourse about the 'Waldheim Affair' took place. What we can conclude at the end of the present chapter is this: in 1986, in Austria, some taboos with respect to antisemitism fell away in certain public realms, especially in the media. This also includes the fact that, then, consciousness about the Austrian Nazi past seems to have started to grow. However, although at that time the more subtle expressions of antisemitic prejudice were usual in formal contexts, certain persons also felt entitled to employ cruder or more blatant forms in such contexts, conjuring up images of an enemy by reverting at the same time to a mystified past and to Austria's sham existence.

Notes

1 In German: '*Es wäre unsinnig abzustreiten, daß die nationalsozialistische Rassenpropaganda bei manchen Österreichern einen gewissen Widerhall gefunden hat; aber als sie sahen, mit welchen Mitteln der Antisemitismus in die Tat umgesetzt wurde, da waren sie geheilt. Man kann ruhig behaupten, daß das Mitleid mit den verfolgten Juden den Antisemitismus in Österreich ausmerzte. Ich glaube nicht, daß diese Frage auch jemals wieder nur die geringste Bedeutung erlangen wird*'. (Leopold Figl, *Shangai Echo*, cited in *Der Neue Weg*, No. 10, 11 June 1947).

2 The German original goes as follows: '... *der grünschnäblige Generalsekretär Singer...der Privatverein mit dem bombastischen Namen Jüdischer Weltkongreß ... die Packeleien des ersten Vereinspräsidenten N. Goldmann mit den arabischen Todfeinden des Judenstaates ...*' (*Neue Kronen Zeitung*, 'Staberl', 2 April 1986: 8, quoted in Wodak *et al.* 1990: 142).

3 The original text reads as follows: '... *die, welche Haß, neuen Haß, säen und dabei in Kauf nehmen – ja vielleicht sogar wünschen – das zu ernten, was nur zusätzlicher Haß sein kann*'. (*Die Presse*, Th. Chorherr, 5/6 April 1986: 1, quoted in Gruber 1991: 187).

4 The German excerpt reads as follows: '*Eine der allerdümmsten Floskeln aus der Gift- und Sudelküche des Goebbelschen Propagandaministeriums ... war die Mär vom unheilvollen Wirken des "Weltjudentums". Die Juden ... hätten sich zu einer hinterhältigen Verschwörung gegen die...germanische Superrasse zusammengefunden. "Die Juden – unser Unglück"*' (*Neue Kronen Zeitung*, 'Staberl', 27 March 1986: 8).

5 The original version goes as follows: '... (*und*) [*sie* = the Jews, R.W. and M.R.] *sind alle wieder da gewesen! Sind gekommen, einer oder zwei sind geblieben, der Zahnarzt und andere, die sind/de de habm ihre Sachen geordnet wieder, (und) Wiedergutmachung, net, und und für Unbill und so weiter! Und dann sind sie wieder gegangen!*'

6 In German: '*Angegriffen von einer Seite, die sich unangreifbar glaubt, sich jedoch schon immer zum willigen Werkzeug einer Handvoll Ewiggestriger machte, die keine Chance ungenutzt lassen, aus einer düsteren Vergangenheit ein Geschäft zu machen*' (*Die Presse*, Leitenberger, 25 March 1986: 1).

7 In German: '*Die Schuldigen san eh aufghängt worn!*'

8 In the original version: '*Wenn ich zu einem sag: "du bist ein Idiot". Und das ist ein Freund von mir, der akzeptiert des, dann sagt er mir nicht nach zwanzig Jahren: "du hast vor zwanzig Jahren gesagt, ich bin ein Idiot!"*'

9 In the original version: '*Antijüdische Gefühle haben uns in unserer Geschichte bisher nie Nutzen oder Segen gebracht. Sie sind außerdem zutiefst inhuman*'. For the reprint of the entire address given by Kirchschläger on 22 April 1986 see Gruber (1991: 246–51).

10 In German: '*Tatsächlich wird in so gut wie allem, was bis dato "enthüllt" worden ist, mit halben Wahrheiten, mit deutlichen oder unterschwelligen Unterstellungen gearbeitet ... Es mag ja sein, daß da jemand Geister, die er rief, nicht mehr beherrschen kann, aber es kann auch ganz anderes im Spiel sein*' (*Die Presse*, 6 March 1986: 1).

11 In the German article this passage reads as follows: '*Der israelische Außenminister Ytzhak Shamir scheint jetzt durchzudrehen. Er rief gestern in Jerusalem die Führer aller Staaten der Welt auf, sich dem Kampf gegen Kurt Waldheim anzuschließen*' (*Neue Kronenzeitung*, 28 May 1986: 2. The whole article is quoted in Gruber 1991: 114).

12 The original version goes as follows: '*Ich darf zum Beispiel eine Geschichte erzählen, eine Geschichte, die we/die noch von meinem Großvater weiß, mein Großvater war sehr, sehr arm, es warn Bauern. Die ham damals um ihre Existenz gerauft. Was hat/es (is) ein Jude vorbeigekommen, hat ihm Gänse gebracht. Junge Gänse. "Du mußt es nicht sofort bezahlen, bezahlst du in einem halben Jahr". Was war? In einem halben Jahr konnte er nicht bezahlen, der Jude hat die aufgezogenen Gänse, wo er das Futter gegeben hat, mitgenommen ((schreit)), ohne zu bezahlen! Das ((schreit)) is die andere Seite. Und von dem spricht keiner!*'

13 In German: '*Man könnte (ja) so viel sagen, hörnS! Ich könnte/ich hab Ihnen zuerst erzählt von unserem General, der auseinandergerissen wurde, net. So wie die Magdeburger Halbkugel. Jetzt frag ich Sie: Sie sind, wern kriegsgefangen wie wir da unten, na? Wie es uns passiert is. Und die sind ja außern Völkerrecht gewesen. Sie warn ja gar net anerkannt, von keiner Macht, das warn ja Banditen und Heckenschützen. Wenn Sie jetzt die Wahl hätten, daß keine andere Alternative! Daß Sie sterben müssen, müssen! – Und Sie haben die Wahl: so auseinandergerissen zu werden wie unser General oder in einer Gaszelle? Was würden Sie machen?*' (See also Wodak *et al.* 1990: 260–1).

14 For the German original see Wodak 1990: 37–8.

15 For the original version see Wodak 1990c: 40.

16 For the German version see Wodak 1990c: 41–2.

17 The original transcript is printed in Wodak 1990c: 42–3.

18 The German transcript can be found in Wodak 1990c: 44–5.

4 'Aliens' and 'Foreigners'

The political and media discourse about the Austria First Petition of Jörg Haider and the Austrian Freedom Party in 1992 and 1993

If one drives on the highway from Vienna's 'Schwechat' airport into the city, a barrage of colourful posters welcome everybody, proclaiming 'Vienna is different'. This so-called 'difference', compared to other European capital cities, is said to lie in Vienna's being less dirty, noisy and crowded. The Austrian government apparently wishes to keep it so, less crowded anyway: the Residence Act that went into effect on 1 July 1993 (and all the following laws and restrictions) not only closed the door to many potential immigrants, it also effectively empowered the immigration authorities to expatriate a large number of those who had lived legally in Austria for years.

The 'Austria First' campaign and the legal restrictions that came into force in 1993 were only the beginning of an anti-foreigner movement that recently culminated in the discriminatory anti-foreigner election campaign of 1999 for the seats in the national parliament. This election campaign was worse than all the other public 'xenophobic' discourses that had evolved since 1989, after the fall of the Iron Curtain. It was even worse than the Anti-Foreigner-Petition campaign of 1992 and 1993, which we will investigate in this chapter, and the other discriminatory discourses of the following years. This time, not only posters saying 'Vienna is different' were to be seen, but provocative advertisements which claimed that the Austrian Freedom Party would be the guarantee to 'stop the overforeignisation' ('*Überfremdung*' is a term that was used by the National-Socialist propaganda minister Joseph Goebbels in 1933) and leaflets with incredible racist statements, like the infamous claim that female foreigners were obtaining free hormone treatment in Viennese hospitals in order to be able to produce more children than 'real Austrians', and that they would thus 'take over' (see Wodak 2000), whereas the hormones were, in fact, being administered for therapeutic reasons to severely traumatised women who had been victims of rape during the war in Kosovo (see the report of the Austrian Press Agency, APA0270 5 II 0504 on 27 September 1999).

In the public political arena in Austria, the anti-foreigner climate has never been as blatant and strong as in the autumn of 1999 (see Wodak and Sedlak, in print); and Haider's Freedom Party, a party similar to Le Pen's party in France, gained 26.92 per cent of the votes, a phenomenon unique in the European Union. This party came to be the second largest in the country, following the

Social Democratic Party (see Arduç-Sedlak 2000 for a detailed analysis of the FPÖ election campaign).

At first glance, all of this seems paradoxical: hostility towards foreigners has come to predominate in a country with one of the lowest inflation and unemployment rates in the European Union. As far as *per capita* income is concerned, Austria is among the richest countries in the world. In this chapter, we will trace the beginning of this turn to the 'Right', which started explicitly in 1992 and 1993, with the petition 'Austria First'. With the help of the discourse-historical approach outlined in chapters 2 and 3, we will trace a part of the drastic development of anti-foreigner discourse in a Western democratic nation-state in Europe: a country with a very specific past during the Second World War, as part of the Third Reich, and an involvement in Nazi crimes.

As the examples from different public spaces illustrate, the populism of the FPÖ is a complex mixture of anti-governmental opposition, an attempt to influence the law-making procedure as well as the formation of public opinion, and of propagandist political advertising that aims at canvassing as much voter support as possible – and all of that on the back of the scapegoat of 'foreigners'. The selective analysis of important public genres allows us to trace the intertextuality and recontextualisation of arguments and topoi from one realm to the other, from the action field of lawmaking to the field of political advertising and formation of public opinion by the media, to the field of political (pre-, intra- and post-parliamentary) control, to the field of bureaucratic administration, i.e. implementation of law (for this, see also chapter 5). Further, it gives us the occasion to illustrate some of the commonalities and differences between the linguistic manifestation of antisemitism (see chapter 3) and the discursive realisation of hostility towards foreigners, and to discuss how a model of deliberative, discursive democracy could work in such a political reality (see chapter 5 and chapter 6).

The petition 'Austria First', discussed in December 1992 and launched in January 1993, was signed by 417,278 Austrians, half the number expected by Haider, but nevertheless a high figure, although it met with massive public resistance. In the following, we are concerned with the question of the issues that were coded in the text of the petition for the referendum and in its official rationale, and how they were presented to achieve the consent of the 417,278 supporters – which cannot be considered a negligible total of a small and marginal right-wing group – and to make the restrictive claims acceptable. Furthermore, what argumentation strategies and rhetorical devices were used to construct 'the foreigner' and to mask explicitly racist or 'xenophobic' contents? In addition, we focus selectively on the slogans employed in pro- and contra-campaigns, on the public discussion in the Austrian press and on some parts of the controversial debate about the petition in the Austrian parliament in September 1993.

According to the official and legal construction of the outgroups of 'aliens' and 'foreigners' (see also chapter 2, pp. 60–2), prospective immigrants should not only be, as the law 1993 states, 'capable of being integrated and willing to integrate', they were also required to file their application for residency in Austria from their native land, irrespective of where they currently resided. Moreover, the application, filed from abroad, had to show proof of permanent employment in Austria, and that one had already arranged for housing sufficient to provide a minimum of 10 square metres per person.

The potential for abuse by the authorities was most acute for those non-Austrian citizens who wished to extend their temporary residency permits. According to the 1993 law, if the Austrian immigration authorities failed to complete work on the request by the end of six weeks after the expiry of the current permit, the applicant lost her or his authorisation to remain in the country, even if the delay was due only to the slowness or inefficiency of the immigration authorities (see the section 'Some newspaper commentaries concerning the petition'; for a description of the respective Austrian bureaucratic procedures in the second half of the 1990s see chapter 5). And with no legal right to remain in the country, he or she could be expelled at the discretion of the authorities.

The provisions of the 1993 law – everywhere understood and widely hailed as the first measure designed to crack down on illegal immigration (since then other, even more restrictive laws have been agreed to, see chapter 5) – appeared even to some of the politicians who voted for it as inhumane. As we mentioned above, this opinion has changed considerably since. Nowadays all the mainstream parties are in favour of an almost total halt in immigration: the Austrian People's Party (ÖVP) and the Social-Democratic Party (SPÖ) have adopted many of the policies of the FPÖ, hoping they could hold on to their voters. (This turned out to be an illusion, as shown in the election of 3 October 1999.) The provision concerning the size of flat was particularly ironic: not only were thousands of 'guest workers' (for the implicit argumentation schemes inherent in this metaphoric econonym see chapter 2, pp. 76–7) affected; thousands of indigenous citizens lived, and still do live, in apartments with an area of fewer than 10 square metres per person (see Matouschek, Wodak and Januschek 1995, Wodak 1996a, Mitten and Wodak 1993, Mitten 1994, van Leeuwen and Wodak 1999, Wodak and van Dijk 2000).

The six-week deadline set by the law then became the focus of heated political debate in Austria. Politicians who had voted for the law (the only members of parliament who voted against it were the Greens), doubtless concerned that resident 'guest workers' indispensable to the economy might fall victim to the bureaucratic arbitrariness the law encourages, called for a speedy change in the law.

Perhaps one of the most grotesque moments of the debate on the Act on Aliens that came into force in 1993 was the almost Pauline conversion of Michael Graff, of the Christian Democratic People's Party, and head of the parliamentary judiciary committee. Graff, who had voted for the measure both in committee and in the House, then claimed that he would have voted differently, if only he had taken the trouble to read the law before the vote.

This law was a major step in a whole set of legal measures that have been introduced since 1989/90 to restrict and regulate immigration. Some of the other 'necessary measures' (as they were called in the public discourse) were the Refugee Assistance Act (August 1990), the Asylum Act (June 1992) and the Alien Act (December 1992), which were important for the time period we are investigating in this chapter, namely 1992–93. These three laws accommodated the 'xenophobic' discourses that evolved after 1989 and that were to be observed not only in the private sphere, but also in most official statements by leading politicians of the major parties, the Social-Democratic Party and the People's Party (see the section 'The "Austria First Petition"').

In chapter 5, we will spell out the legal developments which have taken place since that time. Here, we are concerned with the content of the three acts just mentioned. The principle aims of the Refugee Assistance Act were to regulate the distribution of refugees and to establish criteria for providing government aid to those refugees granted asylum (below, we will discuss sequences of parliamentary debates concerning government aid). The Asylum Act sought to prevent the suspected 'abuse' of the provisions for political asylum by those who were supposed to be not genuinely fleeing from political persecution. The interpretation of this law was naturally broad. The Alien Act enumerated the conditions under which one was entitled to an entry visa. Most disturbing in this law was the placing of all non-citizens into the same category of 'aliens'. Thus, 'guest workers' who had lived in Austria for a number of years, and their children and grandchildren (the so-called 'second' and 'third generations'), also became subject to the same requirements as new immigrants (see Mitten 1994a for more details). In view of these new restrictive acts it was all the more surprising that Jörg Haider of the Freedom Party (FPÖ) should launch his foreigner petition at exactly the time when all these restrictive measures had been decided upon in parliament.

Prior to the law's passage, the debate in Austria was characterised by the climate of fear aroused by the unreal prospect of millions of potential immigrants ready to 'inundate helpless Austria'. Many of the politicians of the governing parties seemed to have lost their parties' earlier humanitarian convictions and to have adopted a political reasoning based on the assumption that no votes were to be won in Austria by appearing to be 'soft on economic refugees'. In retrospect, these politicians and even some analysts of the political and social developments in Austria hold the view that the government's pre-emptive exclusionary hard line against aliens may go some way towards explaining why, in Austria, there were not such terrible riots against immigrants as those committed in the German cities of Hoyerswerda, Mölln, Rostock and Solingen in the early 1990s. Such a simple analysis, however, has the character of a negative *post hoc, ergo propter hoc* argumentation that is based on considering events occurring earlier in time (in our case: the passing of new laws) as the causes of events happening later (in our case: the absence of the riots), and a non-sequitur fallacy: it is as fallacious as the stereotypical reference to the traditional national stereotype about the Austrian *Gemütlichkeit* (Wodak, de Cillia, Reisigl and Liebhart 1999: 144–5). Incidentally: the only foreigners entitled to *Gemütlichkeit* these days, it seems, are those who do not come from Eastern and

Southern Europe and Third-World countries, and who come – as tourists – to spend money (see also Wodak *et al.* 1999).

For better understanding of the argumentation strategies and topoi employed in the discourse about the Austria First Petition, we want to frame our discourse analysis by giving some information about historical and political developments in Austria, since, in our view, Austrian historical peculiarities distinguish the content and, to some extent, the forms of racist and 'xenophobic' discourse in Austria from discourses with similar functions in other countries. It is, for example, not insignificant to know that, in general, Hungarians and Czechs are viewed more positively in Austria than are Romanians and Poles. This is traceable to some extent to perceived cultural affinities with these former groups dating from the time of the Austro-Hungarian empire, and, in part, to a kind of residual 'historical memory' in Austria of Hungarians and Czechs as onetime heroic fighters against Soviet tanks (in 1956 and 1968). At the same time, and somewhat anomalously, the fall of the Iron Curtain and the accompanying end of the Cold War marked a major caesura in the attitudes of Austrians towards potential immigrants from Eastern Europe, transforming former heroic escapees from Communist tyranny into contemporary 'criminal tourists'.

Such facts are illuminating for the discourse-historical analysis of the discussions around and about the Anti-Foreigner Petition, since they help to trace the genesis and changing of the hierarchy of 'foreigners' in populist right-wing discourse in Austria. Much more of such information is given in the following section.

Some historical information about Austria

The Austrian First Republic, established in 1918, issued from the collapsing multiethnic and multicultural Habsburg monarchy. During the final years of the monarchy, language conflicts had dominated public and political discourse, although legally all languages were said to be equal and were to be taught in primary schools. Post-First World War Austria's tense relations with the other Habsburg successor states were in no small measure due to the political antagonisms these language conflicts had engendered.

Between 1938 and 1945, Austria was occupied by the Nazis and became a part of the Third Reich. The Nazi Aryan '*Volksgemeinschaft*' required and received a language policy consistent with its exclusionary ethos. Since 1945, Austria has undergone many political and social changes. After being occupied by Allied forces for ten years after the war, Austria became, in 1955, an independent and neutral country, although its political institutions owed more to Western than to Eastern European influence. An 'economic miracle' was accompanied by the creation of an advanced welfare state, based on the Swedish model. In 1956, during the anti-Stalinist uprising, 160,000 Hungarians entered Austria, most on their way elsewhere, and were warmly welcomed, even though the economic situation in Austria was not particularly favourable. In 1968, almost 100,000 Czechs came to Austria after the crushing of the 'Prague

Spring', and again there were no complaints. In the early 1980s, almost 50,000 Poles fled to Austria after the declaration of martial law, and these, too, were greeted with varying degrees of enthusiasm. The big change occurred in 1989 and 1990, when the Iron Curtain fell and thousands of citizens from former Warsaw Pact countries travelled to Austria.

The liberalisation of the Polish and Hungarian regimes came in 1988. Soon afterwards, those wishing to emigrate to Austria as well as those already inside Austria who had applied for asylum were no longer officially considered *ipso facto* victims of persecution. As a consequence, 3,000 Poles and Hungarians were deported from Austria, and the procedures for receiving asylum were intensified: in 1988, only about 1,700 out of 15,000 immigration applications were approved. In mid-1989, the Czechoslovak Republic relaxed its travel restrictions. Austria's immediate reaction was to reiterate that it was not a country of immigration. In the autumn of 1989, however, Austria was once again able to play a significant role as a 'land of transit' for asylum seekers: masses of citizens of the German Democratic Republic took advantage of the relaxed controls on the Hungarian-Austria border to make their way via Austria to West Germany.

The end of 1989 and the beginning of 1990 witnessed the wave of political reforms and democratic revolutions in the countries inside the Soviet sphere of influence. One of the changes brought about by the fall of the Iron Curtain was the opening of the borders and the relaxation or removal of restrictions on freedom of travel. Official Austrian reaction to the 'wave' of asylum seekers from Romania, Poland, Bulgaria and Czechoslovakia may be gauged by considering the following numbers: in 1989, 2,879 of 21,862 applications for asylum were approved; and in 1990, 1,596 of 22,800. The largest contingent of those seeking asylum in Austria in the spring of 1990 came from Romania. After vehement protests from citizens of the localities where the applicants were to have been temporarily housed while awaiting the processing of their applications, on 15 March 1990 Austrian authorities reinstated a visa requirement for Romanians. In addition, the Austrian government claimed the success of having been able to hinder the estimated 40,000-strong 'storm' of Romanians reportedly underway (an estimation which turned out to have been nothing more than a rumour taken up and then spread by news agencies) by introducing an additional requirement that Romanian visitors to Austria possess at least ATS 5,000 (somewhat less than US\$ 500 at the exchange rate then obtaining) to demonstrate that the purpose of their visit to Austria was tourism. All this, it must be recalled, at a time when it was unclear what had actually changed in Romania apart from the fall of Ceauscescu. Indeed, the violent attacks on the Hungarian minority in Romania began a mere ten days later (see Wodak 1996a, 1997a, 1997b).

At about the same time (March–April 1990), a time in which 'xenophobic' appeals could be heard in public discussions on the immigration issue, the Austrian government considered reintroducing a visa requirement for Poles. After a prolonged political debate, including the months leading up to the

National Assembly elections (during which anti-Polish sentiment grew considerably), the government did finally reintroduce a visa requirement for visitors from Poland. Although the government claimed that its principal motivation was to try to combat an increase in Poles coming to Austria on so-called 'working vacations' (i.e. working illegally for cheaper wages), which had ostensibly been most acute in Vienna and Lower Austria, it also represented a reaction to campaign rhetoric about 'criminal tourism'.

Both of these measures restricting travel to Austria enjoyed the support of the majority of the population. In a poll taken in June 1990, 92 per cent of Austrians were in favour of stronger penalties for those convicted of selling goods on the black market, 78 per cent for stronger penalties against foreigners working without a work permit, and 58 per cent were in favour of introducing a general visa requirement for Eastern Europeans.

Austrians' fears of being 'inundated' or 'overrun' by foreigners ('*überflutet*' and '*überrannt*') and the related increase in negative attitudes towards 'refugees from the East' must be seen against the reality of the country's demographic trends. According to the census (September 1991), Austria's population numbered 7,800,000. This represented an increase of approximately 250,000 in absolute numbers, or about three percent, over the population level recorded in 1981. (Vienna's population increased by only 0.1 per cent over the same period.) Of the quarter of a million people who made up the increase in the total Austrian population, fully 233,400 were immigrants. Thus, as Austrian demographers have suggested, with the average age of the native-born population increasing, the welfare provisions of the Austrian State would become endangered without the continuing influx of younger immigrants capable of financing it (Fassmann and Münz 1996). A later opinion poll carried out by Gallup in October 1992 – at the time when the FPÖ was considering and preparing the Austria First Petition – indicated that 76 per cent of all Austrians were strictly against allowing any more foreigners into the country, while only 19 per cent felt that Austria could afford more immigration. Sixty-six per cent of Austrians would also have preferred to close the borders to war refugees. At the same time, 48 per cent thought that the Anti-Foreigner Petition by the FPÖ was wrong, while 29 per cent agreed with the issues raised there (see below), and 23 per cent remained undecided. Fifty-four per cent of all workers were also in favour of the petition, 31 per cent rejected it. It is unclear why a lower percentage supported the petition than the restrictions against foreigners as a whole, but we will return to this issue later. It relates to the politics of the FPÖ in other domains as well, not with the content of the petition itself.

Today, several different groups of foreigners and minorities live in Austria: autochthonous minorities (Slovenes, Croats, Hungarians, Jews, Roma and Sinti, Czechs and Slovaks); immigrant workers (mainly Turks and ex-Yugoslavs who began arriving in the 1970s); a variety of political refugees (including Iranians, Vietnamese, Hungarians, Czechs, Poles, Albanians and Bosnians); and, since 1989, the new so-called 'economic refugees', predominantly Hungarians, Poles, Czechs, Romanians and Russians (see Bauböck *et al.* 1995, Fassmann and Münz

1996, Lebhart and Münz 1999). By 1994, approximately 720,900 foreigners were living in Austria, around 9 per cent of the total population. Thus, when comparing percentages, in these twenty years the number of aliens living in Austria has more than doubled, and Austria has become a de-facto immigration country. This increase was the result of an active Austrian 'recruitment policy' that followed economic reasoning and was, in fact, very convenient for the overall economic development of Austria. Yet the hegemonic public perception of this change is negative, mostly due to the reporting in the press of the 'huge masses of immigrants' who have recently entered or are about to enter (see chapter 5 for the more recent developments).

The Austria First Petition

At this point, we will briefly digress by providing a few contextualising remarks on the history of the FPÖ (see also chapter 3, p. 96). After the Second World War, in 1949, 'liberals' with a strong German National orientation and with no classical liberal tradition (see Bailer and Neugebauer 1993: 328–30) who felt unable to support the SPÖ or the ÖVP founded the VDU ('*Verband der Unabhängigen*'), which became an electoral home for many former Austrian Nazis. The FPÖ, founded in 1956, was the successor party to the VDU; it retained an explicit attachment to a 'German cultural community'. In its more than forty-year-old history, the FPÖ has, therefore, never been a 'liberal' party in the European sense, although there were always tensions between more liberal and more conservative members of the party. In 1986, Haider was elected as leader of the party and unseated Norbert Steger, a liberal leader. Since 1986, the FPÖ has gained many votes and has now (in October 1999) risen to 26.91 per cent of all the votes cast in Austria (1,244,087 voters). The FPÖ's party policy and politics at that time, 1993, was anti-foreigner, anti-European Union and widely populist, close to Le Pen's party in France. Since the summer of 1995, the FPÖ has almost completely stopped stressing the closeness between the Austrian and the German cultural community because opinion polls demonstrated that the majority of Austrian citizens no longer accepted such a self-definition. In the autumn of 1997, the FPÖ presented a new party program, which, in its calculated ambivalence, emphasises Christian values. At present, the FPÖ is the largest right-wing party in Western Europe (for further information about the FPÖ see, among others, Scharsach 1993, DöW 1993, Mitten 1994a, Bailer-Galanda and Neugebauer 1997, Grünalternative Jugend 1998). This party has, more than any other Austrian party, persuasively set the 'xenophobic' anti-foreigner tone in Austrian domestic policies and, for a decade, has almost always made electoral profit out of the populist business of sowing uncertainty and irrational 'xenophobic' anxieties, which, for different reasons, were and are harboured or willingly adopted by a considerable proportion of voters.

The strategic populist move to initiate the Austria First Petition was just one particularly drastic step in the FPÖ's policy of instigating hostile emotions against specific groups of foreigners. This step had an impact on all of the six main fields of political action we distinguish in chapter 2 (pp. 36–7), i.e. the areas of lawmaking, of party internal opinion-making, of the formation of public political opinion, of political advertising, of political administration and of political control.

As a whole, the discourse about the Austria First Petition or Anti-Foreigner Petition mainly evolved in these six fields of political activity around the topics and in the genres shown in figure 4.1.

According to Article 41 of the Austrian Constitution, parliament is required to consider and vote on any petition that gathers at least 100,000 signatures. Unlike provisions for petitions elsewhere, Article 41 of the Austrian Constitution requires only that parliament considers the petition, which must be in the form of a draft law. Later in this chapter, we will analyse some parts of the debate in parliament about the petition on 23 September 1993.

In October 1992, after the Austrian government had rejected Haider's ultimatum to adopt the FPÖ's program on immigration, his party launched the petition campaign to force the government's hand. Initially, Haider was convinced that they would get one million signatures for the petition (*Neue Kronen Zeitung*, 4 November 1992). This number then slowly dropped as the FPÖ became aware that large-scale opposition was forming against the anti-foreigner sentiment: on 14 January 1993, 500,000 signatures were thought to be a total success (*Täglich Alles*); on 15 January 1993, Haider spoke of more than 500,000 signatures (*Der Standard*). On 26 January 1993, numbers increased to 750,000; on 30 January, Haider explicitly stated that anything under 500,000 would be a failure (*Täglich Alles*) and on 1 February 1993, he said that 780,000 would be a total success. The massive propaganda campaign against the petition paid political dividends: though the 417,278 signatures collected, representing approximately 7 per cent of all eligible voters, amply exceeded the required minimum of 100,000, the number fell far short of the prophecies and speculations of the FPÖ and also of the votes the FPÖ had received in the most recent general election (782,648 or 16.6 per cent) or even the 700,000 that the FPÖ had (internally) projected (*Der Standard*, 2 February 1993).

In the following, we first document the petition in English:

Title: Petition 'Austria First'
Subtitle: Through the creation of legal measures which permanently secure the right to a fatherland for all Austrian citizens and, from this standpoint, ensure a restrained immigration policy in Austria
Text :
1. The adoption of a national law to anchor the national regulatory goal (*Staatszielbestimmung*) 'Austria is not an immigration country' into the federal constitutional law of 1920 (1929 version).
2. Legal standardisation of a halt to immigration until the question of illegal immigration is satisfactorily resolved, until the housing shortage is eliminated, until unemployment is reduced to 5 per cent, as well as the creation of

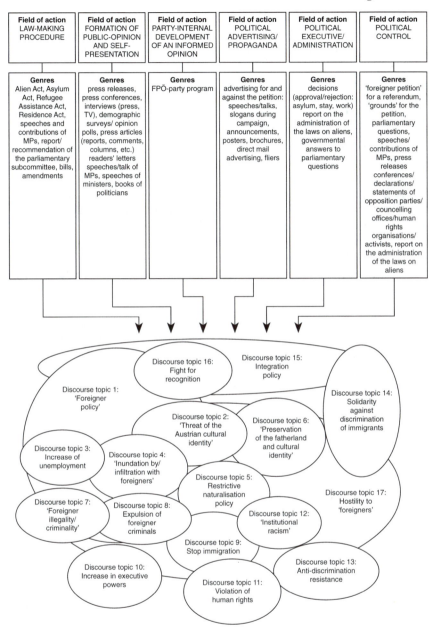

Figure 4.1 The discourse about the Austria First petition in 1992 and 1993

legal measures which ensure that subsidised housing is granted in future solely to Austrian citizens, to the extent that this is not prohibited by international agreements and norms.

3. The adoption of a federal law to institute a general identification requirement for foreign workers at their place of employment, whereby the work
   permit and application for health insurance are prerequisites for this identity
   card.
4. An increase in executive powers (in particular for foreign and criminal
   police), including their improved remuneration, and equipment for the
   apprehension of illegal immigrants and for greater effectiveness in the
   fight against crime, in particular organised crime.
5. The adoption of a federal law for the immediate creation of permanent
   border troops (customs, gendarmerie) instead of federal army troops.
6. The adoption of a federal law to change the law governing the organisation
   of schools so that the proportion of pupils in compulsory and vocational
   school classes whose native language is not German is limited to 30 per
   cent; where the percentage of children whose native language is not
   German is higher than 30 per cent, regular classes for foreigners are to be
   established.
7. Easing the tension in the school situation by having children whose native
   language is not German participate in regular classes only if they possess
   sufficient knowledge of German (preparatory classes).
8. Creation of a regulation in party law that ensures that only Austrian citizens
   participate in party-internal primary proceedings, where lists are created
   for the general elections to general representational bodies.
9. The adoption of a federal law to restrict the practice of premature conferring of citizenship.
10. The adoption of a federal law to end illegal business activities (as, for exam-
    ple, in foreigner associations and clubs), as well as to establish rigorous
    measures against the abuse of social benefits.
11. Creation of the legal basis for the possibility of immediate deportation
    and imposition of residence prohibitions for foreign criminals.
12. The adoption of a federal law to establish an Eastern Europe Foundation
    to prevent migrational movement.[1]

Already the title of the petition 'Austria First' presupposes that there might
be alternative views which posit Austria 'next' or 'last'. The elliptical and pithy
demand implies that Austria – metonymically standing for 'the Austrians' – is
to be given priority over other 'countries' (metonymically implying 'non-
Austrians') and that the governing politicians are neglecting the interests of
the country and its people. This slogan, which was also used by the FPÖ in
1994 in their campaign against Austria's joining the European Union, and, even
more recently, in a political campaign against the change of currency into the
European Euro, constructs the view – from the very beginning of the text –
that the FPÖ is the party which is concerned with the interests of the country
and strategically aims at dividing the electorate into 'good' patriotic Austrians
who love the country and 'bad' unpatriotic Austrians who do not give Austria
and the Austrians preferential treatment.

The subtitle justifies and elaborates the aims of the petition: legal measures are needed, which secure the 'right to a fatherland/home' for all Austrian citizens and which also ensure a reluctant Austrian immigration policy. The evaluative, polysemous and, very often, geographically localised notion of 'fatherland/home' (*Heimat*) woos much more emotional connotations – not least from before and during the Nazi era – and for specific conservative addressees it is much more evocative and solidarity-promoting than the terms 'nation' or 'state'. This term is used mainly by German nationalists or/and very traditional people who are 'rooted in the soil' and endorse a culturally and ethnically defined notion of nation, which in the case of the pan-German nationalists coincides with a sort of 'greater German' nation. Since at least 1995, the Austrian People's Party and its former Vice-Chancellor, Erhard Busek, also frequently picked up and emphasised the 'high-value term' of '*Heimat*'. The President of the Republic, Thomas Klestil, uses this term quite often in his speeches to court Austrian national identification

The subtitle mentions the first group of social actors who are not referred to in terms of metonymic reference. But who are the 'Austrian citizens', these first group of social actors linguistically constructed as beneficiaries? Is it everybody who possesses Austrian citizenship, which also means ethnic minorities and naturalised 'guest-workers' who have lived in Austria for more than ten years, or only German-speaking Austrians? Although it is nowhere explicitly restricted to the German-language community, and although this politonym seems merely to refer to a group of persons in terms of the possession of citizenship and of the assignment of the related political rights and duties (see chapter 2, p. 51), this last assumption could be derived from the rest of the petition (points 6 and 7) where knowledge of the German language as a mother tongue is emphasised as a distinctive feature for schoolchildren of 'the Austrians', who are presupposed to be against the children of 'foreigners' who allegedly do not speak German as a native language – the latter clearly being incorrect in the case of those schoolchildren who belong to the 'second' or 'third generation'. And what does 'restrained' mean? This is – considering the twelve points of the petition – obviously a euphemism for 'most restrictive', for the FPÖ calls for an at least temporary 'halt to immigration'. This mitigating language use is part of the FPÖ's positive self-presentation and may aim at inviting even voters from the political centre to sign the petition. The underlying assumptions become very clear as soon as one reads the first proposal: 'Austria is not a land of immigration' should be stated in the constitution itself. As Mitten (1994a: 29–30) states, 'its initial provision ... was not only demagogic, but also unmitigated nonsense. As the studies of the Austrian demographers Heinz Faßmann and Rainer Münz have shown, Austria has always been a country of immigration and emigration', and the population and economy would stagnate and decline without immigration (Faßmann and Münz 1992, 1996, 1997).

Except for the more polemic rhetoric, points 2, 3, 4, 8 and 12 of the petition do not diverge significantly from governmental policies in Austria. That is to say, certain demands in the petition – such as obliging foreign workers to show identification papers at their place of employment (point 3), increasing the numbers and salaries of the police (point 4), denying voting rights to legal foreign residents (point 8) or establishing a foundation to provide economic aid to Eastern Europe, thus discouraging population migration movements (point 12), widely reproduced projected government policies or proposals under consideration by the government. It is primarily the diction of the government that, all in all, diverges from the discursive practices and instigating populism of the FPÖ opposition. Only such an extreme demand as that for the 'legal standardisation of a halt to immigration until the question of the illegal foreigner question [sic!] is satisfactorily resolved' seems unlikely to be formulated by governmental politicians. As far as this criminalising formulation is concerned, at least two remarks must be made. First, the formulation 'illegal foreigner question' sounds very odd and ambiguous, if not ungrammatical. Taken literally, it allows an interpretation which means nearly the converse of what the petition's authors intended to express. Then, the passage can no longer be crimin-onymically paraphrased by 'the question of illegal foreigners', in which case it still remains unclear what 'illegal' should mean, although the points 3, 4, 10 and 11 indicate several possible interpretations. Moreover, the formulation points back to and questions the way the FPÖ 'asks the foreigner question', meaning that the FPÖ, in making a 'foreigner issue', or 'foreigner problem', places itself outside the frame of legality (by the way: what an unintentional irony that a political party which so grimly emphasises the importance of the German language does not itself seem always to master the most basic linguistic requirements of expression in that language). Second, the term 'satisfactory' is wide open to different interpretations, and the question arises of who will determine when the solutions are satisfactory. The respective actors are not mentioned, but it is clearly implied that they are the FPÖ and their followers.

In general, the actors who are constructed implicitly or explicitly throughout the whole text by reference and predication fall into two groups. On the one hand, there are immigrants (a spatialising actionym), illegal foreigners or aliens (two criminonyms which presuppose the prejudice that 'foreigners are criminal'), foreign employees (an econonym related to the prejudiced criminalising suspicion that foreigners would do illicit work), foreigners or aliens carrying on organised crime (again, a prejudiced criminalisation), foreigners' children who speak a non-German native language (a referential and predicational identifica-tion in terms of negative linguification), clubs of foreigners (a collectivising 'organisationalisation'), aliens doing illicit work (an economising criminalisa-tion), aliens abusing the social welfare system (a criminalisation that reproduces the prejudice that 'foreigners are socioparasites'), non-nationals being natural-ised prematurely (a politicising questioning of political rights) as well as foreign criminals and perpetrators (again, two criminonyms). We want, in passing, to emphasise again the fact that 'foreigners' and 'aliens' mean primarily 'third-country nationals'. On the other hand, the petition posits Austrian citizens (the above-mentioned politonym), Austrian voters (an actionalising politonym),

Austrian security forces – strictly speaking, police and customs authorities ('executionalising' politonyms) and the Austrian army (a militarionym). This dichotomous black-and-white portrayal implicitly and explicitly constructs a two-part world and insinuates a rather clear frontier between an Austrian world of 'law and order' and a non-Austrian world of 'crime and disorder'. Foreigners are depicted as aliens who are illegal and criminal and who do not speak or understand German. The referential exterritorialisation by naming them '*AusländerInnen*' is expanded here by prejudiced predication and discriminatory argumentation – up to the point where it may be concluded that 'foreigners', i.e. primarily 'third-country nationals', are people the FPÖ does not want to have living in Austria.

There are passages in the petition and its rationale which are not only polemical rhetorically, but also explicitly racist or at least ethnicist and which ascribe ethnic significance to social problems that have social and political causes beyond the influence of the 'foreigners'. Point 6 – relying on a combination of the topos of burden with the topos of threat and the topos of culture – requests the segregation of schoolchildren according to their knowledge of German. This would not only contradict international agreements, it would introduce a discriminatory ethnic criterion into the school system. *Nota bene*: children are not directly characterised by their proficiency in German, but by their mother tongue – a characterisation which seems indirectly to imply for the FPÖ, however, that these children must be insufficiently proficient in German, which is not as easy to prove.

Other discriminatory stipulations, like relating unemployment and housing shortages to the 'foreigner problem', clearly offer explanations for problems which are causally not related to the presence of foreigners in Austria. Similar fallacious topoi of consequence or *argumenta ad consequentiam* (see chapter 2, p. 74) are employed in discriminatory discourses against 'foreigners' – whoever they may be – in many Western European countries.

Point 9, the 'curbing' of 'premature conferring of citizenship', is again open to many readings. When is naturalisation 'premature' and when is the conferring of it legally acceptable? In view of the fact that Austria, at the time during which the petition campaign was promoted, already had one of the most restrictive citizenship laws in Europe, such a claim shows the rightist orientation of the FPÖ in an even more negatively striking and alarming light.

Point 10 openly manifests prejudiced hostility to foreigners by a topos of threat and a topos of abuse. On the one hand, 'clubs of foreigners' are viewed to be illegal and threatening to the 'Austrian' economy. On the other hand, 'foreigners' are presented as abusers of the Austrian welfare system. There are good reasons for assuming that one of the basic motivations for this demand – which borders on the violation of the basic right of freedom of assembly – is the FPÖ's fear of a multicultural society.

Point 11 asks for establishing legal instruments that allow for the immediate deportation of foreign criminals. If one reads the reason for this claim, one gets the impression that the FPÖ intentionally avoids making a clear distinction between 'foreign' criminal perpetrators and non-Austrian citizens, who become victims of the restrictive Residence Law, Asylum Law or Foreigner Law and, thus, bear the stamp of 'illegality' legally handed down by the Austrian state and its official administrators. The presupposed equation of 'illegality' and 'criminality' clearly ignores the fact that, from a viewpoint that puts human rights above the rights of a nation-state, following a very restrictive, inhuman law to the letter can mean committing a grave wrong that is not legitimised (see chapter 5, pp. 205–6).

Point 12 demands for the foundation of funds for Eastern Europe to prevent immigration as such. This demand seems to be the thin veneer of democracy of the Anti-Foreigner Petition. However, it cannot mask the central discriminatory claims of the petition.

The FPÖ circulated a brochure, which contained the official rationale that explained the twelve claims of the petition. In addition to the above analysis of the most frequent negative argumentation schemes of the petition campaign, we will only point to some further sequences which were typical of the argumentation used by the FPÖ.

Frequently, the FPÖ combined in its argumentation the topos of burdening with the topos of threat, and this is also found in the explanation of point 2 of the petition:

> A state under the rule of law and order cannot accept these sorts of conditions. The existing problems in the area of the shadow economy and growing criminality are being further exacerbated through the permanent increase of 'illegals'. Moreover, in Austria the housing shortage is rapidly increasing ... Because of the lack of adequate housing capacity numerous foreigners are also being forced to take up residence in slums at unreasonably high rates of rent.[2]

Here, the mention of the numerous foreigners who are also burdened by housing problems seems to be intended to make the petition more acceptable, apart from the fact that, at this point, one group of so-called 'foreigners' is played off against another group.

In the explanation of point 10, the victim-victimiser reversal is committed by combining the topos of threat of hostility to 'foreigners' with the topos of culture and the topos of abuse. To quote just an excerpt:

> Specifically in population centres, especially in the federal capital, Vienna, foreigners are increasingly gathering together in associations and clubs. In this area, however, there is a degree of abuse going on that reaches far beyond the legal basis of Austrian association regulations. With increasing frequency, many [such] associations and clubs take the form of eating establishments which fall considerably short of meeting the [relevant] business, sanitary or building codes (lack of sanitary facilities, no closing hours, no noise protection, prohibited gambling, secret prostitution, black

market, etc.). Consequently, irritation and justified displeasure are created among indigenous residents and businesses. Only a revised legal code and its strengthened enforcement would be able to re-establish order in this area. In the last few years, there has been an increase in the abuse of social welfare by foreigners, which makes counter-measures necessary. In this context examples include new birth certificates, which allow for the premature drawing on pension benefits; children who exist only on paper, and who make [foreigners] eligible for family assistance; the feigning of a domestic place of residence so that considerable compensatory benefits – which cannot be financed through contribution payments – are added to minimal pensions.[3]

A whole range of the anti-foreigner prejudices mentioned in chapter 2 (p. 55) are reproduced in this piece of text: The 'foreigners' are guilty for the 'Austrians' ' negative feelings against them because they are dirty (this prejudice is implied by 'lack of sanitary facilities') and behave deviantly, i.e. conspicuously, noisily and illegally. In consequence, hostility to 'foreigners' seems to be justified. One can ignore the fact that these 'foreign' associations and clubs primarily serve as meeting points for 'foreigners', as places where they can gather, play their traditional music and eat their traditional food, thus at least partly reproducing and protecting the culture into which they or their parents were originally socialised. The allegedly justified animosity mentioned is the displeasure and irritation of the fact that 'foreigners' partly practice different cultural habits of cooking, eating, dressing, celebrating and playing music. Instead of conceiving this pluralistically as cultural enrichment, many Austrians simply brand such differences as the expression of 'the foreigners' desire to resist 'integrating' into 'the Austrian culture' – 'integration' in the majority of cases euphemistically meaning simply 'assimilation' and 'homogenisation'.

Even more explicit in the aim to 'protect the German culture' against a potential 'multicultural society' is the explanation offered for point 6:

> For a number of Socialists, such as Education Minister Scholten, who, as always, promote the idea of a multicultural society, our cultural identity is practically worthless, indeed politically suspect. This can be read in the official writings of the Minister of Education. In order to preserve our cultural identity, to achieve the successful integration of children whose mother tongue is not German, to be able to continue to finance education, but also to guarantee a solid education for our children, the percentage of children whose native language is not German must be limited to about 30 ... Because the educational authorities – who are dominated by the grand coalition – insist specifically that children with inadequate or completely lacking proficiency in the German language be immediately integrated into regular classes within the compulsory educational system, the educational level is sinking and difficulties for the entire educational community are inevitable.[4]

In this passage, the topos of threat is merged with the topos of burden and the topos of culture into the topos of the 'impending decline of the Austrian cultural identity'. Apart from that, now, at least, it becomes clear that one of the main aims of the petition is to attack the governing parties. And this is probably why many potential voters did not sign the petition, while others – although not as many as expected by the FPÖ – signed the petition just because the campaign was directed against the governing parties. Some voters, who would have subscribed to the contents of petition's demands, may have abstained from giving their signature because they thought the petition to be superfluous in view of the fact that its claims in any case overlapped with the actual policy and politics of the grand coalition.

Already in the first sentence, the socialist Minister of Education is accused of neglecting 'the Austrian cultural identity' in favour of a multicultural identity. In this context, only a German culture can be implied. And this implication is always associated with German nationalists and politicians who do not respect the sovereignty of the Austrian state and still wish for a great German nation, a unification with Germany. The second argumentative assumption is that the cultural identity is threatened by people who are not native speakers of German; the German language being presupposed to form an indispensable ingredient of the definition of an 'Austrian nation'. This form of undemocratic linguistic nationalism, which is strictly orientated against any form of 'integrated' education, puts the immigrant children into the difficult position of either being required instantly to enculturate linguistically – which for most of the newly immigrated children is clearly impossible – or being segregated and placed, from the very beginning, at a great disadvantage with probable lifelong consequences.

Here, the FPÖ implies – by a topos of burden in combination with a topos of threat and a topos of culture – that for Austrian schools, non-native speakers of German represent a great handicap for the school education of the 'Austrian' children, a burden (because they are assumed to hinder the 'native Austrian children' from learning at school) and, thus, a threat to the 'Austrian children's solid education'. Of course, it remains unsaid what the FPÖ means by a 'solid education'. And it remains unsaid why the FPÖ assumes 30 per cent to be the absolute limit of non-German natives that should be allowed in a school class. The problem of what is to be understood as a 'mother tongue' is not asked, and the fact that a child may speak more than one native language is not even taken into consideration.

Nobody would argue against the fact that language proficiency does indeed help every schoolchild, but the assumption that the percentage of 'foreign' schoolchildren within a class directly correlates with the average educational level of the class is a hasty hypothesis. The statement that the level of education sinks if there is a higher percentage of children who do not have German as their native tongue is nowhere explained and nowhere proven. No evidence is given for this prejudiced assumption.

All in all, the whole passage is characterised by declarative sentences, which give the impression that the propositions asserted are factual and objective, although one searches unsuccessfully for any evidence. Instead, many existing problems in schools nowadays (many of them due to budget cuts, to reductions in numbers of teachers, of teaching materials and of teaching infrastructures) are simply projected onto 'the foreigners': they are made guilty of problems which are not related to them. Such scapegoat strategies are applied throughout the whole rationale and illustrate typical patterns of argumentation. Similar to the '*Judeus ex machina*' strategy (see chapter 3), we find the '*foreigner ex machina*' strategy here.

The campaign for and against the petition

The slogans for the petition

Both the FPÖ and their opposition started large campaigns around the petition. The FPÖ cleverly used quotes from powerful politicians of the governing parties to underline their proposals. The title of such advertisements was 'But one can sign this with a good conscience', presupposing an argument with somebody who had said the opposite and contradicting this implied contra-argument. Then, the twelve proposals were enumerated in abbreviated form and a quote from a non-FPÖ politician was inserted into the middle of the page, like 'Ever more Eastern Europeans want to leave for the 'Golden West' ... Austria must react to this because it cannot become a land of immigration' – an opinion stated by Leopold Maderthaner, President of the Austrian Chamber of Commerce, Josef Hesoun, the Minister of Social Affairs and Fritz Verzetnitsch, the President of the Unions. To the right of this insertion, the Pope was quoted, and, thus, the agreement with the church insinuated: 'The inalienable human dignity of each individual must be guaranteed, together with all people of good will. One has to take responsibility, between what is ethically required and what is actually feasible'.[5] Here, moral legitimising was attempted, using positively connoted attributes like 'responsibility', 'ethical', 'human dignity'. This lexicon of morality implied that the program of the FPÖ agrees to these claims of the Catholic Church. Moreover, the fallacious appeal to religious authorities was also committed by the following *non-sequitur*: 'The Austrian Conference of Bishops did not [underlined] condemn the petition'. The bottom line, in large and bold letters said: 'From 25th January until 1st February 1993: "I can only sign this!" ' (in German: '*Dies kann ich nur unterschreiben!*'). This *non-sequitur* suggests that those who do not publicly declare themselves to be against the petition must be in favour of it. By such appeals to 'good' Christian authorities, the FPÖ aimed at promoting and legitimising its policy (for the topic of linguistic legitimising see also Rojo and van Dijk 1997 and van Leeuwen and Wodak 1999). If even the members of the Austrian Bishops' Conference do not oppose the petition, there can be nothing wrong with it! Of course, the

FPÖ did not mention that some groups in the church did firmly oppose the petition, and that Caritas was explicitly involved in counter-activities.

Before coming to our next example, we would at this point like to emphasise that, because of restrictions of space, we cannot reproduce the leaflets and posters. Thus, a detailed layout-analysis (for example according to the model proposed by Kress and Van Leeuwen 1996) cannot be undertaken here. In our analysis, we restrict ourselves mostly to a selection of the five types of strategies presented in chapter 2, with a particular focus on the argumentation strategies.

The use of the *argumentum ad verecundiam* in quoting the Pope and in referring to the Austrian Conference of Bishops was a common fallacious argumentation technique in the discriminatory FPÖ discourse manifested in such slogans. In contrast to these techniques, the quotes from the prominent ÖVP and SPÖ politicians function as topoi of authority that cannot so easily be disqualified as fallacies, since they support the FPÖ demands by underlining the fact that the FPÖ proposals are the same as those of the mainstream parties. Thus, the FPÖ hoped that supporters of those parties would also identify with the petition.

There were advertisements by the FPÖ in the *Kleinen Zeitung* on 16 and 23 January 1993, in which the Austrian Freedom Party tried to back most of the twelve demands of the petition by one, two or even three topoi of authority. These were all derived from quotations of utterances allegedly made by members of the two Austrian governmental parties, the SPÖ and the ÖVP (which were not denied by the persons quoted). The content of these quotations seemed definitely to support the twelve claims of the FPÖ, even using the same wording:

> AUSTRIA FIRST.
> Force the government to act.
> Petition 25. 1. – 1. 2.-
> 12 good reasons for your signature.
>
> 1) Constitutional requirement: 'Austria is not an immigration-country'
> ÖVP Flemming (6.1.93): '... Austria is not an immigration-country'
> Advertisement BM Hesoun – BWK-President Maderthaner – Federation of Trade-Unions-President Verzetnitsch: '... since Austria is not an immigration-country'
> SPÖ-Marizzi: '... the boat is full'.
>
> 2) Halt to immigration until satisfactory solution to illegal foreigner problem, until elimination of housing shortage, and decrease in unemployment to 5 per cent [is achieved]:
> ÖVP Busek (28.9.92): '... to date, the admission possibilities from migratory movements are exhausted ... 150,000 illegals should submit application for work permit from their home country, otherwise they would have to be deported'.

Institute for Economic Studies (21.10.92): '... the heavy influx of foreigners is the reason for today's housing-shortage ...'.

SPÖ Cap (*Meet the Press* (*Pressestunde*) 15.11.92) declares himself ultimately to be in favour of deporting foreigners who are residing illegally in Austria.

ÖVP Flemming *TÄGLICH ALLES* (4.1.93): '... deport illegals immediately'.

3) Identification requirement for foreign workers at their place of employment, whereby work permit and health insurance application will result from this identification.

This point is an element of the government agreement on this [subject]:

SPÖ Vranitzky: '... the planned identification requirement is not discrimination but a technically necessary measure ...'.

OVP Korosec (2.10.92) – APA: To control illegal foreigners, Korosec called for the identification requirement for all foreign workers.

4) Increase in executive powers (foreigner police, criminal police), including their better remuneration and equipment for the apprehension of illegal foreigners and for a more effective fight against crime, in particular organised crime.

SPÖ Löschnak (17.8.92) '... since the opening of the Eastern borders, criminality has risen sharply ...'.

Vranitzky (4.1.93) Krone: '... better remuneration for executive powers'.

5) Immediate creation of a permanent border patrol (customs, gendarmerie) instead of federal troops.

Vranitzky (29.9.92): '... Visa requirements and border-protection are measures that are to secure the social prosperity of Austrians'.

6) Easing the tension of the school situation by limiting to a maximum of 30 per cent the proportion of pupils with a foreign mother tongue in compulsory and vocational school classes; the establishment of regular classes for foreigners where a higher than 30 per cent proportion of foreign-language speaking children is reached.

ÖVP Regional Party Convention Steiermark (October 1992) – *Kleine Zeitung*: '... declares himself in agreement with a restrictive limit of one third foreign pupils per class'.

7) Easing the tension of school-situation through participation in regular classes only with sufficient knowledge of German (preparatory classes).

8) No right to vote for foreigners in the general elections.

ÖVP Tirol, Weingartner (15.1.92-APA): '... strictly rejects a right to vote for foreigners'.

9) No premature conferring of Austrian citizenship.

According to existing law, citizenship can only be granted after a 10-year orderly stay in Austria, except when a particularly exceptional reason for consideration exists.

10) Rigorous measures against illegal business activities (as, for example, in foreigner associations and clubs) and against abuse of social benefits. Vranitzky (Autumn 1990): '... we don't need political salami merchants in Vienna'.

11) Immediate identification requirement and residency prohibition for foreign criminals.
SPÖ Zilk (30.4.92 – Kurier): '... call for expelling of violent foreigners'.

12) Establishment of an Eastern Europe Foundation for prevention of migratory movements.

'GRAZ SHOULD NOT BECOME VIENNA!'
Peter WEINMEISTER – FPÖ list 3
(Advertisement of the FPÖ in *Kleine Zeitung*, 23 January 1993)

This advertisement clearly demonstrates the overlap of political viewpoints and policies between the three largest Austrian parties. Here we already find the beginnings of the political development which ultimately led to the results of the 1999 National Assembly election: in the attempt to retain or increase their support, the two big mainstream parties adopted Haider's slogans instead of making a clear distinction. This, of course, turned out to be the wrong strategy.

From an argumentation theoretical point of view, these topoi of authority do not only operate as a simple backing of claims. They also function simultaneously as '*loci a minore*', as argumentation schemes relying on the conclusion rule that, if the less plausible case already happens to be taking place (i.e. that members of the government parties hold our view), then the more plausible case (i.e. that you, as our supporter, sign our petition) should all the more come true.

In this advertisement, the title says 'Austria first. Force the government to act', presupposing that the government up to now had done nothing with respect to the topic of the petition, and that only the FPÖ with a large number of signatures for the petition could achieve this action. Then, '12 good reasons for your signature' are enumerated, and under almost each proposal at least two or three utterances of politicians from the governing parties are printed, taken out of the original context within which they were spoken, thus decontextualised first and then recontextualised and provided with a new argumentation function (for the concept of 'recontextualisation', see, *inter alia*, Bernstein 1990, Muntigl, Weiss and Wodak 2000). In the bottom right-hand corner of the page (the 'new' and 'real' in the taxonomy of Kress and van

Leeuwen 1996), the slogan 'Graz should not become Vienna' is placed. This slogan, the implied persuasive message of which is that Graz should be protected against immigration, provides a good example of the allusive and discriminatory use of metonymies and metaphors. It has the tropological form of a metaphtonymy: that is to say, it is simultaneously metonymical – the two toponyms stand for the people living in the places named by the toponyms – and metaphorical – the toponym 'Vienna' is a negatively connoted metaphorical symbol or short form that stands for a high immigration rate which, in the prejudiced view of the FPÖ, represents a lot of problems, particularly a high crime rate. This last inference of the high crime rate metaphor can only be drawn by those readers who are able to decode the slogan as an allusion to the slogan used by the FPÖ in many election campaigns in the 1990s: 'Vienna should not become Chicago' (in German: '*Wien darf nicht Chicago werden*'). This original discriminatory slogan, which once motivated even the mayor of Chicago to a harsh critique, is intertextually passed on and forms a textual chain with the slogan 'Graz should not become Vienna'. Consequently, we can infer that also Graz should not become like Chicago, the alleged city of criminality and multiculturalism, of Al Capone and many Poles.

Let us now move to our next example, which, once again, contains the topos of authority: In the *Kurier* of 23 January 1993, we find an advertisement quoting the then Austrian Chancellor, Franz Vranitzky, who said 'we do not need Eastern salami, brandy and cigarette merchants on our streets'. And again we read 'I have to sign this!' as the conclusion from the Chancellor's quote, which is a clearly prejudiced discriminatory utterance connecting immigrants from Eastern Europe with the black market.

Finally, we would like to present an advertisement, which alludes to the Nazi era and to antisemitic policies: 'Austrians! Buy in Austrian shops. Thank you!' This imperative appeal reminds the viewers and readers of the Nazi slogan 'Do not buy in Jewish shops' and 'Buy in German shops'. Through such a discriminating demand, it is not only that the two groups, of 'foreigners' and 'real Austrians' (implied German-speaking Austrians), are discursively constructed, implying that many shop-owners of Turkish and Serbian origin who possess Austrian citizenship are not 'real Austrians'. In addition to this explicit linguistic exclusion, the demand, which is not a suggestion to choose between different possibilities or alternatives, is a clear inciting command to active everyday exclusion and discrimination. Over and above that, it conveys many negative nationalist connotations: are non-Austrian products bad? Or are non-Austrian shop-owners criminals and cut-throats? Why is it bad to buy in a non-Austrian shop – does it mean that one is supporting a different economy and also damaging the Austrian economy? To an historically informed reader, the association with many pictures of the Nazi time is close and evident, where Jewish shops are shown with the slogan commanding the public not to buy there splashed on the shop doors and windows, the windows broken and the owners forced to scrub the street in front of their shops.

The slogans against the petition

An ad hoc formation outside the political mainstream provided the rallying point for what was ultimately the most significant opposition to Haider and the FPÖ petition (see Mitten 1994a: 33). In early November 1992, a group of writers, artists and other intellectuals founded 'SOS-Mitmensch' (SOS-Fellow Human Being), a campaign for solidarity with all victims of racist, ethnicist and antisemitic hatred and intolerance. SOS-Mitmensch was a very broad coalition, including the institution of the Catholic Church. Even Minister Löschnak, SPÖ Minister for Internal Affairs and widely accused of his very restrictive 'foreigner policies', thus himself frequently a target of criticism (sometimes he was even apostrophised as the 'best Haider man in the Austrian government'), felt able to join, which was not greeted enthusiastically by the group's other members. The speaker of the group was André Heller, a Jewish artist, known for his progressive opinions and widely acclaimed for his songs and theatre productions. Much of the neo-right propaganda was also directed against him personally. The culmination of the opposition was a candlelight march for tolerance on 23 January 1993, which was inspired by similar events in Germany. The march in Vienna attracted more than 200,000 people, including Chancellor Vranitzky, whose remarks we just quoted and analysed above. The major parties also launched some counter-propaganda. They mainly emphasised that most of Haider's proposals were already included in the Residence Act and Asylum Act (Löschnak 1993; and see the parliamentary debate below) and that Haider's petition was undemocratic.

The advertisements of SOS-Mitmensch differed from the FPÖ propaganda: not only with respect to the content, obviously, but also in their layout. The texts were longer, the argumentation was different (for there were no *argumenta ad verecundiam* and topoi of authority) and the interpersonal metafunction of language, e.g. the mood, was realised differently: there were far fewer imperatives, not least because the statements were very often 'elliptical', having the character of headlines and slogans that delete the verbs. The appeals to the public were also expressed differently: that is to say, much less by fallacious *argumenta ad populum* that played on the fears of the addressees, than by an appeal to rational insights, humanity and democracy. Let us consider two examples.

We will analyse briefly the solidarity-seeking slogan 'together' (*'gemeinsam '*) that was written in large letters on the top left of the first advertisement. Above this, other political catchwords with positive connotations were presented: '*integration: same rights!* ', and written below was '*democratic solutions* ', which implied that Haider's petition was undemocratic. On the top right, the short slogan '*today them, tomorrow you* ' expresses a topos of threat in the form of a specific topos of consequence, which can be paraphrased as follows: if now, at the time of the petition campaign, the foreigners are the victims of the FPÖ attacks, in the future you, the addressee of this advertisement, could probably be the target of the FPÖ aggression. In other words: the 'elliptical' phrase means that the present hostility towards foreigners could just be the beginning and that, in future, everybody could potentially come into the position of being an outsider.

In bold type, we read '*together against the Haider petition, against racist laws*', which should be interpreted as a headline-like, 'elliptical', solidarity-seeking appeal directed against both the FPÖ and the laws of the government, since these in any case embody several of the proposals made in the petition text. By explicitly ascribing to the laws the negative, stigmatising attribute of being 'racist' – that is to say, by employing one of the strongest and most denouncing and critical political fighting words a political group has at its disposal in a modern democracy – the authors of the advertisement aim to mobilise as much democratic, anti-racist Austrian resistance and protest as possible. One form of such protest is concretely mentioned in the ensuing appeal for activities, viz. a demonstration in the form of a candlelight march.

In the middle of the advertisement, many arguments against the petition are explicitly put forward, but written in very small letters, thus not visible from a distance. One really has to read this piece of paper closely to follow the argumentation. The arguments are against both the petition and the government policies. Employing the topos of humanitarianism (see chapter 2, p. 78) in combination with a topos of consequence, the anti-discriminatory opponents state: 'The xenophobic measures of the coalition government violate basic human rights and have laid the ground for the FPÖ's racist propoganda'.[6] Here, the responsibility for the Haider policies is given to the governing parties, which have ostensibly prepared the ground for the anti-foreigner discourse. In this respect, there are some assumptions which the FPÖ advertisements share with those of the opposition, viz. the claim that the FPÖ policy and politics do not greatly differ from the governmental policy and politics. Further, both make the government responsible for the actual political situation in Austria. However, the reference to the government has very different argumentation functions for the two groups of political and ideological antagonists. The FPÖ uses the reference to the government and church to linguistically construct their topoi of authority and *argumenta ad verecundiam* that are intended to promote support of the petition. The anti-racist group aims at attacking two adversaries in the same breath and at constructing a single referential target of critique (that comprises both the FPÖ and the government) against which a topos of humanitarianism is brought to bear.

This harsh critique by the anti-discrimination group does not end in resignation and apathy. It is followed by appeals to rational insight and by a topos of consequence (containing a topos of threat) in combination with a topos of time (technically speaking, a *locus a tempore*) for which the old Ovidian saying '*principiis obsta!*' is recycled and recontexualised:

We want to 'fight the beginnings' before it is too late. We still have the opportunity in Austria to steer away (from this) in time. We want to fight for democratic forms of social coexistence and to denounce every form of racism and nationalism.[7]

Here, the Ovidian topos may be paraphrased by the following complex conditional: if some bad thing is about to arise and develop, one should fight it immediately, before it is too late and becomes progressively worse. Since 1945, this argumentation scheme has often been associated with the recollection of Nazi crimes. It has repeatedly been employed as a warning about negative political developments that could culminate in excesses similar to those of the National-Socialists. The topos of time inherent in this saying is complemented by the explicit emphasis that it is not yet too late. In the last sentence of this quote a we-group is constructed which potentially encompasses everybody in Austria who is against anti-foreigner policies, racism and nationalism. This we-group is twice characterised by a verb that denotes a mental process ('want to'). Thus, the quote becomes a declaration of will and wish, a professed intention with respect to the realisation of political aims that are described by catchwords with very positive connotations.

Below this passage, in bold, we find '*No to the petition against foreigners* '. This is the clear conclusion from the argumentation above. On the right-hand side follow demands under the heading of '*together for* '. These claims are enumerated and are directed against the demands in the petition text:

> Amnesty for all who only through their residence – on account of the existing legal situation in Austria – are 'illegalised'; revocation of all xenophobic laws, because they systematically discriminate against people of particular backgrounds and thereby violate human rights; civil rights for foreigners; more funding for integration policies in schools. Introduction of tutors even at higher educational levels; access to fair asylum procedures; extension of the definition of asylum to include reasons specific to women, extreme poverty, and the environment; social and economic policies which make scapegoating impossible.

All these claims clearly aim at opposing the demands expressed in the petition, and at disqualifying them by means of very comprehensible and precise argument. However, they are again written in very small letters, thus creating the necessity for close reading and hindering their reception.

At the bottom of the page, dates and places are enumerated where anti-racist events will take place.

One would have to study the reception of the different semiotic structuring of the advertisements from the FPÖ and the SOS-Mitmensch empirically. A first analysis shows that the advertisements of the Haider party were more persuasive, using more authoritarian arguments and appeals to irrational emotions. Whereas some of the FPÖ advertisements and slogans alluded to or evoked Nazi propaganda in the Third Reich by recycling it in a transformed manner, the counter-advertisements alluded to the Nazi period only in a deterrent way, by warning of possible negative developments. All in all, the advertisements of the opposition was more elaborate, but required much more effort from the readers.

Let us finally come to a second counter-advertisement, which was put out by the Austrian Unions. This leaflet is interesting specifically because it attempts to appeal to the workers, who are also one of the main addressee groups on which the FPÖ focuses in trying to raise anxieties about unemployment and housing. And as the election of 3 October 1999 illustrated, the FPÖ succeeded in persuading the workers: they won 47 per cent of their votes, much more than the Social Democratic Party which was traditionally the workers' party.

On the left-hand side, the leaflet starts with the topos of humanitarianism, which is embedded into a declarative two-part topos of definition or interpretation that has the argumentative structure of an enthymemic, incomplete syllogism. The conclusion of this quasi-syllogism is the declaration that union members are not going to sign the petition: 'Union means solidarity. Union means human beings for human beings. Therefore, we do not sign a petition against human beings'. This argumentation is semiotically presented as the characterisation of the political position of the unions, as the given. The new information on the right-hand side of the leaflet consists of a list of declarative sentences that express empathy with the working and housing situation of non-Austrian employees (in this advertisement, econonyms are one of the central personal-referential categories) and aim to cheer up the addressees. These four statements are intended argumentatively to undermine and correct some of the anti-foreigner prejudices reproduced in the FPÖ petition:

– Foreign employees have the worst paid and most unhealthy jobs
– live in the worst apartments
– are most frequently exploited by employers and landlords/landladies
– continuously experience disdain and hostility by Austrians

These informative, politically 'educational' statements are again taken as the beginning of an argumentation chain. These explications are followed by the confirmation that 'it is true, that in our country there are too few – and too few well-paid – jobs; in our country there are too few – and too few affordable – apartments'. This sequence paraphrases some of the points made in the petition, but the conclusions drawn are completely different. Again, a topos of humanitarianism is employed. It is embedded in a parallelism that consists of two impersonalised, negative assertions, which carry a serious, although slightly optimistic overtone: 'It would be wrong to accept these conditions. It would be wrong to give up on the hope for humane working and living conditions'.

In contrast now to the advertisements of the FPÖ, the responsibility and guilt for these poor conditions are not projected on to the foreigners, but a new policy is demanded for all employees, be they foreigners or non-foreigners: 'It is necessary to create more jobs for all; to fight for higher salaries for all; to build more apartments for all; and to pay less for housing for all' ('all' in the original is always '*für In- und AusländerInnen* ', i.e. for 'indigenous and foreigners'). Thus, an 'economised' referential group is established: employers and employees. This is the essence of the unions' policies: because of their concept of solidarity, they demand better living conditions for everybody who is working, irrespective of nationality and citizenship. The cohesion in this text is greater than in the FPÖ advertising; linear parallelism and enumeration are used extensively. The leaflet provides the opposition with a very simple, but effective, argumentative structure.

Finally, on the bottom right, we find the question '*who pays?*' and the statement that Austria is a rich country, but that the wealth is not equally divided. A humane distribution of wealth implies a humane foreigner policy. This again stands in complete contrast to government policies as well as to the claims of the petition. The workers should join together and oppose the rich and wealthy. Old socialist slogans are alluded to. In the far-right bottom of the leaflet the last sentence states 'instead of fear and smear campaigns we need cool minds, open hearts and solidarity in our actions'. This is used as an appeal to rationality, moral values like justice, and positive emotions like solidarity. As such, it is also directed against the use of all types of fallacies. In contrast to those analysed above, this advertisement tries to plead for rational insight and for democratic values of equality, justice and anti-discrimination.

From an argumentation theoretical perspective, one can clearly summarise the FPÖ propaganda in favour of the petition as aiming much more to persuade (in the negative sense of the German verb '*überreden*'; see chapter 2, p. 70) than to convince, whereas the anti-petition argumentation is aimed much more to convince than to persuade by fallacious rhetoric.

We have presented this genre of political advertising in public discourse because it illustrates very well the conflicting arguments surrounding the foreigner petition and the discursive strategies used in this multimodal genre. The leaflets were posted everywhere and became part of city life in Vienna. This genre must therefore have been very influential. But as we mentioned above, it would be necessary to design a special empirical study to be able to say more about the specific reception and impact of this genre of political advertisements.

Some newspaper commentaries concerning the petition

The Austrian newspapers

The newspapers in Austria were full of statements, editorials, reports and documentation about the petition, arguing for and against it. As expected, the quality newspapers *Der Standard, Die Presse, Die Furche* and the *Salzburger Nachrichten* argued at length against Haider's proposals, although their political positions and their readerships differ considerably. All of them cited the leading politicians of the governing parties as well as the President of Austria, Thomas Klestil, who were all opponents of the petition. Haider was cited when attacking the government, specifically when he personally attacked the President and the church for not supporting his petition and for being 'undemocratic' (although, as shown above, the FPÖ also used the church for their *argumenta ad verecundiam*).

As the study of press reporting in the years 1989/90 had already shown (Matouschek, Wodak and Januschek 1995), the counter-discourse was lead by *Der Standard*, the paper for liberal intellectuals. This was and is the paper with a clear standpoint supporting foreigners who suffer discrimination and opposing racism and 'xenophobia'. *Die Presse*, in contrast, is a more conservative paper which is read by industrialists and managers. Here, the principles of democracy were discussed, the alleged and so-called 'foreigner problem' was seen mostly from an economic point of view. In contrast, *Die Furche* is a newspaper very close to the church, and thus thematised human rights and Christian values. Finally, the *Salzburger Nachrichten* is a regional newspaper with a big impact at the national level. This paper argued very much in line with *Der Standard* and also opposed governmental policies on the issue of the petition.

The two biggest tabloids, however, both supported the petition. The *Neue Kronen Zeitung* is the most widely read paper in the world in relationship to population numbers and is extremely important in influencing opinion-making; *Täglich Alles* is not so popular, but less expensive. Usually, these two papers have distinctly differing opinions and compete with each other, but on this occasion, both of them tried to be the '*vox populi*', thus committing the fallacy of the *argumentum ad populum*. Daily columns, editorials and letters to the editor were published in favour of anti-foreigner policies. The newspapers of the far right (for example *Aula*), of course, supported Haider.

Most interestingly, *Der Kurier*, which had been a tabloid but has now become almost a quality paper, advanced both anti-racist and racist arguments at the same time, in much the same way as in 1989/90. A careful analysis, however, shows that *Der Kurier* supported government policies.

To summarise, therefore, it may be said that all the quality newspapers were against the Austria First Petition, and the two biggest tabloids in favour of it. Owing to restrictions of space, it will not be possible here to make a systematic analysis of all the newspaper articles over the entire period of the debate on the petition. This analysis alone could fill a whole book. Instead, we will focus on a comparison of some typical editorials from each of the newspapers, together with the advertisements and slogans, as well as the petition itself. This will allow us to selectively reconstruct the recontextualisation of some topics and arguments and to document some intertextual relationships between different texts of the petition discourse in Austria at that time. We undertake an analysis of the commentaries and opinion columns that were published after the results of the petition became known, on 2 and 3 February 1993. This analysis is made against the background that the media, during the campaigns for and against the petition, decisively influenced public discourse on the discursively constructed 'foreigner issue'.

The days after

The dominant topic during the campaign consisted of predictions of the possible numbers of signatures (see the previous section): every day brought new estimates from the FPÖ, but also from opinion polls, politicians and experts. Substantial disagreement could be found about the number that would indicate the success or failure of the petition. The talk about numbers, often utilised in *argumenta ad numerum* and topoi of numbers, is omnipresent: numbers of foreigners, numbers of refugees, numbers (of schillings) in the budget, and numbers of signatures. And, obviously, numbers can be interpreted in various ways, always serving as evidence for the particular argument which is being advanced.

A second major topic was the status of the petition itself: a discussion evolved as to whether the petition was a democratic tool, or whether it was being misused and abused for party politics. Appeals were made, even by the Chancellor himself, that people signing the petition should not be marginalised. The President stated that a petition was not the right instrument with which to come to a decision on such a sensitive issue. The FPÖ justified their demands and attempted to give evidence of censorship in the media and pressure on individuals who were signing the petition. Afterwards, the tabloids claimed that many more people would have signed, if the process had been anonymous like elections. Within this context, the topoi of advantage and justice predominated.

This relates to a third major topic: the election in Graz, where the FPÖ won many seats from the ÖVP and SPÖ, and the significance of this gain for the petition. The election in Graz had been dominated by a focus on the so-called 'foreigner issue'. It became clear that this controversial political issue could be used to win elections. The governing parties tried to downplay the election result in Graz, whereas Haider already showed himself euphoric about the petition, taking the result as an exemplary indicator of the successful outcome of the pro-petition campaign (i.e. employing it for an *argumentum ad exemplum* with the quality of as *non-sequitur fallacy*).

A fourth topic is also worth mentioning: an important journalist, Burgl Czeitschner, had to retire from the Austrian Television Company ORF because she asked her employees to report negatively on the petition. The ORF, however, is state-owned and is supposed to report in an 'objective way' according to the law. Haider had evidence of the intervention by Czeitschner and showed it to the television audience during a talk show. The tabloids seised on this scandal and took it as 'proof of the manipulation of the Austrian media from above', as proof of the party political bias of the state media. In connection with this topic, the topos of responsibility and the topos of example or *argumentum ad exemplum* were frequently used.

What is remarkable when reviewing these topics of topoi and fallacies is the absence of differentiated discussions about the social and political problems related to the discriminated groups of non-Austrian citizens who live and work in Austria and about the laws put forward by the government. The debate in the newspapers was aggressive and polemical, and largely dominated by the speeches of politicians. The subjects of the whole petition, 'the foreigners', had almost no voice and no access to the media; they were neither asked nor allowed to speak for themselves and were totally dependent on their supporters. This phenomenon, very familiar in debates about the discriminatory role of the media with respect to all the different (racialised, ethnicised, religious, autochthonous and immigrant) minorities living in a specific nation state (van Dijk 1991 and 1993), is also characteristic of the discourse about 'foreigners' in Austria after 1989/90: the foreigners are reduced to 'things' or 'numbers'; they are decided upon and de-personalised (for the many metaphors used in public political discussions about migrants and 'foreigners', see chapter 2, pp. 58–60).

On 2 February 1993, the newspapers were full of reports about the results of the petition: the *Neue Kronen Zeitung* brought out a report with the headline 'Petition: results no reason for Haider to celebrate'. *Die Presse* wrote about 'Self-mutilation' (in reference to Haider). *Täglich Alles* stated: 'Petition: FPÖ-boss Jörg Haider is very disappointed'. The weekly *profil*, a liberal journal, had an editorial with the headline 'Shipwrecked' (in German: '*Abgestürzt* '). The *Standard* reported about 'Haider's Wagram – not yet Waterloo'. The *Kurier* emphasised 'Defeat for Haider, warning for the others'.

Already these headlines point to the polarising positions of the newspapers mentioned above: on the one hand, the metaphors of 'war' and 'destruction' are invoked by those newspapers which were against the petition. Here, Haider is seen as a warrior who was defeated (who is the loser) or has destroyed, self-mutilated himself or crashed, and analogies as well as historical comparisons are made with political leaders like Napoleon and Hitler. The two tabloids, on the other hand, avoid such militarising metaphors and touch primarily on the emotional state of Haider, almost evoking pity for him, without viewing the petition and the campaigns as a 'battle' between two opposing sides. Moreover, both the *Standard* and the *Kurier* emphasise that the 'war' is not over yet, that one should not be too happy about these results, and that the FPÖ might win more votes in a normal election.

The first reactions and analyses of the results point to some important dimensions of the whole campaign: those signing the petition were not all FPÖ voters; rather, they were also voices of protest against 'those up there', against the coalition government and corruption. Secondly, many experts thought that the 'real' issue had not been the alleged and so-called 'foreigner issue', but the attempt to marginalise the right wing and to make Haider and the FPÖ lose for once. As indicated above, governmental policies had already suggested most of the measures contained in the petition before it even started. Thus, as the Minister for Interior Affairs, Franz Löschnak said, '[the government] had already completed work on a comprehensive package of laws regulating the "foreigner thing" [in German: "*das Fremdenwesen* "]'. This means that many may have taken part in the candlelight march – as Minister Löschnak did – who could perhaps also utter prejudiced statements against 'foreigners', but wanted to keep their distance from the Haider party for strategic reasons. Many articles in the various newspapers therefore picked up the topic of Haider's future and the perspectives of the FPÖ, rather than the future of immigration policies and immigrants. The petition was seen as a test of how many would actually dare put their names to an FPÖ-sponsored, rather than a simple anti-foreigner, petition.

Let us examine four different columns from the four most important Austrian dailies. We will not analyse them in linguistic detail, but simply focus on the most conspicuous linguistic features. They were all published on 2 and 3 February 1993. The first one appeared in the tabloid *Täglich Alles*:

Author and section: Gerd Leitgeb, The window observer

Title: The 'prophets' ' errors

Text: The petition is over. Several hundred thousand have demanded that the parliament again look extensively into the foreigner problem.

It was no success for Jörg Haider: he set his sights too high. But it was not only the 'Blue Prophet' who was substantially off in his prediction two months ago that about a million Austrians would support the 'Austria First' program. Other prophets also have to concede that they were mistaken.

First, there are those who believed that the foreigner petition would not do any better than Haider's failed ORF petition, which was signed by a mere 109,000 Austrians. But especially those who, on the occasion of the introduction of this petition, believed that the anti-foreigner propaganda of 'the Blues' would tear open graves, lead to the radicalisation of the population, lure right-wing extremists out of their holes, and make good citizens commit arson against housing for asylum-seekers.

All wrong.

The petition, as I wrote in this column weeks ago, is no accident: why shouldn't the Austrians be allowed to say what they think?

Now they have said it. And they have thereby shown that Haider's power is relatively small. Therefore, let us not make him out to be bigger than he is. But they have also shown by the hundreds of thousands that they are not satisfied with the foreigner policies of the government.

For this reason Vranitzky and Co., instead of making fun of Haider's failure, should solve those problems that burden the people [*das Volk*].

(*Täglich Alles*, 2 February 1993: 2–3)

The tabloids which had supported Haider and the petition later quite openly changed their reasons for supporting him. Gert Leitgeb from *Täglich Alles* justified his opinion on moral grounds (see also van Leeuwen and Wodak 1999): 'why shouldn't the Austrians be allowed to say what they think?'. The underlying presupposition here is that Austria is a democratic state and 'the Austrians' should say whatever they think, simply in accordance with the spirit of freedom of speech. Please note that Leitgeb, in his rhetorical question, uses verbs that denote a verbal process ('to say') and a mental process ('to think'), implying that the signing or not-signing of the petition would have been merely a 'verbal' and 'mental' action, and not a political statement that would have very specific consequences within the institutionalised framework and could, for example, lead to very severe, discriminatory political state measures against specific groups of 'foreigners'. Thus, the columnist de-contextualises and de-politicises the petition.

And Leitgeb continues:

> Now they have said it. And they have thereby shown that Haider's power is relatively small. Therefore, let us not make him out to be bigger man than he is. But they have also shown by the hundreds of thousands that they are not satisfied with the foreigner policies of the government.

He concludes: 'For this reason, Vranitzky and Co., instead of making fun of Haider's failure, should solve those problems which burden the people [*das Volk*]'.

Leitgeb systematically denies the factors suggesting a power struggle between the FPÖ and the government. He emphasises the number of signatures (by employing the topos of numbers which in this article also has the character, at least in part, of an *argumentum ad numerum*) and warns the government to react to this dissatisfaction in the population (an implicit topos of danger or threat). For Leitgeb, the 'foreigner politics' of the government is a topic which should be spoken about and in relation to which people who are in favour of more restrictive politics should be taken seriously. He therefore suggests that there is a 'foreigner problem' which burdens the population (please note the topos of burden) and which should be solved by the government. The petition and its arguments are taken as a given, as a relevant fact, although the significance of Haider is trivialised by the topos of numbers. This topos is also designed to relativise the topos of consequence, which was used by the opponents of the petition in combination with the topos of threat of an increasing right-wing-radicalism (this last was considered to be a possible negative consequence of the pro-petition campaign). The religious metaphor of the 'prophets' errors' embraces the whole article as the central trope: the implicit argumentation scheme inherent in this metaphor aims at disqualifying and undermining the topoi of consequence which were very differently employed by the two sides. By using this metaphor, Leitgeb wants to express that both Haider's prognosis and the prediction of those who argued against the petition were wrong.

The second column was published in the *Neue Kronen Zeitung* on 3 February. It was written by Staberl, the best-known of all Austrian columnists, who sometimes employs the persuasive technique of using letters to the editor, which are often quite openly nationalist, ethnicist, racist or sexist, to fill his columns. Thus, he pretends to guarantee a variety of different voices to be heard and read in the *Neue Kronen Zeitung*, but, in fact, selectively utilises the voices implicitly to express his own opinion and avoids being called to account for the discriminatory and prejudiced content of the letters. Apart from this technique, which he also employed to back his argumentation in favour of the petition by *argumenta ad verecundiam*, in his other columns on the Anti-Foreigner Petition Staberl tried to justify his previous support by specific topoi of comparison: that is to say, by naming many other parties and countries who have also suggested similar procedures (legitimation by authorisation). In this way, Staberl attempted to argue that the petition must be good. In the following article, Staberl's argumentation technique is different:

Author: Staberl alias Richard Nimmerrichter

Title: Prosperity as obstacle

Text: Among the twelve points of the petition on the foreigner problem, which has now ended with about 417,000 signatures in favour, there is one upon which everyone agrees wherever in the world there are problems with immigrants, asylum-seekers, and refugees. And here, in addition to the Blues, the Reds, the Blacks, probably even the Greens would agree on this at any given time: namely, that probably the only effective way of solving this problem would be to create a healthy economic situation in the immigrants' countries of origin. Only when these people, whose plight is usually entirely not of their own making, have the opportunity for progress in their home countries, will they stay at home. Who would leave home, if it were also possible to get on well there?

But unfortunately! The demand of the latest petition to create a foundation for the economic recovery of immigration countries was and is completely unrealistic. Neither here nor anywhere else in the well-fed Western countries hit by the refugee problem will this ever come about. The reason for this is depressing enough. Prosperity creates egoism and allows hearts to become lazy.

Concrete evidence for this dreary norm has been provided to us by our German neighbours for some time now. When, in the aftermath of the collapse of the communist countries of Eastern Europe, the unnatural border between the two German states also fell, the former GDR and her completely ruined economy were dependent on the help of their compatriots in the Federal Republic.

In this regard, along with many others, I would have to admit the exemplary way in which I was mistaken. If it had been possible for the Germans, so I thought, to rebuild their completely destroyed and economically ruined country after 1945, and if, out of the misery of the postwar years, the much-cited Economic Miracle was able to arise in a surprisingly short time, there could not and should not be a problem in taking upon themselves those not similarly small efforts and victims, which would have been needed to restore the economy in the new federal states.

A mistake however! The well-fed citizens of West Germany are in no way prepared to make – without a second thought – the sacrifices necessary for their fellow citizens in the East. A people that only four decades ago would not have shied from any effort and willingly accepted every frugality in their everyday life, are today unwilling to take on even a small fraction of that of the former victims in favour of their new neighbours and compatriots. And anyone who believes that only the Germans are like that is mistaken.

Only those who live in prosperity, live comfortably; that is how the leftist German author Bert Brecht described it. He who lives comfortably, one could continue, lives without any annoying compassion.

(*Neue Kronen Zeitung*, 3 February 1993: 4)

The star columnist of the *Neue Kronen Zeitung*, Staberl alias Richard Nimmer-richter, took a different argumentative strategy to justify his previous support for the petition and to explain its failure. He chose the last point out of Haider's twelve issues in the petition, the point which proposed some kind of foundation to provide economic aid to the immigrants' countries of origin – obviously the least controversial point (see above). According to the author, nobody doubts that the best would be 'to create a healthy economic situation in the immigrants' countries of origin'. This would help both the immigrants and the Austrians, since all immigrants would stay at home, which, by a rhetorical question, Staberl implies is the only answer.

This topos of 'to the advantage of them and us' (*pro bono eorum et nobis*), which is contained in point 12 of the petition text, forms the central argumenta-tion scheme of the first paragraph of Staberl's article. However, the author already undermines it in the second paragraph, when he claims that point 12 of the petition and its realisation would be completely unrealistic everywhere, since 'prosperity creates egoism and allows hearts to become lazy'.

Before we come to the third, fourth and fifth paragraphs, in which the columnist seeks to support the contention at the end of the second paragraph with an illustrative example that contains a hasty generalisation, let as observe in advance that Staberl, in this column, is no longer talking about the other issues in the petition. There is no mention here of crime and economic refugees, which figured in previous columns. Cleverly, he reduces the petition to a single issue and decontextualises this point of the petition text. As soon as one lives well, one no longer wants to help or give anybody else anything.

In the third paragraph, the columnist begins to give evidence for his position by introducing an *argumentum ad exemplum*, which serves to support the thesis at the end of the second paragraph by comparing Austria with another country, viz. with Germany. In the fourth paragraph, the journalist specifies the example. He employs a '*locus a minore*', an argumentation scheme relying on the reasoning that, if the less plausible case happens to have taken place (i.e. that the Germans were able in the postwar period to rebuild the country so quickly and to bring about the German 'economic miracle'), then the more plausible case (i.e. that the economy of the New States of Germany will be quickly rehabilitated) is all the more likely to come true. In the fifth paragraph, Staberl returns to the central thesis of his second paragraph. First, he applies it to the German example and refutes the *locus a minore* of the fourth paragraph, arguing that the problems of German reunification are due to the fact that 'the well-fed citizens of West Germany are in no way prepared to make ... necessary sacrifices for their fellow citizens in the East ...'. Then Staberl generalises his statement, supporting it with a fallacious, widely tautological topos of reality: 'this is the way humans are'. In the last short paragraph, Staberl also tries to back his thesis. Employing a topos of authority, he cites Bert Brecht: 'Only those who live in prosperity, live comfortably; that is how the leftist German author Bert Brecht described it. He who lives comfortably, one could continue, lives without any annoying compassion'.

The implications of the column are quite obvious: the Austria First Petition had to fail, because mankind is egoistic in situations concerning economic wealth. This is inherent in human nature. And in more general terms: since human beings are by nature egoistic and lack compassion, certain things cannot change, and racism as well as hostility to foreigners most naturally follow from 'prosperity egoism'. Racism, ethnicism, 'xenophobia' is thus inevitable in a prosperous state (including Austria). This could be seen as an implicit biologising argumentation. In this way, the whole column can also be read as 'objective legitimation' of the status quo (van Leeuwen and Wodak 1999).

In the third article we want to consider briefly a comment by Hans Rauscher in the *Kurier*, of 2 February 1993, on p. 3:

Author: Hans Rauscher

Title: Defeat for Haider: Warning for the Others.

Lead: Measured against what Jörg Haider wanted, his petition is a total flop. Measured against the absolute number of 414,000 signatures, it is nevertheless a sign of considerable anger among the citizens.

Text: Haider himself set his hopes on a million. Then he said that the number of FPÖ voters participating in the last election, 780,000, would be a good number. Once the petition had been underway for two days he said he would be happy with 'over 500,000'. Under 500,000 he would have to 'think about'.

Actually, Haider should now resign. He manoeuvred himself completely into a corner. Jörg Haider knows that no serious politician in this country will believe anything he has to say. With his compulsive, obsessive attacks against everyone and everything, he has marginalised himself as a coalition partner. In their Sunday editorial, the super-serious *Neue Zürcher Zeitung* commented as follows about the virulent slander that Haider exhibited in his 'Führer' speeches: 'The nearly National-Socialist vocabulary is becoming even clearer than before'. A typical call by an ÖVP mayor from Lower Austria to the *Kurier*: 'I always got upset before when people said he's a Nazi. Now I know, he really is one'.

With an 'enormous popular movement' Haider wanted to become so strong that ultimately one could not overlook him. 414,000 signatures are not enough for that. Why weren't there more? Of course, the fact that one had to declare [one's support] with signature and address played a role. It was probably more important, however, that practically all other societal groups and institutions drew a clear line for the first time. We don't want that. The effect of the 'sea of light' of more than 200,000 on the day before the petition can't be estimated highly enough. It was [members of] the middle class which did something that it generally finds so unpleasant. They took to the streets. Most of them are presumably not particularly foreigner-friendly, but it appeared urgently necessary to clarify one thing: 'We don't want it to be the way Mr. Haider does'. And: 'We are many'.

Those familiar with the fear of citizens (in the most general sense) of expressing their points of view publicly can appreciate the political change that has happened here. The heart of the matter was to prove that a dangerously fascinating radical such as Mr. H. has again not won ground. This point has been proven (of all cases, in the arch-middle-class *Presse*, an otherwise clever author has unfortunately completely misunderstood this splendid sign of life among the politically conscious citizenry). 200,000 at 'the sea of light', about 100,000 at the petition in Vienna. But then, 414,000 in the whole of Austria are to be taken seriously. A lot of things are apparently bothering them, not just the foreigners. Fear of unemployment in 'old' industrial centres, rage with 'them up there'. The desire not to let the big coalition become even bigger: 'I'm not in favour of Haider, but they have to feel something at some point ...' was frequently heard. This won't disappear so quickly, but also because a lot of them won't take what is Nazi-like about Jörg Haider seriously. However, one has to take them and their worries into account, even after this heaviest defeat of Jörg Haider to date.

(*Kurier*, 2 February 1993: 3)

Hans Rauscher, the main political columnist of the *Kurier*, discusses the possible interpretation of the number of signatures (topos of numbers), the consequences of the petition and its results for Austria's politics. The main topic of his article is Jörg Haider, his closeness to National-Socialist vocabulary and ideas, and the threats to Austrian democracy that are involved (topos of threat). He begins his column with the two main possible interpretations of the results: failure for Haider on the one hand, and the significance of 414,000 [sic!] signatures on the other hand, which signal massive dissatisfaction with the policies of the government and with 'them up there'. Note, that the label 'flop' for the results of the petition quickly became common usage: 'Measured against what Jörg Haider wanted, his petition is a total flop. Measured against the absolute number of 414,000 signatures, it is nevertheless a sign of considerable anger among the citizens'. Rauscher evaluates the first reading as positive, the second one as negative and as a warning for the government. In his opinion both readings are important, since, in the rest of his column, both are elaborated.

The second paragraph quickly summarises the wild estimates which Haider had made during the campaign for the petition. Haider had claimed that he would have to 'rethink everything', if he got fewer than 500,000 signatures (topos of numbers). Thus, Rauscher concludes, in the third paragraph, Haider should retire now if he keeps his promises. Then he backs and justifies this mitigated demand – mitigated by the use of the subjunctive – by attributing several negative characteristics and traits to Haider. In the author's opinion, no serious politician would ever want to get involved with him; he is seen as compulsive (in German: *triebhaft, zwanghaft*) in his insulting rhetoric and as having marginalised himself. Moreover, Rauscher recalls that Haider made polemical, demagogic and slanderous speeches during the pro-petition campaign. Two fallacious appeals to authorities (*argumenta ad verecundiam*) with the character of illustrative examples serve as supporting evidence for this negative picture. Firstly, the well-known, high-quality paper *Neue Zürcher Zeitung* had stated that Haider's nearness to the vocabulary of National-Socialism was more evident than ever. Secondly, a regional politician, mayor and member of the ÖVP had called Rauscher and had said that he had always been angry in the past if somebody called Haider a Nazi – now he himself knew that Haider was one. This story-like example (for the use of a story as evidence for a generalisation see chapter 3, pp. 111–12 as well as Wodak 1991a, 1991b and Van Dijk 1984), contains a fallacious 'argumentation from the less' (*locus a minore*, which can be paraphrased as follows: if even somebody who, in the past, was always against characterising Haider as a Nazi, comes to the conclusion that he is one, it must be all the more be true that Haider is a Nazi). Through these two argumentative appeals to authorities, which have the character of fallacies, since they do not really supply a proof of the contention that Haider is a Nazi, but simply work with the 'weight' of the conviction of two authorities, Rauscher relates Haider's claims, vocabulary and ideology to National-Socialist beliefs.

In the next paragraph, the author tries to explain why Haider missed his aim of mobilising an 'enormous popular movement' in support of the petition. With the help of three retrospective topoi of consequence, Rauscher offers three reasons for the 'flop'. First, the fact that everybody who signed the petition also had to give her or his name and address, may have deterred many from signing. With this argument, Rauscher implies that many of those who potentially could have signed the petition were well aware of the fact that the claims of the petition violated a social taboo and that anonymity would have reduced the inhibition level that prevented many from signing. Second, and, according to the journalist, more important, Rauscher argues with the observation that the massive opposition to Haider and the petition of so many social groups and institutions may have had a great influence. Third, he assumes that the candlelight march of more than 200,000 people had the strongest impact on the decision whether or not to sign. This third argument is remarkable with regard to at least two different things. It contains, again, an implicit *locus a minore*: if even the many who 'are presumably not particularly foreigner friendly' (please note the rhetorical figure of an understatement, a *litotes*, with the help of which Rauscher expresses his assumption that many of the demonstrators were not consciously anti-anti-foreigner or anti-'xenophobic', but anti-Haider) joined the march, the protest against Haider and the petition must have been felt to be even more urgent. In addition, this passage is interesting for its mode of discourse representation and, thus, of perspectivation: on two occasions the perspective changes from 'they' into 'we', and the form of free indirect speech which is used here indicates that Rauscher empathically identifies with the bourgeoisie about whom he is writing.

In the next paragraph, Rauscher even alludes to Hitler when he writes about Haider in terms of a 'dangerously fascinating radical' who 'has again not won ground'. The denial of such a 'dangerously fascinating radical', was, in Rauscher's view, the central political message of the march. The new dimension of this political statement by a civil society is even more significant, according to the journalist, since even those who are normally in fear of declaring themselves publicly joined the demonstration. The message, in Rauscher's opinion, was not understood by a journalist of the competing newspaper *Die Presse*.

In the last paragraph, Rauscher comes back to the topos of numbers and the second interpretation of the number of signatures, with which he began. He suggests that many were angry with 'the people up there' (please note the reference in terms of metaphorical spatialisation). Again he uses examples: – quite a few (we do not know who) had said: 'I am not for Haider, but they [i.e. the coalition parties and the government] have to feel something at some point'. Here, Rauscher combines a topos of authority (which, because of the character of its construction and the vague reference to the alleged speakers, borders on an *argumentum ad populum*) with the topos of numbers (which, for the same reasons as those mentioned in relation to the topos of authority, approaches a fallacious *argumentum ad numerum*).

The journalist concludes that this kind of reaction will stay, because many do not understand the nearness to National Socialism. 'However, one has to take them and their worries into account, even after this heaviest defeat of Jörg Haider to date'. This last impersonalised indirect appeal (the impersonal 'man' opens a variety of interpretations of who will have to take into account the worries of those who signed the petition, be it the government, or the journalists, including the author himself, or all who engage in anti-discriminatory civil society) is the synthesis of Rauscher's arguments where he relates the two interpretations to each other. The whole column serves to put Haider alongside Hitler, to compare the FPÖ to the Nazis, and, thus, to stress the enormous danger.

Finally, we would like to illustrate the position of *Der Standard* with an analysis of the column by Peter Michael Lingens entitled 'Haider's Wagram – not yet Waterloo', which already alludes to Napoleon in the headline (see Gräf 1999 for a very subtle analysis of other columns of Lingens). The metaphor of charismatic leadership is stressed both by Rauscher and Lingens, but this time the political hero myth is also present (Kargl 1996). The metaphorical title contains a topos of threat that can be paraphrased as follows: since the result of the petition is only Haider's Wagram, and not his Waterloo, one has to fear that Haider's FPÖ will 'conquer' many voters in the coming years, and one should try, therefore, to prevent this 'war of conquest'. The sub-headline states that the crash (in German: '*Absturz*') of Haider's petition only damages the leader of the FPÖ in the long run. As we have already pointed out, the metaphors of accident, crash and shipwrecking were used frequently in editorials by journalists who were against the petition, together with the metaphors of struggle and war. The first group has connotations of fate and catastrophes, the latter of active confrontation.

Author: Peter Michael Lingens

Title: Haider's Wagram – not yet Waterloo.

Text: The crash of his petition only harms the FPÖ-leader in the long term.

Most of the commentaries express, rightly so, satisfaction: the number of signatures in the foreigner petition is not only miles below Haider's announcements, but also far below the hopes of more realistic FPÖ functionaries. Haider's image, leaving as victor on any battlefield he engages upon, has received the biggest scratch so far.

For a conqueror whose popularity is based on the ever-new victories raining down on to the people, it could mean a prophetic significance similar to the defeat at Wagram of Napoleon: Haider can be stopped when he is countered purposefully and energetically enough.

Despite that, after Wagram, Napoleon still conquered half of Europe. It would therefore be fatal to be lulled into hoping that this first big flop of '*Gröschaz*' (the biggest screamer of all times) signals a new trend. More accurately, Haider has more completely succeeded in what all feared: making an issue of the 'foreigners' and awakening the relevant anxieties and fears.

There is a big difference between publicly signing a petition, rejected by the Federal President, the church, the government and the trade unions, and checking off the 'FPÖ' in the anonymity of the ballot-box. It is known that Haider in Graz, by playing the foreigner keyboard, won a landslide victory, although the ensuing petition found very few signatories.

Already at the next election in Lower Austria the sequence of events could simply be turned around: the moderate result of the petition could be followed by a new election victory (especially in the event that all those people vote for Haider, who, in fact, would gladly have signed the petition but failed to do so because of their priest, their works committee or their boss). The election victory in Graz also cut short any possibility that Haider, because of his petition flop, could get into serious trouble in the FPÖ. He will talk himself out of it using 'intimidation of opinion' [in German: '*Meinungsterror*'], and other than that, in the Party-leadership, he sits with fifteen functionaries who agreed with him on the petition.

Not even the position of Heide Schmidt could become better in the short term. On the contrary: nobody creates as much anger as a woman who is proven right. And also the odds are very slight that Haider will in

any case, after the experience of the petition, veer away from his hugely –
even in his own party – controversial anti-EC-course. Precisely because he
has suffered a defeat, he will hurl himself into the next – and therefore far
more promising – battle. The party will grumble and follow.

For it is only in the long term and with reflective party officials (who
have become a rarity in the FPÖ) that Haider has suffered considerable
damage this week. The petition has made clear, not only to the international
Liberals, that the Haider-FPÖ has nothing in common with a Liberal party.
The Sunday-edition of the *Neue Zürcher Zeitung* thus more or less acknowl-
edges that Haider is not only guilty of 'near-Nazi vocabulary' and 'abuse
of xenophobia', in alliance with 'defensive reflexes to all that is justifiably
or unjustifiably considered supranational', but also consistently names the
FPÖ in one breath together with the movements of Le Pen, Schönhuber
and, in his era, Schwarzenbach.

All these movements were or are successful in elections, but they are
not conducive to a coalition. Therein lies the real risk of the Haider course
for the FPÖ: Franz Vranitzky and Erhard Busek no longer stand alone in
their conviction that no coalition could be workable with this party as long
as a Jörg Haider is at its top.

(*Der Standard*, 2 February 1993: 24)

In a very similar way to Rauscher, Lingens suggests in his column that the
defeat of Haider is obvious, but that these are not results which can be taken as
representative of 'normal elections'. Thus, the argumentation is again complex,
viewing the failure of the petition as positive, but the FPÖ and Haider as
enormous threats to democracy (topos of threat). The first three paragraphs
elaborate the historical analogy to Napoleon. According to Lingens, the result
of the petition has to be seen as the largest defeat which Haider has suffered
up to now, and his image is therefore tarnished: 'Haider's image, leaving as
victor on any battlefield he engages upon, has received the biggest scratch so
far'. Lingens concludes the second paragraph with a prospective and hypothetical topos of consequence that Haider, like Napoleon, is only to be stopped
if opposed seriously and determinedly, which was what happened in Wagram
for the first time. Nevertheless, the defeat is equated to a scratch, thus not very
serious. The third paragraph, however, starts out with a counter-argument by
extending the argumentative metaphor of the title: nevertheless, Napoleon
still went on to conquer half of Europe afterwards. This implies, on the basis
of a topos of threat, if we take the analogy further, that it would be wrong to
equate the failure of the petition with the end of 'the biggest screamer of all
times' (please note the debasing metaphor '*Gröschaz*', which has the form of an
ad-hoc acronym).

Moving away from the historical comparison, Lingens begins in this third
paragraph to talk about the 'success of the petition': the success of the petition
was to construct a 'foreigner issue' and to evoke fears and anxieties related to
this 'issue'. Lingens thus points to the political utilisation of the topos of threat

or *argumentum ad baculum* by Haider and the FPÖ, and warns the government and opposition to the petition against feeling safe and complacent (topos of threat). Extending the topic of the result of the petition and its relevance for future elections in the fourth paragraph, the journalist argues that the failure of the petition is the outcome of the massive public opposition, specifically of the authorities of the church, the President, the government and the 'economy' (please note the abstract, collectivising and metonymic reference). Apart from that, the lack of anonymity, in Lingens' view, was an additional reason for the result of the petition. However, the journalist maintains, the conclusion to draw from this result should not be a prognosis that the FPÖ will also lose in future elections. Lingens supports this warning topos of threat with an illustrative example. He reminds the readers that the election in Graz was won by the FPÖ by 'playing the foreigner keyboard' in its campaign. (Note the musical and mechanical metaphor that insinuates a skilfulness in manipulative rhetoric that elicits and evokes anti-foreigner fears.)

In the fifth paragraph, Lingens speculates that the next provincial election in Austria could again turn the tables and result in a new electoral success for the FPÖ. This speculation is backed by the arguments given in the fourth paragraph, as well as by a conclusion rule added in this paragraph: if all those people who would gladly have signed the petition (if they had not been persuaded by the authority of influential social groups and institutions) should vote for Haider, then the FPÖ will again win votes. With this interpretation Lingens suggests, in contrast to Rauscher, that the result of the petition should not be interpreted as a 'political statement' against Haider and the FPÖ, but simply as the outcome of massive opposition by influential forces. In this assumption, Lingens is not very far from Haider's own argumentation, apart from the fact that the leader of the FPÖ resorts to hyperbolic metaphors like 'intimidation of opinion' (in German: *'Meinungsterror'*) which Lingens would probably not use. It suggests, moreover, that there are many more Austrians with an anti-foreigner attitude than those who actually signed.

It is clear for Lingens that the voters and members of the FPÖ are not all Nazis, but that many of them are, nevertheless, racist or 'xenophobic'. Declaring the FPÖ members to be Nazis would mean both downplaying the crimes of the Nazis and misinterpreting the actual populist politics of this party as well as their impact. And arguing, as Rauscher does, that many signed the petition not because of its content but because of their anti-government attitudes also minimises the actual impact and relevance of ethnicist, 'xenophobic' or racist beliefs of Austrians.

However, in the sixth paragraph Lingens opposes two more arguments made by the anti-Haider press: the journalist recalls the widespread knowledge of the hierarchical structure of the FPÖ and predicts that Haider will have no trouble with his fellow party members (who will follow him in any case) but also not with Heide Schmidt, a former MP and member of the FPÖ who left the party because of its anti-Europe and anti-foreigner policies and formed a new party, the Liberal Forum. The reader following this argumentation is left with serious doubts whether the result of the petition could in any way be interpreted as a defeat. But, as the structure of the article suggests, a conclusion is still missing.

Lingens provides us with his evaluation at the end of the article in the seventh and eighth paragraphs. He does not relate the two arguments to each other, as Rauscher did, but brings a third option into play, namely Haider's damaged image abroad. Using the topos of historical comparison, he relates Haider's party with the 'fate' of other populist and neo-right parties in Europe, with Schönhuber, Schwarzenbach and Le Pen. The Liberal International has distanced itself from Haider (first example), and the *Neue Zürcher Zeitung* suggests that Haider is using National-Socialist vocabulary. In addition to this accusation Lingens cites two more reproaches of Haider and the FPÖ by this Swiss quality paper, viz. the accusation of Haider's 'abuse of the fear of foreigners' and of Haider's rejection of everything supranational (second example in support of his assertion of the damaged image; see also above on p. 180 on the question of whether this example has the character of an *argumentum ad verecundiam*).

Lingens interprets the reaction from abroad as reassuring. He believes that as long as Haider is the leader of the FPÖ, the party may still win at elections but that it is not a party with which to form coalitions (in German: '*nicht koalitionsfähig*'), because it would damage Austria's image abroad (where Haider in some respects has the image of a 'potential small Hitler'), alluding to the election of Waldheim who was then even put on the Watchlist in the USA.

The statements of this article are ambivalent, and, almost exactly seven years after the publishing of the article, the conclusions will, at least in the essential, second part, prove to be wrong: on the one hand, Lingens argues that Haider is still very dangerous (Wagram is not Waterloo); on the other hand, he implicitly predicts a large defeat (Waterloo) and a 'fate' similar to the other European neo-right parties, all of which have a much lower percentage of support than the FPÖ. He makes it very clear that the future of the FPÖ depends largely on the political culture in Austria, i.e. on the question of whether another party would actually form a coalition with the FPÖ. This question remained unanswered until 4 February 2000, when, after three months of political negotiation between the SPÖ, ÖVP and FPÖ, the ÖVP dared to form a coalition with the FPÖ, because the ambitious leader of the Austrian People's Party, Wolfgang Schüssel, wanted to seize the unique and most probably never-returning opportunity of becoming Austrian Chancellor, willingly accepting the biggest political crisis in the Second Austrian Republic.

The processes of recontextualisation of arguments from the petition and the laws to public discourse, in slogans as well as in the media, is very complex; the tabloids react to the presentation of the petition text and its rationale, which are often selectively quoted or alluded to in the articles, slogans and advertisements. The quality newspapers elaborate the background and underlying assumptions of the petition and interpret the whole debate as a power struggle between the government and the FPÖ.

In the analysis of the textual relationship between the texts that we examined, we were able to observe at least two forms of intertextuality: explicit surface relationships between texts, and implicit thematic chains which relate texts to each other via underlying assumptions and presuppositions. We have been able to deal only selectively with the issue of intertextuality in this chapter and will refrain from any further detailed discussion (except for an example in the last section of this chapter, i.e. an excerpt from a television interview with Jörg Haider in November 1997), since we must still present and discuss another facet of the 'petition story', viz. the legislatively prescribed dealing with the petition in parliament. In order not to inflate this chapter unnecessarily, we will forego any detailed linguistic and rhetorical analysis, expecting from our readers that our argument thus far will enable them to apply the main categories of linguistic analysis for themselves. We will therefore look only briefly at a number of sequences from the parliamentary debate in which the petition was discussed and decided upon.

The petition in parliament

On 23 September 1993, the Austrian parliament considered the Austria First Petition, as required by the constitution. Because of the defeat of the petition, nobody was in any doubt that it would fail in parliament. Nevertheless, there were heated statements by leading politicians of the FPÖ, the SPÖ, the ÖVP, the Liberal Forum and the Green Party, which illustrate very well the different ideological positions taken on the politically constructed 'foreigner issue', and which we have already shown in some of the previously analysed genres. In the following, we analyse selectively the turns of Jörg Haider (FPÖ), Robert Elmecker (SPÖ), Terezija Stoisits (Green Party) and Heide Schmidt (Liberal Forum). This will enable us to contrast the four most polarised positions with each other. The rest of the debate will be summarised.

First, we quote the statement of the subcommittee which had been debating the petition since 22 April 1993:

> Ladies and gentlemen! The National Council has asked the Federal Minister of Internal Affairs to present a report on the execution of the mentioned laws in order to be able to react appropriately in case of problems. The first 'migration report' has already been presented to the National Council and this showed that changes in the existing laws are not necessary at this time. However, the National Council will further scrutinise the situation and will receive a further report from the Federal Minister of Internal Affairs in the autumn of this year. Out of these considerations the Internal Affairs Committee concludes that based on the Austria First Petition legal measures are not required. As a result of its consultations the Council for Internal Affairs moves that the National Council take note of this report.[8]

The subcommittee recommends that the petition proposals should not be considered because the existing legal situation is adequate to cope with social problems resulting from migration. The first speaker, accorded exactly 20 minutes, is Jörg Haider. In his speech, he points to several other petitions which have never been acknowledged, the issues of which were taken up years later. The same, he predicts, would be the case with this petition. The speech can be divided into four basic parts, each of which carries an important argument in Haider's attempt to justify the petition and to persuade the members of parliament to vote for it. After the introduction, which is mainly a positive self-presentation as being the party which cares most for Austrian citizens, he enumerates the points of the petition which are all concerned with the well-being of Austrians (topos of 'to the advantage of us', technically speaking, *topos pro bono nobis*). Thus, immigration has to be stopped immediately ('*sofortiger Einwanderungsstopp*') because of housing problems; only if sufficient apartments are available for Austrians, should foreigners be allowed to enter the country. Note that Haider always talks about 'Austrians', which might be taken to imply German speakers only, rather than 'Austrian citizens', and adheres to this usage in other contexts. This assumption can be verified when looking at later parts of his speech. The same, he continues, is true for employment policies: only if the 200,000 unemployed Austrians had jobs, could foreigners be accepted. He presents himself as a 'speaker of the population' (positive self-presentation) and succeeds in dividing the audience into 'we' (the Austrians concerned about Austria's future) and 'you' or 'they' (the other politicians who are not concerned with what people think and need). The topos of 'to the advantage of us' and the topos of threat/danger predominate in this part of his speech:

> Ladies and gentlemen! All this is immediate cause for us to clarify that with the throwing out of the petition, we, members of the Freedom Party, will be, as of today, the advocates of the Austrians in Parliament on this important matter and we will keep on reminding them that, in defiance of better knowledge, they have trampled an important matter of concern to the Austrian population ... But we will remind them that on the other hand 400,000 people have publicly announced in a democratic decision, by signing a petition, that it is a matter of concern for them that the problem of housing in Austria ... should first be taken care of for Austrians before this problem is intensified by further immigration. [9]

The third part of Haider's speech is dedicated to the alleged hypocrisy which he detects in the governing parties and which we have sought to expose in this chapter. The FPÖ – as shown above – used the anti-foreigner statements of leading politicians cleverly in their propaganda. Haider accuses the governing politicians of having joined SOS-Mitmensch only because of the political fight against himself, but not for humanitarian reasons. With this accusation, he attempts to undermine the credibility of the topos of humanitarianism employed by members of the governing parties and clearly provokes the following speakers who are also concerned with their positive self-presentation:

> In the meantime, it has dawned even on the SOS-activists that they were politically abused, for it was not concern for a humanitarian immigration

policy that brought the government to support this action, but, once and for all, visibly the fear of an all-too-successful petition that was initiated by the Freedom Party.[10]

In the last part of his speech, Haider uses stories as illustrative examples of the worries of the population: quotes from teachers who cannot cope with foreign children in their schools (topos of burdening and argumentative example – technically speaking, *exemplum*). This part has to be seen as evidence for the second part of Haider's contribution, where the FPÖ leader merely enumerated the problems. Haider attacks several politicians and criticises them for seeming to neglect the interests of the Austrian population, again using quotes and stories as seemingly representative and valid proof. Finally, he closes his speech with an appeal to solve the problems raised by him and the FPÖ, to take the petition seriously and to decide on concrete measures based on the petition.

Without going into detail here, we are able to distinguish several rhetorical argumentative techniques in Haider's anti-foreigner discourse. Haider uses positive self-presentation strategies to present himself as protector of the rights and interests of Austrians, thus constructing 'insiders' and 'outsiders'. Austrians are those with German as a native language, not those with Austrian citizenship. He discursively constructs various other groups: politicians of other parties, those with humanitarian interests, and 'foreigners'. After having defined the social actors, he argues and rationalises as follows: the social problems which obviously exist are all projected by Haider on to the immigration of foreigners (scapegoating strategy), so that anxieties and fears are evoked (topos of threat). The threat is then quasi-objectified with numbers (topos of numbers or *argumentum ad numerum*), and with the *vox populi* (*argumentum ad populum*). And, finally, Haider unmasks the leading politicians and accuses them of hypocrisy. The FPÖ is presented as the party which can save Austria and the 'real' Austrians. All these rhetorical techniques may be seen as a perfect recipe for gaining votes, for increasing the level of distrust in the existing government and for producing and reproducing 'xenophobic', ethnicist and racist attitudes and beliefs.

The second speaker is Robert Elmecker, member of the SPÖ, the largest party in Austria. He also has 20 minutes for his contribution. Much less persuasive and rhetorically skilled, Elmecker tries to legitimise the policies of the government. All the existing laws are good enough to cope with the problems, the proposals of the petition are not necessary:

> Through the laws agreed upon by parliament – in particular the Federal Protection Law [*Bundesbetreuungsgesetz*], the Asylum Law, the Residence – and Foreigners Law – the legal means have been created to overcome the special situation that Austria was confronted with through the immigration wave – in particular after the opening of the East and because of the situation in former Yugoslavia.[11]

Thus, the SPÖ does not reject the petition as such, on humanitarian or anti-racist grounds. They do so for pragmatic reasons. Moreover, by enumerating all the existing laws, Elmecker provides examples and proofs of the capacity to cope with immigration (topos of law, partly with the character of an *argumentum ad verecundiam* and topos of example). This implicitly proves Haider's point about the double standards of governmental policies: the SPÖ does not oppose the petition on ideological grounds, but because the claims of the petition seem unnecessary. Elmecker then moves on, in an attempt to provide a positive self-presentation, and enumerates several examples where the laws have helped refugees, which serves to legitimise the restrictive legal situation: 'Twenty-one per cent of political asylum requests positively processed! No other European country can show such a high acceptance quota as we in Austria'.[12]

At the end of his turn, he summarises the goals of Social Democratic foreigner policies:

> Specifically in this sensitive area of foreigner policy we are for well-defined, but also well-considered measures; that has been the case so far and will also be so in the future.[13]

This statement remains very vague; the measures are 'well-considered': what does this mean? How are they to be evaluated in respect to hostility to 'foreigners' and immigrants? The area of 'foreigner policy' is 'sensitive': in what respect, we might ask?

Because of this vagueness and the absence of clear ideological positioning, the SPÖ is attacked from two sides: by the Green Party and the opposition in SOS-Mitmensch on the one hand, and by the FPÖ on the other hand. The latter find the laws not restrictive enough, the others find them too restrictive and inhumane (topos of humanitarianism). The SPÖ chooses the easy way out of this dilemma and confines itself to pragmatic and formal arguments, vague and ambivalent (see Billig *et al.* 1988 for discussion of such typical ideological dilemmas).

The next speaker is Terezija Stoisits, member of the Green Party and renowned for her anti-discriminatory involvement. As early as June 1992, she had accused the governing parties and the FPÖ of deciding on racist laws: 'The fact that the government's draft residence law, along with several amendments proposed in the committee, was passed with the support of the FPÖ, ÖVP and SPÖ, confirms that the FPÖ has prevailed with its 'xenophobic' [in German: *ausländerfeindlich*] policies', was her judgement in a session of the subcommittee (see Mitten 1994a: 35). She uses her 20 minutes for something very different compared to the two previous speakers. She rejects debating the petition as such and focuses on the laws which the government has put forward, specifically the Residence Law, passed in July 1993 (discussed at the beginning of the chapter):

> Ladies and gentlemen! In some respects I am grateful to the Freedom faction, that we today, on the basis of the petition, which in principle we don't have to discuss – for me, this case was closed six months ago when literally hundreds of thousands (of people) opposed this petition publicly,

with faces and names – have the opportunity to discuss precisely these really current problems of Austrian domestic politics in connection with the Foreigner Law.[14]

Stoisits emphasises the problem of the clause stipulating a six-week limit for obtaining a new residence permit after the expiration of the old one: the applicant has to leave the country even if the delay is due to the inefficiency of the administration. Thus, she proposes an amendment to the existing law which would exclude the passage containing the six-week restriction. And she justifies this proposal as follows:

> Honourable ladies and gentlemen! Even if it may appear to you to be a minor detail in a law containing fifteen paragraphs, for thousands of people in Austria who do not possess an Austrian passport nor citizenship but live here, it means a push into illegality and, as a further consequence, expulsion from this country.[15]

In contrast to Haider, Stoisits constructs different social actors linguistically: people without Austrian citizenship and an Austrian passport, and those who possess these two things, not 'real' Austrians, and 'others'. Her definition of an Austrian is thus related to citizenship and not to ethnic criteria (topos of definition). Moreover, she redefines the problem: it is not a minor one, but a very large one, with large and inhumane consequences for many people (topos of humanitarianism, topos of numbers). The rest of her 20 minutes is used to elaborate the situation of non-Austrian citizens in Austria and the terrible bureaucratic barriers they are confronted with. Stoisits also explicitly emphasises that the law as it was then was legally wrong. She ends her statement by using the topos of numbers, but differently in comparison with the two preceding speakers:

> Ladies and gentlemen! One glance at the absolute figures tells us how far the understanding for the persecuted, for refugees and for the acceptance of these people in Austria has degenerated. No other word than 'degenerated' is appropriate here.[16]

The evaluation is very significant here: 'degenerated' is usually used in relation to deviance and criminality. Thus, she makes a predication with extremely negative connotations for the policies of the two major parties. And in analogy to the last words of Haider, she also uses an appeal: 'Migration policies will be in the future, as they are today, one of the main emphases in political debate – I'm convinced of that'.[17]

Stoisits is the only speaker until now who actually draws on a different argumentation, a moral and humanitarian one which intersects with the political and administrative-legal argumentation. Her turn is of substantial interest in our context because she resorts to a counter-argumentation which might serve as a model for other debates about discrimination: she pins down formally incorrect issues, and does not enter into a polemical debate on the same level as the other speakers. Her contribution is based on the ethical values of human rights.

The next two speakers are Hubert Pirker (ÖVP) and Heide Schmidt (Liberal Forum). Pirker underlines the arguments of Elmecker, because the ÖVP is also part of the government. He repeats that the existing laws are good enough and that the new problems since 1989/90 have been handled very well. Pirker concedes that there are still minor issues here and there which need to be analysed and dealt with, and he concludes with a short summary of the position of the ÖVP:

> The present situation is no reason for a panic-orchestra, neither a panic-orchestra from the left nor a panic-orchestra from the right. To preserve the stability and security of Austria we do not need these extreme points of view, neither from the one side nor from the other, but a balanced and sound foreigner policy. We must free ourselves from these initial difficulties.[18]

Pirker evokes a very emotional metaphor which combines fear and music, thus meaning irrationality and chaos. He employs political 'flag words' and 'high value' words like 'stability' and 'security'. And he reiterates the vagueness of the SPÖ, a 'balanced' and 'sound' foreigner policy which is not clearly defined, but – with respect to the wording – has positive connotations.

Heide Schmidt touches upon a different issue. She was the former member of the FPÖ who left the party because of the petition and the anti-Europe politics of Haider, and has created a new party, '*das Liberale Forum*' (see above). At the time of this debate, she was the third President of the National Assembly. She asks the question whether a petition is the right democratic instrument with which to decide upon such sensitive issues as migration or the death penalty. In her view, Haider had abused the democratic tool for party political reasons. She continues by explicitly pointing to the racist formulations and issues in the petition – the only speaker in this debate to do so. She does not make vague statements, but is very clear in her evaluation: the petition is biologistic, racist and nationalist. Further, Schmidt points to the fact that certain terms used by the FPÖ, like '*Umvolkung*', have a Nazi past. We cite this passage from her speech in full:

> This petition was through its title clearly intended to create patriotism. I believe patriotism is something positive. I myself am a supporter of it. However, I believe that this petition did not awaken patriotism, but a deviation from it, a deformation of it, namely a nationalism that in the end leads to a fear-ridden persecution mania. It is expressed by the word 'repopulation' [in German; '*Umvolkung*'] (shout: depopulation!) that ever and again comes from the ranks of the FPÖ, a persecution mania which is

clearly supported by a kind of purity concept, for it cannot be otherwise explained that one could be afraid of the fact that there are now perhaps a few among us with different origins. For 'repopulation' does not mean social circumstances, but ethnic ones.

And this is precisely what it's all about. I'd like to express what patriotism means to me. It is not just love for my country, it is not just the protection of certain traditional values, but for me patriotism means responsibility for what happens in a nation, responsibility for what happens to the people in our republic and by our republic. For exactly this reason it was intolerable for me to experience what this petition intended to trigger and what, in part, it has already started.

For the first time expression was given to the idea that we should set as a national objective our own protection. That is not a national objective for an open society. I wouldn't have that as a national objective for my home country. For the first time, the fear of people has been orchestrated, for the first time there has been an attempt to divide people according to their origin. When I say here 'for the first time' I am talking about our Republic and not of our ill-fated past. That is what is being awakened again here, which worries and frightens me. For it is incorrect – everyone who can read, will agree – that the impression is created that point six of this petition means only the language-proficiency of the children. Point seven is designed for this problem, which does exist, and which is why we have a need for regulation in this area. Point six is really deliberately added as an origins paragraph, for it does not concern language proficiency but it is about the background of non-German mother-tongue, which equals origins.

I say this, because it was exactly that point which was most elaborately discussed in the FPÖ committees. That is, anyone who is a member of a committee knows it was turned into a problem and knows therefore in what direction the decisions were made.

Among others – but I don't want to speak prematurely – it was also Thomas Barmüller who made this issue the main focus in his faction. In his faction, because he is not a member of the executive; it was me who took over in the executive. Both in the executive as in other committees, it was this point that was discussed extensively. The outcome was that it was discovered that regulations were required for people who are of a different origin than German [Shout from FPÖ: 'That was never said!'].

For me this is the expression of biologistic thinking, for me it is an expression of a purity concept, for me it means a gateway to inhumanity [applause by the Liberal Forum]. I feel this as an unfortunate reawakening of ideas from the past. We know where they led and where they can lead.

That, too, was a reason for political change, through it something became clear, which a lot of people recognised no later than 1988 as a tendency – I admit, not me – a tendency that started with a counting of the domestic unemployed and the numbers of foreigners. Let me just remind you of the New Year's gathering of 1988 – I'm not saying this for the first time. It is not true that I applauded then, it is not true that I accepted it – those people who said this know it from me – but one thing is correct: I really did not believe that this remark announced a tendency. I did believe that other matters were meant, I truly believed that a strong aphorism could also be used as an honest instrument to make this government aware of the need to act. Through this petition, however, it has become clear what tendency was really meant. And therefore we cannot give in to this petition. Thank you [Applause by the Liberal Forum].[19]

Schmidt also provides MPs with an explanation for the FPÖ petition: perse-cution-mania, irrational fears, 'xenophobia', scapegoating. And she attempts to show how the petition could be a 'gateway to inhumanity'. Ever since then, Heide Schmidt has been one of the few Austrian politicians who were able to confront and defeat Haider in TV-debates and on similar occasions: first, because she had been an insider in the FPÖ and had all the necessary knowledge about the party practices; second, because she is a brilliant and courageous speaker; third, because she clearly positioned herself ideologically in a very different sphere from the FPÖ and also the governing parties; fourth, because of her education as a lawyer, she possesses the legal know-how of argumentation in the issue of immigration laws. It is very unfortunate that in the 1999 election to the National Assembly, the Liberal Forum did not obtain enough votes to be represented in the new parliament. It is certainly not by chance, but as a consequence of the Austrian political climate, which we have illustrated with so many examples.

The argumentative positions presented above manifest the different convictions of the political parties and their views on 'foreigners' and migration policies. Haider clearly formulates and legitimises his anti-foreigner policies by evoking fear and anxieties about the housing and the job situation. He creates two opposing groups of social actors, the 'real' Austrians and the 'others', foreigners who threaten the well-being of Austrians. His positive self-presentation consists of constructing the image of the protector and advocate of the rights and interests of the Austrians. The position of the SPÖ and ÖVP is pragmatic and vague: they are also concerned about the problems of Austrians, but both governing parties emphasise that the existing measures are good and capable of solving all problems. Thus, their argumentation is not anti-discriminatory, anti-racist or humanitarian, but pragmatic; it is not directed against the petition as such, but against the necessity of new and more restrictive measures. They both also aim at legitimising the existing laws by enumerating examples of positive policies with moral values, and by mitigating the problems inherent in the laws. Terezija Stoisits from the Green Party, however, unmasks the policies of the government. Her counter-argumentation is not directed against the FPÖ – she willingly ignores the petition – but against the existing legal situation. Stoisits introduces ethical, humanitarian values into the debate. Finally, Heide Schmidt is the only speaker who clearly attacks the FPÖ and exposes their discriminatory policies and politics. The two women thus lead the counter-argumentation in two different ways – by introducing other dimensions in order to view the problems of immigration policies as a whole, and by clearly pointing to the biologistic racist argumentation in the petition.

After Heide Schmidt, the Minister of Interior Affairs takes his turn to outline the policies of the government. Finally, the petition is defeated by a large majority.

Perspectives: the continuity of the discourse

While the Austria First Petition has so far been a unique 'xenophobic' incident in the political-parliamentary history of the Second Austrian Republic, there is to this day a continuity of this discriminatory discourse as far as the recurrence of the main topics and topoi of the petition and petition campaign are concerned. Although we cannot really show this constancy in detail in the present chapter, we want to give at least one concluding instance that shows the continuity of the 'anti-foreigner discourse'.

In November 1997, the FPÖ decided on a new party program which again contains anti-foreigner slogans, but also the ambivalently calculated propagation of Christian virtues like charity ('*Nächstenliebe*'). Now, the party is trying to target new sections of the population – who had been, until then, out of reach for the FPÖ – and to win more votes. In an interview in the late evening news on Austrian state television, the '*Zeit im Bild 2*' on 29 October 1997, Jörg Haider was questioned on the new program and on his anti-foreigner position. He was asked by the newsreader and interviewer Robert Hochner (RH), how the new Christian values fit with the exclusion of others, e.g. foreigners:

RH: Dr Haider, in this party program, Christian values and the obligation to defend these Christian values are relatively strongly emphasised – uh, but there is no Christian xenophobia, Christianity does not distinguish between Austrians and foreigners and Christianity in fact obliges people – who don't have a lot, even to share what one has – how does – does this in fact fit into the politics of your party?

JH: First of all we are Christian during [the time of] disintegrating privileges because we are the only ones who are voluntarily making an income sacrifice – whereas, in times of the savings package, from the Federal Chancellor right to all of the ministers, regional leaders, regional government members, every one has given him- and herself the gift of salary increases. That's the first thing that's Christian about us. The second is – ah, that we take the words of the Pope seriously and – ah there – the cur-/current Pope made it very clear that neighbourly love really means to care of your immediate neighbour and not to embrace the whole world but also to think of the Austrians.

RH: So, your neigh-/the neighbour has to have an Austrian passport for you to love him.

JH: Not necessarily but he has to have a legal residence permit for th/this country because otherwise for us it'll be that one – ah – lets in illegals –

and then in the end it creates a problem for the Austrians and the foreigners residing legally here. So, in that respect we are very much – on the basis of the rule of law – and because:/the reactions of the government show how only that we are completely on the right track, also with the – ah- 'Austria First' outline, that we are thinking about this country: and that we want to stop the sell-out, or rather an unrestrained immigration in any case [See the German text in Appendix 4.2].

The interviewer's question puts Haider into a dilemma – how do Christian values fit with ethnicist policies hostile to 'foreigners'? Haider – as usual – does not answer the question directly, but shifts topic by considering other arguments which he defines as Christian. According to his new definition and reformulation of 'Christian', the cutback in politicians' privileges would symbolise Christian values, in times of economising. This whole sequence is an excellent example of a topos of definition: Haider decontextualises the term '*Nächstenliebe*' (best translated as 'brotherly and sisterly love', 'neighbourly love' or 'Christian charity') from the Christian context (the church uses this term for every human being) and constructs a very limited extensional meaning of the term that refers only to the German-speaking Austrians.

The FPÖ politicians are the only ones who have renounced salary increases – this, Haider claims, is Christian. And then he uses a legitimising *argumentum ad verecundiam* and quotes the Pope, who made it clear that 'charity' means the helping of neighbours. Haider takes this argument further: helping others does not mean embracing the whole world, it means thinking of the Austrians first. 'Neighbours' are redefined in their extensional meaning; this is the second application of the same rhetorical device in this interview. This strategy allows a positive self-presentation as the protector of Austrian rights and interests. The interviewer becomes cynical and asks if this might mean that the neighbour in the Christian sense could only be somebody with an Austrian passport, thus ironically dismantling the misuse of the Christian concept and making the chauvinist implications explicit. Haider picks up the interviewer's choice of irony and goes on to say that 'the neighbour' should at least have a legal residence permit, legitimating this claim with a topos of threat. If unrestrained immigration is not stopped, then Austria will have enormous problems. Here, Haider kicks at an open door and seems fallaciously to attack a straw man, as no Austrian politician, from the governmental parties least of all, would endorse 'unrestrained immigration'. Haider seems to recognise that – with the statement just uttered – he lags behind the actual developments in Austrian policies towards immigrants. Thus, he quickly points to the policies and politics of the government which, he implicitly claims, has been or is implementing the proposals of the petition of 1992 and 1993, and this would prove how right the policy pursued by the FPÖ would have been in the past and still is.

Although the Austrian 'anti-foreigner discourse' has slightly changed over the years, the explicit reference to the petition of 1992 and 1993, the – albeit outdated – picking up of the claim of 'stopping unrestrained immigration', the fallacious use of the topos of threat, and even the *argumentum ad verecundiam* (one may think of the false appeal of the *Neue Freie Zeitung* to the Pope, who allegedly completely justified the Austria First Petition, and of Alois Huber, who backed his argument against the 'mixture of races' by the fallacious appeal to the 'Creator') and the topos of definition, all strongly remind one of the Austria First campaign of 1992 and 1993. Then and now, Haider emphasises that he is – first and foremost – thinking of the Austrians. The short excerpt from an interview with Haider four years later illustrates that the fall of the petition in parliament on 23 September 1993 did not prevent the FPÖ from continuing their nationalist, ethnicist and racist policies. It is worrying that, since 1993, the FPÖ has constantly increased its level of support, in October 1999 receiving the support of 26.91 per cent of Austrian voters.

This excerpt, once again, illustrates some of the persuasive rhetorical techniques that Haider uses in public discussions. Even Robert Hochner, one of the most famous TV interviewers in the ORF, cannot keep up with Haider, and, therefore, resorts to cynicism and irony in his attempt to uncover Haider's contradictory, racist and ethnicist argumentation.

Having analysed the 'xenophobic' examples of five different genres from different fields of political action and public spaces, we will now attempt to draw some conclusions about the genesis, dissemination and impact of discriminatory argumentation within the discourse about 'foreigners' and immigrants. In contrast to postwar-antisemitism in Austria (chapter 3), hostility towards 'foreigners' is rarely only latent or insinuated linguistically. In the contexts we analysed, blatant and explicit prejudices against non-Austrian citizens or 'foreigners' are frequently visible in the streets as signs and posters in the texts of politicians of the FPÖ and the governing parties as well as in the media, in particular in the tabloid press. Moreover, legal measures and official documents support this kind of discrimination – even in laws, decrees or official notifications (see chapter 5 and van Leeuwen and Wodak 1999) containing explicit ethnicist or even biologist arguments and legitimations for discriminatory measures. The variety and range of linguistic realisations is wide, but not as widespread as in texts with anti-Jewish contents, where allusions of every kind are an extremely frequent rhetorical technique. Metaphors of all kinds, prejudiced predications, insulting nominations of social actors, and discriminatory argumentation schemes (topoi and fallacies) are typical. The range of arguments is very large (see also chapter 2, 'Arguing for and against discrimination'), and the petition represents a first attempt to summarise in textual form the most frequent prejudices about 'foreigners'. The discursive reproduction of these prejudices forms a continuum up to the slogans employed in the 1999 election (see below). The most significant distinguishing feature between the mainstream parties and the FPÖ is not the position on immigration (where there are differences only of degree) but the discursive legitimation devices used for certain demands with possibly segregatory and exclusionary effects. The FPÖ has no difficulty with using a lexicon and vocabulary which are close to Nazi terminology, whereas this would be taboo for the mainstream parties.

In addition, biologistic arguments and the appeal for 'purity of language and blood' are not used in *Realpolitik*. The mainstream parties make extensive use of positive 'flag words', of the topos of numbers or the *argumentum ad numerum*, of economist arguments (see Matouschek *et al.* 1995) and so on: their position is 'pragmatic'.

The recontextualisation of the politicians' arguments in the media is complex: the newspapers are clearly divided on the 'immigration issue', between tabloids in favour of the petition and a 'halt to immigration', and quality papers which – for different reasons – all oppose the government's 'foreigner policy' and the FPÖ. The parliamentary debates contain anti-discriminatory argumentation as well, in our case led by two women from the Green and Liberal Parties. Thus, parliamentary discussion and the media, as well as 'the streets' (the *Lichtermeer*), are situated within different, interrelated fields of political action in which discursive confrontation, conflicts and debates are held, unfortunately almost never in accordance with the model of deliberative, discursive democracy which we will try to elaborate in chapters 5 and 6.

On 3 October 1999 the FPÖ won 26.91 per cent of votes, after conducting an election campaign with blatant and explicit ethnicist and racist slogans against foreigners. The FPÖ is currently the second largest party in Austria. In this election, the SPÖ lost 6 percent, and the conservative party, the ÖVP, was mostly able to retain its level of support. The only progressive party which succeeded in gaining votes is the Green Party, which gained 2 per cent (now about 8 per cent). The Liberal Forum with Heide Schmidt failed to win any parliamentary representation.

During the campaign, the SPÖ as well as the ÖVP (who formed a coalition government until October 1999) seemed paralysed. On 1 October 1999, thousands of people gathered on St Stephen's Square and applauded the FPÖ leader Jörg Haider as he gave his last speech before the elections, welcoming 'our Viennese citizens', whom he promised 'to protect against foreigners and against unemployment'. The slogans '*Stop der Überfremdung*' ('Stop over-foreignisation') and '*Stop dem Asylmißbrauch*' ('Stop the misuse of asylum') were accompanied by loud cheers and some whistles from those who dared to disturb. Police were stationed all around the square, the atmosphere was tense, but most of the bystanders had broad smiles on their faces. Moreover, the headline of the *Neue Kronen Zeitung* was already celebrating Haider's 'March into the Chancellery' four days before the election.

What has Haider now become, and what kind of party is the FPÖ in the year 2000? Does this rise of populism, racism and hostility towards 'aliens' correspond to broader social changes in Europe, or is it a unique Austrian phenomenon? Many of the demands in the Austria First Petition were implemented by the governing parties in subsequent years. But there were also a number of scandals concerning the FPÖ. To mention only a few:

On 30 September 1995 in the Carinthian town of Krumpendorf, the 'Kameradschaft IV' (K-IV), a Waffen-SS veterans' organisation, held its annual gathering on the evening before the general war veterans' commemoration in nearby Ulrichsberg (see Mitten 1999). Traditionally, the K-IV meeting is the occasion for former members of the SS, Waffen-SS and the Wehrmacht to trade stories from Hitler's war, and to cultivate what they take to be proper Germanic values. Among the guests at this particular K-IV reunion were several highly decorated former SS and Waffen-SS dignitaries, a few convicted war criminals, and Heinrich Himmler's daughter. Near the end of the scheduled festivities, Jörg Haider arrived to stormy applause. After attacking the 'moral terrorism' (in German: '*Tugendterror*') of the 'politically correct', 'welfare cheats', artists who receive public money but then criticise Austria (or the FPÖ), Haider quickly moved on to his main theme, the exemplary moral fortitude of those present, 'who have character and who remain true to their convictions against strong headwinds, and who have remained true to them until today'. In his analysis of Haider's politics, Mitten (1999) analyses Haider's speech and subsequent activities and policies: ' "Moral uprightness [*Anständigkeit*]", Haider added, "will always prevail in our world; even if at the moment we cannot win a majority, we are spiritually [*geistig*] superior to the others and that is something very crucial". These utterances and the lexicon are clearly close to Nazi ideology and the ideas of the "*Übermensch*". The remarks were but the latest in a string of statements which evoke repugnant images of "revisionist" history and apologia for Nazis' crimes. Next to his belief, expressed in 1985, that convicted war criminal Walter Reder had merely "done his duty" as a soldier; his praise of the German armed forces during the Second World War for having laid "the foundations for peace and freedom" in Europe; or his endorsement of the Nazis "sound employment policies", Haider's attempt to refurbish the tainted honour of the Waffen-SS seemed almost restrained'.

In the autumn of 1997, the FPÖ presented a new party program, which, in its calculated ambivalence, emphasised Christian values and succeeded in integrating new voters (see above). Currently, the FPÖ is the largest right-wing party in Western Europe (Mitten 1994a; Bailer-Galanda and Neugebauer 1997) which, more than any other Austrian party, persuasively sets the 'xenophobic' anti-foreigner tone in Austria. The electoral success achieved with populist slogans is even more surprising if one knows that Austria today is one of the richest countries in the world, has one of the lowest inflation rates in Western Europe and also one of the lowest rates of unemployment. Comparisons with the *Weimarer Republik* or with Austria between the two World Wars – which were often used in FPÖ propaganda during the election campaign – are thus completely wrong.

What then is responsible for the success of Haider and his party (a classical *Führerpartei*)? We would like to attempt some explanations which illustrate that there are Austrian peculiarities on many levels, but also supranational, and indeed global (economic and ideological) implications and phenomena (see Wodak 2000). Since 1945, Austria, a very small neutral state with a population of eight million, has had difficulties in establishing its new identity *vis-à-vis* Germany and in trying to come to terms with its Nazi past (Wodak *et al.* 1999). The effort to establish a strong identity and positive ingroup, however, is often connected with the construction of negative outgroups. After the fall of the Iron Curtain in 1989, Austria lost its function of being a 'bridge' between the East and the West; and new compensatory functions have not yet been found. Joining the European Union (EU) in 1995 did not solve the problem either. On the contrary, the tensions between national state ideology and supranational convictions have noticeably increased.

Viewed from a historical perspective, racist, ethnicist and 'xenophobic' prejudices are strongly rooted in the Austrian tradition. Ethnic groups were often used as scapegoats for economic and social problems. Before World War Two, Jews were discriminated against, and antisemitism was a 'normal' feature of Austrian political culture. Nowadays, at the beginning of the new millennium, hostility towards 'foreigners' has become a *quasi*-'normality'. When the first immigrants from the former Eastern Bloc entered Austria in 1989/90, discriminatory slogans were used by all political parties except for the Green Party, but they were never as explicit as the slogans used by the FPÖ in the 1999 election campaign: The main poster of the FPÖ during this election campaign said '*Stop der Überfremdung*' ('Stop overforeignisation'), a term coined by the Nazis and used by Göbbels in 1933. Opposition to the FPÖ discourse was small: parts of the Catholic and Protestant Churches, the Jewish *Kultusgemeinde*, the Green, Liberal and Communist Parties, and some intellectuals. The two major parties feared they would lose support if they gave voice to counter-slogans, and condemned the racist and 'xenophobic' propaganda only a week before the election.

Moreover, the personality of Haider (and his suntanned telegenic appearance) are a significant factor for the popularity of the FPÖ: Haider is certainly a charismatic politician who is very persuasive and suggestive rhetorically in the field of political self-presentation (for example, in the media). He constructs his new image as a statesman very cleverly, for example by participating in summer courses at Harvard University for three successive years.

With respect to the supranational European level, the fear of the 'eastern expansion' of the EU is politically functionalised by the FPÖ and used to evoke fears of unemployment and of being 'colonised by the Islamic culture'. The 'globalisation rhetoric' of EU policy, with its main focus on 'flexibility and competitiveness' as a safeguard against unemployment, causes many fears (Weiss and Wodak 2000a, Muntigl, Weiss and Wodak 2000). People are afraid of losing the traditional securities of the Austrian welfare state which have been implemented over the past twenty-five years of Socialist and Grand Coalition government. Change seems inevitable, but the coalition parties have not succeeded in proposing adequate measures. Moreover, they have seemed to be trapped in the Austrian model of 'social partnership' which has made any significant changes very difficult. The FPÖ, on the other hand, is promising to protect jobs, and accuses the coalition parties of 'giving in' to 'international pressure'. They proclaim the necessity of a 'turn' (*Wende*) in Austrian politics. The trade unions, therefore, now participate in the anti-foreigner discourse, in contrast to 1993, and traditional Socialist voters, such as workers, join the

FPÖ in increasing numbers. Note, however, that the percentage of foreigners of all kinds in Austria is a mere 10 per cent of the population. Of course, the populist argumentation provides no constructive programs, but simply responds to the fears and gives simplistic answers (Eatwell 1998).

The search for a new identity and the (discursive) construction of scapegoats are not only Austrian issues, but supranational ones. The competition of the European economy with the USA and Japan has resulted in a 'competitive-ness rhetoric' (neo-liberal concepts) which is taking over the economic debates (Krugmann 1998). It is the phenomenon of globalisation which is one of the main factors at the core of anxiety about the 'future', and which reinforces nationalism, ethnicism, 'xenophobia' and racism. Thus, although Austria is in many ways unique, it is also a case study for European problems. We should all take the Austrian case very seriously.

Appendices: the German originals

Appendix 4.1

The original text of the 'Austria First Petition' reads as follows (see Document No. 1015 of the Supplements to the Stenographic Minutes of the Austrian National Assembly, Legislation Period XVIII, p. 1 / 1015 der Beilagen zu den Stenographischen Protokollen des Nationalrates, XVIII. Gesetzgebungs-periode, p.1)'.

Title: *Volksbegehren 'Österreich zuerst'*

Subtitle: *Durch Schaffung gesetzlicher Maßnahmen, die das Recht auf Heimat für alle österreichischen Staatsbürger dauerhaft sichern und unter diesem Gesichtspunkt eine zurückhaltende Einwanderungspolitik nach Österreich gewährleisten*

Text: *1. Die Verabschiedung eines Bundesgesetzes, um die Staatszielbestimmung 'Österreich ist kein Einwanderungsland' im Bundes-Verfassungsgesetz 1920 (idF 1929) zu verankern.*

2. Gesetzliche Normierung eines Einwanderungsstopps bis zur befriedigenden Lösung der illegalen Ausländerfrage, bis zur Beseitigung der Wohnungsnot und zur Senkung der Arbeitslosigkeit auf 5% sowie Schaffung gesetzlicher Maßnahmen, die gewährleisten, daß geförderte Wohnungen (Wohnbauför-derung) in Zukunft nur österreichischen Staatsbürgern zuerkannt werden, sofern nicht internationale Abkommen und völkerrechtliche Normen dem entgegenstehen.

3. Die Verabschiedung eines Bundesgesetzes, um eine generelle Ausweispflicht für ausländische Arbeitnehmer auf dem Arbeitsplatz einzuführen, wobei aus

diesem Ausweis die Arbeitsgenehmigung und die Anmeldung zur Krankenversicherung hervorzugehen hat.

4. Die Aufstockung der Exekutive (insbesondere Fremden- und Kriminalpolizei), sowie deren bessere Bezahlung und Ausstattung zur Erfassung der illegalen Ausländer und zur wirkungsvolleren Kriminalitätsbekämpfung, insbesondere des organisierten Verbrechens.

5. Die Verabschiedung eines Bundesgesetzes zur sofortigen Schaffung einer ständigen Grenzschutztruppe (Zoll, Gendarmerie) statt des Bundesheereinsatzes.

6. Die Verabschiedung eines Bundesgesetzes zur Änderung des Schulorganisationsgesetzes mit der eine Begrenzung des Anteils von Schülern mit nichtdeutscher Muttersprache in Pflicht- und Berufsschulklassen auf höchstens 30% gewährleistet ist; bei einem mehr als 30%igen Anteil von Kindern mit nichtdeutscher Muttersprache Einrichtung von Ausländer-Regelklassen.

7. Entspannung der Schulsituation durch Teilnahme am Regelunterricht von Kindern mit nichtdeutscher Muttersprache nur bei ausreichenden Deutschkenntnissen (Vorbereitungsklassen).

8. Schaffung einer Bestimmung im Parteiengesetz, die sicherstellt, daß an parteiinternen Vorwahlverfahren zur Erstellung der Listen für die allgemeinen Wahlen zu den allgemeinen Vertretungskörpern, ausschließlich österreichische Staatsbürger teilnehmen.

9. Die Verabschiedung eines Bundesgesetzes zur Eindämmung der Praxis vorzeitiger Staatsbürgerschaftsverleihungen.

10. Die Verabschiedung eines Bundesgesetzes, um illegale gewerbliche Tätigkeiten (wie z.B. in Ausländervereinen und -clubs) zu unterbinden, sowie Setzung rigoroser Maßnahmen gegen den Mißbrauch von Sozialleistungen.

11. Schaffung der gesetzlichen Grundlagen für die Möglichkeit der sofortigen Ausweisung und Verhängung von Aufenthaltsverboten für ausländische Straftäter.

12. Die Verabschiedung eines Bundesgesetzes zur Errichtung einer Osteuropa-Stiftung zur Verhinderung von Wanderungsbewegungen.

Appendix 4.2

Interview with Jörg Haider about the new party programm, in *Zeit im Bild 2*, 29. October 1997 (Interviewer: Robert Hochner):

RH: Herr Doktor Haider! In diesem Parteiprogramm sind christliche Werte und die Verpflichtung, diese christlichen Werte zu verteidigen, relativ stark unterstrichen. – Äh, es gibt keine christliche Ausländerfeindlichkeit. Das Christentum unterscheidet nicht zwischen Österreichern und Ausländern, und das Christentum verpflichtet eigentlich Menschen, – die wenig haben, das, was man hat, noch zu geben. Wie ver/paßt das eigentlich zur Politik ihrer Partei? –

JH: Zum ersten einmal, daß wir christlich sind bei Privilegienabbau, weil wir sind die einzigen, die freiwilligen Einkommensverzicht leisten, – während in Zeiten des Sparpaketes vom Bundeskanzler angefangen bis zu allen Ministern, Landeshauptleuten, Landesregierungsmitgliedern, jeder sich Gehaltserhöhungen verpaßt hat. So, einmal das erste Christliche an uns. Das Zweite ist, – ah daß wir das Papstwort ernst nehmen, und äh der – äh je/jetzige Papst hat ja ganz deutlich gemacht, daß Nächstenliebe bedeutet, wirklich sich um den Nächsten zu kümmern und nicht die ganze Welt zu umarmen, sondern auch an die Österreicher zu denken.

RH: Also, der Näch/der Nächste muß einen österreichischen Paß haben, daß Sie ihn lieben.

JH: Nicht unbedingt, aber er muß eine legale Aufenthaltsberechtigung hier in d/im Lande haben, denn sonst geht's uns so, daß man – äh Illegale hereinläßt – und dann letztlich den Österreichern und den hier legal lebenden Ausländern ein Problem schafft. Wir sind also da sehr – auf der rechtsstaatlichen Grundlage – und der/die Reaktionen der Regierung zeigen ja nur, daß wir völlig richtig liegen auch mit der Linie – äh 'Österreich zuerst', daß wir an dieses Land denken und den Ausverkauf beziehungsweise eine ungehemmte Zuwanderung jedenfalls stoppen wollen.

Notes

1 For the German original see appendix 4.1.
2 The original reads as follows: '*Ein Rechtsstaat kann einen derartigen Zustand nicht akzeptieren. Durch die permanente Zunahme der 'Illegalen' werden bestehende Probleme im Bereich der Schwarzarbeit und der wachsenden Kriminalität noch weiter verstärkt. In Österreich nimmt darüber hinaus die Wohnungsnot rapide zu ... Durch fehlende Wohnungskapazitäten werden auch zahlreiche Ausländer gezwungen, bei unzumutbar hohen Mieten in Elendsquartieren Unterkunft zu nehmen ...*'.
3 The original text reads as follows: '*Speziell in Ballungszentren, insbesondere in der Bundeshauptstadt Wien, schließen sich Ausländer immer wieder in Vereinen und Clubs zusammen. In diesem Bereich wird aber weit über die gesetzlichen Grundlagen des österreichischen Vereinsgesetzes*

hinaus Mißbrauch betreiben. Vereins- bzw. Clublokale stellen in Wahrheit immer häufiger Gastronomiebetriebe dar, welche die gewerberechtlichen sanitäts- und baupolizeilichen Auflagen weitgehend nicht erfüllen (fehlende Sanitäranlagen, keine Sperrstunden, kein Lärmschutz, verbotenes Glücksspiel, Geheimprostitution, Schwarzhandel usw.) und dadurch bei einheimischen Anrainern und Gewerbetreibenden Verärgerung und berechtigten Unmut hervorrufen. Nur eine gesetzliche Neuregelung und deren strenger Vollzug könnten in diesem Bereich die Ordnung wiederherstellen. In den letzten Jahren wurden zunehmende Mißbräuche von Sozialleistungen durch Ausländer bekannt, die Gegenmaßnahmen erforderlich machen. Neue Geburtsurkunden, die einen früheren Pensionsbezug ermöglichen, nur auf dem Papier existente Kinder, die zum Bezug von Familienbeihilfen berechtigen, Vortäuschen eines inländischen Wohnbesitzes, sodaß zu minimalen Pensionen beträchtliche, aus den Beitragszahlungen nicht finanzierbare Ausgleichszahlungen gewährt werden, sind in diesem Zusammenhang anzuführen'.

4 The German original goes: '*Für einige Sozialisten, wie etwas Unterrichtsminister Scholten, die nach wie vor die Idee der multikulturellen Gesellschaft vertreten, ist unsere kulturelle Identität praktisch wertlos, ja sogar politisch bedenklich. Dies ist in den offiziellen Schriften des Unterrichtsministeriums nachzulesen. Um unsere kulturelle Identität zu erhalten, den Einbindungsprozeß von Kindern mit nicht-deutscher Muttersprache erfolgreich durchzuführen, um den Unterricht auch weiterhin finanzieren zu können, aber auch um eine solide Ausbildung unserer Kinder zu gewährleisten, muß der Anteil von Kindern mit nicht-deutscher Muttersprache in den Klassen mit rund 30% begrenzt werden ...Weil die von der großen Koalition dominierte Schulverwaltung justament darauf besteht, Kinder mit mangelhaften oder überhaupt fehlenden deutschen Sprachkenntnissen sofort in Regelklassen des Pflichtschulbereichs einzugliedern, sinkt das Ausbildungsniveau, und Schwierigkeiten für die gesamte Schulgemeinschaft sind unabwendbar ...*'.

5 In German: '*Die unveräußerliche Menschenwürde eines jeden einzelnen muß in Zusammenarbeit mit allen Menschen guten Willens erhalten werden. Man muß Verantwortung tragen, zwischen dem ethisch Gebotenen und dem tatsächlich Machbaren*'.

6 The original text reads as follows: '*die fremdenfeindlichen Maßnahmen der Koalitionsregierung verstoßen gegen grundlegende Menschenrechte und haben den Boden aufbereitet für die rassistische Hetze der FPÖ*'.

7 The German version goes as follows: '*Wir wollen den Anfängen wehren, bevor es zu spät ist. Noch haben wir in Österreich die Gelegenheit, rechtzeitig entgegenzusteuern. Wir wollen uns für demokratische Formen des Zusammenlebens einsetzen und jedlichen [sic!] Rassismus und Nationalismus eine Absage erteilen*'.

8 The original contribution goes as follows: '*Meine Damen und Herrn! Der Nationalrat hat den Bundesminister für Inneres ersucht, einen Bericht über die Vollziehung der erwähnten Gesetze vorzulegen, um die Möglichkeit zu haben, im Fall von Problemen entsprechend reagieren zu können. Der erste 'Migrationsbericht' lag dem Nationalrat bereits vor und hat gezeigt, daß Änderungen der beschlossenen Gesetze zur Zeit nicht erforderlich sind. Der Nationalrat wird jedoch die Situation auch weiter beobachten und vom Bundesminister für Inneres im Herbst dieses Jahres einen weiteren Bericht erhalten. Aus diesen Erwägungen kommt der Innenausschuß zum Schluß, daß aufgrund des Volksbegehrens 'Österreich zuerst' gesetzliche Maßnahmen nicht erforderlich sind. Als Ergebnis seiner Beratungen stellt der Ausschuß für Innere Angelegenheiten somit den Antrag, der Nationalrat wolle diesen Bericht zur Kenntnis nehmen*'.

9 In German: '*Meine Damen und Herrn! Das alles ist für uns Anlaß, klarzustellen, daß wir Freiheitlichen vom heutigen Tag an mit dem Abschmettern des Volksbegehrens der Anwalt der Österreicher im Parlament in dieser wichtigen Sache sein werden und nicht zur Ruhe kommen werden, Sie daran zu erinnern, daß Sie hier wider besseres Wissen ein wichtiges Anliegen der österreichischen Bevölkerung mit Füßen treten ... Aber wir werden Sie daran erinnern, daß demgegenüber in einer demokratischen Entscheidung mittels Volksbegehren über 400,000 Menschen mit ihrer Unterschrift öffentlich bekannt haben, daß es ihnen ein Anliegen ist, daß in Österreich zuerst einmal für die Österreicher die anstehenden Probleme des Wohnens ... in Ordnung gebracht werden müssen, bevor durch eine weitere Zuwanderung die Probleme einer Verschärfung zugeführt werden*'.

10 In the original version: '*In der Zwischenzeit ist auch den SOS-Aktivisten ein Licht aufgegangen, daß sie politisch mißbraucht worden sind, weil es nicht das Anliegen einer humanitären Einwanderungs-*

politik war, das die Regierung zur Unterstützung dieser Aktion gebracht hat, sondern einzig und allein offenbar die Angst vor einem allzu erfolgreichen Volksbegehren, das die Freiheitlichen initiiert haben'.

11 Verbatim in German: *'Durch die vom Parlament beschlossenen Gesetze, insbesondere durch das Bundesbetreuungsgesetz, das Asylgesetz, das Aufenthalts- und das Fremdengesetz wurde eine Rechtslage geschaffen, aufgrund derer die besondere Situation, mit der Österreich durch die Migrationswelle – insbesondere nach der Ostöffnung und aufgrund der Lage im ehemaligen Jugoslawien – konfrontiert ist, bewältigt werden kann'.*

12 In the original version: *'21 Prozent der Asylansuchen positiv erledigt! Kein anderes Land Europas kann so eine hohe Anerkennungsquote verzeichnen wie wir in Österreich'.*

13 In German: *'Wir sind gerade in diesem sensiblen Bereich der Ausländerpolitik für gezielte, aber auch gut überlegte Maßnahmen – das war bisher so und wird auch in Zukunft so sein'.*

14 In the original version: *'Meine Damen und Herrn! Ich bin in gewisser Hinsicht der freiheitlichen Fraktion dankbar dafür, daß wir heute aufgrund des Volksbegehrens, über das wir uns im wesentlichen nicht mehr unterhalten müssen – für mich ist diese Sache vor einem halben Jahr erledigt gewesen, als sich tatsächlich Hunderttausende gegen dieses Volksbegehren öffentlich gewandt haben, mit Gesicht und Namen – Gelegenheit haben, genau diese wirklich aktuellen Probleme der österreichischen Innenpolitik im Zusammenhang mit der Ausländergesetzgebung hier zu diskutieren'.*

15 Verbatim in the original version: *'Meine sehr geehrten Damen und Herrn! Auch wenn Ihnen das so vorkommen mag, als wäre das eine kleine Nebensächlichkeit in einem 15 Paragraphen umfassen- den Gesetz, bedeutet das für tausende Menschen in Österreich, die keinen österreichischen Reisepaß und keine Staatsbürgerschaft besitzen und hier aufhältig sind, ein Ab in die Illegalität und in weiterer Folge Ausweisung aus diesem Land'.*

16 The German version goes as follows: *'Meine Damen und Herrn! Ein Blick auf die absoluten Zahlen zeigt uns, wie weit das Verständnis für Verfolgte, für Flüchtlinge und für die Aufnahme solcher Menschen in Österreich bereits verkommen ist. Kein anderes Wort als "verkommen" ist hier angebracht'.*

17 In the original version: *'Migrationspolitik wird so wie heute auch in Zukunft einer der Schwerpunkte politischer Auseinandersetzung sein – davon bin ich überzeugt'.*

18 In German: *'Die gegenwärtige Situation gibt also keinen Anlaß für ein Panikorchester, weder für ein Panikorchester von der linken noch für ein Panikorchester von der rechten Seite. Zur Erhaltung der Stabilität und Sicherheit Österreichs brauchen wir nicht diese extremen Standpunkte, weder von der einen noch von der anderen Seite, sondern eine ausgewogene und fundierte Ausländerpolitik. Anlaufschwierigkeiten müssen wir beseitigen'.*

19 Due to its length, we are not able to reproduce the German original here. Please see the Stenographic Minutes of the Austrian National Assembly. Sitting No. 131, 23 September 1993, Legislation Period XVIII, pp. 15036–7 / Stenographisches Protokoll des Nationalrates, 131. Sitzung, 23. September 1993, XVIII. Gesetzgebungsperiode, pp. 15036–7.

5 Institutionalising and administrating social exclusion

The discourse about Austrian authorities' refusals of residence permits for aliens

For years, Department 62 of the Viennese Municipal Authorities, its chief council officer, Hans Werner Sokop, and the head of Department III of the Austrian Ministry of the Interior, Manfred Matzka – he and 'his' section are responsible for passports, citizenship, refugees and aliens – have been 'objects' of public political critique and controversial discussion. They were accused of issuing notifications that reject aliens' applications for residence permits (Department 62) or appeals against refusals of residence permits (Department III) on the basis of fallacious arguments, which sometimes even bordered 'culturalist-racist' reasoning and, thus, represented a blatant example of 'institutional racism'. It is the discourse about the authorities' refusals of residence permits for aliens in Austria in 1996, 1997 and 1998 that we will analyse in this chapter against the methodical and theoretical background presented in chapter 2.

The topic of this fifth chapter is the political administration of social exclusion (see also Fairclough 2000), the attempt to legitimise as well as to delegitimise institutional measures of immigration control (see van Leeuwen and Wodak 1999) – strictly speaking, the expulsion of 'aliens', most of them Turkish citizens – within the legal framework of modern nation-states like Austria.

In addition, this fifth part of the book is designed to discuss – from a critical discourse-analytical viewpoint committed to the concept of 'deliberative democracy' – the possible tension between legality and legitimacy and the anti-discriminatory potential of a democratic model based on a strong civil society.

While 'legality' simply denotes the correspondence between actions or practices and the established law, the notion of 'legitimacy' or 'legitimateness' transcends the purely legalistic framework, as it stands for the justification of the display of – for example the state's – power and rule (see Würtenberger 1982: 677) on the basis of a commitment to fundamental ethical principles of justice, equality and recognition.

Ideally, legality is or should be based on legitimacy (as far as the question of legitimacy through legality is concerned, see Habermas 1992: 541–99). Actually, there can be a great discrepancy between them, often proving the old Roman Ciceronian proverb *summum jus summa injuria* ('the highest law (can be) the greatest injustice') to be true: that to follow a law to the letter may mean to commit a grave wrong.

Legality does not automatically imply legitimacy. Wherever a particular law contradicts or comes into conflict with more universal principles or laws – e.g. an 'Alien Act' with the constitution, basic rights or human rights – a gap is opened, which, from a critical, deliberative democratic point of view should lead to critique that, in extreme cases, may even take the form of ethically legitimate, though 'illegal', 'civil disobedience' and resistance.

That pure legality or legalism by no means entails legitimacy becomes most evident in the historical example of National-Socialism or fascism:

> The unobjectionable manner in which a norm comes into being, that is, the legal form of a procedure, guarantees as such only that the authorities which the political system provides for, and which are furnished with certain competencies and recognised as competent within that system, bear the responsibility for valid law. But these authorities are part of a system of authority that must be legitimised as a whole if pure legality is to be able to count *as an indication* of legitimacy. In a fascist regime, for example, the legal form of administrative acts can have at best a masking function. This means that the technical legal form alone, pure legality, will not be able to guarantee recognition in the long run if the system of authority cannot be legitimised independently of the legal form of exercising authority.
>
> (Habermas 1975: 100 [1973: 138])

Nowadays, the question of democratic legitimation and – as in our specific case – of the legitimate administration of justice and the implementation of laws – is an important matter of public debate and control. The political system of democratic states has to incorporate institutionalised, more or less public mechanisms of control, such as a parliamentary opposition, an impartial jurisdiction, especially the Constitutional Court and the Administrative Court, as well as free and critical media. Thus, in the present case study of discriminatory administrative notifications the focus of analysis also lies on judgements made by the Administrative Court, on the uncovering and public critique by opposition parties and on the 'deliberative democratic' function of media coverage as an important political instrument of control. In the present case, the – very delayed – political decision in the summer of 1998 to remove Werner Sokop as chief administrator of the Residence Act or Aliens' Act was decisively influenced by the pressure of public critique.

Locating the discourse within the fields of political action

In the following, we will be mainly concerned with those negative official notifications issued by Department 62 of the Municipal Authorities dealing with residence permits for aliens which, for years, have been metaphorically criticised as 'headscarf notifications' ('*Kopftuchbescheide*'), 'over-foreignerisation notifications' ('*Überfremdungsbescheide*') and 'family planning notifications' ('*Familien-*

planungsbescheide'). In part, we will also be concerned with notifications issued by the Ministry of the Interior, Department III, Section 11, which deal with appeals against the municipal refusals and have been criticised as 'assembly line notifications' or 'piecework notifications' ('*Fließbandbescheide*' or '*Akkord-bescheide*'). Nevertheless, it seems to be useful to give, first of all, an overview on the whole public discourse in Austria about residence permits for aliens and about family reunion.

The discourse mainly took place in the four political action fields of

- the lawmaking or legislative procedure
- the formation of public opinion and self-presentation
- the administration of justice and implementation of law
- the political control.

And, in part, it was also situated in the field of

- political advertising and propaganda.

The topics of the discourse primarily revolved around 'residence permits for aliens', 'quotas of residence permits', 'residence bans', 'family reunions', 'immigration', 'integration', 'expulsion', 'over-foreignerisation', 'fraudulent marriages', 'foreigner illegality and criminality', 'working off the books', 'public order', 'local standard dwellings', 'ethnic discrimination' and 'human rights'.

As far as the political field of the lawmaking procedure is concerned, the main genres employed in this discourse were the different laws on aliens (especially the Residence Act), the amendments to these laws and the commission report on these amendments. The formation of public opinion primarily involved the genres of press releases, press conferences, interviews, political speeches and contributions in the parliament, as well as press, book and journal articles and readers' letters. The political field of action where the discourse in question was principally located, i.e. the administration of justice and implementation of law, was mainly associated with the genres of applications for a residence permit, the notifications dismissing or refusing the residence permit, appeals against these refusals, decisions and judgements of the Administrative Court and governmental answers to parliamentary questions. Within the field of political control – which is neatly connected with, and overlaps, the formation of public opinion – the genres employed included press releases and conferences, declarations of opposition parties, counselling offices, human rights organisations and engaged experts, parliamentary questions and differing statements of representatives, judgements of the Administrative Court, appeals, decisions, press and book articles and books. Finally, for the purpose of political advertising and propaganda – a political macro-function that cannot strictly be separated from the political aim of the formation of public opinion – the Austrian Freedom Party (FPÖ) utilised advertisements in local Viennese district journals ('*Wiener Bezirksjournale*').

Figure 5.1 sums up the relationship between the fields of political action, the genres and the discourse topics of the particular discourse.

The Austrian discourse about aliens' residence permits is embedded into an economic, social, political, demographic and legal framework, which we at least partly described in chapter 4. Additional, complementary contextual information about the Austrian policy on 'aliens', about demographic development in Austria and about the laws on non-Austrian citizens residing and/or working in Austria or aspiring to come to Austria, which may be illuminating for the analysis contained in this chapter, is given in the following section.

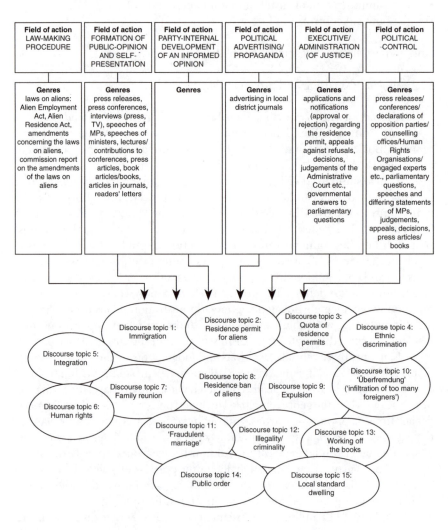

Figure 5.1 The discourse about aliens' residence permits in Austria in 1996, 1997 and 1998

The Austrian 'foreigner policy', the statistics on the population and naturalisations and the legal setting

Austria's population statistics from 1945 up to the present show that, during this period, immigration to has almost always been greater than emigration from Austria (Fassmann and Münz 1996: 210). During the last thirty years, the average increase in population has been around +13,000 persons per year, in the 1980s even around +23,000. Thus, the overall extent of immigration has obviously been greater (between 20,000 and 25,000 persons per year).

According to the increase in the annual average, in 1998 the resident population amounted to 8,082,819 (8,072,182 in 1997, 8,067,812 in 1996, 8,054,802 in 1995), of which 739,837 (732,671 in 1997, 730,869 in 1996, 726,200 in 1995) were 'foreigners', which corresponds to a share of 9.1 per cent (9.1 per cent in 1997, 9.1 per cent in 1996, 9 per cent in 1995) of the total population (the statistics within this section are almost all taken from *Der Fischer Weltalmanach 1996, 1997, 1998, 1999* and *2000*; they slightly differ from the statistics reproduced in Lebhart and Münz 1999). The main countries of origin of the 'foreign' population are shown in table 5.1; the population (annual average) and total of 'foreigners' is shown in table 5.2.

The figure of 'foreigners' born in Austria in 1998 amounted to 13.2 per cent of a total number of 81,233 births. In 1997 the figure amounted to 13.1 per cent of a total number of 84,045 births, in 1996 it amounted to 13.6 per cent of the total number of 88,809 births, in 1995 it amounted to 13.8 per cent of a total

Table 5.1 Main countries of origin of the 'foreign' population in Austria

Country of origin	1998		1997		1996		1995	
Former Yugoslavia	337,863	(4.2%)	335,800	(4.2%)	335,060	(4.2%)	322,892	(4.1%)
Turkey	138,220	(1.7%)	138,505	(1.7%)	139,004	(1.7%)	142,231	(1.8%)
Rest	263,754	(3.3%)	258,366	(3.2%)	256,805	(3.2%)	251,628	(3.1%)

Sources: Der Fischer Weltalmanach 1996, 1997, 1998, 1999 and 2000 (headword: Österreich)

Table 5.2 Population (annual average) /total of 'foreigners' in Austria

Year	Total	Foreigners
1990	7,729,200	456,100
1991	7,795,800	517,700
1992	7,913,800	623,000
1993	7,991,500	689,600
1994	8,039,900	720,900
1995	8,054,800	726,300
1996	8,067,800	730,900
1997	8,075,400	734,300
1998	8,082,800	739,800

Sources: Der Fischer Weltalmanach 1996, 1997, 1998, 1999 and 2000 (headword: Österreich)

number of 88,669 births. In 1994 there were 13.7 per cent non-Austrians of the total number of 92,415 births.

The figure for naturalisations shows 18,321 naturalisations in 1998 and is thus clearly higher than in 1997 (16,274) and in 1996 (16,243), when it was clearly higher than in 1995 (14,366). Compared to 1994, the number of naturalisations in 1995 was lower than in 1994, when there were 16,720 naturalisations. For 1999 and the following years, one must expect the number of naturalisations to have decreased and to further decrease, since on 1 January 1999 a new Citizen Act came into force that is more restrictive and standardised. Since 1 January 1999, an 'alien' can apply for an Austrian citizenship only if the applicant has been living and working in Austria for at least ten years. An applicant is legally entitled to citizenship only after thirty years. According to the new law, an applicant has to be 'successfully integrated' in Austrian society and must establish proof of knowledge of German. The countries of origin where the applicants for naturalisations came from in the past years are shown in table 5.3 ('–' means 'without specification').

As the statistics of recent decades show, Austria has actually become an immigration state, though most of the politicians still deny it.

In comparison with Germany, the phases of Austrian 'foreigner policy' seem to be slightly delayed. The internationally organised foreigner employment started well after the 'recruitment policy' began in West Germany, Switzerland or Scandinavia (Faßmann and Münz 1996: 216). Austria concluded the first 'recruitment agreement' in 1962 with Spain, the second one in 1964 with Turkey and a third one in 1966 with Yugoslavia. The agreement with Spain was of little significance. The statistics of the annual increase in the 'foreign work force' in Austria demonstrate that the 'take-off-phase' did not begin until the middle of the 1960s. At the end of the 1960s and the beginning of the 1970s, the number of foreign workers increased by 20,000 to 40,000 persons per year. In 1973, the 'employment of guest workers' reached its first high point with 230,000 persons (10 per cent of all employed persons in Austria).

Owing to the economic crisis and the age groups with a high birth rate 'available' for the labour market, the quota of 'guest workers' in Austria clearly decreased after 1973. In 1984, there were only 138,710 registered foreign workers in Austria.

Table 5.3 Naturalisations in Austria

Country of origin	1998	1997	1996	1995	1994
Turkey	5,683	5,064	7,499	3,201	3,379
Former Yugoslavia	4,151	3,659	3,133	4,529	5,284
Romania	1,501	1,096	692	872	904
Poland	–	–	499	680	759
India	–	–	402	–	–
Iran	–	–	–	531	–

Sources: *Der Fischer Weltalmanach* 1996, 1997, 1998, 1999 and 2000 (headword: Österreich)

In 1976, the 'Aliens' Employment Act' (*'Ausländerbeschäftigungsgesetz'*) came into force. It was intended to stimulate rotation and remigration, though the reality of immigration then already no longer corresponded to the legal situation.

The 'Aliens' Employment Act' was first amended in 1988, but only marginally. In 1990, it was again amended. The act still allowed only temporary work permits. Apart from the work permit (*'Beschäftigungsbewilligung'*), maximally valid for twelve months, and apart from the 'releasing certificate' (*'Befreiungsschein'*) (which was valid for two years until 1988 and for three years from 1988 to 1990), the amended Act introduced the 'special work permit' (*'Arbeitserlaubnis'*), valid for two years in the particular state (*'Bundesland'*) if the applicant had already worked for a year in the state.

From 1984 until now, the number of foreign workers has again increased. There were 291,044 registered foreign workers in Austria in 1995.

As far as the countries of origin are concerned, Faßman and Münz summarise the developments of the last few decades in Austria as follows:

> Migrants from Slovenia and Croatia were followed by migrants form Serbia, Bosnia and Kosovo. After Yugoslav citizens came Turkish people and persons of other nationalities; at the moment new immigrants are coming from Eastern Central Europe. Male labour migrants living alone were followed by women and children; legal immigrants were followed by illegal ones.
>
> (Faßman and Münz 1996: 218)

In the late 1980s, new foreign workers were 'absorbed' by Austria. The increase in population was considerable. In 1989, the increase amounted to +56,100, in 1990 to +71,900, in 1991 to +87,700. In 1992, the growth decreased to +82,100, in 1993 to +40,300 and in 1994 to +13,100. Because of the fall of the Iron Curtain and the war in Bosnia, the demographic structure of the aliens changed in the 1990s.

Since 1992, Austria has – as one of the first West European states – an immigration law, even though the official phrasing speaks only of a 'residence right' (*'Aufenthaltsrecht'*). The primary aim of this law was to restrict the number of immigrating 'foreigners' on a legal basis by introducing an annual quota of residence permits (Rieser 1996: 31 and 46–54; see paragraph 2 of the Residence Act). In reaction to the increasing numbers of labour migrants, asylum seekers and refugees on the one hand, and, on the other hand, because of the fear of the populist and nationalist policy of the Austrian Freedom Party (FPÖ), the largest opposition party in Austria, the governing parties SPÖ and ÖVP passed this very restrictive act, which anticipated many of the claims put forward by the FPÖ in the Anti-Foreigner Petition (see chapter 4). The newly introduced formal criteria (see especially paragraph 6 of the Residence Act) functioned as administrative barriers that led to many refusals or dismissals of applications for residence permits. Consequently, many of those applicants who were not used to the highly formalised and complex procedures of legal administration were forced into illegal situations that could only be solved with great difficulties and sometimes into problems that threatened their livelihood. Though some of the parliamentary representatives who passed the Residence Act were probably unaware of the negative consequences the formal regulations of the new law would have, the juridical experts of the Ministry of the Interior were most probably able to assess the negative effects of the law. One must therefore assume that they judged the consequences to be at least partly acceptable (Rieser 1996: 35).

Two years before, in 1990, the coalition parties (SPÖ and ÖVP) had already introduced a new legal regulating instrument to control the number of foreign workers – the 'aliens' quota' ('*Ausländerquote*'). They decided to fix by decree the number of employed and unemployed foreign workers according to presumable economic necessities and according to the number of aliens already living in Austria. In 1995, for example, the quota was fixed at 9 per cent (295,000 persons) of the whole potential Austrian 'work force'. Persons from states of the European Union (or the Europäischen Wirtschaftsraum (EWR)) were exempted from this restriction.

According to the Residence Act that came into force on 1 January 1993, an alien can apply for a permanent residence permit at the earliest after five years, if she or he can convincingly prove that she or he has a secure livelihood in Austria and sufficient 'living space' ('*Wohnraum*') for the period of the permanent residence. The acceptance of the application is at the discretion of the authorities. There is no legal entitlement to obtain a permanent residence permit.

In 1995, the Residence Act was amended because of a decision by the Austrian Constitutional Court, according to which the regulation regarding the expulsion of aliens was deemed partly unconstitutional. Though in the amended law some points are improved (the duration of marriage is decreased from twelve to six months), others are further restricted (the government fixes a quota of approvals for family reunification; the residence permit is maximally valid for five years – independent of the period of validity of the partner's or the parents' approval).

In 1996, there was no essential change in the Residence Act (nor in the Asylum Act). In comparison to 1995, the government's decree about the quota of approvals for family reunion was slightly increased, and the quota of approvals for residence permits for new work immigrants slightly reduced.

Apart from that, an important change occurred in 1996 as regards the Association Agreement between the European Union and Turkey (see Wiener Integrationsfonds 1997: 83). Since 1995, that is, since Austria's becoming a member of the EU, there has been a discussion about whether or not Austria is obliged to apply the regulations of the agreement – which partly provided for an equal status with respect to work and the freedom of movement of Turkish citizens and citizens from member states of the European Union living and working in EU states other than their home states. In 1996, the Austrian Administrative Court terminated this discussion by deciding that Austria has to apply the regulations of the agreement, the decision of the Association

Council 1/80 based on this agreement and the respective judgements of the European Court of Justice.

Though these regulations do not touch on the right of the member states to control new immigration (including family reunion), the decisions have a decisive effect on the question of employment and, in consequence, also on the question of residence permits of Turkish citizens. According to the Association Agreement, family members of Turkish employees living in Austria, after three or five years obtain access to the Austrian labour market, which they did not have according to the Austrian Alien Employment Act. For children of Turkish citizens, this is the case during their training and after they have completed it. The decisions affect the realm of residence inasmuch as the European Court of Justice decided that employment rights shall entail a right of residence.

According to the Administrative Court Turkish citizens entitled to association do not need a residence permit as prescribed by the Residence Act (*Aufenthaltsgesetz*). However, the question still remains open how and according to which legal requirements the right of residence is to be regulated and documented. As a consequence, the Austrian Ministry of the Interior gives the competence to regulate the right of residence of persons entitled to association to the local authorities responsible for the implementation of the 'Aliens' Act' and recommends them to issue endorsements with a special mark.

In 1996 and 1997, the implementation of the Residence Act, which is a matter for the respective local authorities of the nine Austrian states (either of the 'aliens' offices' of the police or, in Vienna, of Department 62 of the Municipal Authorities), was especially publicly discussed and criticised with respect to the Viennese administration. This was for several reasons. First, the Viennese authorities had problems with the implementation of the decisions of the Administrative Court regarding the Association Agreement. Strictly speaking, they were first inclined simply to ignore the decisions. Second, particularly as far as the authorities' suspicion of 'fraudulent marriage' was concerned, the procedures of investigation and the interview questions asked of the applicants for residence permits were dubious and partly offended the private spheres of the applicants. Third, several grounds for the negative notifications – especially those regarding the refusal of family reunion – were suspected of being prejudiced, legally not supported, fallacious with regard to their argumentation structure or even culturalist-racist with regard to their content (we will analyse some of these 'grounds' later in this chapter).

Both the Mayor of Vienna, Michael Häupl, and the Viennese City Councillor for Integration, Renate Brauner, on the one hand, and the Ministries of the Interior as well as for Social Affairs on the other, had to intervene several times (for example by directives) in order at least partly to improve the illegitimate and sometimes illegal and unconstitutional implementation of the very restrictive Residence Act.

As mentioned above, every year the Austrian government fixes by decree the quota of residence permits for applicants applying for the first time (see BGBl 1994/1023, 1995/854, 1996/707, quoted according to Davy 1997a:

472). In 1995, 17,000 permits were assigned to persons applying for a residence permit in Austria for the first time. In 1996, the quota was slightly increased (18,480), while, in 1997, it was again decreased (17,320). In 1998, Karl Schlögl, the social-democratic Minister of the Interior, roughly halved the quota and fixed the number at 8,660 residence permits (see *Der Standard*, 23 October 1997: 1). Since then, Schlögl retains this extraordinary restrictive quota policy. In 1999, Schlögl limited the number of permits to 8,770 (see *Der Standard*, November 1998: 1), and in 2000, the number will approximately amount to 9,000 permits (see *Der Standard*, 14 September 1999: 1 and 2).

As far as the quota for family reunion is concerned, the Austrian government annually reserves about 60 per cent of all first applications for family members of non-Austrian citizens wishing to join their relatives in Austria. In 1995, 10,300 permits (61 per cent) were assigned to family members, 10,520 (57 per cent) in 1996, 9,890 (57 per cent) in 1997 (for more detailed statistics, see Wiener Integrationsfonds 1997: 85). Due to the further aggravation of the restrictive policy by Karl Schlögl, the number of family members enjoying a residence permit decreased by half – 4,600 (53.1 per cent) in 1998 (see *Der Standard*, 23 October 1997: 1). In 1999, 5,210 family members (59.4 per cent) of non-Austrian citizens were granted a residence permit (*Der Standard*, 12 November 1998: 8), and in 2000, 5,000 persons (about 55.5 per cent) will be given the allowance for family reunion (see *Der Standard*, 5 November 1999: 39).

On 1 January 1998, a new Act on Aliens (*Fremdengesetz* 1997, '*Integrations-paket*') came into force (see Wiener Integrationsfonds 1998b and 1998c for the following explanations). Parts of this Act have been in force since 15 July 1997. A number of sections are still unclear as regards the enforcement and interpretation of important provisions. Among the most important changes are the following ones:

With effect from 1 January 1998, aliens residing and working in Austria are required to have a 'permanent residence permit' ('*Niederlassungsbewilligung*') instead of the so-called residence permit required up to now. For temporary residence purposes (e.g. study), a 'temporary residence permit' ('*Aufenthalts-erlaubnis*') is necessary.

The core of the new act comprises the regulations for 'progressive residence security' of persons who have already resided in Austria legally and for a long period of time without interruption. Even if such a person were to lose her or his means of income, she or he would retain the right to a renewal of the permanent residence permit.

According to the new act, 'immigrants' who have lived in Austria since early childhood are protected from the termination of their right of residence.

Furthermore, under the Alien Employment Act, persons who have resided legally in Austria for at least eight years are, with the help of an employer, able to apply for the first-year restricted work permit ('*Beschäftigungsbewilligung*') and, in special cases, e.g. in the case of integrated youths, this is possible even earlier. In contrast, 'aliens' who have not legally resided in Austria for at least eight years may, under the circumstance of extended periods of unemployment, be subject to expulsion.

As regards sending for family members, regulations have also been stiffened: it is no longer possible to send for children who are 14 and older or parents requiring nursing care. To mitigate this change, there are transitional regulations for children between the ages of 14 and 19 inclusively. The quotas for family members sent for by non-Austrian citizens continue to be lowered.

As regards other newly arriving immigrants, the system of annual quotas remains intact. Now, only specially qualified persons are able to come to Austria to work.

From now on it is easier for family members of Austrian citizens to join their families in Austria. Moreover, this family circle is more comprehensive than before. The quota for family reunion, however, is low (see above).

For Turkish citizens who have been living and working in Austria for a long time, the Association Agreement signed by the European Community and Turkey or the Association Council Resolution 1/80 based on this can be applicable. If so, the person in question is entitled to the renewal of her or his work and residence permits. In the Act on Aliens, this right is called '*Bleiberecht*' ('right to remain').

Official notifications as a genre

As characterised in chapter 2 (p. 36), we conceive a genre to be a schematically conventionalised use of language, which represents a specific discursive practice situated within a specific field of social activity. The written administrative or bureaucratic genre of 'official notification' is a specific type of legal text which has the performative force to regulate directively a specific aspect of the life of an applicant – in our case, the temporally limited permit legally to reside in a specific part of a specific country or not. The performative or illocutionary force of official notifications is guaranteed by the particular political system that provides for the establishment of an administrative apparatus of bureaucratic institutions, which implement the legal requirements fixed in the codices of laws of the respective state. In other words, official notifications are sovereign political expressions of will articulated by anonymous bureaucrats who make decisions in the name of the authority of a region or state and (allegedly) look after the public interest of a political community.

As with almost all legal genres, the language of notifications is syntactically complex, abstract (see Grewendorf 1992, Bierwisch 1992, Krausneker 1997, van Leeuwen and Wodak 1999) and impersonal – both with regard to the bureaucrats who issue the notifications in the name of a region or state authority and who are linguistically very often backgrounded or deleted by passivation etc. (see van Leeuwen 1993 and van Leeuwen 1996), and with regard to the applying individuals who in an abstract, actionalising, 'politicising' (for example nationalising) manner are referred to as 'party', as 'applicant', as 'applying party', as 'Turkish citizen' and so on.

The internal discursive structure of the negative notifications (see also Krausneker 1997: 2; for a detailed description of the discursive script of application see van Leeuwen and Wodak 1999: 21) can be described as an activity sequence consisting of:

- the authority's self-identification
- identifying the notification numerically and with respect to the applicant's address
- temporally and locally situating the notification
- informing in a subsuming mode about the legal matter addressed by the notification (law)
- noting the applicant's request and the authority's decision ('*Bescheid*') by briefly referring to paragraphs of the respective law (e.g. of the Residence Act)
- grounding the decision ('*Begründung*')

  (a) by giving information about the legal regulations referring to specific paragraphs and/or clauses of the respective law
  (b) by explaining the 'facts of the case'
  (c) by subsuming the specific case explained in (b) under the law or parts of law referred to in (a)
  (d) by refuting the approval
  (e) by formulating the conclusion that the decision had to be taken as it was taken

- informing the applicant of his or her rights to appeal against the refusal ('*Rechtsmittelbelehrung*', statement of rights of redress or appeal)
- authenticating the decision by the signature of the responsible bureaucrat acting as representative of the head of the regional government
- informing the applicant about the delivery of the notification to three different addressees.

Figure 5.2 shows one example of such a notification, and its structure is analysed, in the right-hand column, as a sequence of discursive practices (the Austrian version is included in appendix 5.1; the argumentation and fallacy structure of the 'grounds' of this notification is analysed in detail in the next section).

The question of who the applicants are who need a residence permit in Austria can be answered a follows (see Paragraph 1 of the Residence Act; see Rieser 1996: 36–46): they are aliens who want to stay in Austria for more than six months or want to work as employed or self-employed persons in Austria. Exceptions are made as far as artists, professors, university teachers, international commuters across a local border, asylum seekers, convention refugees, citizens from member states of the European Union and their family members are concerned.

The purpose of residing in Austria, which has to be indicated in the applications, can be (see Rieser 1996: 104 and 169; see Paragraph 10, Section 1, last Clause):

- 'work as employed person'
- 'work as self-employed person'
- 'family reunion with alien citizens'
- 'family reunion with Austrian citizens'
- 'studies'
- 'school education'
- 'pension'
- 'private stay'

The maximum length of validity of an application made for the first time – such an application has to be made from abroad, unless the applicant is a relative of an Austrian citizen or an alien's child under 18 who was born in Austria and is living there – amounts to one year. The validity of the second and third application is two years. As mentioned earlier in this chapter, after five years, an applicant can apply for a permanent residence permit.

At the time of the issue of the negative notifications that we are primarily analysing in this chapter, the conditions for obtaining a residence permit were the following (see Rieser 1996: 68–98, Wiener Integrationfonds 1996: 17, Beratungszentrum für Migranten und Migrantinnen, undated: 9–17):

The applicant has to prove that she or he lives or will live in accommodation with as much 'living space' as is usual for Austrian citizens ('*ortsübliche Unterkunft*', see paragraph 5 of the Residence Act). According to a circular of the Austrian Ministry of the Interior, the number of square meters is not decisive in judging an applicant's accommodation to be a locally appropriate ('*ortsüblich*') dwelling or not. Moreover, the judging authority is required to take into account both the specific local circumstances as well as the specific circumstances in which the applicant is situated.

Further, the applicant has to show that she or he has a regular and sufficient income, a secure livelihood ('*gesicherten Lebensunterhalt*', see paragraph 5 of the Residence Act). While sufficient, earnings-related benefit, 'emergency benefit' ('*Notstandsgeld*') and maternity or paternity leave benefit ('*Karenzurlaubsgeld*') are considered to be a secure livelihood, income support is normally not, unless it is added to the individual's own, (insufficient) income. This is especially the case for aliens who have already been living legally in Austria for several years. The authority can also accept a declaration of commitment (a 'surety') with respect to the secure livelihood, if another person acts as guarantor for the applicant.

Finally, to obtain a residence permit there must be no reason for refusing the '*Sichtvermerk*', the visa stamp (see paragraph 5, section 1 of the Aliens' Act, i.e. '*Fremdengesetz*'). An application for residence permit is not approved:

Office of the Vienna Regional Government Indirect Regional Administration Residence Permits 1082 Vienna, Friedrich-Schmidt-Platz 3 DVR: XXXXXX	Self-identification of the authority *indication of the authority's responsibility* *localisation of the authority* *numerical codification of the authority*
Dept. 62 of the Municipal Authority – XXXXX Vienna, XX XX XXXX (name of the applicant) Turk. Ctzn Residence Act	Identification of the notification *(numerically + with respect to the* *applicant's name and address)* + temporal and local placing of the notification Subsuming information about the legal matter (law)
Notification The application of XX.X.1995 by Mrs (name of the applicant), b. XX.X. XXXX, for granting of a residence permit according to Par. 1 Section 6 and Section 1 of the Residence Act, BGBl. Nr. 466/1992, c.q. F.BGBl. No. 351/95 is rejected with reference to Par. 3 Section 5 Residence Act.	Giving notice of the decision – *information about the applicant's* *request and reference to the paragraph* *of the law which the applicant thinks* *legally to support her or his request* *(topos of law)* – *information about the authority's* *decision and reference to the paragraph* *of the law which the authority thinks* *legally to support its decision (topos of* *law)*
Grounds According to Par. 3 Section 5 of the Residence Act, those applicants are to be favourably considered for whom in view of personal circumstances immediate integration can be effected, or for whom family reunion is particularly urgent, provided that the number of applications according to Par. 3 Section 1 Number 2 Residence Act probably exceeds the legally established quota for the number of permissions to be granted (Par. 2 Section 2 Number 3). The present application constitutes a case of family reunion according to par. 3 Section 1 Number 2 Residence Act, with the relevant marriage having taken place on XX.X.XXXX, previous common addresses described as: [two addresses in Turkey are given], and special relevant reasons argued as follows: 'I would like to live with my family'. As such no grounds for a possible immediate integration or an especially urgent family reunion have been given in the present case, nor can they be assumed to exist on objective and overall consideration of the case. Both on the basis of precedence and because of the situation as per XX.X.XXXX (2600 places offered for Vienna, 1250 applications granted) the Authority has no choice other than to favour the cases specified in Par. 3 Section 5 Residence Act, and given the amount of discretion allowed, this cannot be taken to include the present application. The documentation clearly establishes that the husband of the applicant currently resides in	Grounding the decision (explicative argumentation) (a) Information about the legal regulations and juridical subsumption of the 'case in question' – *reference to the paragraph of the law:* *two topoi of law as two conclusion* *rules characterising the conditions of* *preferred approval (personal* *integratability + urgency)* – *condition of exception as topos of* *numbers limiting the preferential* *approval and favouring the refusal* – *explanation of the 'facts' of the case* *and subsuming of the specific case* *under a specific paragraph of the law* – *information about the applicant's wish* *by quotation* (b) Refutation of the approval – *anticipation of the conclusion that the* *two conclusion rules are not applicable* *to the present case (applicant's failing* *to give reasons and 'objective' lack of* *reasons for applying the above* *mentioned paragraphs)* – *backing of the thesis of the priority of* *conclusion rule (CR) 1 by argument 1* *(previous experiences of the authority)* *and argument 2 (the situation given)*

Figure 5.2 The discursive structure of a notification

Austria, and as a consequence it cannot be denied that personal and family ties with Austria exist.

In view of the intrusion clause of Par. 8 Section 2 MRK, it is possible to effect a constitutional interpretation of Par. 3 Section 5 Residence Act, provided the Authority balances the private interests of the parties concerned against the public interest. In this case, and given that the number of applications for family reunion currently exceeds the allotted number of permissions, it was decided after careful consideration that the present application could not be favoured above the applications of other foreigners, since immediate integration of the applicant appears impossible, all the more since the husband, although resident in Austria, is himself still in the process of achieving integration in Austria. Granting rights of residence to the applying party, from whose application no circumstances can be deduced to facilitate an easy integration, would only further encumber the already costly efforts towards integration of the foreign fellow citizens already here, since everyday experience shows that those who arrive as adults from the same culture area as the applying party are hardly likely to enter into communication with the local population, especially not in terms of speaking the language, and are hardly likely to successfully adapt to Central-European customs, traditions and ways of life, even after a residency of many years. Thus, the decision had to be taken according to the ruling.

Thesis: present case cannot be subsumed to CR 1 because of condition of exception; condition of exception because of non-consequence of CR 1; backing of non-consequence of CR 1. Topos of advantage (pro bono publico and pro bono eorum) Argumentum ad consequentiam as topos of advantage (including topos of culture which is backed by 'experiences of everyday life'), petitio principii

Enthymemic argumentation (CR: if it is encumbering, then 'no'. It is encumbering. Ergo. 'no')

(c) Conclusion

Statement of rights of appeal

An appeal may be lodged within a period of two weeks after serving of this notification, and should be addressed to the Office of the Vienna Regional Government, Department 62 of the Municipal Authority – Dez. A, Friedrich-Schmidt-Platz 3, Vienna 1081, in writing, by telegraph, by fax, by electronic data transmission or by any other technically possible means. The appeal should include the reference number of this notification and the reasons for appealing against it, and it should be provided with a Federal Stamp of ATS 120.-

Informing the applicant of her or his rights to appeal
information about the conditions of acceptance of an appeal: time, place, medium of transmission, necessity of money, of descriptive identification/ denomination of the negative notification (identification number) and of reasons for appealing

For the Governor:

Dr. Sokop
Chief Council Officer

Authentication of the decision
by the signature of the responsible bureaucrat acting as representative of the head of the regional government

Cc.:
1) (name and Turkish address of the applicant)

2) Federal Police Directorate Vienna
Aliens Branch
Wasagasse 20
1090 Vienna

3) On file

Information about the delivery of the notification to three different addressees

Figure 5.2 continued

- if the applicant has no health insurance that covers all risks
- if the applicant's residence could become a financial burden for a regional administrative body (e.g. welfare aid), unless this encumbrance results from the fulfilment of a legal claim (e.g. earnings-related benefit)
- if the applicant's residence would disturb public peace, order and security
- if there exists a residence ban against the applicant (for reasons of a previous conviction, of an unconditional three-month prison sentence or a conditional six-month prison sentence, of illicit work, of false statements to Austrian authorities concerning the applicant's purpose or duration of residence and so on)
- if the application is made after an illegal entry by circumvention of the border control
- if the applicant applies for a residence permit after having entered the country with a tourist visa stamp or without any visa stamp

An application cannot be refused simply because the annual quota for residence permits (see earlier in this chapter) is already exhausted. As soon as the quota is complete, all applications that the authority has not yet decided upon are to be dealt with in the next year.

According to these legal conditions as well as according to additional, sometimes prejudiced, reasons that are not always legally supported or that are not sufficient per se for the grounding of a refusal, the most frequent arguments – normally, the bureaucrats of Department 62 of the Viennese Municipal Authorities put forward more than one argument in their refusal notifications – appearing in the refusals of applications for residence permits are the following (At this point, we do not refer to the specific legal paragraphs of the Residence Act, the Aliens' Act and the General Administration Act [AVG], which are brought into play as *topoi of law*. We will refer to them when typologising the second authority's dealing with the appeals against the refusals of applications for residence permit; see below on p. 223 and in appendix 5.2 on pp. 254–8):

- lack of secure livelihood
- lack of local standard dwelling (sometimes implying problems of health and hygiene)
- disturbance of public peace, law and order
- lack of health insurance
- fraudulent marriage or false statement about the wedlock
- financial burden for a regional administrative body
- unlikelihood of integration
- danger of infiltration of too many foreigners ('over-foreignerisation')
- residence ban (for reasons of previous conviction, of an unconditional three-month prison sentence or a conditional six-month prison sentence, of illicit work/working off the books, of false statements to Austrian authorities concerning the applicant's purpose or duration of residence and so on)

- prevailing of the public interest in comparison to the private interest of the applicant
- unlikelihood of the applicant's integration
- illegal immigration by circumvention of the border control
- applicant's application for a residence permit after having entered the country with a tourist visa stamp or with no visa stamp
- taking into consideration the annual quota of residence permits
- taking into consideration the situation of the national or local labour market
- formal application fault: delayed application, incomplete documents, application on the state territory in cases where it is prescribed that the application must be made from abroad, e.g. in most cases of a first application for a residence permit.

Figure 5.3 roughly illustrates the most important official channels (including the social actors involved) and proceduralised textual chains condensed into the institutionalised genres of application, approval, refusal, appeal, sustaining, dismissal/refusal, complaint, sustaining of finding, refusing of finding and devolution.

As far as the administrative dealing with appeals (*'Berufungen'*) against the refusals of residence permits (*'Berufungsbescheide'*) is concerned – appeals have to be made within the period of two weeks after the legally valid serving of the notification – Department III, Section 11 (passport, citizenship, refugees and aliens) of the Ministry of the Interior is responsible for deciding on the appeals. If the Ministry of the Interior, the second deciding authority, decides negatively, the applicant has only two possibilities. Either she or he directly addresses the Administrative Court or the Constitutional Court with her or his complaint

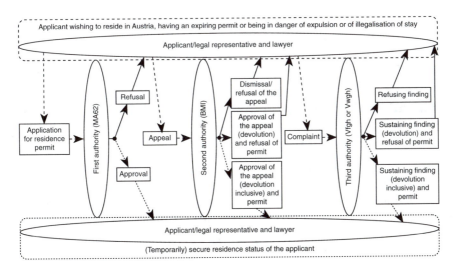

Figure 5.3 Most important channels and proceduralised textual chains regarding the implementation of the Residence Act

('*Beschwerde*'), which has to be signed by a lawyer, within a period of six weeks after the negative decision about the appeal against the refusal has been delivered to the applicant, or, if the applicant cannot or does not want to pay for a lawyer, she or he can make an application for approval of 'aid in the proceedings' ('*Verfahrenshilfe*'), i.e. for approval of a free lawyer, which must also be done within the period of six weeks. If the aid is approved, a lawyer is assigned free of charge. If the application for aid is rejected, the period of time (six weeks) during which an appeal addressed to one of the two courts may be lodged again comes into force. During this time, the applicant has to search for her or his own lawyer.

According to legally fixed formal defects and reasons for the dismissal of appeals, the refusal of appeals, the sustainings of appeals against refusals, the devolution of appeals against dismissals of appeals and other administrative dealings with appeals against refusals, one can codify the typology of official notifications issued by the second authority in the case of administrative decisions about residence permits, i.e. the Austrian Ministry of the Interior, Department III, Section 11 (see figure 5.4) (note that many of the applicants involved in the applications from which the following typology has been extracted are children or wives of non-Austrian citizens who live and work in Austria; note also that particularly the notifications of refusal R1–R14 bring repeatedly into play the arguments and references to laws already given by the first authority; see Liberales Forum 1997).

With respect to the readability of our own text – that is to say, in order not to overload the chapter with long-winded ponderous officialese that would explain the legal options of procedures in the political administration and implementation of the Residence Act – we will not spell out down to the last detail the typology listed of official notifications in the present context. However, we refer all readers who are not deterred by the officialdom that rears its ugly head to appendix 5.2, in which we try briefly to elucidate the listing and to indicate the complexity of everyday political administration in a modern nation state with the example of Austria.

The administrative practice of the municipal authorities from a linguistic and argumentation analytical perspective

Filling in gaps in the meaning of the respective laws that are to implement modern administration today acts more politically-formatively than it did in its past. It interprets and complements the wording of the increasingly complex and often intentionally vague laws (specific paragraphs of which are sometimes called '*Gummiparagraphen*', elastic paragraphs), in order to find practicable solutions for the single cases that are to be decided. However, it becomes increasingly difficult for executive members of the system of political administration to know and apply in their everyday bureaucratic work all the legal norms and instructions that are or would be relevant for a specific single case, because

1. Dismissal (*'Zurückweisung'*: D)
    D1 – appeal introduced too late
    D2 – lack of grounds for the appeal
    D3 – lack of application for appeal
    D4 – notification appealed against not identified
    D5 – brief of improvement of the _(date)_ not complied with within the period stipulated
    D6 – brief of improvement of the _(date)_ party legally not competent ('*geschäftsunfähig*')
    D7 – lack of signature in the applicant's own hand and doubts
    D8 – general:_____
2. Refusal (*'Abweisung'*: R)
    R1 – fraudulent marriage: marriage ceremony on the _____, judgement on the _____ Zl. _____, District Court _____
    R2 – Bosnian: State _____ Passport from _____, until _____
    R3 – § 6/2 on the Austrian state territory: date of arrival
    R4 – § 6/3 application too late, residence permit until _____
    R5 – § 10/1/1 residence ban: Authorities _____
          From _____, becoming final _____
    R6 – § 10/1/6 entry   without endorsement (*'Sichtvermerk'*)   tourist endorsement
    R7 – § 10/1 open for Clause (*'Ziffer'*) _____
    R8 – § 5 private stay:
    R9 – § 5 dwelling/living space: persons _____ land _____
    R10 – § 5 certification that no taxes, loans etc. are outstanding: LGAMS of _____
    R11 – § 13 iVm § 6/2 _____ weeks/months too late
    R12 – § 5/1 dummy/fictitious business
    R13 – § 5 sufficient maintenance not verified: means for maintenance ___ land ___
    R14 – § 5 sufficient maintenance not verified: minimum _____ actually _____
3. Sustaining (*'Stattgebung'*)
    S1 – vignette: via embassy   on the Austrian state territory   maintenance
    S2 – vignette: aim   dwelling/living space
    S3 – vignette: from _____ until _____   other
4. Devolution (*'Devolution'*, transference of the decision competence)
    DV1 – dismissal
    DV2 – sustaining
    DV3 – refusal
    DV4 – sustaining vignette   via embassy   on the Austrian state territory
5. Other (*'Sonstiges'*)
    SUS – suspension of the appeal (*'ausgesetzt'*), Authorities _____, Zl. _____
    FRT – removal/withdrawal via the official channels (*'amtsweg. Behebung'*)
    REF – referral to the first authority ('Instanz'), need for explanation, points _____

Figure 5.4 A typology of official notifications dealing with residence permits

there are too many regulations that must be taken into account. Some bureaucrats therefore resort to a pragmatic reduction of regulations, as has also happened in our instance of the negative notifications concerning aliens' residence permits. The administrative reduction of the legal complexity leads to the analytical result that negative notifications can exhaustively be systematised against the background of the typology listed above.

The augmenting vagueness of laws – 'an unfavourable and unplanned gap within the Aliens' Act' (a *'planwidrige Lücke im Fremdengesetz'*) is even admitted by the Austrian Minister of the Interior in his parliamentary response to the written question by the liberal opposition of Volker Kier and others, who criticise the Aliens' Act for contravening the Human Rights Convention, while according to the Minister of the Interior it does not (see *Der Standard* of 25/26 July 1998: 8) – enlarges the anonymous political power of the administrative authorities, and the probability of arbitrary, including illegal or illegitimate, interpretations and decision increases. This is all the more likely since, as administration experts reckon, most of the members of the bureaucratic system know only about a third of the relevant legal regulations.

Particularly bureaucrats who are not professionally qualified in jurisprudence tend towards an uncritical and truncated acceptance and application of the courts' decisions issued in the form of basic principles, without taking into consideration the context of the specific single cases with which the decisions are dealing (see Voigt 1990: 147). The laws' scope of interpretation, the very restrictive Residence Act, the complexity of the legal apparatus and the administrative system, pressure of time and juridical uninformedness are only six important factors, which had a decisive institutional influence that allowed personal and social prejudices hostile to specific groups of non-Austrian citizens to influence many decisions and written accounts among the negative notifications by Department 62 of the Viennese Municipal Authorities. As far as the prejudiced predications mentioned in chapter 2 are concerned, the following prejudices appeared in the notifications as parts, or strictly speaking, as premises both in the conclusion rule and in the minor premise of discriminatory argumentation:

*   'Foreigners are to blame for high unemployment rates'
*   'Foreigners are "socioparasites" ("*Sozialschmarotzer*") who exploit, endanger and overtax the welfare system with respect to housing, health and so on'
*   'Foreigners are not willing to adapt themselves, to assimilate and to conform'
*   'Foreigners are too different in culture and religion'
*   'Foreigners are careless and allow the flats and houses they are living in to fall into disrepair'
*   'Foreigners are always conspicuous and loud'
*   'Foreigners are aggressive and criminal. They endanger public order and security and tend to have fraudulent marriages'
*   'In contrast to "us", foreigners have too many children, which endangers the school success of "our" children and which leads to the infiltration of too many foreign influences'
*   'Foreigners are dirty'.

Most of these prejudiced predications will be encountered in the following analysis of passages extracted from negative notifications. In this analysis we will focus mainly on the (topical) argumentation and fallacy structure of the notifications, since the '*Begründung*' is the 'core' of this legal genre. As we will see, arguments relying on legal authority, dis/advantage, numbers, culture and hypothetical consequences are among the most frequent ones.

The first example is an extract from the above-quoted negative notification issued by Department 62 of the Viennese Municipal Authorities, which was publicly criticised as '*headscarf notification*', as its argumentation relies on two prejudices: that the residence permit is denied by the authorities on the ground of the arguments that the applicant is culturally too different (this difference is metaphoricised by the 'wearing of a headscarf'), and is not able or willing to adapt herself and assimilate to the alleged hegemonic culture (speaking metaphorically, not willing to the take off the headscarf). This argumentation, here addressed to a female Turkish citizen, is clearly 'culturalist racist' and was recycled in at least twenty-five negative notifications as a textual module (see *Der Standard* of 7 July 1998: 8).

> The documentation clearly establishes that the husband of the applicant currently resides in Austria, and in consequence it cannot be denied that personal and family ties with Austria exist.
>
> In view of the intrusion clause of Par. 8 Section 2 MRK, it is possible to effect a constitutional interpretation of Par. 3 Section 5 of the Residence Act, provided that the Authority balances the private interests of the parties concerned against the public interest. In this case, and given that the number of applications for family reunion currently exceeds the allotted number of permissions, it was decided after careful consideration that the present application could not be favoured above the applications of other foreigners, since immediate integration of the applicant appears impossible, all the more since the husband, although resident in Austria, is himself still in the process of achieving integration in Austria. Granting rights of residence to the applying party, from whose application no circumstances can be deduced to facilitate an easy integration, would only further encumber the already costly efforts towards integration of the foreign fellow citizens already here, since everyday experience shows that those who arrive as adults from the same culture area as the applying party are hardly likely to enter into communication with the local population, especially not in terms of speaking the language, and are hardly likely to successfully adapt to Central-European customs, traditions and ways of life, even after a residency of many years. Thus, the decision had to be taken according to the ruling.
>
> (Notification of 26 March 1996)[1]

Looking linguistically at this quotation, at least three things are conspicuous. First, the references both to the applicant and to the authorities are extremely impersonal, and this is, of course, not only a peculiarity of this specific sort of notification, but a typical feature of almost all genres within the social action field of political administration. While the applicant, a female Turkish citizen applying for family reunion in Austria, is impersonally addressed and judged upon in the third person singular and referred to in terms of 'the party', 'applications of other foreigners', 'the party', 'those who arrive as adults from the same culture area as the applying party' and 'the applying party', the issuing authority is only once identified as 'the authority' and otherwise always suppressed or backgrounded by passivation as in 'it was decided', 'could not be favoured', 'can be deduced', by agent deletion through grammatical (experiential) metaphors like 'careful consideration' and 'everyday experience shows' and by impersonal constructions like 'it appears'. Second, as far as the argumentation structure is considered, in this quotation one can find the culture topos already mentioned in chapter 2, which is employed for 'culturalist racist' argumentation. In addition, within this passage there are also the genre-obligatory topos of law as well as the topos of advantage, and these are both in the form of a *pro bono publico* (in the public interest) and in the form of a *pro bono eorum* (for the benefit of foreign fellow citizens). Third, one cannot overlook how weak the whole argumentation is: that is to say, that the modality, or strictly speaking, the modalisation, indicates an extremely uncertain epistemic status of the authority's contentions. The modalising mitigation signals that the whole argumentation is highly hypothetical and badly supported. Rather than being grounded on factual observations, the authority asserts with the mitigating verb of felling 'appear' (see chapter 2, p. 84) that immediate integration of the applicant '*appears*' impossible. Further, it refers extremely vaguely to somebody's 'everyday experience', which seems to suggest that persons like the applicant are '*hardly likely*' to enter into communication with the local population and 'successfully to adapt to Central-European customs, traditions and ways of life'. In addition, the fallacious *argumentum at consequentiam* – which points out without proving it, (*petitio principii*), that a positive decision on the application leads to the unfavourable consequence of encumbering 'the already costly efforts towards integration of the foreign fellow citizens already here' – is modalisingly mitigated by subjunctive and future tense '*would encumber*'. In contrast to the highly speculative epistemic modality and in order to stress the necessity for the decision, the modulation employed by the authority indicates strong obligation, which contradicts the epistemic uncertainty (the integration appears to be 'impossible', the decision 'had to be taken').

The *topos of law/right* is employed in every notification, as it is a prerequisite of this legal genre. This means that if a law or some otherwise codified norm prescribes/forbids a specific politico-administrative action, the action has to be performed/omitted. This topos can be considered to be a specific form of the *topos of authority*. As such, it is not always easy to delimit it from the *argumentum ad verecundiam*. To mention just one example: 'The application of 31 July 1995 by [name of the female claimant] for a residence permit according to Par. 1 Section 1 and Par. 6 Section 1 ... of the Residence Act is rejected with regard to Par. 3 Section 5 of the Residence Act'.[2]

The *topos of advantage* (both as *pro bono publico* and as *pro bono eorum*) is also employed in the following quotation, which is a textual module that had been recycled in several notifications referring to the 'public interest':

In reference to the intervening clause provided in Art. 8 Sec. 2 of MRK, it would be possible to effect an interpretation of Par. 3 Sec. 5 of the Residence Law that is in agreement with the constitution, provided that the authorities balance the private interests of the parties concerned against the public interest. In this case, and given that the number of applications for family reunion currently exceeds the allotted number of permissible applications, it was decided upon careful consideration that the present application could not be favoured above the applications of other foreigners, since immediate integration of the applicant appears impossible.[3]

The *topos of definition/interpretation* is associated with the *non-sequitur fallacy* and the *fallacy of petitio principii* in the following example taken from a decision of the Austrian Administrative Court (*Erkenntnis* of 14 February 1997, Zl. 95/19/0629-0631), which criticises the fact that the chosen interpretation of the authorities is untenable, since

in the wording of Par. 3 Sec. 5 no order is recognisable, whereby applications ... that are not preferentially taken into account are rejected. One enters into contradictory assessments in which the previously made application should be refused in which it was first foreseen with this application that, in reference to the specific quotas of the year in question, it will not be processed. While an application made later is kept on record and is delayed where it is already certain that the application will not be processed in the year in question because of the already filled quota.[4]

(Quoted in Wiener Integrationsfonds 1997: 86)

The textual module of 'over-foreignerisation' is recycled very often. It contains a fallacious *argumentum ad numerum*:

Concerning the amount of over-foreignerisation it is to be noted that, according to statistics from central office, 300,675 foreigners live in Vienna. That makes 18.4 per cent of the total population of Vienna. Of these, 180,350 or 60 per cent are from the former Yugoslavia or Turkey. The percentage of foreign students in compulsory schools is even 30.55 per cent. The percentage of foreign students in the year 1993/94 was 28.4 per cent. Out of the percentage of foreign students attending compulsory schools, 82.75 per cent were Yugoslav and Turkish. Out of the total number of students attending compulsory schools, this amounted to 23.5 per cent.

(Notification of January 1997)[5]

The socially engaged jurist Ulrike Davy disqualified the employment of the unjuridical term (in fact, the term was already used by the Nazis, see also p. 199) and criticised the numerical fallacy as inhumane:

'Over-foreignerisation' is not explicitly mentioned in the Zielkatalog of
Art. 8 Sec. 2 of EMRK ... From this it is possible, at the very least, to
conclude that exceeding a specific quota does not warrant, in and of itself,
an intrusion in the law of Art. 8 Sec. 1 of ERMK. An authority responsible
for residency that implements a 'policy of purity' based strictly on numbers
therefore (also) violates Austrian fundamental rights.

(Quoted in Hödl and Winter 1998: 116)[6]

Another textual module very often recycled in the notifications concerns
the questions of sufficient 'living space' ('*ortsübliche Unterkunft*') and secure livelihood ('*gesicherten Lebensunterhalt*'). To quote two examples referring to the concept
of an adequate dwelling and employing the *topos of number*:

In Vienna, the average living space per person is around 33 m². 3.4 per
cent of Austrian citizens living in Vienna have a living space of less than
10 m² – throughout Austria, this number is only 0.83 per cent. Therefore,
the measurement of customary accommodation must correspond to the
prevailing majority of the Austrian people and not to this neglected
minority.

(Notification of 28 February 1997)[7]

For the judgement of what is customary, the guidelines for the ordering
and assigning of community residences may be consulted since out of
870,000 available residences in Vienna, 215,000 are community residences
(25%). A claim to a community residence exists according to the responsible
municipal department's guidelines for assigning residences when there is
surplus demand. This permits the reverse conclusion that a residence with
surplus demand in Austria does not constitute customary residence.

(Notification of 28 February 1997,
quoted in Hödl and Winter 1998: 117)[8]

Interestingly, only Austrian citizens are entitled to live in flats built by the
local government ('*Gemeindewohnungen*'). Thus, the argumentation in the second
quotation could, in a certain sense, be invalidated as an *ignoratio elenchi*: why
should one apply the specific municipal department's guidelines with respect
to community residences to non-Austrian citizens for negative purposes, if
non-Austrian citizens are strictly excluded from the positive regulations of the
guidelines? Turning the argumentation the other way round, one could employ
a *topos of justice* and argue: if the criterion of a locally adequate dwelling is
applied to non-Austrian citizens, then, they should also have access to community residences.

The prejudice of dirtiness is implicitly ascribed in the following example,
which also refers to the dwelling:

For the judgement of whether a residence is customary, it is of course
necessary to pay attention to the legally stipulated hygienic conditions and,

in reference to community health, the required measures for health provisions. For a 3-member family, these requirements are not fulfilled when, in the residence applied for, neither a bathroom nor a WC is present. Especially for families – as in the case applied for – that having a child who is required to attend school, a residence can only be understood as customary when in addition to the parent's and children's bedrooms, there is also a living space for the family's social and cultural activities.

(Notification of 14 March 1997,
quoted in Hödl and Winter 1998: 117)[9]

A flat in which a Turkish citizen lives, who desires his wife, his sister and his mother to come to Austria, is not accepted as '*ortsüblich*' by the authorities, because no 'separate bedroom is available for every generation and the in-laws. In a residence that is inhabited by numerous people, an additional living space that is separated from the bedrooms is also necessary' (Notification of 28 February 1997, quoted in Hödl and Winter 1998: 118).[10]

The juridical weakness and lack of tenability of such an argumentation that relies on the argument of the 'local standard dwelling' is criticised by Ulrike Davy as follows:

In the view of the administrative law courts 'the rules of Par. 5 Sec. 1 of the Residency law are considered unconstitutional in view of Art. 8 Sec. 1 of EMRK, if the authorities always intrude on the rights of Art. 8 Sec. 1 when presenting the reasons for refusal. To a greater extent, the authorities are obligated to achieve a balance of interests that also can result in the granting of a permit for additional persons, even though the residence does not correspond to the usual standards for Austrian citizens.'

(Davy 1997a: 472)[11]

Similarly to the textual modules quoted above, however, the authorities sometimes argued (both in 1995 and in 1996) that the refusal would be justified because

the residence applied for, consisting of one room and one kitchen, [is, M.R. and R.W.] inhabited by at least three persons, as determined by a residence inspection ... Consequently, the applicant's daughter who is required to attend school does not have, as it is common in Austria, her own separate walled-off bedroom. The public interest, which speaks against granting, [is, M.R. and R.W.] greater than the party's contrary private and family interests.

(Notification from May 1996,
quoted in Wiener Integrationsfonds 1997: 87)[12]

Very often, the Viennese Authorities in recycled textual modules pass judgement on an applying non-Austrian, very often Turkish, citizen, deeming – with the help of a *topos of culture* – that

even though residing for several years in Austria, upon careful consideration, however, no obstacles [exist] for returning to Turkey in order to raise
a family. This possibility is the more real, since the applicant has spent
his/her whole life there and therefore has grown up in the cultural and
linguistic environment of the land.

> (Notification of 27 January 1997, of 24 and 28 February 1997, of 14
> March 1997, quoted in Hödl and Winter 1998: 119)[13]

The 'lack of maintenance' as a very often fallacious argument (i.e. a specific
argumentum ad numerum) for the refusal of a residence permit for family members
may be illustrated by the following example: a Turkish citizen with a gross
income of AS 18,000 is not considered to be capable of maintaining a family.
The authorities even insinuate that the affected party does not have adequate
financial resources to survive without social assistance (Notification of 14 March
1997, in Hödl and Winter 1998: 119).[14]

The fallacious *argumentum ad consequentiam* already illustrated, based on a more
than very weak epistemic certainty (see the example discussed above in this
section), is also employed in the following example, which was repeatedly
employed as a textual module:

> ... that increased family reunification without a concurrent solution to the
> problem of family members receiving access to the job market ... [can]
> only lead to the ghettoisation and impoverishment of underprivileged
> immigrants, which, in turn, will not stimulate economic growth in Austria
> and will only have negative socio-political effects.
>
> (Notification of 27 January 1997, of 24 February 1997, of 14 March
> 1997, quoted in Hödl and Winter 1998: 119)[15]

Here the *fallacy of consequence* is realised in combination with the *topos of numbers*
and the *topos of disadvantage*. Ulrike Davy criticises this as follows:

> The notifications rest simply on the assumption that: an effort is made to
> keep one's residency; married couples will regularly beget children (who
> will then go to school in Austria and will afterwards enter the workforce);
> and wives will also look for part- or full-time work. The notifications further-
> more rest on the (unverified) assumption that these 'plans' cannot or can
> only poorly be put into effect and that the family will slip into social poverty.
> With these heavily prejudicial and generalisable assumptions concerning
> individual résumés, it is not adequately justifiable to refuse additional
> persons in accordance with Art. 8 Sec. 2 of EMRK for the economic
> wellbeing of the land or to maintain the public peace and order.
>
> (Davy 1997a: 471)

Notifications from the Aliens' Office issuing the residence ban sometimes
also contain an *argumentum ad consequentiam*. This is based on the prejudice of

criminality in the following example: a Pakistani citizen is banned from staying in Austria, with the prejudiced assumption that

> because of the inadequate amount of cash [AS 2,500 support from Caritas] it can not be assumed that [he] is able to finance [his] further stay and/or [his] return trip to his homeland. There [exists] therefore the suspicion that [he] will remain longer in the federal territory and that his residency will be financed through punishable offences.
>
> (Notification from June 1997,
> quoted in Hödl and Winter 1998: 121)[16]

The expulsion of a woman with the child of her marriage with an Austrian citizen and whose child is, thus, also an Austrian citizen, is cynically and contemptuously justified by the authorities with the help of the refutation of a *topos of consequence*, which the authorities seem to interpret as a sort of *non-sequitur fallacy*:

> Against the appellant's explanations that, because of her child's Austrian citizenship her child should remain in Austria, and that the Aliens' Department supports the point of view that the child should grow up here without her parents, it must be objected that a child must orient to the residence of his/her parents and, on the other hand, for Austrian citizenship, there is no obligation to remain constantly in Austria. There exists, therefore, for the appellant no necessity to leave her child here ... But it also runs contrary to the interests of the maintenance of principles in dealing with foreigners when a foreigner, simply because of the fact that he/she has a child with Austrian citizenship, requires further illegal residency in the federal territory permanently.
>
> (Notification of the '*Sicherheitsdirektion Wien*' from 16 April 1997,
> quoted in Hödl and Winter 1998: 123)[17]

At this point we will conclude our theoretical analysis of the argumentation of these notifications. We believe we have sufficiently revealed and illustrated some of our concerns as critical discourse analysts with regard to the argumentation practice involved in the political administration of social exclusion. We hope that we have shown the misanthropic discriminatory practices carried out by a section of the Austrian bureaucratic state apparatus – practices indeed that, on the basis of the commitment to fundamental ethical principles of justice, equality and recognition, assume the character of democratic illegitimacy that contradicts fundamental human rights. That means against the background of our argumentation theory approach to a model of 'deliberative democracy' outlined in chapter 2 (pp. 69–71) that the notifications violate many of the ten rules of rational argument, and, thus, are not 'convincing' in the sense of 'rationally persuasive'. They are, therefore, democratically not legitimate. Apart from raising the question of legitimacy or legality, we also hope to have demonstrated with the help of the expertise of critical jurists like Ulrike Davy that some of the notifications in question are not even lawful within the particular legalistic framework of the Austrian nation state: that is to say, that some of the administrative practices performed by the authorities through these notifications do not correspond to the established laws, since the interpretation of the specific law is not adequate or contradicts the interpretation of another law.

It is vital for a democratic state that the partial illegitimacy, irrationality or illegality of its political administration should lead to public critique that – as a means of political control – aims at abolishing the respective undemocratic discriminatory practices. We will illustrate this in the final part of this chapter with the example of the critical public discussion of the authorities' refusals of residence permits for aliens.

Public critique as political control

'The public sphere is like the pupil in the eye of the body politic; when its vision is murky, cloudy, or hindered, the sense of direction of the polity is also impaired' (Benhabib 1996: 209). This quotation is intended to stress, in general, the importance of the public for political orientation and decision-making within a state and, in particular, the necessity of transparency, clearness and lack of bias for public democratic deliberation and political control.

But what do 'public' or 'public sphere' and 'political control' mean within the organisational framework of a democratic nation-state?

Although we will also discuss the concept of 'public' in chapter 6, we can already emphasise here that we conceive it pluralistically as complex, more or less institutionalised communication networks which are not necessarily bound to fixed places or locations such as parliaments, town and city halls or specific squares and assembly rooms. Whenever the object of discussion is a political matter of shared interest, the place where the politically engaged persons gather together can be any room (also a living room), square, street, field, meadow and so on.

While the first public spheres in modern societies, viz. salons, clubs, cafés and dinner parties (see Habermas 1962: 90–106, and Benhabib 1996: 45–56) were based on quite small face-to-face interactions, technological developments very soon allowed the expansion of the addressable auditorium, though at the expense of the personal presence of the – at least theoretically – participating political actors. Consequently, public spheres have become less reciprocal, more unidirectional, abstract, indirect and dependent on the electronic and printed mediation of the mass media. This has led, under the influence of the growing marketisation of the media (see Fairclough 1995b), to the rise of a new form of power (media power), which is sometimes called the fourth power (see Jäger and Link 1993). This means that media people act according to their own interests and, for different reasons, very selectively pick out events thought to be worth communicating to the public, thereby strongly influencing the perception and activities of all social actors involved in the system of public communication.

The ongoing commercialisation of the media clearly increases the danger that the ideal of autonomous and participating political individuals or citizens fades into a counter-factual democratic dream in view of the increasingly disillusioned perception of pure spectators and consumers who are fobbed off with prefabricated pictures and messages that help to promote sensation-voyeurism and to colonise the lifeworld of the recipients (Benhabib 1992b: 128). In order to avoid a situation where the public sphere becomes merely a virtual space of enter- and info-tainment, it is necessary for democratic societies that the public sphere is organised around the principles of:

- open, free and equal access
- discursivity (in the Habermasian sense of a rational debate about validity claims in which it is the 'compulsion of the better argument' that leads to political decisions)
- effectiveness: that is to say, of influence on the processes of political decision-making, both in the sense of an immediate perception and taking-into-consideration by the democratically delegated decision-makers and an influence on the formation of political opinions and voting preferences of the citizens (see Gerhards 1998: 272).

Such a concept of 'public sphere' conceptualises the public as pre-, intra- and post-parliamentarian 'place' – and not just as a *pre*-parliamentarian sphere as implied by Axel Honneth (1999: 39) – where public opinions are formed by the free exchange of beliefs and arguments. It is, further, based on the normative claim that the democratic exercise of power and the implementation and administration of justice by democratic institutions have to be visible, transparent, examinable and questionable, in order to be able permanently to examine their legitimacy (see also below, chapter 6). The controlling function of the public is crucial for democracies, all the more so since the public sphere is not directly or immediately associated with that sort of justification-compulsive political power that has to do with the setting of legal norms. However, as a recent study on the organisations of the EU illustrates (Weiss and Wodak 2000a, forthcoming) new public spaces are being created because of changes in supranational organisations that do not fall into any of the above-mentioned conceptualisations of the 'public': for example, the so-called 'expert regime'. The impact of the new, supranational expert groups still has to be researched in detail.

In general, 'political control' denotes the limitation and examination of state exercises of power. It is conceptually related with the notions of 'critique', 'power regulation', 'transparency of responsibility', 'demanding of account' and 'comparison between 'should' and 'being' (see Nödl 1995: 19). It is the inspection of an activity's correspondence with the relevant and decisive norms through comparison of the actual with the required state or situation (see Voigt 1990: 130).

With respect to the question of political and legal justification, 'political control' means both the examination of the legality, i.e. conformity with the law – including the examination of the conformity of a specific law with another (mostly, more fundamental and basic) one, and the examination of the democratic legitimacy of laws: for instance, by comparing their compatibility with human rights or the principle of the sovereignty of the people (see Habermas 1998b: 173).

According to the liberal-democratic concept of separation of powers, legislation, the executive and jurisdiction are the three distinct political powers that have discrete areas of competence and that control each other mutually. The control of the political administration, i.e. the implementation of laws and administration of justice, by juridical institutions (especially the Administrative and Constitutional Court), is concerned with the examination of the correct application of legal regulations. Thus, it is not a control of success or efficiency, but of legality.

Nowadays, media coverage is one of the most potent instruments for opposition parties and social or civil movements to control and influence both public opinion and the decision-making processes in which the governing politicians and administrative organs are primarily involved.

Genuine political instruments of control, like interpolations, petitions and parliamentary questions, represent direct means of political intervention, which are, in the first place, located in the close area of parliamentarism. Their influence can be increased by media coverage. The public sphere is the hinge by which minority political parties as well as social movements interact with political decision-makers. Media coverage can be a quite efficient means to force ruling politicians not simply to ignore the requests and matters with which minorities are concerned, but to react to them (see Schmitt-Beck 1998: 475). This, however, presupposes, first, that criticism has access to the media and, second, that the media people themselves are not just hench- or spokespersons of the hegemonic political group. Thus, it is of eminent, 'vital' significance for modern democracies to have media that are largely independent, which in Austria is clearly not the case. (There is very little competition and almost no 'market' in the media. See Trappel 1991, Pelinka, Duchkowitsch and Hausjell 1992, Bruck, Selhofer and Stocker 1995.)

If we try to apply critically the three above-mentioned criteria for democratic public spheres, viz. that of, first, free and equal access, second, of discursivity and, third, of effectiveness, to the case we are analysing in this chapter, we must state that it complied with them – at best – only partially. The first criterion was the least fulfilled, since those who were immediately concerned with the authorities' refusals, the applicants, had little or no direct access to the media. They had to rely on aid organisations and politicians of opposition parties (both at the communal and the national level) who are concerned with anti-discrimination interventions and activities and who themselves quite strongly depend on having good contacts with and enjoying the favour of media people – which is a very problematic point for deliberative democracies. The second criterion was also only partly fulfilled, because the press reports on the authorities' discriminatory treatment of the applying non-Austrian citizens were, except in a few instances, very brief, so that not all 'voices' could obtain a public hearing and no real deliberative debate about this case of institutionalised bureaucratic discrimination arose. This was all the more marked since some of the (responsible) actors even refused to appear publicly and justify their practices. The third criterion, finally, was hesitantly but in the main fulfilled as far as the question of perception and taking-into-consideration on the part of the democratically delegated responsible politicians was concerned. We cannot really answer the question of the reports' influence on the formation of political opinion and voting preferences of the citizens here. On the other hand, the fear of losing the favour of different groups of voters may have had some influence both on the delay in making decisions and on finally making the specific decisions against institutional discrimination. However, members of the Green Party and the Liberal Forum made quite successful use of the controlling function of media coverage. Vienna's Mayor twice issued a directive against the authorities' administrative abuse of power and, in July 1998, though after more than two years of discussion, the responsible municipal politician decided to withdraw Werner Sokop's authority for the administration of the Residence Act or Aliens' Act. The pressure of public critique finally forced Renate Brauner, the Viennese City Councillor for Integration, to take this decision.

In the following, we will focus selectively on two examples of public political control from the discourse about aliens' residence permits.

The mind in the bureaucratic machine, or a civil servant's poems: looking behind the anonymous scenes of political administration

The first example concerns Hans Werner Sokop, the jurist and Chief Council Officer of Department 62 of the Viennese Municipal Authorities who is chiefly responsible for the negative, discriminatory notifications of the first authority, which legally enact and officially inform the applying non-Austrian citizens of the refusal of their applications for residence permits. The decision to revoke Sokop's being in charge of the administrative implementation of the Residence Act in Vienna was extremely delayed and ponderous. Renate Brauner did not simply withdraw the chief council officer's competence to deal with applications for residence permits. Apart from party-political, strategical reasons, this action was severely hindered by the fact that Sokop, because of the legal regulation of 'pragmatisation' (in Austrian German: '*Pragmatisierung*') 'stuck firmly' to his post as a civil servant and, thus, could only be dismissed with great difficulty. Brauner herself repeatedly argued as follows: 'Sokop is not a politician who can be required to resign. He is a civil servant, and the reasons for dismissal from office are very meticulously regulated' (Brauner in the interview in *Der Standard* of 7 July 1998: 8). Therefore another, more indirect remedy had to be invented in order to reach the same aim. Under the clever guise of institutional reform and reorganisation, Brauner decided to transfer the competence for the administration of the Residence Act from Department 62 (MA 62) to another department of the Municipal Authorities. This other department did not yet exist, but had to be newly established. Renate Brauner did nothing to threaten Sokop's face. She even felt obliged to state publicly that this measure was not a 'punishment' of Sokop. Moreover, she explained, the examination of the reform of Department 62 had led to the conclusion that 'such a difficult matter as the Aliens' Act needs its own department' (*Der Standard*, 7 July 1998: 8).

After the 'reform', Sokop still remained head of Department 62, which is now responsible for elections and the regional Security Act, while the officials of the new department – who will receive special training, psychological advice and supervision – are now dealing with the implementation of the Aliens' Act.

Though the reasons for Brauner's decision seemed to be quite clear, she did not verbally concede to her political opponents, the Greens and the Liberal Forum, that it was their persistent and revealing public critique of Sokop and his department's administrative practices of discrimination that, in the end, forced Brauner to act against Sokop.

One of the most crucial motives for finally withdrawing Sokop's responsibility for the implementation of the Aliens' Act was the exposure and critique of his side activities as an author of dialect poems with antisemitic and ethnicist contents. The politician Maria Vassilakou, a member of the City Council and the Integration Spokesperson for Vienna's Green Party, considered Sokop's activities as a writer to be a 'grave violation of public service' (see *Der Standard*, 12 May 1997). Sokop's poems would reveal the prejudice of the Chief Council Officer of Department 62 of the Municipal Authorities. Thus, the Greens in Vienna's City Council demanded the suspension of the leader of the 'residence authorities'.

Particularly thanks to Maria Vassilakou, but also thanks to Marco Smoliner, another member of the City Council and Spokesperson on Integration as well as Security for Vienna's Liberal Forum, Sokop was finally, though indirectly, released from his specific administrative function regarding 'aliens' matters'. Vassilakou and Smoliner at regular intervals made use of their contacts with critical journalists of the Austrian daily *Der Standard* and the two Austrian weeklies *Falter* and *profil*. In more than fifty press articles published in these three press organs over a period of about two-and-a-half years, they undermined the professional seriousness of Sokop by publicly criticising Sokop's writing of dialect poems as containing antisemitic verses as well as verses that are hostile to foreigners.

From the point of view of argumentation theory, the critique against Sokop has the form of a specific *argumentum ad hominem*. Here, this argumentation scheme aims at questioning the civil servant's impartiality. However, the very specific form of an *argumentum ad hominem* in this single concrete case cannot simply be disqualified as a fallacy. The attack on Sokop's personality has convincing force, as the poems actually prove a hostility to foreigners that seriously questions Sokop's professional aptitude as Chief Council Officer in charge of the implementation of the Aliens' Act.

We will quote just a few examples from two anthologies of poems. In 1991, Sokop published a collection of poems entitled *Wiener Woikerln: Gedichte in Wiener Mundart*, i.e. 'Small Viennese Clouds: Poems in Viennese Dialect'. This collection is divided into four sections with four topics. They are entitled 'At that time' ('*Seinerzeit*'), 'Such a year' ('*A so a Joa*'), 'Holiday season ('*Urlaubszeit*') and '... They are also human' ('... *san aa Menschn*'). It is not hard to guess that the first section is dedicated to a historical retrospection focusing on Austria's past, strictly speaking, from the Hallstatt period to postwar Austria. The second section is concerned with looking back over the passing of a year, while the third part of the collection deals with experiences during the vacation period. The last part contains poems about different people of different ages, of different ethnic origin and in different situations of life. The following two poems are taken from this fourth section. They both evoke the ethnicist prejudice of Austria's infiltration by too many foreigners and foreign influences. As we showed earlier in this chapter, the prejudice of 'over-foreignerisation' ('*Überfremdung*') even appears lexically and explicitly in at least twenty-five negative notifications issued by Department 62 of the Municipal Authorities in the summer of 1996. While the 'over-foreignerisation' prejudice of the notifications is mainly directed against non-Austrian citizens from Turkey, in the two poems, the target is Chinese people in Austria. It is no accident that Sokop's chooses Chinese people as a symbol for the prejudiced danger of foreign infiltration, because Sokop can reckon with the readers' background knowledge that the population of China is the largest in the world. The first short poem indirectly states that there are too many Chinese restaurants in Vienna or Austria, which oust the typical old-established Viennese restaurants:

> Bitter Rice
> It's bitter/when a Chinese/gets an appetite/for a fiaker-goulash/
> And in the area/only three Chinese restaurants/are open...
>
> (Sokop 1991: 55)[18]

The metaphorical title of this poem becomes clear in the text: the negative predication of 'bitterness' in the title is extended to a semantic isotope by the lexical repetition of the adjective 'bitter'. The author, Sokop, designates the rice a 'collective symbol' (see p. 26) for the Chinese culture of cooking, to become 'bitter' in a metaphorical sense by depicting it to be the only food available in Austria, and Chinese restaurants to be the only places where one can go to eat – even when, in certain situations, when a Chinese person, who seems to be presupposed normally to eat rice, wants to consume something else – strictly speaking, a fiaker goulash. The 'fiaker goulash' serves Sokop as a 'collective symbol', i.e. simultaneously as a metaphor and a synecdoche representing the typical Viennese (and partially also Austrian) cooking. Together with the 'rice', it forms an opposition which helps construct an antagonism between Viennese and Chinese culture. Sokop is not aiming at criticising globalising uniformisation or the lack of cultural variety. His critique is motivated by nationalism and/or regionalism. The opposition between 'Chinese rice' and 'Viennese or Austrian fiaker goulash' is not value-free. The 'rice' is judged in a negative evaluation to be 'bitter'. However, the poem does not make explicit and unambiguously clear who may be the senser or sensers – the construction '*scho bitter*' ('it's bitter') is impersonal and lacks any social actor acting as a senser – that is to say, for whom the rice tastes 'bitter', whether it is 'the Chinese person' (as a *pars pro toto* for 'culturally different aliens in Austria') wanting to eat a fiaker goulash, or the Austrian author, or the author and his Viennese or national ingroup (including the readers who are prevalently supposed to belong to this ingroup), or both 'the Chinese person' and the 'Austrian ingroup' (including the author and the readers).

From an argumentation theoretical point of view the poem contains an implicit appellative 'topos arguing from the less' (i.e. an implicit *locus a minore*), which addresses the imaginary Viennese or Austrian readers. This argumentation scheme can be paraphrased as follows: if already the less probable case occurs, then the more probable case should all the more occur. In a certain sense, the poem even comprised two such topoi. The first one may be explicated as: if Chinese people, who normally like to eat rice, already want to consume fiaker goulash in Austria, you, as a 'good' or 'real' Viennese or Austrian, should appreciate this food even more. This argumentation is, by the way, based on the implication that fiaker goulash is so good that even members of other cultures who normally eat something else want to enjoy it. The second 'topos from the less' can be formulated as: if Chinese people in specific situations already regret not getting fiaker goulash when they want some, you should all the more regret it if you cannot get your typical regional dish.

The main message of this poem is that there are so many Chinese restaurants in Austria that replace the typical Viennese restaurants and food – at least as far as specific hours of business are concerned – that it is too much and frustrating even for Chinese people living in Austria. Taking the proposition of the poem's main clause as unquestioned, one could, however, easily turn the message around and conclude: when you want to eat something in Vienna, luckily, there are Chinese restaurants that are open even when typical Viennese restaurants are closed.

Werner Sokop is far from such reasoning. That can also be illustrated by the second poem selected from the same anthology. It is printed on the same page as the first poem and also deals with the prejudice of too many Chinese restaurants driving out the old-established Viennese ones, which are in danger of becoming exotic. In addition to the first poem, the second one not only ethnicistically imagines the threat of an everyday-cultural 'over-foreignerisation' in the area of cooking, it also depicts the threat of a 'racial' or 'ethnic mixing' by reproduction. This 'bio-political' warning is typical of the so-called 'differentialist' or 'ethnopluralist racism', which propagates a strict segregation of ethnicities and takes the view that multiculturalism threatens 'cultural and ethnic purity' and leads to 'contamination, degeneration and decline' (see chapter 1, pp. 9–10).

The Chinese are Coming
The coin laundromats/In the sixties/Now really .../But today with these/
Chinese restaurants/For a restaurant/To become something exotic .../
Just laugh. – This misfortune,/When the daughter/gives birth to a wee
Mongolian/And the doctor says:/'Anyhow, it's a picture of health'.

(Sokop 1991: 55)[19]

The title of the poem dynamically and Austro-centrically formulates the
present and future arrival of 'the Chinese' in Austria. The definite article,
which is typical of prejudiced discourse, helps Sokop linguistically to construct
an all-encompassing Chinese 'collective'. The poem itself is divided into three
parts, which are chronologically ordered along the time axis and assigned to
past, present and future. They are separated by two pseudo-dialogical elements,
the one of which (*'na bitte'*/'now really') being an emphatic and negating
conversational routine formula, the other an appellative formula with the
rhetorical form of a *permissio*: that is to say, of an ironic, apparent imperative
demand; rhetoric describes it as 'irony of false advice' (see Plett 1989: 65),
which means the opposite of what it literally says (*'lach nur'*/'just laugh') and
which typically introduces a verbal threat. Sokop applies an intensification
strategy relying on a rhetorical three-part *incrementum*: that is to say, a sequence
of aggravation. While the first part simply refers to the 1960s when laundromats
were introduced in Vienna, the second and the third part of the poem threaten
with two dangers. In the second part, Sokop has visions of a reversal of the
exotic status of restaurants in Austria, the old-established ones (the *'Beisln'*)
becoming rarities, the others becoming a majority. As mentioned, the third
part is introduced by the pseudo-dialogic, threatening *permissio* meaning 'just
you wait if you don't take my warning seriously!'. In this culminating part the
amateur poet fantasises about the birth of a healthy baby that has an Austrian
mother and a Chinese father. Sokop discriminatorily predicates this birth as
being a misfortune that cannot be diminished by the fact that the baby is
absolutely healthy. Though there are no explicit you-deictic linguistic elements
in the third part of the poem, the dialogical introductory formula rubs off on
this whole part, which seems to be addressed to the Austrian parents of the
daughter who gives birth to the child. The imagined child is identified to be a
'wee Mongolian'. In this, Sokop presupposes that the genetic material of the
Chinese father is the decisive factor in determining a child's 'racialised' or
'ethnicised' identity, the genetic material of the mother being completely
irrelevant. Apart from this biological perspective, which makes the genetic factor
to be the one that determines the identity of a person, the predication of 'misfortune' introduces a discriminatory hierarchy of groups of persons in which
'Chinese persons', however defined, are subordinated to 'Austrians', however
defined.

The prejudiced fear of 'over-foreignerisation' expressed in the two poems is
also present in the second anthology, which Werner Sokop published in 1996,
when the mythicalised date of the first written documentation of the toponym
'ostarrichi' (for 'Austria') was officially commemorated in Austria (see Reisigl

1999b). The anthology, entitled *1,000 Years Austria: A Viennese Rhyme Chronicle* (*'1,000 Jahre Österreich: Eine Wiener Reimchronik'*) contains 1,000 couplets, each of which is dedicated to one of the 1,000 years from 996, the year of the first written record of the toponym, and 1996, the year of the commemorated millennium. We selectively quote only forty-nine out of the 1,000 couplets (the German original is reproduced in appendix 5.3 of this chapter). However, these selected verses are the most discriminatory ones. Primarily, they aim pejoratively at 'Turks', 'Jews', 'Poles', 'Hungarians', 'Swabians', 'Swiss', 'Bavarians', 'black slaves', 'Protestants', 'Huguenots' and 'women':

1013   The Pole Boleslaw, the louse,/Simply brought Lausitz under his control ...

1042   The Hungarians need to be shown a thing or two,/King Peter has been chased out ...

1049   Church rule needs to be reinstated/And no women, thank you very much ...

1094   The Byzantine emperor calls: Listen,/the Turks are coming and it bothers me ...

1103   Heinrich thinks dearly of the Jews:/Out of business, honestly, are they driven ...

1124   One wants the Poles in Pommern, so that they come to know the truth,/to become Christians ...

1205   In Vienna, there exist cultural ambitions,/A Jewish school, a synagogue ...

1238   The Jews are given special rights/As servants to the emperor ...

1244   The Jews should rejoice because of the royal decree:/They have the right to lend money ...

1260   The Gozzoburg in Krems is getting good./In Kroissenbrunn Hungarian blood flows ...

1267   The church wants, that everyone obeys. -/And Jews wear a hat with horns ...

1287   With the duke we will have problems,/We do not want Swabians in office ...

1303   The Albrecht gives him [the Pope] his word,/The Jews in Vienna are not happy ...

1364   Out of fear, perhaps, of the Bavarian oafs/Are Luxembourg and Habsburg joining forces...

1394   In Nuremberg, military fatigues are being sewed./This clothing is needed with certain foreigners ...

1407   A wild alliance of Swiss confederates/has gruesomely encircled Bregenz ...

1420   The Jews – hey what was that?/In Vienna they're being murdered.

1421   So many, it's not possible, are you for real?/They are being burnt on the goose pasture ...

1451 In Vienna the Jews are now tolerated./As long as they are not owed very much ...

1459 The Turks are taking, excuse me,/all of Serbia excluding Belgrad ...

1480 Alongside the damage caused by the Turks, the plague, and grass-hoppers/We will elevate Baden to a city ...

1526 So that I do not drone out my rhyme:/The Turks are winning the battle of Mohács ...

1528 The Süleyman is sending wild signals./The Habsburgs should get out of Hungary.

1529 From in front of Vienna the Turks should disappear,/Since the Camels have a runny nose ...

1532 The Turks are again coming from the south./The blacksmith from Waidhofner and the military are being slaughtered by them ...

1544 In Hungary the Turks are gaining power./Now he is willing to help, the Frenchman ...

1547 An armistice, good for the Turks,/for one thousand Ducats yearly ...

1551 The Jews have a patent for clothes:/A yellow patch so that they can be recognised ...

1571 After the sea battle of Lepanto,/The Turks go angrily away.

1572 In Vienna: The riding stable is made Spanish/Paris: Massacre of St Bartholomew.

1573 Out of France the Huguenots are fleeing./They do not allow them-selves to be eradicated.

1574 The Jews should not stay in Vienna/At Protestant instigation.

1575 The negro trade blooms like lilies./It goes even as far as Brazil ...

1592 Although they nicely continue the peace,/The Turks are constantly invading.

1593 The slogan for the emperor's troops is: Be prepared!/At Sisak the Hassan remains defeated.

1594 Then the Ottomans are winning again./The fortress of Raab falls. – something to cry about.

1595 In Hausruck wild farmers are on the move./In Hungary the Turks are lurking.

1596 As if the Turks had bull's blood,/they conquer Erlau like the bur-docks ...

1598 From Raab the Turks are thrown out of/In France hangs the Edict of Nantes ...

1624 In the lower districts soon there will be only Yiddish spoken./There the Jews are displaced by force ...

1656 A protestant, a Jew needs his/- well? – residence permit ...

1663 A Turkish troop draws nearer, very quickly./Help, Leopold, because you are holy!

1664 The field-marshall Montecuccoli/Is conquering the Turks ...

1670 Leopoldstadt is now called this way. –/Out with the Jews. Be content ...

1675 250 Jewish families/are happily seen here ...

1682   The Sun King is not nice./Helps the Turks. – What a bastard!
1684   One would like to finish them off/But as always: One sits in the mire
   ...
1691   And on the river Theiß the 'Turkenluis'/creates quite a stir, and you can only say: Wee! ...
1720   The diplomat is the emperor's guest./Since 18 are the Turks quieter
   ...

Actually, these verses speak for themselves. To summarise, however, we will select a small number of the references and predications employed by Sokop negatively to present different 'non-Austrian' outgroups (see table 5.4).

From these selected couplets, the most discriminatory ones were quoted in several press articles in *Der Standard, profil* and *Falter*:[20] Particularly the verses dedicated to the years of 1656, 1670 and 1682, but also the above-quoted poem *The Chinese are Coming*, were repeatedly quoted in these three press organs and criticised as being racist and antisemitic.

As mentioned above, the press-mediated public critique of these poems as well as of the 'culturalist racist' 'headscarf notifications', 'over-foreignerisation notifications' and 'family planning notifications', all brought Renate Brauner to the decision to transfer the responsibility for implementation of the Residence Act from Sokop and the MA 62 to a newly established department.

Since 1 January 1999, Department 20 of the Municipal Authorities, the '*Wiener Magistratsabteilung 20*', has administered the Aliens' Act. The new head, the 43-year-old jurist Gertraud Stroblberger, announced in the media that the six sections of the new department would be service and advice oriented (see the article entitled ' "*Integration" statt "Überfremdung"* ', i.e. ' "Integration" instead of "Over-Foreignerisation"', by Eva Linsinger in *Der Standard* of 16 December 1998: 8). Stroblberger declared that, in future, the head office of the department would give personal and telephonic information in order to enable the six sections to issue quickly the extensions to residence permits. 'Our aim is the one-day vignette', were Stroblberger's words. That is to say: the decision about the extension of a residence permit would be taken within one day, and not, as in the past, only after weeks or months. In order to avoid the issuing of questionable, i.e. discriminatory notifications, the 140 officials of the new department have been intensively trained and instructed during months. Further, Stroblberger is planning to institutionalise a 'quality circle', which will discuss the implementation of the act and the formulation of the notifications, in order to come to strict [sic!] and comprehensible criteria and to a standardised interpretation of the law, and in order to prevent the giving of ideological and political reasons for negative decisions. According to Stroblberger, the fundamental philosophy of the administration of the Aliens' Act will be the conviction that the implementation of the Aliens' Act is part of the integration process of immigrants, and, consequently, the new motto of the MA 20 will be 'the human being is in the centre'.

Table 5.4 A selection of (discriminatory) references and predications in Sokop's poem

Out-groups	Reference	Predications
Poles	the Pole Boleslaw	is a louse (= insulting animalising metaphor)
	the Poles	are to come to know the truth, are to become Christians
Hungarians	the Hungarians	are to be beaten
	Hungarian blood	is flowing
Women	*Weiber* (depreciative)	are to be excluded from church posts
Swabians	Swabians	are not wanted in office
Bavarians	Bavarian oafs	are oafs
Swiss	an alliance of Swiss confederates	is wild
		is a cruel encircler of Bregenz
Huguenots	the Huguenots	are fleeing from France
		are unwilling to accept being totally exterminated
Protestants	Protestant instigation	are not wanting the Jews to stay in Vienna
	a Protestant	is needing his [sic!] residence permit
Black	Negro trade	is blooming like lilies
French	the Sun King (= antonomasia)	is a bastard
Turks	the Turks	are unwanted invaders
	the Turks	are conquerors
	the Turks	are a damage (to Austria)
	the Turks	are winners
	the Süleyman (= antonomasic synecdoche)	is a sender of wild signals
	the Turks	are repulsed invaders
	the Turks	are gainers of power
	the Turks	are angry withdrawers
	the Turks	are permanent invaders
	the Hassan (= antonomasic synecdoche)	are defeated
	the Ottomans	are winners
	the Turks	are lurkers
	the Turks	are wild as if they have bull's blood
	the Turks	are like the burdocks
	the Turks	are thrown out
	a Turkish troop	is drawing nearer quickly
	the Turks	are conquered
	the Turks	are here again
	they	are likely to be finished off
	the *Turkenluis* (= antonomasic synecdoche)	creator of a stir
	the Turks	are quieter

Table 5.4 continued

Out-groups	Reference	Predications
Jews	the Jews	are dearly (=ironically) driven out of craft/business
	a Jewish school, a synagogue	are an expression of cultural ambitions
	the Jews	are holders of special rights as imperial servants
	the Jews	are holders of the right to lend money
	the Jews	are wearers of a hat with horns
	the Jews in Vienna	are not happy
	the Jews	are being murdered
	they	are being burnt
	the Jews in Vienna	are tolerated as long as they are not owed very much
	the Jews	have a patent for clothes, a yellow patch so that they can be recognised
	the Jews	are not welcome in Vienna
	the Jews	are speaking Yiddish
	the Jews	are displaced by force
	a Jew	is needing his [sic!] residence permit
	the Jews in Leopoldstadt	are expelled from Leopoldstadt
	250 Jewish families	are happily seen in Vienna

It remains to be seen whether the future holds the positive, programmatic self-presentation of Stroblberger and her new department or whether the training of the officials will primarily serve a more skilful and clever bureaucratic 'veiling' of the administration of the social exclusion of non-Austrian citizens from Austria. Stroblberger's declaration of aiming at strict criteria, however, seems not to be auspicious. Equally ominous is the fact that the '*Wiener Integrationsfonds*' – up to the beginning of 1998 a quite important advisory and critical organ that controlled the communal (and also national) immigration policy and politics – is becoming increasingly depoliticised, since the critical work and voices of the two minor opposition parties (the Liberal Forum and the Greens) have been increasingly excluded from the Viennese Fund for Integration and the fund, consequently, has increasingly become exclusively tied to the party politics of the two Austrian government parties SPÖ and ÖVP.

This depolitisation can be understood by comparing the annual reports of the Wiener Integrationsfonds for 1996 and 1997. While the annual report for 1996 extensively and critically covered the discriminatory notifications by the MA 62, the authors of the report for 1997 'forgot' the function of political control and did not even mention Werner Sokop and the MA 62, as they were almost exclusively concerned with presenting positively the 'integration policy' of the local government.

Thus, the critical liberal and humanitarian opposition as well as the different counselling and aid movements are all the more required to keep a watch on the future 'integration politics' of the local and national government. Unfortunately, there are no reasons for being too optimistic, all the more so as the Liberal Forum opposition party, since the election day of 3 October 1999, can no longer fulfil its political controlling role as a democratic opposition party at the national level, because it failed to take office in parliament. The democratic importance of the Liberal Forum in the case of the discriminatory authorities' notifications will be illustrated by the following section.

Administrative piecework

On 17 September 1997, Volker Kier and Marco Smoliner, two politicians of the Austrian Liberal Forum, organised a press conference in the Viennese Café 'Landtmann'. Two days later, on 19 September, one of the two politicians, the parliamentary representative Volker Kier, introduced a parliamentary question dealt with in a meeting of the parliament, directed to the Austrian Minister of the Interior, Karl Schlögl.

The parliamentary question by Volker Kier went (see Question No. 159/M – Notifications regarding alien matters – Recording with the help of prefabricated text modules – issued only after investigation by organs versed in the law):[21]

> What will you undertake to prevent [the authorities] in future from doing piecework in issuing notifications concerning alien matters with the help of prefabricated text modules, as it has been practised since the regulations of 29th February 1996, and to ensure that notifications are not issued before a thorough investigation by organs versed in the law?

The minister answered that this matter was a very delicate one that needed clear, transparent and 'good-looking' ('*herzeigbar*') decisions according to human considerations, because they strongly influenced the life both of alien fellow-citizens and Austrians. After these apparently sympathetic words, Schlögl qualified them restrictively by saying that, in future, there would probably be only limited possibilities of receiving new fellow-citizens. Then, the minister employed the *topos of ignorance* and pointed to the problem of the administrative flood of decrees: within the period from 1 January 1996 to 18 September 1997, 1,526 decrees amounting to 12,372 pages had been issued in the area of the Ministry of the Interior. The Minister was directly informed of only about 300 of all these decrees. Thus, Schlögl continued, although the Minister is politically responsible for everything concerning the Ministry of the Interior, he cannot always know everything, especially if it concerns an internal decree, such as the one in question. After an additional question by Kier asking for specification, Schlögl concluded that he assumed that, in the following weeks, it would no longer be necessary to work out and compose notifications dealing with appeals against refusals of applications for residence permits applying the criteria criticised by Kier.

Both the press conference and the question were concerned with the authority's institutionalised conditions and ways of issuing notifications dealing with appeals against refusals of applications for residence permits. The main objects of criticism were Manfred Matzka, the head of Department III of the Austrian Ministry of the Interior, and Section 11 of Department III of the Ministry, which is responsible for passports, citizenship, refugees and aliens and the second authority of appeal if applicants appeal against negative notifications regarding residence permits.

The Liberal Forum discovered that Matzka had instructed the civil servants of Department III, Section 11 to do piecework as far as the issuing of notifications dealing with appeals from the nine counties of Austria regarding the Residence Act are concerned (see Liberales Forum 1997). By means of official regulations dating from the 29 February 1996, Matzka had prescribed that the overtime paid out to the responsible examining servants be determined according to the number of issued notifications ('*Überstundenverrechnung nach Bescheideanzahl*').

Already in 1993, a system of points had been introduced. This was designed to catalogue the notifications issued depending on the expenditure of labour and to pay the overtime depending on the number of points a servant 'scored'. On 29 February 1996, Matzka suspended this system and introduced the aforementioned regulations according to which every official in charge had to reach an output target of at least twenty notifications a week. This means that a notification must be issued at least every two hours, assuming that an official has to work forty hours a week.

In addition to this output target, for every three additional notifications started, two hours of overtime are to be paid. Accordingly, overtime during a five-day working week is charged to the servants – irrespective of whether they really complete their particular working hours or not, but according to whether or not they issue the expected number of notifications – as shown in table 5.5 (originally, Matzka intended to prescribe that every servant should issue at least ten notifications a day, implying that every forty-eight minutes a new appealing application should be dealt with).

If a civil servant issues at least forty-eight notifications a week, twenty hours of paid overtime are credited to her or him. If he or she issues this number of notifications during the regular forty office hours, and this is quite possible because nobody would check whether the overtime was really consumed by work or not, every appeal is simply allocated a maximum of forty minutes: forty minutes, during which an essential and decisive ruling is made on the life of the applicant and her or his family members.

Dealing with appeals against refusals of applications for residence permits takes much more time and effort than conceded by these regulations. To comply with them, the administrating authority catalogued and standardised many different cases of appeals and ways of dealing with them. It prefabricated

Table 5.5 Overtime schedule for civil servants of Department III/Section 11

20 notifications a week	obligatory minimum
21–23 notifications a week	2 hours overtime
24–26 notifications a week	4 hours overtime
27–29 notifications a week	6 hours overtime
30–32 notifications a week	8 hours overtime
33–35 notifications a week	10 hours overtime
36–38 notifications a week	12 hours overtime
39–41 notifications a week	14 hours overtime
42–44 notifications a week	16 hours overtime
45–47 notifications a week	18 hours overtime
48–50 notifications a week	20 hours overtime

textual modules and 'model notifications' that could be recycled in order to compose the daily notifications quickly (see figure 5.4 on p. 223). Thus the responsible officials only needed to fill in the remaining name slots and free text slots manually. A whole notification could consist of premanufactured textual elements and be completed with a few minimal additions by the clerks. And, indeed, many notifications were produced in this way, just as if they were mass produced, for which reason they were criticised as 'assembly-line notifications' ('*Fließbandbescheide*').

It is obvious that a careful examination of the appeals is not possible under such conditions of administrative automation and time pressure, all the more so since the responsible decision-makers are government administration officials and administration employees and not jurists – which means that in view of the complex legal subject-matter of the Residence Act they are much more likely to be influenced in their decisions than true legal experts (see 'The administrative practice of the municipal authorities', pp. 222–32 and appendix 5.2 of this chapter).

Already an accurate scrutiny of the notification issued by the provincial government (in Vienna: Department 62 of the Municipal Authorities) that refused the application for residence permit showed that this process takes more than an hour. Further proceedings of investigation, e.g. interviews, inspections of records and so on, are not possible in consideration of the average time available, viz. two hours per notification, apart from the fact that the time is much shorter still if an official issues more notifications than the minimum output target.

The consequences of the 'piecework notifications' from the Ministry of the Interior were immense. The Administrative Court was paralysed by complaints against the many negative notifications issued in 'assembly-line production' which refused or dismissed the appeals against notifications issued by the first responsible authority. As far as the matter of aliens' residence is concerned, in September 1997 the Administrative Court had to deal with more than 10,000 complaints. In addition, it had to examine approximately 4,000 complaints against refusals of applications for asylum, which were also issued by officials of Department III of the Ministry of the Interior. Years of waiting became the rule. Thus, the new Aliens' Act of 1997 incorporated the regulation required by the Administrative Court that beginning on 1 January 1998 all notifications of non-prolongation or withdrawal of residence permits that were appealed against and taken to the Administrative Court were referred back to the Ministry of the Interior (Paragraph 113, Section 6 and the following of the Aliens' Act of 1997). This meant that the thousands of complaints that piled up were simply declared to be irrelevant and, consequently, the appellants were set back considerably. Furthermore, a charge of 2,500 Austrian schillings was introduced for all complaints to the Administrative Court. So, the 'piecework notifications' imposed or inflicted quite a high financial barrier on all those seeking justice by appealing to the Administrative Court.

In their press conference on 17 September 1997, the two above-mentioned politicians of the Liberal Forum publicly accused Karl Schlögl of being responsible for this scandal. They demanded:

- the immediate revocation of the 'piecework regulations' of 29 February 1996
- the accurate exploration of this 'piecework fabrication' of notifications and of its consequences
- the replacement of the responsible head of Department III, Manfred Matzka
- the individual handling of appeals according to the legal and temporal framework (six months according to the AVG, the General Administration Act) and by officials versed in the law
- the resignation of the Minister of the Interior, Karl Schlögl.

Though the call for the minister's resignation and the head's replacement was not met with success, the 'piecework regulations' were, in the end, withdrawn, and that not least because of the press reports about the scandal.

The liberal, critical quality daily *Der Standard* (here we just focus on *Der Standard*, which is the most important independent 'quality' Austrian daily) alone published eight articles about this issue within a period of about two weeks – that is, from 18 September to 2 October 1998.[22] Two of them even appeared on the front page.

On 18 September, the day after the press conference, *Der Standard* reported on the conference of Marco Smoliner, a member of the City Council, and Volker Kier, a parliamentary representative. In addition to the most important information given by the two politicians at the press conference (see above), the article, entitled '*Ausländerbescheide: Honorar für Stückzahl*' ('Foreigner notifications: Fees for piecework totals'), also covered Manfred Matzka's attempt to justify – in an interview with *Der Standard* – his internal decree of 29 February 1996. At the time when Matzka issued the decree, the twenty-three civil servants of Section 11 of Department III supposedly had to deal with up to 2,000 appeals per month. 'Thus, we thought about how to motivate our officials to be more efficient if they were proportionately remunerated'. Today, there would only be 600 notifications per month to deal with, he continued, and therefore the regulations were now of no importance. All notifications would have been and would be examined repeatedly. In any case, Matzka added, no modern text-processing program could do without prefabricated documents – one might think, for example, of tickets for parking offenders.

The following day, on Friday 19 September, *Der Standard* printed two articles about the affair: a report on page 8 and a critical commentary on page 28. The article on page 8 was entitled '*Ausländer-Bescheide im Akkord: Dringliche an Minister Schlögl*' ('Foreigner-notifications on piecework: Urgent parliamentary question to minister Schlögl'). Its main information was that the Liberal Forum was going to introduce an 'urgent parliamentary question' containing twenty points about the 'piecework notifications' to deal with at the meeting on Friday. The commentary by Michael Simoner on page 28, entitled '*Inhumane Quotenjagd*' ('Inhumane hunt for quotas'), criticised:

- the inhumane maxims 'time is money' and 'overtime is even more money', which lay behind Matzka's regulations
- the fact that the responsible Minister of the Interior, Karl Schlögl, was conspicuously silent about the accusations of his subordinate official Matzka and Department III
- that Matzka's comparison of the officials' 'piecework notifications' with 'tickets for parking offenders' is inadequate and cynical, as if 'humanitarianism could be checked off with a cross' ('*Menschlichkeit zum Ankreuzen*')
- that the new Aliens' Act of 1997 that would come into force on 1 January 1998 would imply that thousands of complaints addressed to the Administrative Court would be referred back to Matzka's department, meaning that for the appellants, a new round would begin without any new chance of a positive decision.

On Saturday, 20 September, two articles were again published on the same topic. The article on page 17 reported that on Thursday, the parliamentary question introduced by the Liberal Forum was not accepted by the Socialist Party as an urgent one that should have been dealt with in a special parliamentary debate. Instead of that, Schlögl gave a semi-official written answer to the parliamentary question from Kier and his party colleagues. In this answer, the minister declared himself to be completely behind the head of Department III, Manfred Matzka. *Der Standard* informed its readers further that Volker Kier criticised Schlögl's answer to be, though quickly given, too vague and evasive. With respect to Matzka's comparison of the notifications with preprinted tickets, Schlögl, for instance, only explained that comparisons would always be difficult. In addition, Kier explained that the parliamentary question would still be open from a parliamentary-procedural point of view and that Kier hoped the formally adequate answer would be more concrete.

In the commentary entitled '*Textbausteine*' ('Text modules') on page 35, Günter Traxler, throughout the article, completely ironically – Traxler's irony is mainly based on the fallacies of ambiguity, equivocation and false analogy – remarked that the administrative usage of prefabricated textual modules in notifications would represent philanthropy and be the most adequate realisation of the principle of 'equal rights for all!', because this practice would ignore individual differences and take into account the fact that in the eyes of the law all are equal. The fact that the same text-producing technique was also employed to write tickets for parking offenders would, all the more, prove the principle of legal equality, as the tickets are practically exclusively issued to Austrians, implying that foreigners are not put at a disadvantage in comparison to nationals. The fact that thousands of applicants appealed to the Administrative Court would say nothing against Matzka's method of issuing notifications, but at least it would say something about the odd humanitarian convictions of the foreigners. It would be the Administrative Court's own fault to be threatened by paralysis in view of the thousands of complaints it had to deal with. The Court merely needed to employ Matzka's method of recycling textual modules: in addition, this would have the positive effect that foreigners would not have to wait so long for the administrative decision.

On Thursday, 25 September, two further articles appeared in *Der Standard*, viz. a short one on page 1 announcing a longer one on page 9. Entitled '*Aufenthaltsverfahren: Keine "Akkordbescheide" mehr*' ('Residence proceedings: No more "piecework notifications" '), the article on page 1 noted that on Wednesday, Minister Schlögl revoked the controversial internal regulations of Matzka and stopped the criticised paying of overtime. Apart from this, the report stated that the Liberal Forum had presented new incriminating evidence against Manfred Matzka and had handed it over to the courts as a description of fact.

The new accusations against Matzka and the new incriminating evidence are reported on page 9 in the article entitled '*Schlögl stoppt "Akkordbescheide"*' ('Schlögl stops "piecework notifications" '). Matzka's argument of having issued the decree of 29 February 1996 in view of the approximately 2,000 appeals per month becomes very flimsy knowing that the head of Department III of the Ministry of the Interior had already decreed in July 1994 that the officials were to issue at least twenty-five notifications per week. According to the Security Spokesperson of Vienna's Liberal Forum, Marco Smoliner, to whom the information about this early internal decree was leaked, this decree seems not to have been crowned with success, because in April 1995, Matzka issued another decree that prescribed the output target as ten appeals per day and fifty per week. According to Smoliner, the most incriminating fact is, however, a memo dating from February 1995. It said: 'In order to withstand possible examinations by the Auditor-General's office, it is absolutely necessary to indicate the exact time spans in the overtime forms. In order to have enough leeway, the time period between 7 a.m. and 9 p.m. would be sensible'.

This memo clearly reveals that Matzka was conscious of the fact that the actual working hours of his subordinate officials did or do not correspond to the officially indicated working hours. Even worse, it shows how Matzka instructs his team to commit illegal actions without being caught by the Auditor-General's office. Consequently, the Liberal Forum sent a factual description to the Penalty

Department of the Ministry of Justice for examination. Representative Volker Kier argued that it could be possible that these facts had relevance for criminal law, and if so, they should be prosecuted. The Minister of the Interior agreed to Kier's demand of the Auditor-General's office to examine the case, but he refused, however, to take legal proceedings against Manfred Matzka for a possible breach of duty.

The last article about this case appeared in *Der Standard* on Thursday, 2 October 1997 on page 8. Entitled '*Chefanteil für Akkordbescheide*' ('Boss's share for piecework notifications'), it reported that not only were the issuing officials of Department III, Section 11 rewarded with overtime for their piecework notifications, but also the five leaders of the individual sub-sections ('*Referate*') were additionally paid for the extra work of their subordinates. The most industrious subsection even provided its leader with an overtime payment of twenty-five hours per month. The article further informed its readers, repeating information from the previous days, that the Liberal Forum demanded an examination by the Auditor-General's office and the resignation of Karl Schlögl. The Ministry of the Interior for its part once again tried to justify the overtime regulations with the amount of work that had to be done at the time of issuing the decree in question.

Der Standard's press coverage of this case of administrative discrimination by anonymous, non-individual and ethically completely indifferent 'mass production' of – for the most part negative, refusing or dismissing – notifications dried up after 2 October 1997. As already noted, the Liberal Forum's demand for the minister's resignation and the replacement of the head was not fulfilled. The internal 'piecework decree', however, was ultimately withdrawn, and that is surely thanks to the Liberal Forum, or, strictly speaking, two of its exponents, one, Marco Smoliner, acting politically at the communal, regional level, and the other, Volker Kier, who – until the Liberal Forum's election defeat on 3 October 1999 – was the most active parliamentary representative as far as the number of contributions in parliamentary sessions and debates is concerned.

Taking into consideration the fact that the Liberal Forum is only a very small opposition party, its partial success in the case of the 'piecework notifications' shows that – in order to assert oneself against a coalition government that, owing to its majority of seats, can often easily vote down or simply ignore the opposition's initiatives – widely independent media are an extremely important instrument of political control, of politically countering abuse of power and discrimination. By critically making things public via independent media, the criticised responsible party, within a democratic system, is put on the spot and has to justify its political activities publicly. And, if the attempt at justification does not convince the critical opposition, it will again react publicly, so that a whole public discourse may arise and, hopefully, not cease until the problem under discussion is acceptably resolved and the critique on this specific point is no longer necessary.

Such mechanisms of public critique, control and debate can best be described within a deliberative model of democracy. In addition to our concluding remarks that summarise the potential political role of critical discourse analysis in a democratic society, we dedicate the last chapter of the present book to this model of discursive democracy, as we believe that its realisation can contribute substantially to acting effectively against any form of social discrimination.

Appendices

Appendix 5.1: Example of a negative notification

Amt der Wiener Landesregierung
Mittelbare Bundesverwaltung
Aufenthaltsgenehmigungen
1082 Wien, Friedrich-Schmidt-Platz 3
DVR: XXXXXXX

MA 62 – XXXXXXXXX

Wien, XX XX XXXX

(Name der Antragstellerin)
Türk. Stbg.
Aufenthaltsgesetz

Bescheid

Der Antrag vom XX.X.1995 der Frau (Name der Antragstellerin), geb. XX.X. XXXX auf Erteilung einer Bewilligung gemäß §§ 1 Abs. 1 und 6 Abs. 1 Aufenthaltsgesetz, BGBl. Nr. 466/1992, i.d.F. BGBl. Nr. 35/95 wird im Hinblick auf § 3 Abs. 5 AufG. abgewiesen.

Begründung

Gemäß § 3 Abs. 5 des Aufenthaltsgesetzes sind solche Bewilligungswerber bevorzugt zu berücksichtigen, denen aufgrund persönlicher Umstände eine sofortige Integration möglich ist oder bei denen eine Familienzusammenführung besonders dringlich ist, sofern voraussichtlich die Zahl der Anträge nach § 3 Abs. 1 Z 2 AufG die festgelegte Zahl von Bewilligungen (§ 2 Abs. 2 Z 3) übersteigt. Beim vorliegenden Antrag handelt es sich um einen Familienzusammenführungsfall nach § 3 Abs. 1 Z 2 AufG, wobei die Eheschließung am XX.X.XXXX erfolgte, bisherige gemeinsame Haushalte wie folgt umschrieben wurden: [zwei Adressen in der Türkei mit zwei Jahreszahlen als Datum des Beziehens der Wohnung] und besonders berücksichtigenswürdige Gründe wie folgt ausgeführt wurden: 'Möchte ich mit meiner Familie zusammenleben'.

Damit wurden im vorliegenden Fall weder für eine sofort mögliche Integration oder eine besonders dringliche Familienzusammenführung sprechende Gründe dargetan, noch sind solche bei einer objektiven Gesamtbetrachtung des gegebenen Sachverhaltes anzunehmen.

Sowohl nach der bisherigen Erfahrung als auch nach der gegebenen Situation per XX.X.XXXX (2600 Quotenplätze für Wien, 1250 erteilte Bewilligungen) ergibt sich für die Behörde zwingend die bevorzugte Behandlung der im § 3

Abs. 5 AufG angeführten Fälle, unter welche für die Behörde im Rahmen des ihr eingeräumten Ermessens der gegenständlichen [sic!, M.R. and R.W.] Antrag nicht subsumiert werden kann. Aufgrund der Aktenlage steht fest, daß der Gatte der Partei im Bundesgebiet aufhältig ist und somit unabsprechbare private und familiäre Beziehungen zu Österreich bestehen.

Im Hinblick auf den Eingriffsvorbehalt des Art. 8 Abs 2 MRK kann der § 3 Abs. 5 AufG verfassungskonform interpretiert werden, soferne die Behörde eine Abwägung der öffentlichen Interessen zu den privaten Interessen im Einzelfall vornimmt. Diese Abwägung ergab, daß durch das Übersteigen der Anträge auf die Familienzusammenführung und der dafür vorgesehenen Anzahl von Bewilligungen der vorliegende Antrag gegenüber Anträgen anderer Fremder nicht bevorzugt behandelt werden konnte, da eine sofortige Integration der Partei unmöglich erscheint, zumal der in Österreich lebende Gatte seinerseits noch bemüht ist, sich in Österreich zu integrieren. Da nach den Erfahrungen des täglichen Lebens bei den als Erwachsene aus dem gleichen Kulturkreis wie die antragstellende Partei kommenden Personen auch nach mehrjährigem Inlandsaufenthalt eine insbesondere die Bereiche Sprache, Kommunikation mit der eingesessenen Bevölkerung und Anpassung an mitteleuropäische Sitten, Gebräuche und Lebensweisen umfassende Integration kaum stattfindet, würde eine bevorzugte Bewilligungserteilung an die antragstellende Partei, aus deren Antrag keinerlei ihre Integration erleichternde Umstände abgeleitet werden können, die aufwendigen Integrationsbemühungen für die hier lebenden ausländischen Mitbürger nur weiter erschweren. Es war daher spruchgemäß zu entscheiden.

Rechtsmittelbelehrung

Gegen diesen Bescheid ist die binnen zwei Wochen nach Zustellung beim Amt der Wiener Landesregierung, Magistratsabteilung 62 – Dez. A, Friedrich-Schmidt-Platz 3, Wien 1082, schriftlich, telegraphisch oder fernschriftlich, im Wege automationsunterstützter Datenübertragung oder in jeder anderen technisch möglichen Weise einzubringende Berufung zulässig, welche außer der Bescheidbezeichnung einen begründeten Berufungsantrag zu enthalten hat und mit S 120. -- Bundesstempel zu versehen ist.

Für den Landeshauptmann:
Dr. Sokop
Obersenatsrat

Ergeht an:
1) Frau
   [Adresse der Antragstellerin in der Türkei, M.R. and R.W.]
2) Bundespolizeidirektion Wien
   Fremdenpolizeiliches Büro
   Wasagasse 20
   1090 Wien
3) zum Akt

Appendix 5.2: Explanations of the typology of official notifications issued by the Austrian Ministry of the Interior, Department III, Section 11 in the case of administrative decisions about residence permits

The first group of negative notifications mentioned in this list (D1–D8) concerns dismissals of appeals against refusals of applications for residence permits. This group is based on the legal reference to Paragraph 66, Section 4 of the AVG, the General Administration Act ('*Allgemeines Verwaltungsgesetz*').

The authorities dismiss an appeal with reference to Paragraph 66, Section 4 of the AVG if an applicant has not appealed according to Paragraph 63, Section 5 of the AVG, which prescribes that appeals have to be made within the period of two weeks after the applicant has legally and validly been served with the negative notification (D1). The authorities also dismiss an appeal if they come to the decision, according to Paragraph 66, Section 4 of the AVG, that the form of the appeal lacks the grounds for the appeal that are legally required according to Paragraph 63, Section 3 of the AVG (D2). Further, the authorities justify a dismissal of an appeal with reference to Paragraph 66, Section 4 of the AVG, arguing that the applicant has omitted to make an application for appeal (which is required according to Paragraph 63, Section 3 of the AVG) in her or his appeal (D3). A dismissal is also justified with reference to Paragraph 66, Section 4 of the AVG if the notification against which the applicant has appealed has not been indicated by reference to the identification number as is prescribed in Paragraph 63, Section 3 of the AVG (D4). If a brief of improvement dating from XX.XX.XXXX is not complied with within the period stipulated and in the form prescribed by Paragraph 13, Section 1 of the AVG, the authority also dismisses the appeal against a refusal by reference to Paragraph 66, Section 4 of the AVG (D5). If a brief of improvement dating from XX.XX. XXXX is not complied with within the period required and by an applicant who is not legally competent, as required according to Paragraph 9 and Paragraph 13, Section 3 of the AVG, the authority also dismisses the appeal against a refusal by reference to Paragraph 66, Section 4 of the AVG (D6). If the application form lacks the signature in the applicant's own hand or if the authority doubts whether the application was made or signed by the applicant, as required according to Paragraph 13, Section 4 of the AVG, the appeal is also dismissed by the authority with reference to Paragraph 66, Section 4 of the AVG (D7). An appeal can finally be dismissed by the respective authority for other, general reasons, and this again by reference to Paragraph 66, Section 4 of the AVG (D8). An example of this would be that an appeal is based on questioning the means of the authority's transmission of the refusal (e.g. via telefax) and the respective authority dismisses the appeal by declaring this means of transmission to be a legally accepted one.

The second group of negative notifications (R1–R14) is selected from refusals of appeals for residence permits. This group consists of official notices about decisions of the second authority (i.e. Department III, Section 11 of the Ministry of the Interior), which affirm the decisions of the first authority (i.e. the Department 62 of Vienna's Municipal Authorities). If the authority thinks the alien applicant to have entered into matrimony with an Austrian citizen for the exclusive purpose of obtaining legal claims in the area of the aliens' rights (for instance, the unrestricted right to stay in Austria and the unhindered access to the Austrian labour market) and, thus, to have abused the legal system, it refuses the appeal against the refusal of an application for residence permit with reference to Paragraph 5, Section 1 of the Residence Act – it refers to the regulation that an application for a residence permit should not be approved by the authority if there is a reason for refusing the visa stamp ('*Sichtvermerksversagungsgrund*') – in relation to Paragraph 10, Section 1, Clause 4 of the Aliens' Act ('*Fremdengesetz*'; FrG), which refers to 'the disturbance of public peace, law and order', the latter being considered to be a reason for refusing the visa stamp (R1). The authority also refuses an appeal if the applicant asking for the prolongation was a Bosnian citizen at the moment of applying for a residence permit for the first time and if she or he is no longer a Bosnian citizen at the moment of applying for a prolongation, but has, for instance, a Croatian passport. Such refusals are backed by reference to Paragraph 66, Section 4 of the AVG in relation to Paragraph 6, Section 2 and Paragraph 13, Section 1 of the Residence Act (R2). The authority also refuses an appeal if a first-time application for a residence permit was not made from abroad, i.e. before the applicant's entering of Austria, but if the applicant, at the moment of application, was already in the Austrian state territory. Paragraph 6, Section 2 of the Residence Act are invoked in relation to Paragraph 66, Section 4 of the AVG for such refusals of appeals (R3), while Paragraph 6, Section 3 of the Residence Act and Paragraph 66, Section 4 of the AVG are referred to by the authority in order to refuse an appeal against a refusal of an application for residence permit in cases of the applicant's failing to apply for a prolongation of her or his residence permit (R4). If the authority thinks that there is a reason for a residence ban on the applicant (see above), the authority refuses the appeal by reference to Paragraph 66, Section 4 of the AVG in connection with Paragraph 5, Section 1 of the Residence Act and Paragraph 10, Section 1, Clause 1 of the Aliens' Act (R5). Paragraph 66, Section 4 of the AVG is also brought into play together with Paragraph 5, Section 1 of the Residence Act and with Paragraph 10, Section 1, Clause 1 of the Aliens' Act if the authority refuses an appeal against a refusal of an application for a prolongation of the residence permit because there is a reason for refusing the visa stamp or endorsement ('*Sichtvermerk*'). This reason consists of the legally not accepted situation that an endorsement should temporally follow the applicant's entering of Austria with no visa or with a tourist visa (R6). Very similar refusals of appeals also bring into play Paragraph 66, Section 4 of the AVG in connection with Paragraph 5, Section 1 of the Residence Act and Paragraph 10, Section 1, Clause XXX of the Aliens' Act. Here, an appeal against the refusal of a first-time application is backed by reference to specific clauses of Paragraph 10, Section 1 of the Aliens' Act, containing specific reasons for refusing an endorsement (R7). Appeals are also refused by the authority if the applicant indicates as the purpose of residence that she or he wants to reside in Austria for 'a private stay' and the authority doubts whether the applicant is able to secure her or his livelihood or not without gainful employment that would contradict the indicated purpose of residence. In such a case, the authority refers to Paragraph 66, Section 4 of the AVG in connection with Paragraph 5, Section 1 of the Residence Act (R8). The same paragraphs and laws are called into play if the authority refuses an appeal assuming that the applicant does not or will not live in a local standard accommodation with as much 'living space' for each person living in the applicant's dwelling as the authority thinks to be usual for Austrian citizens ('*ortsübliche Unterkunft*') (R9). If the authority refuses an appeal because the applicant indicates 'work as employed person' as the purpose of residence, though she or he has no work permit, the authority refers to Paragraph 66, Section 4 of the AVG in connection with Paragraph 5 of the Residence Act (R10). If an applicant applies for the prolongation of a residence permit after the validity of the permit has run out, the appeal against the refusal of the application for reasons of delay is also refused by the authority, which brings into play the argument of the applicant endangering the public peace, law and order. In such a case, the authority refers to Paragraph 66, Section 4 of the AVG in connection with Paragraph 6, Section 2 of the Residence Act as well as to Paragraph 5, Section 1 of the Residence Act in connection with Paragraph 10, Section 1, Clause 4 of the Aliens' Act (R11). The refusal of an appeal is also justified by the authority if it assumes the applicant to have a business that is actually fictitious. This refusal is issued with reference to Paragraph 5, Section 1 of the Residence Act in relation to Paragraph 10, Section 1, Clause 4 of the Aliens' Act (R12). If the second authority takes the view (a) that the applicant has not proved in his appeal against the refusal of an application for residence permit that the first authority illegally misused its discretionary powers when judging the applicant not to be able to secure her or his livelihood and (b) that the applicant still has not proved in the appeal that she or he has sufficient means of maintenance at her or his disposal, the second authority refuses the appeal by reference to Paragraph 66, Section 4 of the AVG in connection with Paragraph 5, Section 1 of the Residence Act (R13). If, finally, and very similarly to R13, but without reference to any appealing critique mentioned in (a) of R13, the authority refuses an appeal arguing that it has not verified the applicant's secure livelihood, as the proved actual means of maintenance of the applicant fail to reach the allegedly required minimum of ATS XXXX. This refusal refers to the same paragraphs as R13.

The third set of notifications (S1–S3) groups around sustainings of appeals against refusals of applications for residence permits. These concern applicants who are children applying for a residence permit for reasons of 'family reunion' or 'school education'. An appeal is sustained if the second authority comes to the conclusion that the first authority's judgement about the unsecured livelihood or the non-local standard dwelling of the applicant (who is again a child applying for family reunion) relies on inadequate assumptions and that the applicant's livelihood or local standard dwelling is actually secured or verified.

This sustaining is simply backed legally by reference to Paragraph 66, Section 4 of the AVG and contains the order directed towards the first authority to issue a residence-permit vignette on the state territory (S1 and S2). The second authority also sustains an appeal in cases where the Residence Act has been amended on a point to which the first authority referred in order to support its negative decision, so that, for instance, a formerly delayed application for residence permit with the purpose of family reunion can no longer be judged to be delayed, as the legal regulations about the place of (e.g. 'from abroad' versus 'on the Austrian state territory') and the deadline for applications have changed. In such a case, the authority refers to Paragraph 66, Section 4 of the AVG and to Paragraph 6, Section 3 of the Residence Act (as announced in BGBl. Nr. 351/1995, i.e. in the Federal Law Gazette No. 351/1995) and orders the first authority to issue a residence-permit vignette via embassy XXXX (S3a). If the first authority has refused a child's first application for a residence permit, e.g. an application for the purpose of school education, and that by arguing that the applicant had to apply from abroad while she or he actually applied on the state territory, the second authority can sustain the appeal against such a refusal by reference to Paragraph 66, Section 4 and to Paragraph 6, Section 2 of the Residence Act in relation to Paragraph 3 of the decree BGBl. Nr. 408/1995 (Federal Law Gazette No. 408/1995), which regulate that the applicant's first application for residence permit need not always be made from abroad. If, for instance, an applying schoolchild is a member of a family in which a parent has a work permit and a residence permit, the child is allowed to apply for the first time in the state territory (S3b).

The fourth group is taken from dismissals, refusals and sustainings of appeals asking for devolution, that is to say, for transferring the competence or responsibility of the decision to another, higher authority that is relevant concerning the matter of residence permits. Applications for devolution are justified by the argument that an authority – failing to make the necessary inquiries or to take a decision within a period stipulated or delaying serving the notification – has violated its ruling duty. The application for devolution can be dismissed by reference to Paragraph 73, Section 1 of the AVG (DV1). It can be sustained by reference to Paragraph 73, Section 1 and 2 of the AVG, having the effect that the second authority itself assumes the decision competence of the first authority and that (a) it refuses the application for residence permit (DV2) or that (b) it gives orders to the first authority to serve the vignette on the devolution applicant via embassy XXXX (DV4). Finally, it can be refused, and this also by reference to Paragraph 73, Section 1 and 2 of the AVG (DV3).

The fifth and last group of appeals encompasses 'other' cases like suspensions, removals and referrals of appeals. The second authority, i.e. the Ministry of the Interior, can decide temporarily to suspend the procedure of appeal, with reference to Paragraph 38 of the AVG (SUS). It can decide to sustain the appeal and, thus, to refer the 'case' to the first authority because of the need for explanation in point XXXX, as the living situation of the applicant since the time of application has changed. If that occurs, the second authority refers to Paragraph 66, Section 2 of the AVG and orders the first authority to reexamine the 'case' (REF). Apart from all these standardised options of the second authority to react on appeals against refusal of applications for residence permits, there can be the case that the second authority writes a completely free text, both with respect to the notice referring to a specific law and the grounds justifying the decision (FRT = free text).

Appendix 5.3: Extracts from Werner Sokop's Eine Wienerische Reimchronik

1013   Der Pole Boleslaw, de Laus,/fecht afoch si die Lausitz aus...

1042   Den Ungarn ghert jetzt ane griebm,/den Kenig Peter haums vertriebm ...

1049   A Kirchnzucht ghert wieder her/Und kane Weiber, bitte sehr...

1094   Der Kaiser von Byzanz ruaft: Heats,/de Tirkn kumman und mi steats...

1103   Der Heinrich liab aun d Judn denkt:/Vom Haundwerk, ehrlich, werns verdrängt...

1124   Ma wü de Poin, daß d Woaheit gspirn,/in Pommern christianisiern...

1205   In Wien, do gibt's Kuiturgewoge,/A Judnschui, a Synagoge...

1238   Fir d Judn götn bsundre Rechte/Ois kaiserliche Kaummerknechte...

1244   Min Schutzbriaf soin si d Judn gfrein:/Se kriagn des Recht zum Göd-verleihn...

1260   De Gozzoburg in Krems wird guat./In Kroissnbrunn rinnt Ungarn-bluat...

1267   Die Kirchn wü, daß jeder spurt. -/Und Judn trogn an Herndlhuat...

1287   Min Herzog wern ma Wickln hobm,/wir woin in Ämter kane Schwobm...

1303   Der Albrecht leistet eam [= the Pope] sein Eid,/De Judn haum in Wien ka Freid...

1364   Aus Aungst vielleicht vur d Bayernlackln/Tuat Luxmburg mit Habsburg packln...

1394   In Nürnberg naht ma Paunzerhemdn./Des Gwandl brauchst bei maunchn Fremdn...

1407   A wüder Bund von Eidgenossen/Hot Bregenz grausam eingeschlossn...

1420   Die Judn – jo wos war denn des?/De kriagn in Wien an Murdsprozeß.

1421   So vü, des gibt's net, bist du gscheit?/Verbrennt werns auf der Gänseweid...

1451   In Wien san d Judn jetz geduidet./Solaung ma eana wenig schuidet...

1459   De Tirkn hoin si, tuat ma lad,/gaunz Serbien ohne Beograd...

1480   Nebm Tirkn-, Pest- und Heischreckschodn/Zur Stodt erhebm tamma Bodn...

1526   Damit i meine Reim net ohatsch:/De Tirkn gwinnan d Schlocht von Mohács...

1528   Der Süleyman schickt wüde Zeichn./Aus Ungarn soi si Habsburg schleichn.

1529   Vur Wien derf si der Tirk verzupfn,/denn de Kamö haum scho an Schnupfn...

1532   Von Süden kumman d Tirkn wieder./Waidhofner Schmied und s Heer hauns nieder...

1544   In Ungarn wern de Tirkn groß./Jetzt tät er höfn, der Franzos...

1547   A Woffnstüstand, türkisch-herrlich,/gegen tausnde Dukotn jährlich...

1551   Fir Judn güt a Gwaund-Patent:/A göbes Fleckerl, daß mas kennt...

1571   Noch dera Seeschlacht von Lepanto,/do foan de Tirkn mit an Grant o.

1572   In Wien: Der Reitstoi spanisch gmocht/Paris: Bartolomäusnocht.

1573   Aus Frankreich flüchtn d Hugenottn./Se lossn si net gaunz ausrottn.

1574   De Judn soin in Wien net bleibm -/Auf protestantisches Betreibm.

1575   Der Negerhaundl bliat wia Lilien./Es geht sogoa scho bis Brasilien...

1592   Obwois in Friedn brav verlängern,/tan d Tirkn dauernd einedrängan.

1593   Fir d Kaisertruppn güt jetzt: Faß an!/Bei Sisak bleibt er liegn, der Hassan.

1594   Daun gwinnan wieder de Osmanan./De Festung Raab foit. – s is zum Wanan.

1595   Im Hausruck rian si wüde Bauern./In Ungarn tan de Tirkn lauern.

1596   Ois ob de Tirkn Stierbluat hättn,/eroberns Erlau wia de Klettn...

1598   Aus Raab wern d Tirkn auseghaut./In Fraunkreich stehts Edikt von Nantes...

1624   Im Untern Werd wird boid nur gjidlt./Durt wern de Judn zwaungs-augsiedlt...

1656   A Protestant, a Jud braucht sein/no? – Aufenthoits-Erlaubnisschein...

1663   A Tirknheer ruckt au, sehr eulich./Hüf, Leopoid, denn du bist heulich!

1664   Der Födherr Montecuccoli/Schlogt d Tirkn unterm Köprili...

1670   De Leopoidstodt haaßt jetzt so. -/De Judn ausse. Sads doch froh...

1675   250 Famülien/von Judn san doch gern do gsehn...

1682   Der Sonnenkenig is ka Guater,/hüft dena Tirkn. – So a Luader!

1684   Ma gabat eana gern den Rest/Doch immerhin: Ma sitzt in Pest...

1691   Und aun der Theiß der Tirknlouis,/der riat fest um, do sogst nur: Wui!...

1720   Der Großbotschafter Gost beim Kaiser./Seit 18 san de Tirkn leiser.

'Eine Wienerische Reimchronik', *1000 Jahre Österreich*.
Werner Sokop (1996)

Notes

1   The German original reads as follows: '*Aufgrund der Aktenlage steht fest, daß der Gatte der Partei im Bundesgebiet aufhältig ist und somit unabsprechbare private und familiäre Beziehungen zu Österreich bestehen. Im Hinblick auf den Eingriffsvorbehalt des Art. 8 Abs 2 MRK kann der § 3 Abs. 5 AufG verfassungskonform interpretiert werden, soferne die Behörde eine Abwägung der öffent-lichen Interessen zu den privaten Interessen im Einzelfall vornimmt. Diese Abwägung ergab, daß durch das Übersteigen der Anträge auf die Familienzusammenführung und der dafür vorgesehenen*

Anzahl von Bewilligungen der vorliegende Antrag gegenüber Anträgen anderer Fremder nicht bevorzugt behandelt werden konnte, da eine sofortige Integration der Partei unmöglich erscheint, zumal der in Österreich lebende Gatte seinerseits noch bemüht ist, sich in Österreich zu integrieren. Da nach den Erfahrungen des täglichen Lebens bei den als Erwachsene aus dem gleichen Kulturkreis wie die antragstellende Partei kommende Personen auch nach mehrjährigem Inlandsaufenthalt eine insbesondere die Bereiche Sprache, Kommunikation mit der eingesessenen Bevölkerung und Anpassung an mitteleuropäische Sitten, Gebräuche und Lebensweisen umfassende Integration kaum stattfindet, würde eine bevorzugte Bewilligungserteilung an die antragstellende Partei, aus deren Antrag keinerlei ihre Integration erleichternde Umstände abgeleitet werden können, die aufwendigen Integrationsbemühungen für die hier lebenden ausländischen Mitbürger nur weiter erschweren. Es war daher spruchgemäß zu entscheiden' (Notification of 26 March 1996).

2   The German original goes: *'Der Antrag vom 31. 7. 1995 der [..., = Name der Antragstellerin] auf Erteilung einer Bewilligung gemäß §§ 1 Abs. 1 und 6 Abs. 1 Aufenthaltsgesetz, BGBl. Nr. 466/1992, i.d.F. BGBl. Nr. 351/95 wird im Hinblick auf § 3 Abs. 5 AufG. abgewiesen'.*

3   In German: *'Im Hinblick auf den Eingriffsvorbehalt des Art. 8 Abs. 2 MRK kann der § 3 Abs. 5 AufG verfassungskonform interpretiert werden, soferne die Behörde eine Abwägung der öffentlichen Interessen zu den privaten Interessen im Einzelfall vornimmt. Diese Abwägung ergab, daß durch das Übersteigen der Anträge auf Familienzusammenführung und der dafür vorgesehenen Anzahl von Bewilligungen der vorliegende Antrag gegenüber Anträgen anderer Fremder nicht bevorzugt behandelt werden konnte, da eine sofortige Integration der Partei unmöglich erscheint'.*

4   In German: *'[da] dem Wortlaut des § 3 Abs. 5 ... keine Anordnung zu entnehmen ist, wonach Anträge ..., welche nicht ... bevorzugt zu berücksichtigen seien, abzuweisen wären. Man gelangte damit in einen Wertungswiderspruch, daß der früher gestellte Antrag, bei dem erst vorauszusehen wäre, daß er im Rahmen der für für das betreffende Jahr festgelegten Quote nicht zum Zug kommen werde, abzuweisen wäre, während ein später gestellter Antrag, bei dem schon sicher ist, daß er infolge der bereits eingetretenen Erschöpfung der Quote im jeweiligen Jahr nicht zur Behandlung gelangt, aufrecht und die Entscheidung hierüber aufgeschoben bliebe'* (Quoted in Wiener Integrationsfonds 1997: 86).

5   In the original version: *'Zum Grad der Überfremdung ist zu bemerken, daß in Wien laut Statistischem Zentralamt 300.675 Ausländer leben. Das sind 18,4% der Gesamtbevölkerung Wiens. Davon wiederum stammen 180.350 oder 60% aus dem ehemaligen Jugoslawien oder der Türkei. In den Pflichtschulen liegt der Anteil der ausländischen Kinder gar bei 30,55%. Im Schuljahr 1993/4 lag der Anteil ausländischer Schüler bei 28,4%; der Anteil jugoslawischer und türkischer Schüler bezogen auf ausländische Schüler an den Pflichtschulen betrug gar 82,75%, ihr Anteil bezogen auf die Gesamtschülerzahl an den Pflichtschulen 23,5%'* (Notification of January 1997).

6   In German: *' "Überfremdung" ist im Zielkatalog des Art. 8 Abs. 2 EMRK nicht ausdrücklich erwähnt ... Daraus ist zumindest zu schließen, daß das Überschreiten eines bestimmtes [sic!] Zahlen-verhältnisses für sich allein einen Eingriff in die Rechte des Art. 8 Abs. 1 ERMK nicht rechtfertigt. Eine Aufenthaltsbehörde, die eine strikt an Zahlen ausgerichtete "Reinheitspolitik" umsetzt, verstößt daher (auch) gegen die österreichische Grundrechtsordnung'* (Quoted according to Hödl and Winter 1998: 116).

7   The original reads as follows: *'In Wien liegt die durchschnittliche Wohnnutzfläche bei 33 m² pro Person. 3,4% der in Wien lebenden österreichischen Staatsbürger verfügen über eine Wohnfläche von weniger als 10 m² – österreichweit sind es gar nur 0,83%, sodaß die Bemessung einer ortsüblichen Unterkunft nicht nach dieser vernachlässigbaren Minderheit, sondern der überwiegenden Mehrheit der österreichischen Bevölkerung entsprechen muß'* (Notification of 28 February 1997).

8   The German text is: *'Für die Beurteilung der Ortsüblichkeit können die Richtlinien für die Vormerkung und Vergabe von Gemeindewohnungen herangezogen werden, da von 870,000 vorhandenen Wohnungen in Wien 215,000 Gemeindewohnungen sind (25%). Ein Anspruch auf eine Gemeindewohnung besteht laut den Vergaberichtlinien der zuständigen Magistratsabteilung, wenn ein Überbelag besteht. Dies läßt den Umkehrschluß zu, daß eine Wohnung mit Überbelag in Österreich keine ortsübliche Unterkunft darstellt'* (Notification of 28 February 1997, quoted according to Hödl and Winter 1998: 117).

9 In German: '*Bei der Beurteilung einer Unterkunft als ortsüblich ist selbstverständlich auch auf die gesetzlich vorgeschriebenen hygienischen Verhältnisse und im Sinne der Volksgesundheit auf die erforderlichen Gesundheitsvorsorgemaßnahmen zu achten. Für eine 3-köpfige Familie erscheinen diese Voraussetzungen in der antraggegenständlichen Wohnung, die ja weder ein Badezimmer noch ein WC aufweist, nicht erfüllt. Gerade bei Familien – wie im antraggegenständlichen Fall – mit einem schulpflichtigen Kind kann eine Unterkunft nur als ortsüblich verstanden werden, wenn neben den jeweiligen Schlafräumern für Eltern und Kinder auch ein zusätzlicher Wohnraum Platz für die gesellschaftlichen und kulturellen Gestaltungsmöglichkeiten der Familie bietet*' (Notification of 14 March 1997, quoted in Hödl and Winter 1998: 117).

10 The original version: '*... jeder Generation und den Generationen bzw. Verschwägerten ein eigener Schlafraum zur Verfügung steht. Ein von den Schlafräumen getrennter zusätzlicher Wohnraum für gesellschaftliche und kulturelle Gestaltungsmöglichkeiten ist bei einer Unterkunft, die von zahlreichen Personen bewohnt wird, ebenfalls nicht wegzudenken*' (Notification of 28 February 1997, quoted in Hödl and Winter 1998: 118).

11 The German text reads as follows: '*Nach Auffassung des Verwaltungsgerichtshofes "wären die Regeln des § 5 Abs. 1 AufG unter dem Blickwinkel des Art. 8 Abs. 1 EMRK verfassungswidrig, wenn die Behörde bei Vorliegen des Versagungsgrundes stets in die Rechte des Art. 8 Abs. 1 einzugreifen hätte. Die Behörde ist vielmehr zu einer Interessenabwägung verpflichtet, die auch zum Ergebnis führen kann, daß eine Nachzugsbewilligung zu erteilen ist, obwohl die Unterkunft den für österreichische Staatsangehörige üblichen Standards nicht entspricht"*' (Davy 1997a: 471, quoted in Hödl and Winter 1998: 118).

12 The original version goes as follows '*... die antragsgegenständliche Zimmer-Küche-Wohnung, wie anläßlich einer Wohnungsüberprüfung ... festgestellt wurde, von mindestens drei Personen bewohnt [wird, M.R. and R.W.]. Somit steht der schulpflichtigen Tochter der Antragstellerin nicht, wie in Österreich üblich, ein eigener, räumlich abgegrenzter Schlafraum zur Verfügung. Das öffentliche Interesse, welches gegen die Erteilung spreche, [ist, M.R. and R.W.] höher zu veranschlagen als die gegenläufigen privaten und familiären Interessen der Partei*' (Notification from May 1996, quoted in Wiener Integrationsfonds 1997: 87).

13 That she or he '*zwar seit einigen Jahren in Österreich aufhältig sei, jedoch streng genommen keine Hindernisse [bestehen], in die Türkei zurückzukehren, um dort ein Familienleben aufzubauen. Diese Möglichkeit ist umso wirklicher, als die antragstellende Partei ihr ganzes Leben dort zugebracht hat und somit im kulturellen und sprachlichen Umfeld ihres Landes aufgewachsen ist*' (Notification of 27 January 1997, of 24 and 28 February 1997, of 14 March 1997, quoted in Hödl and Winter 1998: 119).

14 Verbatim: '*... daß die Unterhaltsmittel ... nicht dazu ausreichen, um ohne Unterstützung der Sozialhilfe auszukommen*' (Notification of 14 March 1997, quoted in Hödl and Winter 1998: 119).

15 In the German version: '*... daß eine verstärkte Familienzusammenführung ohne gleichzeitige Lösung des Zugangsproblems von Familienangehörigen zum Arbeitsmarkt ... nur zur Ghettobildung und Verarmung unterprivilegierter Migranten führen [kann], was wiederum keinesfalls das Wirtschaftswachstum in Österreich vorantreiben und nur negative gesellschaftspolitische Auswirkungen mit sich bringen wird*' (Notification of 27 January 1997, of 24 February 1997, of 14 March 1997, quoted in Hödl and Winter 1998: 119).

16 The original version reads as follows: '*[daß] aufgrund der Geringfügigkeit [seiner] Barmittel [= AS 2500 Caritas Unterstützung] nicht angenommen werde könne, daß [er] in der Lage [sei], [seinen] weiteren Aufenthalt bzw. die Rückreise in [sein] Heimatland zu finanzieren. Es [bestehe] daher der Verdacht, daß [er] sich weiter im Bundesgebiet aufhalten werde und den Aufenthalt aus der Begehung strafbarer Handlungen bestreiten werde*' (Notification from June 1997, quoted in Hödl and Winter 1998: 121).

17 In German: '*Den Ausführungen der Berufungswerberin, daß aufgrund der österreichischen Staatsbürgerschaft ihres Kindes dieses in Österreich zu bleiben hätte, und daß die Fremdenpolizei wohl die Ansicht vertrete, ihr Kind solle hier ohne Eltern aufwachsen, ist entgegenzuhalten, daß sich ein Kind nach dem Wohnsitz der Eltern zu richten hat und andererseits für eine österreichische Staatsbürgerschaft*

keine Verpflichtung besteht, ständig in Österreich zu leben. Es besteht somit für die Berufungswerberin keine Notwendigkeit, ihr Kind hier zurückzulassen... Dem Interesse an der Aufrechterhaltung eines geordneten Fremdenwesens läuft es aber auch entgegen, wenn ein Fremder bloß aufgrund der Tatsache, daß er ein Kind hat, das die österreichische Staatsbürgerschaft besitzt, den weiteren illegalen Aufenthalt im Bundesgebiet auf Dauer erzwingen könnte" (Notification of the *Sicherheitsdirektion Wien* from 16 April 1997, quoted in Hödl and Winter 1998: 123).

18   The original version reads as follows: '[Title:] *Bitterer Reis* [Poem:] *Scho bitter/Waun a Chines/Grod an Gusto hot/Auf a Fiakergulasch/Und in der Umgebung/Nur drei Chinarestaraus/ Offn haum ...*' (Sokop 1991: 55).

19   The original German poem reads as follows: '[Title:] *Die Chinesen kommen* [Poem:] *De Münzwäscherein/In de Sechzgerjoar, –/Na bitte .../Ober heit mit de/Chinarestaraus!/Bis amoi a Beisl/Was Exotisches is .../Loch nur. – Des Unglick,/waun die Tochter/a Mongerl auf d' Wöt bringt/und der Oazt sogt:/ "s is eh pumperlgsund"'* (Sokop 1991: 55).

20   See, for example, *profil* 19/97 from 4 May 1997, *profil* 20/97 from 11 May 1997, *profil* 21/97 from 16 May 1997, *profil* 22/97 from 25 May 1997, *profil* 23/97 from 1 June 1997, *profil* 48/97 from 23 November 1997, *profil* 1/98 from 4 January 1998; *Der Standard* of 5 May 1997: 6, *Der Standard* of 5 May 1997: 20, *Der Standard* of 6 May 1997: 8, *Der Standard* of 12 May 1997: 6, *Der Standard* of 16 December 1998: 8.

21   The original title of the question goes as follows: '*Nr. 159/M – Bescheide in Ausländer-angelegenheiten – Erfassung mit Textbausteinen – Erlassung erst nach Prüfung durch rechtskundige Organe*'.

22   See *Der Standard*, Thursday, 18 September 1997: 8, *Der Standard*, Friday, 19 September 1997: 8, *Der Standard*, Friday, 19 September 1997: 28, *Der Standard*, Saturday/Sunday, 20/21 September 1997: 17, *Der Standard*, Saturday/Sunday, 20/21 September 1997: 35, *Der Standard*, Thursday, 25 September 1997: 1, *Der Standard*, Thursday, 25 September 1997: 9, *Der Standard*, Thursday, 2 October 1997: 8.

6 Discourse analysis, deliberative democracy and anti-racism

The critical and controlling potential of linguistics for anti-discrimination policy and politics

A deliberative-democratic model of anti-discrimination

Habermas (1981[1980]) and Benhabib (1995: 25) counter postmodernist criticisms against the Enlightenment and modernity, arguing that modernity is still an incomplete project. They maintain that the emancipatory undertaking of modernity should not be given up hastily, and that the Enlightenment cannot be condemned and rejected as a whole by the simple and undifferentiated contention that modernity has contributed substantially to the development of the very different forms of social discrimination, racism being just the tip of the iceberg. Moreover, the fair, humanist and cosmopolitan potential of the Enlightenment – including its self-reflective, self-critical and self-corrective capacity – has to be recognised, and its legacy has to be critically renegotiated.

For such an undertaking in the realm of political action, a deliberative, discursive (in the Habermasian sense) concept of democracy that is committed to critical theory and, as Seyla Benhabib (1992b, 1995, 1996) suggests, seems to be a suitable means of polity, policy and politics. Such a concept of democracy tries to take into account the political, social, economic and, in particular, communicative complexities of modern societies. It is not based on a simplistic and illusory image of a uniform public sphere, but on a differentiated model of an unhomogeneous, disparate and dispersed network of many and multiple publics, sub-publics and counter-publics (Frazer 1992: 123 speaks about 'subaltern counterpublics').

On the basis of more or less universalistic values and principles of justice, e.g. human rights, within the fields of these public spheres, the legitimacy and legality of political intentions, plans and decisions related to issues of public interest should be negotiated deliberatively: that is to say, in a discursive, advisory, consultative manner, by rational debate and argument, by weighing up critically the pros and cons, making transparent the divergent interests and motives of the parties involved and by public control of the procedures for making and for implementing decisions. The public debates should develop in accordance with the rules of non-manipulative, non-fallacious, transparent, rational argumentation (as explained in chapter 2, pp. 69–71) and under the condition that

264 Discourse and discrimination

all persons or parties involved can participate equally in the formation of public opinion.

The procedures of deliberative democracy should be founded on permanent auto- and hetero-reflective control and examination, and on clear and transparent discursal operations, which means that all protagonists and antagonists involved in the controversial issue are provided with extensive, comprehensive and relevant information, that the participating social actors clear their own point of view and try to think from the point of view of the other parties involved, to put themselves empathically in the others' position, or, to use the words of Hannah Arendt (1961: 220 [German text 1971]), to practice and cultivate 'an expanded way of thinking' ('*eine erweiterte Denkungsart*').

Such a democracy, and that is one important thing we also wish to clarify in this final chapter, needs different deliberative corporations and bodies of control acting within the different areas of politics, especially a critical parliamentary opposition, a system of jurisdiction proceeding as impartially and rationally as possible (especially as far as the Constitutional Court and the Administrative Court are concerned), media that are as free, independent and critical as possible and, of course, critical, politically informed and engaged citizens willing to take clear positions and to participate with courage in the deliberative formation of a strong civil society. Consequently, they will not hesitate to join civil rights and anti-discrimination movements to fight for justice and recognition whenever social and political power is abused, whenever public institutions discriminate and exclude specific minority groups of persons or – and exactly this was the topic of the fifth chapter – whenever the principle of democratic legitimacy is violated and the principle of legality conflicts with it, for example in the form of *summum ius summa iniuria*.

Apropos opposition: as Benhabib (1995: 13) sets out, the practice of parliamentary opposition means to control, examine, question, criticise and reformulate the presuppositions on the basis of which the majority party or parties (if there is a coalition government) claims or claim to govern. Procedures of parliamentary opposition, of debating and questioning, and procedures of investigating malfeasance, as well as fact-finding committees, incorporate principles which include that of deliberative rationality according to which majority decisions are to be seen as only temporary results, whose claims to validity and rationality are publicly examinable. Genuine parliamentary mechanisms of control closely tied to form and genre are the interpellation (e.g. in the form of written or verbal questions), the resolution (e.g. in the form of petitions and resolution proposals or motions) and the investigation (e.g. in the form of a parliamentary survey or *symposion*; see Nödl 1995). Apart from that, and as we showed and discussed in the previous chapter with the specific example of the political administration of social exclusion, in civic societies, there are, *inter alia*, the very important instruments of press conferences and media coverage.

All the four 'political bodies' of control mentioned here are required to recognise that democracy is not simply to be understood as a decision-making and problem-solving machinery based on arithmetical calculations and majority decisions. In contrast, they, and the political actors in power, should always keep in mind, in all important areas of political issues, the obligation to justify rationally the use of the majority principle as a democratic instrument of decision-making. And that means that they must also take into account the claims and preferences of societal minorities and can never simply suspend or even abolish the basic human, political and civil rights by a simple majority decision.

The majority principle, conceived in a deliberative-democratic fashion, should never simply be a political rule that follows the principle of 'legitimacy qua quantity'. Moreover, it should, wherever possible, respect the claim that something can only be a rational and democratic decision-making procedure if a majority of persons comes to the conclusion, at a specific moment in time and on the basis of reasons which are the result of a public discursive deliberation, that to act according to the result 'A' is the right thing to do, although the conclusion remains valid only as long as no another group of persons doubts 'A' for good reasons (see Benhabib 1995: 13). A critical discourse analysis oriented towards argumentation theory and rhetoric, as presented in chapter 2, can contribute greatly to answering the question of what are 'good reasons', because such an approach provides criteria, which enable one to distinguish between manipulative and suggestive procedures of persuasion and discursive procedures of convincing argumentation.

A deliberative democracy conceived in this way brings into being, as one of its most powerful remedies against such forms of discrimination as racism, antisemitism, ethnicism and sexism in modern, democratic states and societies, a strong civil society. It interprets legitimacy as the rationally achieved conviction that the main institutions of a society and the decisions taken in the name of the people deserve to be complied with or normatively acknowledged (see Benhabib 1995: 9).

In the specific case of the political administration of social exclusion on the basis of fallacious and discriminatory reasoning, such a conviction of legitimacy was very remote, all the more so considering the fact that the administrative authorities did not even adhere to the obligation to act exclusively within the legal framework.

To summarise: democratic legitimacy has to be the result of discursive procedures, performed under the condition of largely egalitarian reciprocity and located within the different public spheres or fields of political action, of a free, open and rational formation of public opinion about political problems and questions of shared interest. In this sense, democracy should be a form of political organisation, a public and collective exercise of power in the most important institutions of a specific society within a specific nation-state. This exercise of power should follow the deliberative principle that decisions which concern the welfare of a political community take the form of the result of a free and reasonable weighing of arguments among individuals who are recognised to be morally and politically equal (see Benhabib 1995: 3). That means that the political participation of the citizens has to go far beyond the periodic legitimisation of the state exercise of power qua votes or elections. Moreover, the participatory practices should take the form of communicative interaction before the forum of permanent deliberative public spheres and serve as a source for all political decisions of common interest (see Honneth 1999: 38).

It would not be sufficient simply to postulate the conditions of free and rational deliberation and the democratic revelation of its failure in abstract and theoretical terms, just from the perspective of a philosophy of law, social philosophy or the theory of democracy. Deliberative democracy and its endangerment, the latter having been the main subject of the present book, are realised linguistically or discursively. They are to be characterised from the point of view of communication and discourse theory. Therefore, a very broad area of interesting tasks and questions opens up for a critical discourse analysis that is informed by argumentation theory and rhetoric, and the relevance of critical discourse analysis to the concept of deliberative democracy and its antidiscrimination potential seems to be obvious.

The contribution of critical discourse analysis to the study of antisemitism, racism and anti-racism

The case studies presented in the course of our book have not only illustrated the wide range of ethnicist, antisemitic and racist prejudices and their realisation in language. They have also shown how a critical linguistic approach can be employed in the detection and analysis of these prejudices.

Depending on the situation and context (for example, interactional function, setting, participants and audience), racist, antisemitic and 'xenophobic' beliefs and ideologies are expressed and used for different aims. Many of these beliefs have historical traditions and multiple roots. Through discourse analysis, we are able to make explicit the whole range of linguistic devices used to code such beliefs and ideologies as well as the related practices. We have offered an overview of various linguistic approaches to the study of racism and of a number of different theoretical concepts to explain the production and reproduction of such attitudes and ideologies (chapter 1).

Two of our general basic questions, which we hope to have answered at least partly in the present book, were as follows: how is it possible that in postwar Europe such explicit discrimination against certain groups of 'foreigners' (especially third-state nationals), migrants, Jews, Roma and Sinti is still encountered and even helps to win votes, is politically functionalised to create scapegoats and outgroups, and is acceptable and tolerated? Moreover, since our case studies used empirical data from Austria, the question arose of how such explicit discrimination is possible in this country with its tradition of involvement in Nazi-Fascism and its contribution to the extermination of Jews during the National-Socialist era. Clearly, history teaches lessons that are not learnt and not understood.

The phenomenon of racism is even more threatening today, as one follows the development of populist parties throughout Western Europe and collects the slogans and arguments that are used to create or reinforce fears in the population. Fear of unemployment, of criminality, of drug abuse, of 'inundation by foreigners', of 'overforeignisation' are prevalent and are exploited successfully by the media and by politicians.

In Europe, recent elections in Austria (3 October 1999) and in Switzerland (24 October 1999) have made political parties using 'xenophobic', racist and antisemitic propaganda much stronger; such parties have won the support of almost a third of the electorate. The striking paradox is that the rise of populism is not related to economic crises in these countries.

Of the many possible reasons for the most recent rise of racism, ethnicism and 'xenophobia', we mentioned the impact of fears of globalisation and of changes in the public domains, such as the economic sphere (see chapter 4). Unemployment has become one of the biggest and most relevant social problems in Europe and throughout the world. Changes in the economy are necessary, and these lead to changes in social welfare states such as Austria. People will have to adapt to new lifestyles, to less social security – to 'flexibility', to use the new current catchword (Weiss and Wodak 2000b, forthcoming, Chouliariki and Fairclough 1999). Moreover, the possible expansion of the European Union to the former Eastern Bloc countries is being debated, and fears exist because of the huge costs of such an expansion. Politicians warn of a 'waste of money' and of thousands of migrants who would possibly travel to the West. The problems of supranationalisation and 'globalisation', the search for a new European identity, are thus related to or accompanied by the rise of nationalism, ethnicism, as well as 'xenophobia' and racism. The fears of changes, which cannot be defined with sufficient clarity, are projected on to scapegoats – and these scapegoats are 'the foreigners' who 'threaten the jobs'. Of course, this is only one of the many reasons for the rise of discriminatory ideologies and practices. But as we saw in the Austrian election of October 1999, it was precisely these fears which were cleverly emphasised, exploited and used to win votes for the FPÖ.

At the beginning of this book, we stressed the complex, multidetermined nature of racism and antisemitism, and argued that these phenomena have to be studied from an inter- or trans-disciplinary perspective. We should therefore now summarise what the specific linguistic contribution to the study of racist and ethnicist prejudices might be? Using the discourse-historical approach, which we elaborated from a theoretical viewpoint in chapter 2, we attempted to offer a conceptual, categorical and methodical framework, which seeks not only to facilitate the critical linguistic reconstruction and diagnostic description of a clear and explicit discursive manifestation of racist, ethnicist, 'xenphobic' and antisemitic prejudices, but also to make it possible critically to 'read between the lines' and to identify and grasp the more latent discriminatory prejudices with the help of linguistic tools. Blatant racist remarks do not need much linguistic analysis; they are readily understandable and classifiable. But the coded language of racism, antisemitism and xenophobia, as used in the media, by politicians and in political bureaucracy – that is to say, the implicit assumptions and insinuations, the veiling argumentation, the concealed fallacies and the ethymemic, condensed argumentation by (often discriminatory) metaphors – can only be adequately detected if the linguistic tools are sufficiently subtle. If discrimination is linguistically coded and 'drawn' by positive self-presentation, then a close and detailed linguistic analysis is needed to be able to discover the discriminatory intentions and their consequences. Therefore, the first contributions of critical discourse analysis to the study of discursive discrimination are the broadly immanent reconstruction and description (see also chapter 2, p. 32).

However, after detection and description of the purely linguistic dimension of discrimination, critical discourse analysis has to attempt to interpret the linguistic data within their sociopolitical context, thus uncovering the persuasive, propagandist, populist, 'manipulative' function of the discursive practices in question. This aim can only be reached with the help of explanatory approaches from other fields of knowledge beyond the purely linguistic discipline. In this phase of sociodiagnostic analysis (see chapter 2, pp. 32–3), we seek to understand why specific discriminatory discursive practices are performed at a specific time in a specific place in pursuit of specific political or social aims. Here, a historical, sociopsychological and sociological analysis can help to complement the linguistic description and reconstruction and to embed the linguistic 'material' into a broader context.

One should be aware, however, that social sciences cannot achieve explanatory power in the same way as the natural sciences. The causal assumptions made in the social sciences can hardly attain the strength and stringency of explanations in the natural sciences. This lies in the 'nature' of social phenomena. In the social sciences we attempt to understand, we interpret the 'sense', we differentiate and distinguish the complexity of interrelationships and tendencies. However, the difference between natural sciences and social sciences should not be overemphasised, for the description of natural phenomena, events or processes is also simply an interpretation. Thus, the difference is mainly one of degree.

The third main contribution of critical discourse analysis to the problem of discursive discrimination is the prospective critique that we outlined in chapter 2, pp. 33–5. Now critical discourse analysis could achieve a practical political dimension by trying to contribute to the solution of specific social problems and dysfunctionalities: for example, by attempting to the improve communicative relations, e.g. within the political system of a democracy. It is precisely here that our theoretical reflections about a deliberative, discursive democracy should come into play and be put into action.

Our three case studies endeavour to illustrate how a multidisciplinary context-dependent approach could work: the antisemitic Austrian discourse during the 'Waldheim Affair' was related to the history of antisemitism in Central Europe, to the Second World War, to the role of the Wehrmacht, to the context in Greece where Waldheim himself was stationed in 1943, to the postwar rationalisations and the Austrian '*Lebenslüge*', and, finally, to the 1986 election campaign and the *Realpolitik* of the competing political parties. Only in such a broad and differentiated context was it possible to grasp the functions of antisemitic language use and to understand why such prejudices could be effective and could actually create an 'enemy-image', the 'Jew abroad', forty years after the end of the Second World War and Auschwitz.

In all three case studies, we tried to present a more or less detailed description of the many competing arguments, the overlapping of discourse topics, the interdiscursivity and also the intertextuality, which are continuously produced between the different genres and fields of political action or public spaces.

As we have suggested, a critical discourse analysis of discursive practices that aim at discriminating against specific social groups or at disguising such discrimination has both theoretical as well as practical relevance. On the one hand, the many case studies and context-dependent interpretations allow for careful generalisations and – in the best case – also predictions. Thus, we attempt to build theories about the discursive construction of racist, ethnicist and anti-semitic prejudices as well as about their reproduction, dissemination and impact. On the basis of contrasting studies, discourse analysts can, for example, attempt to make generalisations about public-domain political discourse concerning immigration. These comparisons are important both for the analysis of discriminatory and anti-discriminatory argumentation patterns, and for the development of an interdisciplinary theory. On the other hand we stressed – when pointing to the third possible contribution of critical discourse analysis – that accurate linguistic analyses may permit practical applications in combating all forms of social discrimination through language (including racism, antisemitism, 'xenophobia' and sexism). For example, guidelines for journalists can be created which help to avoid the discriminatory linguistic presentation of specific groups of persons in the media. The same can be done for administrative and bureaucratic institutions (see Kargl *et al.* 1997). Training courses and seminars can be offered both for persons who engage in anti-discrimination activities and for those of a specific profession who are susceptible to discriminatory discursive practices and thus could be sensitised to their use of language. The EU Monitoring Centre on Racism and Xenophobia was created to observe, criticise and control public discourse and to point to discriminatory usage of language in public in the fifteen EU countries. Linguistic evidence can be used for forensic aims in courts of law to prove racist and antisemitic language use (see Gruber and Wodak 1992). Schoolbooks can be revised or written to give an adequate presentation of minorities and their problems (see Janks 1997, Janks [in preparation], Martin [in preparation]).

On the basis of the studies presented in this book, several attempts have been made successfully to utilise our analyses, methods and categories for anti-discriminatory aims: there was an exhibition in 1987, in the wake of the 'Waldheim Affair', which depicted the wide range of antisemitic language use during the election campaign. This exhibition was shown in Austria and Germany and made its way into many schools and museums. The accompanying catalogue (Wodak and De Cillia 1988) is still also used as a schoolbook. In Austria, this was the first of its kind critically and clearly to present and evaluate antisemitic prejudices and their realisation in discourse.

An expert opinion about the documents rejecting applications for family reunion (Matouschek and Wodak 1996, van Leeuwen and Wodak 1999) was presented by the Green Party in a parliamentary debate and question time. The Mayor of Vienna, Michael Häupl, promised afterwards that the documents would be revised and that such explicit discriminatory statements would be avoided. However, as our case study in chapter 5 illustrates, changes in administration take place with enormous slowness, if at all. Moreover, we were able to show how certain personae of the anonymous administration apparatus arrive at their decisions, and who are some of the leading and responsible persons behind the 'grey suit' of bureaucracy.

The election in Austria of 3 October 1999 should be seen as a qualitative leap in explicit and tolerated discursive discrimination. Never until that election campaign had slogans and posters been seen over the whole city of Vienna with such blatant 'xenophobic' language. 'The real Austrians' (the we-group) were contrasted with 'the foreigners' (of course, only certain groups of 'foreigners', like ex-Yugoslavians, Turks and members of the former Eastern Bloc countries). The Freedom Party of Jörg Haider promised to protect the 'real' (meaning German-speaking) Austrians from the danger of losing jobs to such 'foreigners' and from criminality. Complete lies were constructed and printed in brochures. For example, it was stated that Austrian (real German-speaking) schoolchildren were forced to read Turkish and Croatian texts in their schoolbooks. In a press conference a week before the election, the president of the Vienna School System was able to prove that such texts did not exist in any schoolbook used in Austrian schools. Thus, the Freedom Party distorted realities and made use of explicit lies. Moreover, Kurt Scholz, the president of the Vienna School System, illustrated that he had only found one single text in one schoolbook that was printed in four languages, in English, French, Turkish and Croatian: It consisted of five words: 'yes', 'no', 'please', 'thank you' and 'hello'. As laughable as this might seem to readers, the seriousness of such propaganda should not be underestimated. The most salient feature, however, of this election campaign was the incapability of the SPÖ and the ÖVP to counteract the discriminatory propaganda. The Green and Liberal Parties (both under 10 per cent) were active, as were religious groups; but the major governing parties did not take the fears of the population seriously and also did not disseminate important information that could have contradicted and evicted the fears. As we stated several times in chapter 4, the major parties actually implemented many of the proposals made by the Freedom Party in the hope of taking support from them. This strategy proved wrong; the Social Democratic Party lost many workers to the Freedom Party, which now calls itself the Workers' Party. What is most worrying in this whole context is not so much the fact of the existence of populist parties (although their growth is certainly a threatening factor). What concerns us more is the acceptance, the silence and the tolerance of discrimination by large sectors of the population and also by many politicians – now still at the level of discourse. But perhaps very soon other social and political practices might be involved, for since 4 February 2000, the Austrian Freedom Party has become a party of government. We will, obviously, keep an eye on the future political developments.

Bibliography

Adorno, T. W. (1963) *Eingriffe: Neun Kritische Modelle*, Frankfurt am Main: Suhrkamp.

Adorno, T. W. (1973)[1950] *Studien zum autoritären Charakter*, Frankfurt am Main: Suhrkamp.

Adorno, T. W. (1993) 'Antisemitismus und faschistische Propaganda', in: E. Simmel (ed.) *Antisemitismus*, Frankfurt am Main: Fischer, pp. 148–61.

Adorno, T. W., Fränkel-Brunswik, E., Levinson, D. J. and Stanford, P. N. (1950) *The Authoritarian Personality*, New York: The American Jewish Committee.

Aegerter, R. (1996a) 'Antisemitismus: Geschichte und Gegenwart einer hartnäckigen Feindschaft', in: R. Aegerter and I. Nezel (eds) *Sachbuch Rassismus. Informationen über Erscheinungsformen der Ausgrenzung*, Zürich: Pestalozzianum-Verlag, pp. 131–62.

Aegerter, R. (1996b) 'Die "Auschwitz-Lüge" ', in: R. Aegerter and I. Nezel (eds) *Sachbuch Rassismus. Informationen über Erscheinungsformen der Ausgrenzung*, Zürich: Pestalozzianum-Verlag, pp. 163–78.

Allport, G. W. (1993) 'Vorwort', in: E. Simmel (ed.) *Antisemitismus*, Frankfurt am Main: Fischer, pp. 9–11.

Altermatt, U. (1996) *Das Fanal von Sarajevo: Ethnonationalismus in Europa*, Paderborn/Munich/Vienna/Zurich: Schöningh.

Ammerongen, M. (1977) *Kreisky und seine unbewältigte Vergangenheit*, Graz: Styria.

Anderson, B. (1988) *Die Erfindung der Nation: Zur Karriere eines folgenreichen Konzepts*, Frankfurt am Main/New York: Campus [Engl. 1983].

Arduç-Sedlak, M. (2000) *Einfach Menschlich? Eine diskursanalytische Analyse xenophober Töne im Nationalratswahlkampf der FPÖ*, Vienna (2nd and revised version of the paper given on 3 December 1999 in Vienna during the 2nd Round Table organised by the European Monitoring Centre on Racism and Xenophobia).

Arendt, H. (1961) 'Crisis and Culture', in: H. Arendt (ed.) *Between Past and Future: Six Exercises in Political Thought*, New York [German: Arendt, H. (1971) *Zwischen Vergangenheit und Zukunft: Übungen im politischen Denken*, Munich/Zurich: Piper].

Bade, J. K. (1994) *Ausländer, Aussiedler, Asyl: Eine Bestandsaufnahme*, Munich: Beck.

Bader, V.-M. (1995) *Rassismus, Ethnizität, Bürgerschaft: Soziologische und philosophische Überlegungen*, Münster: Westfälisches Dampfboot.

Bailer, B. and Neugebauer, W. (1993) 'Die FPÖ: vom Liberalismus zum Rechtsextremismus', in: DöW (=Dokumentationsarchiv des österreichischen Widerstands) (ed.) *Handbuch des österreichischen Rechtsextremismus*, Vienna: Deuticke, pp. 327–428.

Bailer-Galanda, B. and Neugebauer, W. (1997) *Haider und die 'Freiheitlichen' in Österreich*, Berlin: Elefanten Press.

Balibar, E. (1991) ' "Es gibt keinen Staat in Europa": Racism and politics in Europe today', *New Left Review*, No. 186, pp. 5–19.

Balibar, E. and Wallerstein, I. (1990)[1988] *Rasse, Klasse, Nation. Ambivalente Identitäten*, Hamburg, Berlin: Argument-Verlag.

Barker, M. (1981) *The New Racism*, London: Junction Books.

Bauböck, R., Cinar, D., Hofinger, C. and Waldrauch, H. (1995) *Die rechtliche Integration von Ausländern im europäischen Vergleich*, Vienna: Institut für Höhere Studien.

Bauer, Y. (ed.) (1988) *Present-Day Antisemitism*, The Vidal Sassoon International Center for the Study of Antisemitism: The Hebrew University of Jerusalem.

Bauman, Z. (1989) *Modernity and the Holocaust*, Cambridge: Polity Press.

Bauman, Z. (1991) *Modernity and Ambivalence*, Cambridge: Polity Press.

Beaugrande, R. de and Dressler, W. U. (1981) *Einführung in die Textlinguistik*, Tübingen: Niemeyer.

Beck-Gernsheim, E. (1999) *Juden, Deutsche und andere Erinnerungsgemeinschaften*, Frankfurt am Main: Suhrkamp

Benhabib, S. (1992a) *Kritik, Norm und Utopie: Die normativen Grundlagen der Kritischen Theorie*, Frankfurt am Main: Fischer.

Benhabib, S. (1992b) *Selbst im Kontext: Kommunikative Ethik im Spannungsfeld von Feminismus, Kommunitarismus und Postmoderne*, Frankfurt am Main: Suhrkamp.

Benhabib, S. (1995) 'Ein deliberatives Modell demokratischer Legitimität', *Deutsche Zeitschrift für Philosophie. Zweimonatsschrift der internationalen philosophischen Forschung*, Vol. 43/1, pp. 3–29

Benhabib, S. (1996) *The Reluctant Modernism of Hannah Arendt*, New York: Sage.

Benhabib, S. (1997) 'Die gefährdete Öffentlichkeit', *Transit. Europäische Revue*, Vol. 13, pp. 26–41.

Benjamin, J. (1982) 'Die Antinomien des patriarchalischen Denkens: Kritische Theorie und Psychoanalyse', in: W. Bonß and A. Honneth (eds) *Sozialforschung als Kritik: Zum sozialwissenschaftlichen Potential der Kritischen Theorie*, Frankfurt am Main: Suhrkamp, pp. 426–55.

Beratungszentrum für Migranten und Migrantinnen (undated) 'Die rechtliche Stellung von Ausländer/innen in Österreich', Vienna: Beratungszentrum für Migranten und Migrantinnen, pp. 9–17.

Berger, P. and Luckman, T. (1980) *Die gesellschaftliche Konstruktion der Wirklichkeit: Eine Theorie der Wissenssoziologie*, Frankfurt am Main: Fischer.

Bergmann, W. and Erb, R. (eds) (1988) *Neue Studien zum Nachkriegsantisemitismus*, Opladen: Westdeutscher Verlag.

Bergmann, W. and Erb, R. (eds) (1991) *Antisemitismus in der Bundesrepublik Deutschland. Ergebnisse der empirischen Forschung von 1946–1989*, Opladen: Leske + Budrich.

Bergmann, W., Erb, R. and Lichtblau, A. (eds) (1995) *Schwieriges Erbe: Der Umgang mit National- sozialismus und Antisemitismus in Österreich, der DDR und der Bundesrepublik Deutschland*, Frankfurt am Main: Campus.

Bernstein, B. (1990) *The Structure of Pedagogic Discourse: Class, Codes and Control*, Vol VI, London: Routledge.

Bhabha, H. K. (ed.) (1990) *Nation and Narration*, London: Routledge.

Bierwisch, M. (1992) 'Recht linguistisch gesehen', in: G. Grewendorf (ed.) *Rechtskultur als Sprachkultur: Zur forensischen Funktion der Sprachanalyse*, Frankfurt am Main: Suhrkamp, pp. 42–68.

Billig, M. (1978) *Fascists: A Social Psychological Analysis of the National Front*, London: Academic Press.

Billig, M. (1985) 'Prejudice, categorisation and particularisation: From a perceptual to a rhetorical approach', *European Journal of Social Psychology*, Vol. 15, pp. 79–103.

Billig, M. (1988) 'The notion of "prejudice": Some rhetorical and ideological aspects', *Text*, Vol. 8, pp. 91–111.

Billig, M., Condor, S., Edwards, D., Gane, M., Middleton, D. and Radley, A. (1988) *Ideological Dilemmas: A Social Psychology of Everyday Thinking*, London: Sage.

Böke, K. (1997) 'Die "Invasion" aus den "Armenhäusern" Europas: Metaphern im Einwanderungsdiskurs', in: M. Jung, M. Wengeler and K. Böke (eds) *Die Sprache des Migrationsdiskurses: Das Reden über 'Ausländer' in Medien, Politik und Alltag*, Opladen: Westdeutscher Verlag, pp. 164–93.

Bonß, W. and Honneth, A. (1982) *Sozialforschung als Kritik: Zum sozialwissenschaftlichen Potential der Kritischen Theorie*, Frankfurt am Main: Suhrkamp.

Brackmann, K. H. and Birkenbauer, R. (1988) *NS-Deutsch. 'Selbstverständliche Begriffe und Schlagwörter aus der Zeit des Nationalsozialismus*, Straelen, Niederrhein: Straelener Manuskripte Verlag.

Brainin, E., Ligeti, V. and Teicher, S. (1993) *Vom Gedanken zur Tat: Zur Psychoanalyse des Antisemitismus*, Frankfurt am Main: Brandes and Apsel.

Broder, H. (ed.) (1986) *Der ewige Antisemit*, Frankfurt: Suhrkamp.

Brown, M. (ed.) (1994) *Approaches to Antisemitism. Context and Curriculum*, New York: The American Jewish Committee.

Bruck, P. A, Selhofer, H. and Stocker, G. (1995) *Marktmacht Mediaprint: Endbericht. Eine medienökonomische und publizistische Analyse der Marktposition von Österreichs größtem Verlagskonzern*, Salzburg: Institut für Informationsökonomie und Neue Medien.

Brumlik, M. (1990) 'Die Entwicklung der Begriffe "Rasse", "Kultur" und "Ethnizität" im sozialwissenschaftlichen Diskurs', in: E. J. Dittrich and F.-O. Radtke (eds) *Ethnizität: Wissenschaft und Minderheiten*, Opladen: Westdeutscher Verlag, pp. 179–90.

Budzinski, M. (ed.) (1988) *Alle Menschen sind Ausländer: Fast überall. Ein Aktionshandbuch*, Göttingen: Lamuv Verlag.

Bühler, K. (1982)[1934] *Sprachtheorie: Die Darstellungsfunktion der Sprache*, Stuttgart: Gustav Fischer Verlag (UTB).

Burgen, St. (1998) *Bloody hell, verdammt noch mal: Eine europäische Schimpfkunde*, Munich: dtv.

Burkhardt, A. (1996) 'Politolinguistik. Versuch einer Ortsbestimmung', in: J. Klein and H. Diekmannshenke (eds) *Sprachstrategien und Dialogblockaden: Linguistische und politikwissenschaftliche Studien zur politischen Kommunkation*, Berlin: de Gruyter, pp. 75–100.

Calhoun, C. (1995) *Critical Social Theory: Culture, History, and the Challenge of Difference*, Oxford: Blackwell.

Castles, S. and Kosack, G. (1972) 'The function of labour immigration in Western European capitalism', *New Left Review*, Vol. 73, pp. 3–21.

Castles, S. and Kosack, G. (1973) *Immigrant Workers and Class Structure in Western Europe*, London: Oxford University Press.

Centre for Contemporary Cultural Studies (ed.) (1982) *The Empire Strikes Back: Race and Racism in 70s Britain*, London: Hutchinson/Centre for Contemporary Cultural Studies.

Chafe, W. (1982) 'Integration and involvement in speaking, writing, and in oral literature', in: D. Tannen (ed.) *Spoken and Written Language. Exploring Orality and Literacy*, Norwood, NJ: Ablex, pp. 35–53.

Chouliaraki, L. and Fairclough, N. (1999) *Discourse in Late Modernity: Rethinking Critical Discourse Analysis*, Edinburgh: Edinburgh University Press.

Cicourel, A. V. (1974) *Methode und Messung in der Soziologie*, Frankfurt am Main: Suhrkamp.

Claussen, D. (1994) *Was heißt Rassismus?*, Darmstadt: Wissenschaftliche Buchgesellschaft.

Collins (1991) *The Collins German Dictionary. Großwörterbuch Deutsch-English Englisch-Deutsch. German-English English-German Dictionary*. 2nd edition, Glasgow and Stuttgart: Harper Collins Publishers and Ernst Klett Verlag für Wissen und Bildung, p. 447.

Conze, W. and Sommer, A. (1984) 'Rasse', in: O. Brunner, W. Conze and R. Koselleck (eds) *Geschichtliche Grundbegriffe: Historisches Lexikon zur politisch-sozialen Sprache in Deutschland*, Stuttgart: Klett-Cotta. Vol. 5: Pro-Soz, pp. 135–77.

Cox, O. C. (1970) *Caste, Class and Race*, New York: Monthly Review Press.

Davy, U. (1997a) ' "Überfremdung" und Familiennachzug', *ecolex*, Vol. 6, pp. 469–73.

Davy, U. (1997b) 'Die Asylrechtsreform 1997 (I)', *ecolex*, Vol. 9, pp. 708–12.

Davy, U. (1997c) 'Die Asylrechtsreform 1997 (II)', *ecolex*, Vol. 10, pp. 821–26.

De Cillia, R., Reisigl, M. and Wodak, R. (1999) 'The discursive construction of national identities', *Discourse and Society*, Vol. 10/1, pp. 149–73.

Der Fischer Weltalmanach 1996, Frankfurt am Main: Fischer.

Der Fischer Weltalmanach 1997, Frankfurt am Main: Fischer.

Der Fischer Weltalmanach 1998, Frankfurt am Main: Fischer.

Der Fischer Weltalmanach 1999, Frankfurt am Main: Fischer.

Der Fischer Weltalmanach 2000, Frankfurt am Main: Fischer.

Der Standard. 'Österreichs Unabhängige Tageszeitung für Wirtschaft, Politik und Kultur', Vienna: *Der Standard*.

Dieckmann, W. (1964) *Information und Überredung: Zum Wortgebrauch der politischen Werbung in Deutschland seit der Französischen Revolution*, Marburg: N.G. Elwert Verlag.

Dieckmann, W. (1975) *Sprache in der Politik. Einführung in die Pragmatik und Semantik der politischen Sprache*, Heidelberg: Carl Winter Universitätsverlag.

Dieckmann, W. (1981) *Politische Sprache – Politische Kommunikation: Vorträge – Aufsätze – Entwürfe*, Heidelberg: Carl Winter Universitätsverlag.

Dittrich, E. J. and Radtke, F.-O. (eds) (1990) *Ethnizität: Wissenschaft und Minderheiten*, Opladen: Westdeutscher Verlag.

DöW (=Dokumentationsarchiv des österreichischen Widerstands) (ed.) (1993) *Handbuch des österreichischen Rechtsextremismus*, Vienna: Deuticke

Duden (1989a) *Deutsches Universalwörterbuch A-Z*, 2nd edition, Mannheim, Vienna, Zurich: Duden.

Duden (1989b) *Etymologie. Herkunftswörterbuch der deutschen Sprache*, 2nd edition, Mannheim, Vienna, Zurich: Dudenverlag.

Duisburger Institut für Sprach- und Sozialforschung (eds) (1999) *Medien und Straftaten. Vorschläge zur Vermeidung diskriminierender Berichterstattung über Einwanderer und Flüchtlinge*, Duisburg: DISS.

Eatwell, R. (1998) 'The dynamics of right-wing electoral breakthrough', *Patterns of Prejudice 32/3/1998*, pp. 3–31.

Ebbinghaus, A. (ed.) (1996) *Opfer und Täterinnen: Frauenbiographien des Nationalsozialismus*, Frankfurt am Main: Fischer.

Ehlich, K. (1983) 'Text und sprachliches Handeln: Die Entstehung von Texten aus dem Bedürfnis nach Überlieferung', in: A. Assmann, J. Assmann and C. Hardmeier (eds) *Schrift und Gedächtnis. Beiträge zur Archäologie der literarischen Kommunikation*, Munich: Fink, pp. 24–43.

Engelmann, B. (1984) *Du Deutsch? Geschichte der Ausländer in Unserem Land*, Munich: Bertelsmann Verlag.

Eriksen, T. H. (1993) *Ethnicity and Nationalism: Anthropological Perspectives*, London: Pluto Press.

Essed, P. (1991) *Understanding Everyday Racism: An Interdisciplinary Theory*, London: Sage.

Essed, P. (1992) 'Multikulturalismus und kultureller Rassismus in den Niederlanden', in: Institut für Migration und Rassismusforschung e.V. (ed.) *Rassismus und Migration in Europa: Beiträge des Kongresses 'Migration und Rassismus in Europa' Hamburg, 26. bis 30. September 1990*, Hamburg and Berlin: Argument, pp. 373–87.

Fairclough, N. (1989) *Language and Power*, London: Longman.

Fairclough, N. (1992) *Discourse and Social Change*, Oxford: Polity Press/Blackwell.

Fairclough, N. (1995a) *Critical Discourse Analysis: The Critical Study of Language*, London: Longman.

Fairclough, N. (1995b) *Media Discourse*, London: Edward Arnold.

Fairclough, N. (2000) 'The discourse of social exclusion', in: M. Reisigl and R. Wodak (eds) *The Semiotics of Racism: Approaches in Critical Discourse Analysis*, Vienna: Passagen.

Fairclough, N. and Wodak, R. (1997) 'Critical discourse analysis', in: T. van Dijk (ed.) *Discourse as Social Interaction. Discourse Studies: A Multidisciplinary Introduction. Volume 2*, London: Sage, pp. 258–84.

Falter. Stadtzeitung Wien: Mit Programm, Vienna: Falter Verlag.

Fanon, F. (1986) *Black Skin, White Masks*, London: Pluto Press.

Faßmann, H. and Münz, R. (1992) *Einwanderungsland Österreich? Gastarbeiter – Flüchtlinge – Immigranten*, Vienna: Dachs-Verlag.

Faßmann, H. and Münz, R. (1996) 'Österreich: Einwanderungsland wider Willen', in: H. Faßmann and R. Münz (eds) *Migration in Europa: Historische Entwicklung, aktuelle Trends, politische Reaktionen*, Frankfurt am Main: Campus, pp. 209–29.

Faßmann, H., Münz, R. and Seifert, W. (1997) 'Die Arbeitsmarktposition ausländischer Arbeitskräfte in Deutschland (West) und Österreich', in: K. M. Bolte et al. (eds) *Mitteilungen aus der Arbeitsmarkt und Berufsforschung*, Vol. 30, Stuttgart: Kohlhammer, pp. 732–45.

Feagin, J. R. (1990) 'Theorien der rassischen und ethnischen Beziehungen in den Vereinigten Staaten: Eine kritische und vergleichende Anaylse', in: E. J. Dittrich and F.-O. Radtke (eds) *Ethnizität: Wissenschaft und Minderheiten*, Opladen: Westdeutscher Verlag, pp. 85–118.

Fenichel, O. (1993) 'Elemente einer psychoanalytischen Theorie des Antisemitismus', in: E. Simmel (ed.) *Antisemitismus*, Frankfurt am Main: Fischer, pp. 35–57.

Fischer, G. and Wölflingseder, M. (1995) *Biologismus – Rassismus – Nationalismus: Rechte Ideologien im Vormarsch*, Vienna: Promedia.

Fleischer, W. and Barz, I. (1992) *Wortbildung der Deutschen Gegenwartssprache*, Tübingen: Niemeyer.

Fowler, R. (1996) *Linguistic Criticism*, Oxford: Oxford University Press.

Fox-Genovese, E. (1992) *Within the Plantation Household: Black and White Women of the Old South*, Chapel Hill, NC: University of North Carolina Press.

Frazer, N. (1992) 'Rethinking the public sphere. A contribution to the critique of actually existing democracy', in C. Calhoun (ed.) *Habermas and the Public Sphere*, Cambridge, MA: MIT-Press.

Fromm, E. (1988)[1941] *Die Furcht vor der Freiheit*, Frankfurt am Main: Ullstein. [English: Escape from Freedom.]

Frosh, S. (1987) *The Politics of Psychoanalysis*, London: Macmillan.

Frosh, S. (1989) 'Psychoanalysis and racism', in B. Richards (ed.) *Crisis of the Self*, London: Free Association Books.

Frosh, S. (1991) *Identity Crisis: Modernity, Psychoanalysis and the Self*, London: Macmillan.

Gallup (= Österreichisches Gallup Institut, Dr. Karmasin Markforschung) (1991) '*Fremdenfeindlichkeit und Antisemitismus*'. Präsentation der Ergebnisse einer international vergleichenden

Repräsentativbefragung in Österreich. Kurzzusammenfassung der wichtigsten Ergebnisse anläßlich der Pressekonferenz am 24. Oktober 1991 im Presseclub Concordia, Vienna: Österreichisches Gallup Institut.

Gärtner, R. (1997) 'Rassismus und Nationalismus in Österreich', in: Institut für Interkulturelle Forschung und Bildung (ed.) *Rassismus und Nationalismus in West- und Osteuropa. Ursachen und Auswirkungen in verschiedenen Ländern Europas*, Munich: Marino-Verlag, pp. 65–85.

Geiss, I. (1988) *Geschichte des Rassismus*, Frankfurt am Main: Suhrkamp.

Genovese, E. D. (1995) *The Southern Front: History and Politics in the Cultural War*, Columbia, MO: University of Missouri Press.

Georgakopoulou, A. and Goutsos, D. (1997) *Discourse Analysis: An Introduction*, Edinburgh: Edinburgh University Press.

Gerhard, U. and Link, J. (1991) 'Zum Anteil der Kollektivsymbolik an den Nationalstereotypen', in: J. Link and W. Wülfing (eds) *Nationale Mythen und Symbole in der zweiten Hälfte des 19. Jahrhunderts: Strukturen und Funktionen von Konzepten nationaler Identität*, Stuttgart: Klett-Cotta, pp.16–52.

Gerhards, J. (1998) 'Öffentlichkeit', in: O. Jarren, U. Sarcinelli and U. Saxer (eds) *Politische Kommunikation in der demokratischen Gesellschaft: Ein Handbuch*, Opladen: Westdeutscher Verlag, pp. 269–74.

Gilman, S. L. and Katz, St T. (eds) (1991) *Antisemitism in Times of Crisis*, New York: New York University Press.

Gilroy, P. (1987) *'There Ain't No Black in the Union Jack': The Cultural Politics of Race and Nation*, London: Hutchinson.

Girnth, H. (1996) 'Texte im politischen Diskurs: Ein Vorschlag zur diskursorientierten Beschreibung von Textsorten', *Muttersprache*, Vol.106/1, pp. 66–80.

Goffman, E. (1974) *Rahmen-Analyse: Ein Versuch über die Organisation von Alltagserfahrungen*, Frankfurt am Main: Suhrkamp.

Goffman, E. (1981) *Forms of Talk*, Philadelphia: University of Pennsylvania Press.

Goldberg, D. T. (1993) *Racist Culture: Philosophy and the Politics of Meaning*, Oxford: Blackwell.

Gottschlich, M. (1987) *Der Fall 'Waldheim' als Medienereignis*, Vienna: unpublished research report.

Graefen, G. (1997) *Der wissenschaftliche Artikel: Textart und Textorganisation*, Frankfurt am Main: Lang.

Gräf, L. (1999) *Bekenntnisse eines Rassisten? Eine kritische Diskursanalyse der Debatte um 'The Bell Curve' in österreichischen Printmedien*, Vienna: unpublished MA-thesis.

Grewendorf, G. (1992) 'Rechtskultur als Sprachkultur. Der sprachanalytische Sachverstand im Recht', in: G. Grewendorf (ed.) *Rechtskultur als Sprachkultur: Zur forensischen Funktion der Sprachanalyse*, Frankfurt am Main: Suhrkamp, pp. 11–41.

Grimm, J. and Grimm, W. (1991)[1877] *Deutsches Wörterbuch von Jacob und Wilhelm Grimm*, Volume 10, Munich: Deutscher Taschenbuch Verlag (dtv).

Gruber, H. (1991) *Antisemitismus im Mediendiskurs: Die Affäre 'Waldheim' in der Tagespresse*, Wiesbaden and Opladen: Deutscher Universitätsverlag/Westdeutscher Verlag.

Gruber, H. and Wodak, R. (eds) (1987) *'Jetzt erst recht!' – Sozio- und textlinguistische Untersuchungen zur Medienberichterstattung im Bundespräsidentschaftswahlkampf 1986*, Vienna: Institut für Sprachwissenschaft (= Wiener Linguistische Gazette WLG, Vols 38/39).

Gruber, H. and Wodak, R. (1992) 'Ein Fall für den Staatsanwalt? Diskursanalyse der Kronenzeitungsberichterstattung zu Neonazismus und Novellierung des österreichischen Verbotsgesetzes im Frühjahr 1992', *WLG, Supplement 11.*

Grünalternative Jugend (ed.)/Gratzer, C. (1998) *Der Schoß is fruchtbar noch ... NSDAP (1920– 1933) – FPÖ (1986–1998). Kontinuitäten, Parallelen, Ähnlichkeiten*, Vienna: Grünalternative Jugend.

Guillaumin, C. (1991) 'RASSE: Das Wort und die Vorstellung', in: U. Bielefeld (ed.) *Das Eigene und das Fremde: Neuer Rassismus in der Alten Welt*, Hamburg: Junius, pp. 159–73.

Guillaumin, C. (1992) 'Zur Bedeutung des Begriffs "Rasse" ', in: Institut für Migration und Rassismusforschung e.V. (ed.) *Rassismus und Migration in Europa: Beiträge des Kongresses 'Migration und Rassismus in Europa' Hamburg, 26. bis 30. September 1990*, Hamburg and Berlin: Argument, pp. 77–87.

Gumperz, J. (1982) *Discourse Strategies*, Cambridge: Cambridge University Press.

Habermas, J. (1962) *Strukturwandel der Öffentlichkeit*, Frankfurt am Main: Suhrkamp.

Habermas, J. (1975) *Legitimation Crisis*, Boston: Beacon Press [German: Habermas, J. (1973) *Legitimationsprobleme im Spätkapitalismus*, Frankfurt am Main: Suhrkamp.]

Habermas, J. (1981[1980]) 'Die Moderne – ein unvollendetes Projekt', in: Habermas, J. *Kleine politische Schriften I–IV*, Frankfurt am Main: Suhrkamp, pp. 444–64.

Habermas, J. (1992) *Faktizität und Geltung: Beiträge zur Diskurstheorie der Rechts und des demokratischen Rechtsstaats*, Frankfurt am Main: Suhrkamp.

Habermas, J. (1996) *Die Einbeziehung des Anderen: Studien zur politischen Theorie*, Frankfurt am Main: Suhrkamp.

Habermas, J. (1998a) *Die postnationale Konstellation: politische Essays*, Frankfurt am Main: Suhrkamp.

Habermas, J. (1998b) 'Zur Legitimation durch Menschenrechte', in: J. Habermas (1998a) *Die postnationale Konstellation*, Frankfurt am Main: Suhrkamp, pp. 170–92.

Hak, T. (1987) *Discourse Representation in Media Discourse*, Amsterdam: unpublished manuscript.

Hall, S. (1978) 'Racism and Reaction', in: Commission for Racial Equality (ed.) *Five Views of Multi-Racial Britain*, London: Commission for Racial Equality, pp. 22–35.

Hall, S. (1980) 'Race, Articulation and Societies Structured in Dominance', in: UNESCO (ed.) *Sociological Theories: Race and Colonialism*, Paris: UNESCO, pp. 305–45.

Hall, S. (1989) 'Rassismus als ideologischer Diskurs', *Das Argument*, Vol. 178, pp. 913–21.

Hall, S. (1994) *Rassismus und kulturelle Identität: Ausgewählte Schriften 2*, Hamburg: Argument.

Halliday, M. A. K. (1994) *An Introduction to Functional Grammar*, London: Arnold.

Hamilton, D. and Trolier, T. (1986) 'Stereotypes and stereotyping. An overview of the cognitive approach', in: J. F. Dovidio and S. L. Gaertner (eds) *Prejudice, Discrimination, and Racism*, Orlando, FL: Academic Press, pp. 127–63.

Heckmann, F. (1991) 'Ethnos, Demos und Nation, oder: Woher stammt die Intoleranz des Nationalstaats gegenüber ethnischen Minderheiten?', in: U. Bielefeld (ed.) *Das Eigene und das Fremde: Neuer Rassismus in der Alten Welt?*, Hamburg: Junius, pp. 51–78.

Heenen-Wolff, S. (1994) *Im Land der Täter: Gespräche mit überlebenden Juden*, Frankfurt am Main: Fischer.

Heinemann, M. (ed.) (1998) *Sprachliche und soziale Stereotype*, Frankfurt am Main: Lang.

Heiss, G. and Rathkolb, O. (eds) (1995) *Asylland wider Willen. Flüchtlinge in Österreich im europäischen Kontext seit 1914*, Vienna: Verlag für Gesellschaftskritik.

Hermanns, F. (1982) 'Brisante Wörter: Zur lexikographischen Behandlung parteisprach- licher Wörter und Wendungen in Wörterbüchern der deutschen Gegenwartssprache', in: H. E. Wiegand (ed.) *Studien zur neuhochdeutschen Lexikographie II*, Hildesheim: Olms, pp. 87–108.

Hirschfeld, M. (1938)[1933/34] *Racism*, London: Gollancz.

Hodge, R. and Kress, G. (1991) *Social Semiotics*, Cambridge: Polity Press and Ithaca: Cornell University Press.

Hödl, G. and Winter, P. (1998) *Auf der Suche nach einem sicheren Hafen: Zur rechtlichen Stellung und Lebenssituation von Fremden in Österreich*, Vienna: International Helsinki Federation for Human Rights and IHF-Wissenschaftsgesellschaft.

Hofinger, C., Liegl, B., Ogris, G., Unger, T., Waldrauch, H., Wroblewski, S. and Zuser, P. (1998) *Einwanderung und Niederlassung II*. Soziale Kontakte, Diskriminierungserfahrung, Sprachkenntnisse, Bleibeabsichten, Arbeitsmarktintegration und Armutsgefährung der ausländischen Wohnbevölkerung in Wien, Vienna: Institut für Höhere Studien.

Hogg, M. A. and Abrahams, D. (1988) *Social Identification*, London: Routledge.

Honneth, A. (1989) *Kritik der Macht. Reflexionsstufen einer kritischen Gesellschaftstheorie*, Frankfurt am Main: Suhrkamp.

Honneth, A. (1990) *Die zerrissene Welt des Sozialen: Sozialphilosophische Aufsätze*, Frankfurt am Main: Suhrkamp.

Honneth, A. (1994) *Kampf um Anerkennung: Zur moralischen Grammatik sozialer Konflikte*, Frankfurt am Main: Suhrkamp.

Honneth, A. (1999) 'Demokratie als reflexive Kooperation: John Dewey und die Demokratietheorie der Gegenwart', in: H. Brunkhorst and P. Niesen (eds) *Das Recht der Republik*, Frankfurt am Main: Suhrkamp, pp. 37–65.

Hooke, A. E. (1991) 'Torturous logic and tortured bodies. Why is ad baculum a fallacy?', in: F. H. van Eeemeren, R. Grootendorst, A. J. Blair and C. A. Willard (eds) *Proceedings of the Second International Conference on Argumentation. Organized by the International Society for the Study of Argumentation (ISSA) at the University of Amsterdam. June 19–22, 1990*, Amsterdam: International Centre for the Study of Argumentation (Sic Sat), pp. 391–96.

Horkheimer, M. (1992) *Traditionelle und Kritische Theorie: Fünf Aufsätze*, Frankfurt am Main: Suhrkamp.

Horkheimer, M. and Adorno, T. W. 1991[1944] *Dialektik der Aufklärung: Philosophische Fragmente*, Frankfurt am Main: Fischer.

Horkheimer; M. and Flowerman, S. H. (eds) (1949 f.) *Studies in Prejudice*, New York: The American Jewish Committee.

Horkheimer, M., Fromm, E., Marcuse, H., Mayer, H., Wittfogel, K. A. and Honigsheim, P. (1987) *Studien über Autorität und Familie: Forschungsberichte aus dem Institut für Sozialforschung*, Frankfurt am Main: Klampen.

Il Nuovo Dizionario di Garzanti (1984) Milano: Garzanti.

Jacoby, R. (1983) *Die Verdrängung der Psychoanalyse oder Der Triumph des Konformismus*, Frankfurt am Main: Fischer.

Jacquard, A. (1996) 'Ein unwissenschaftlicher Begriff', in: *Unesco-Kurier*, Nr. 3, pp. 18–21.

Jäger, M. (1993) ' "Feministische" Argumente zur Untermauerung von Rassismus: Warum liegt Deutschen die Stellung der Einwanderinnen so am Herzen?', in: C. Butterwegge and S. Jäger (eds) *Rassismus in Europa*, Cologne: Bund, pp. 248–61.

Jäger, M. (1996a) *Fatale Effekte: Die Kritik am Patriarchat im Einwanderungsdiskurs*, Duisburg: DISS.

Jäger, M. (1996b) 'Rassismus im Alltagsdiskurs', in: M. Jäger and F. Wichert (eds) *Rassismus und Biopolitik. Werkstattberichte. DISS-Forschungsbericht 1996*, Duisburg: DISS, pp. 34–45

Jäger, M., Cleve, G., Ruth, I. and Jäger, S. (1998) *Von Deutschen Einzeltätern und ausländischen Banden: Medien und Straftaten. Mit Vorschlägen zur Vermeidung diskriminierender Berichterstattung*, Duisburg: DISS.

Jäger, S. (1992) *BrandSätze: Rassismus im Alltag*, Duisburg: DISS.

Jäger, S. (1993) *Kritische Diskursanalyse. Eine Einführung*, Duisburg: DISS.

Jäger, S. and Jäger, M. (eds) (1992) *Aus der Mitte der Gesellschaft (I–IV): Zu den Ursachen von Rechtsextremismus und Rassismus in Europa*, Duisburg: DISS.

Jäger, S. and Januschek, F. (eds) (1992) *Der Diskurs des Rassismus: Ergebnisse des DISS-Kolloquiums November 1991*, Osnabrück: Redaktion Obst (OBST 46).

Jäger, S. and Link, J. (eds) (1993) *Die vierte Gewalt. Rassismus in den Medien*, Duisburg: DISS.

Janks, H. (1997) 'Teaching language and power', in: R. Wodak and D. Corson (eds) (1997) *Encyclopedia of Language and Education. Volume 1: Language Policy and Political Issues in Education*, Dordrecht, Boston and London: Kluwer Academic Publishers, pp. 241–51

Janks, H. (in preparation) ' "We rewrote the book". Constructions of literacy in South Africa', in: R. de Cillia, H.-J. Krumm and R. Wodak (eds) (in preparation) *Loss of Communication in the Information Age*, Vienna: Verlag der Österreichischen Akademie der Wissenschaften.

Januschek, F. (1992) *Rechtspopulismus und NS-Anspielungen am Beispiel des österreichischen Politikers Jörg Haider*, Duisburg: DISS.

Jarren, O., Sarcinelli, U. and Saxer, U. (eds) (1998) *Politische Kommunikation in der demokratischen Gesellschaft: Ein Handbuch*, Opladen: Westdeutscher Verlag.

Jung, M., Wengeler, M. and K. Böke (eds) *Die Sprache des Migrationsdiskurses: Das Reden über 'Ausländer' in Medien, Politik und Alltag*, Opladen: Westdeutscher Verlag, pp. 164–93.

Kalpaka, A. and Räthzel, N. (eds) (1986) *Die Schwierigkeit, nicht rassistisch zu sein*, Berlin: Express Edition.

Kargl, M. (1996) *Der Held von Brüssel: Das Bild Alois Mocks in der EU-Berichterstattung von 'Kronen Zeitung' und 'Täglich Alles'*, Vienna: unpublished MA-thesis.

Kargl, M., Wetschanow, K., Wodak, R. and Perle, N. (1997) *Kreatives Formulieren: Anleitungen zu geschlechtergerechtem Sprachgebrauch*, Vienna: Bundesministerium für Frauenangelegenheiten und Verbraucherschutz.

Karl-Renner Institut (eds) (1990) *Fremdenangst und Ausländerfeindlichkeit: Gegenargumente*, Vienna: Karl-Renner-Institut.

Kienpointner, M. (1992) *Alltagslogik. Struktur und Funktion von Argumentationsmustern*, Stuttgart-Bad Cannstatt: frommann-holzboog.

Kienpointner, M. (1996) *Vernünftig argumentieren: Regeln und Techniken der Diskussion*, Hamburg: Rowohlt.

Kienpointner, M. and Kindt, W. (1997) 'On the problem of bias in political argumentation: An investigation into discussions about political asylum in Germany and Austria', *Journal of Pragmatics*, Vol. 27, pp. 555–85.

Kienzl, H. and Gehmacher, E. (eds) (1987) *Antisemitismus in Österreich, Eine Studie der österreichischen demoskopischen Institute*, Vienna: Braumüller.

Kier, V. *et al.* (1997) *Mündliche parlamentarische Anfrage Nr. 159/M: Bescheide in Ausländerangelegenheiten – Erfassung mit Textbausteinen – Erlassung erst nach Prüfung durch rechtskundige Organe*, Vienna: Austrian Parliament.

Kindt, W. (1992) 'Argumentation und Konfliktaustragung in Äußerungen über den Golfkrieg', in: *Zeitschrift für Sprachwissenschaft*, Vol. 11, pp. 189–215.

Klein, J. (1998) 'Politische Kommunikation: Sprachwissenschaftliche Perspektiven', in: O. Jarren, U. Sarcinelli and U. Saxer (eds) *Politische Kommunikation in der demokratischen Gesellschaft: Ein Handbuch*, Opladen: Westdeutscher Verlag, pp. 186–210.

Kluge (1999) *Etymologisches Wörterbuch der deutschen Sprache*, 23rd edition, Berlin: de Gruyter.

Knight, R. (ed.) (1988) ' "Ich bin dafür, die Sache in die Länge zu ziehen": Die Wortprotokolle der österreichischen Bundesregierung von 1945 bis 1952 über die Entschädigung der Juden*, Frankfurt: Athenäum.

Knoblauch, H. A. (1994) 'Erving Goffmans Reich der Interaktion', in: E. Goffman *Interaktion und Geschlecht*, Frankfurt am Main: Campus, pp. 7–49.

Kopperschmidt, J. (1980) *Argumentation. Sprache und Vernunft 2*, Stuttgart: Kohlhammer.

Kopperschmidt, J. (1989) *Methodik der Argumentationsanalyse*, Stuttgart: frommann-holzboog.

Koselleck, R. (1989) *Vergangene Zukunft: Zur Semantik geschichtlicher Zeiten*, Frankfurt am Main: Suhrkamp.

Krausneker, V. (1997) ' "Es war daher spruchgemäß zu entscheiden": Eine linguistische Analyse von Bescheiden der Wiener Magistratsabteilung 62', in: *Informationen der Gesellschaft für politische Aufklärung*, No. 53, pp. 1–5.

Krausneker, V. (1999) *Rassismus in Österreich? Rassismus in Österreich! Analyse und theoretische Einbettung der Diskriminierungen aus dem Rassismusbericht 1998/99 von Helping Hands*, Vienna: unpublished report.

Kress, G. and van Leeuwen, T. (1996) *Reading Images*, London: Routledge.

Krugman, P. (1996) *Pop Internationalism*, Cambridge, MA: MIT Press.

Kurz, H., Collins, J., Vanwelkenhuyzen, J., Fleming, G., Fleischer, H., Wallach, J. and Messerschmidt, M. (1988) 'Der Bericht der Internationalen Historikerkommission', *profil* 15, February.

Labov, W. and Waletzky, J. (1967) 'Narrative analysis. Oral versions of personal experience', in: J. Helm (ed.) *Essays on the Verbal and Visual Art*, Seattle: University of Washington Press, pp.12–44.

Langner, M. (1994) *Zur kommunikativen Funktion von Abschwächungen. Pragma- und Soziolinguistische Untersuchungen*, Münster: Nodus Publikationen.

Lanham, R. A. (1991) *A Handlist of Rhetorical Terms*, Berkeley: University of California Press.

Lawrence, E. (1982) 'Just plain common sense: The "Roots" of racism', in: CCCS (eds) *The Empire Strikes Back: Race and Racism in '70s Britain*, London: Hutchinson/Centre for Contemporary Cultural Studies, pp. 47–94.

Lebhart, G. and Münz, R. (1999) *Migration und Fremdenfeindlichkeit: Fakten, Meinungen und Einstellungen zu internationaler Migration, ausländischer Bevölkerung und staatlicher Ausländerpolitik in Österreich*, Vienna: Institut für Demographie/Österreichische Akademie der Wissenschaften.

Lentz, A. (1995) *Ethnizität und Macht: Ethnische Differenzierung als Struktur und Prozeß sozialer Schließung im Kapitalismus*, Köln: Papy Rossa Verlag.

Levy, R. S. (1991) *Antisemitism in the Modern World*, Lexington: D. C. Heath and Company.

Liberales Forum (1997) *'Neue Fakten zum Vollzug des Aufenthaltsgesetzes'. Unterlagen zur Pressekonferenz am 17. September 1997 im Café Landtmann. Mit Labg. Marco Smoliner und Abg. zum Nationalrat Volker Kier*, Vienna: Liberales Forum.

Link, J. (1982) 'Kollektivsymbolik und Mediendiskurse', *kultuRRevolution*, No. 1, pp. 6–21.

Link, J. (1983) 'Was ist und was bringt Diskurstaktik', *kultuRRevolution*, No. 2, pp. 60–6.

Link, J. (1988) 'Über Kollektivsymbolik im politischen Diskurs und ihren Anteil an totalitären Tendenzen', *kultuRRevolution*, Vol. 17/18, pp. 47–53.

Link, J. (1990) *Schönhuber in der Nationalelf: Halbrechts, Rechtsaußen oder im Abseits? Die politische Kollektivsymbolik der Bundesrepublik und der Durchbruch der neorassistischen Schönhuberpartei*, Duisburg: DISS.

Link, J. (1992) 'Die Analyse der symbolischen Komponenten realer Ereignisse. Ein Beitrag der Diskurstheorie zur Analyse neorassistischer Äußerungen', in: S. Jäger and F. Januschek (eds) *Der Diskurs des Rassismus: Ergebnisse des DISS-Kolloquiums November 1991*, Osnabrück: Redaktion Obst (OBST 46), pp. 37–52.

Loewenstein, R. M. (1952) *Psychoanalyse des Antisemitismus*, Frankfurt am Main: Suhrkamp.

Löschnak, F. (1993) *Menschen aus der Fremd: Flüchtlinge, Vertriebene, Gastarbeiter*, Vienna: Holzhausen.

Louw, B. (1993) 'Irony in the text or insincerity in the writer?', in: M. Baker, G. Francis and E. Tognini-Bonelli (eds) (1993) *Text and Technology. In Honour of John Sinclair*, Philadelphia and Amsterdam: Benjamins, pp. 157–76.

Lyotard, J.-F. (1984) *The Postmodern Condition: A Report of Knowledge*, Manchester: Manchester University Press.

Manoschek, W. (1996) 'Die Wehrmacht im Rassenkrieg', in: W. Manoschek (ed.) *Die Wehrmacht im Rassenkrieg. Der Vernichtungskrieg hinter der Front*, Vienna: Böhlau, pp. 9–15.

Marcuse, H. (1936) 'Ideengeschichtlicher Teil', *Studien über Autorität und Familie: Forschungsberichte aus dem Institut für Sozialforschung*, Paris: Klampen.

Marcuse, H. (1980) *Ideen zu einer kritischen Theorie der Gesellschaft*, Frankfurt am Main: Suhrkamp.

Marin, B. (1983) 'Ein historisch neuartiger "Antisemitismus ohne Antisemiten" ', in: J. Bunzl and B. Marin (eds) *Antisemitismus in Österreich*, Innsbruck: Universitätsverlag, pp. 171–92.

Martin, J. R. (in preparation) 'Giving the game away: explicitness, diversity and genre-biased literacy in Australia', in: R. de Cillia, H.-J. Krumm and R. Wodak (eds) (in preparation) *Loss of Communication in the Information Age*, Vienna: Verlag der Österreichischen Akademie der Wissenschaften.

Masson, J. M. (1984) *The Assault on Truth: Freud's Suppression of the Seduction Theory*, New York: Farrar, Strauss and Giroux.

Matouschek, B. (1999) *Böse Worte? Sprache und Diskriminierung: Eine praktische Anleitung zur Erhöhung der sprachlichen Sensibilität im Umgang mit den Anderen*, Vienna: Grüne Bildungswerkstatt Minderheiten.

Matouschek, B. and Wodak, R. (1996) *Sprachwissenschaftliche Untersuchung über 'kulturrassistische' Verwaltungsbescheide der Magistratsabteilung 62*, Vienna: Die Grünen/Der Grüne Club im Rathaus.

Matouschek, B., Wodak, R. and Januschek, F. (1995) *Notwendige Maßnahmen gegen Fremde? Genese und Formen von rassistischen Diskursen der Differenz*, Vienna: Passagen Verlag.

Mayr, S. and Reisigl, M. (1998) ' "Muso ardito e strafottente – intonato alle scarpe coi chiodi": Faschismus und literarische Antimoderne bei Strapaese', in: J. Born and M. Steinbach (eds) *Geistige Brandstifter und Kollaborateure: Literatur und Faschismus in Italien und Frankreich*, Dresden: Dresden University Press, pp. 145–65.

Mecheril, P. and Thomas T. (eds) (1997) *Psychologie und Rassismus*, Reinbeck bei Hamburg: Rowohlt.

Memmi, A. (1992) *Rassismus*, Hamburg: Europäische Verlagsanstalt.

Menke, C. and Seel, M. (1993) *Zur Verteidigung der Vernunft gegen ihre Liebhaber und Verächter*, Frankfurt am Main: Suhrkamp.

Meulenbelt, A. (1993[1986]) *Scheidelinien: Über Sexismus, Rassismus und Klassismus*, Hamburg: rororo.

Miles, R. (1982) *Racism and Migrant Labour: A Critical Text*, London: Routledge and Kegan Paul.

Miles, R. (1991) 'Die Idee der "Rasse" und Theorien über Rassismus: Überlegungen zur britischen Diskussion', in: U. Bielefeld (ed.) *Das Eigene und das Fremde: Neuer Rassismus in der alten Welt*, Hamburg: Junius, pp. 189–218.

Miles, R. (1992) *Rassismus: Einführung in die Geschichte und Theorie eines Begriffs*, Hamburg and Berlin: Argument [English: Miles, R. (1989) *Racism*, London: Routledge.]

Miles, R. (1993) *Racism after 'Race Relations'*, London: Routledge.

Miles, R. (1994) 'Explaining racism in contemporary Europe', in: A. Rattansi and S. Westwood (eds) *Racism, Modernity and Identity: On the Western Front*, Cambridge: Polity Press, pp. 189–221.

Miles, R. and Phizacklea, A. (eds) (1979) *Racism and Political Action in Britain*, London: Routledge and Kegan Paul.

Mitscherlich, A. and Mitscherlich, M. (1977) *Die Unfähigkeit zu trauern*, Frankfurt am Main: Suhrkamp.

Mitten, R. (1992) *The Politics of Antisemitic Prejudice: The Waldheim Phenomenon in Austria*, Boulder, CO: Westview Press.

Mitten, R. (1994a) 'Jörg Haider, the anti-immigration petition and immigration policy in Austria', *Patterns of Prejudice* Vol. 28/2, pp. 24–47.

Mitten, R. (1994b) 'The eyes of the beholder: Allied wartime attitudes and the delimiting of the "Jewish question" for post-war Austria', *Tel Aviver Jahrbuch für deutsche Geschichte* XXIII, pp. 345–70.

Mitten, R. (1995) 'Antisemitism in Austria', *Antisemitism World Report*, London: Institute of Jewish Affairs, pp. 10–19.

Mitten, R. (1997) 'Das antisemitische Vermächtnis: Zur Geschichte antisemitischer Vorurteile in Österreich', in: R. Mitten *Zur 'Judenfrage' im Nachkriegsösterreich: Die Last der Vergangenheit und die Aktualisierung der Erinnerung*, Projektbericht: BMWV, pp. 77–165.

Mitten, R. (1999) 'Jews and other victims: The "Jewish question" and discourses of victimhood in post-war Austria', paper delivered to the Conference 'The Dynamics of Antisemitism in the Second Half of the Twentieth Century', SICSA, Jerusalem, June.

Mitten, R. and Wodak, R. (1993) 'On the discourse of racism and prejudice', *Folia Linguistica: Acta Societatis Linguisticae Europaeae. Tomus XXVII / 3–4: Special Issue, Discourse Analysis and Racist Talk*, pp. 191–215.

Mosse, L. G. (1990) *Die Geschichte des Rassismus in Europa*, Frankfurt am Main: Fischer.

Muntigl, P., Weiss, G. and Wodak, R. (2000) *European Union Discourses on Unemployment. An Interdisciplinary Approach to Employment Policy-making and Organisational Change*, Amsterdam: Benjamins.

Nikolinakos, M. (1975) 'Notes towards a general theory of migration in late capitalism', *Capital and Class*, Vol. 17/1, pp. 5–18.

Nipperdey, T. and Rürup, R. (1972) 'Antisemitismus', in: O. Brunner, W. Conze and R. Koselleck (eds) *Geschichtliche Grundbegriffe: Historisches Lexikon zur politisch-sozialen Sprache in Deutschland*, Stuttgart: Klett-Cotta, pp. 129–53.

Nödl, A. (1995) *Parlamentarische Kontrolle: Das Interpellations-, Resolutions- und Untersuchungsrecht. Eine rechtsdogmatische Darstellung mit historischem Abriß und empirischer Analyse*, Vienna: Böhlau.

Nowak, P., Wodak, R. and de Cillia, R. (1990) 'Die Grenzen der Abgrenzung: Methoden und Ergebnisse einer Studie zum antisemitischen Diskurs im Nachkriegsösterreich', in: Wodak, R. and Menz, F. (eds) *Sprache in der Politik: Politik in der Sprache*, Klagenfurt/Celovec: Drava, pp. 128–151.

O'Neill, J. (1979) *Kritik und Erinnerung: Studien zur politischen und sinnlichen Emanzipation*, Frankfurt am Main: Suhrkamp.

Ottomeyer, K. (1997) 'Psychoanalytische Erklärungsansätze zum Rassismus: Möglichkeiten und Grenzen', in: P. Mecheril and T. Thomas (eds) *Psychologie und Rassismus*, Reinbeck bei Hamburg: Rowohlt, pp. 111–31.

Outlaw, L. (1990) 'Toward a Critical Theory of "Race"', in: T. D. Goldberg (ed.) *Anatomy of Racism*, Minneapolis: University of Minnesota Press, pp. 58–82.

Palonen, K. (1995) 'Der Parteiname als Synekdoche? Eine rhetorische Perspektive zum Wandel der Konfliktkonstellationen', in: R. Reiher (ed.) *Sprache im Konflikt: Zur Rolle der Sprache in sozialen, politischen und militärischen Auseinandersetzungen*, Berlin: de Gruyter, pp. 447–60.

Pauley, B. F. (1993) *Eine Geschichte des österreichischen Antisemitismus: Von der Ausgrenzung zur Auslöschung*, Vienna: Kremayr and Scheriau.

Pelinka, P., Duchkowitsch, W. and Hausjell, F. (eds) (1992) *Zeitungs-los: Essays zu Pressepolitik und Pressekonzentration in Österreich*, Salzburg: Otto Müller Verlag.

Pelinka, A. and Mayr, S. (eds) (1998) *Die Entdeckung der Verantwortung: Die Zweite Republik und die vertriebenen Juden*, Vienna: Braumüller.

Perelman, C. (1976) *Juristische Logik als Argumentationstheorie*, Freiburg: Alber.

Perelman, C. (1980) *Das Reich der Rhetorik*, Munich: Beck.

Perelman, C. (1994) *Logik und Argumentation*, Weinheim: Beltz Athenäum.

Phizacklea, A. and Miles, R. (1980) *Labour and Racism*, London: Routledge and Kegan Paul.

Plett, H. (1989) *Einführung in die rhetorische Textanalyse*, Hamburg: Buske.

Poliakov, L. (1979–89) *Geschichte des Antisemitismus. Band 1–8*, Worms/Frankfurt am Main: Heintz/Jüdischer Verlag Athenäum.

Poliakov, L. (1993) *Der arische Mythos: Zu den Quellen von Rassismus und Nationalismus*, Hamburg: Junius.

Poliakov, L., Delacampagne, C. and Girard, P. (1992)[1976] *Rassismus: Über Fremdenfeind-lichkeit und Rassenwahn*, Hamburg: Luchterhand.

Potter, J. and Wetherell, M. (1987) *Discourse and Social Psychology: Beyond Attitudes and Behaviour*, London: Sage.

profil. Das unabhängige Nachrichtenmagazin Österreichs,Vienna: trend-Verlagstechnik.

Quasthoff, U. (1973) *Soziales Vorurteil und Kommunikation: Eine sprachwissenschaftliche Analyse des Stereotyps*, Frankfurt am Main: Athenäum.

Quasthoff, U. (1978) 'The uses of stereotype in everyday argument', *Journal of Pragmatics*, Vol. 2/1, pp. 1–48.

Quasthoff, U. (1980) *Erzählen in Gesprächen: Linguistische Untersuchungen zu Strukturen und Funktionen am Beispiel einer Kommunikationsform des Alltags*, Tübingen: Narr.

Quasthoff, U. (1987) 'Linguistic prejudice/stereotypes', in: U. Ammon, N. Dittmar and K. Mattheier (eds) *Sociolinguistics/Soziolinguistik: An International Handbook of the Science of Language and Society/Ein Internationales Handbuch zur Wissenschaft von Sprache und Gesellschaft. First Volume/Erster Halbband*, Berlin/New York: de Gruyter, pp. 785–99.

Quasthoff, U. (1989) 'Social pejudice as a resource of power: Towards the functional ambivalence of stereotypes', in: R. Wodak (ed.) *Language, Power, and Ideology*, Amsterdam: Benjamins.

Quasthoff, U. (1998) 'Stereotype in Alltagsargumentationen. Ein Beitrag zur Dynamisierung der Stereotypenforschung', in: Heinemann, M. (ed.), *Sprachliche und soziale Stereotype*, Frankfurt am Main: Lang, pp. 47–72.

Quirk, R., Greenbaum, S., Leech, G. and Svartvik, J. (1985) *A Grammar of Contemporary English*, London: Longman.

Rath-Kathrein, I. (1997) 'Fragen der Aufenthaltssicherheit im Fremdengesetz 1997', *ecolex*, Vol. 9, pp. 713–18.

Rathkolb, O. (1988) 'Die Wiedererrichtung des Auswärtigen Dienstes nach 1945', *Project-report*, Vienna: Ministry of Science and Education.

Rattansi, A. (1994) ' "Western" racism, ethnicities and identities in a "postmodern" frame', in: A. Rattansi and S. Westwood (eds) *Racism, Modernity and Identity: On the Western Front*, Cambridge: Polity Press, pp. 15–86.

Rattansi, A. and Westwood, S. (eds) (1994) *Racism, Modernity and Identity: On the Western Front*, Cambridge: Polity Press.

Reeves, F. (1989) *British Racial Discourse: A Study of British Political Discourse about Race and Race-Related Matters*, Cambridge: Cambridge University Press.

Reich, W. (1986)[1933] *Die Massenpsychologie des Faschismus*, Cologne: Kiepenheuer und Witsch.

Reisigl, M. (1998) ' "50 Jahre Zweite Republik" – Zur diskursiven Konstruktion der österreichischen Identität in politischen Gedenkreden', in: O. Panagl (ed.) *Fahnenwörter in der Politik: Kontinuitäten und Brüche*, Vienna: Böhlau, pp. 217–51.

Reisigl, M. (1999a) *Sekundäre Interjektionen: Eine diskursanalytische Annäherung*, Frankfurt am Main: Peter Lang.

Reisigl, M. (1999b) 'Nationale Identitätsstiftung und Mythenbildung im öffentlichen Gedenken der Zweiten Österreichischen Republik', in: J. Kopperschmidt and H. Schanze (eds) *Fest und Festrhetorik: Zur Theorie, Geschichte und Praxis der Epideiktik*, Munich: Fink, pp. 281–311.

Reisigl, M. (2000, in print) 'Literarische Texte als heuristische Quellen und kunstfertige Herausforderung für die Analyse gesprochener Sprache: Eine Fallstudie am Beispiel von Friedrich Glauser', in: O. Panagl and W. Weiss (eds) (2000) *Noch einmal: Dichtung und Politik. Vom Text zum politisch-sozialen Kontext und zurück*, Vienna: Böhlau. pp. 227–308.

Rex, J. (1990) ' "Rasse" und "Ethnizität" als sozialwissenschaftliche Konzepte', in: E. J. Dittrich and F.-O. Radtke (eds) *Ethnizität: Wissenschaft und Minderheiten*, Opladen: Westdeutscher Verlag, pp. 141–53.

Rieser, R. (1996) *Das Aufenthaltsgesetz: Rechtsgrundlagen – Verwaltungspraxis*, Vienna: Orac-Verlag.

Rittstieg, H. (1997) 'Einführung', in: *Deutsches Ausländerrecht. Die wesentlichen Vorschriften des deutschen Fremdenrechts. Textausgabe mit ausführlichem Sachverzeichnis und einer Einführung von Professor Dr. Jur. Helmut Rittstieg*, Munich: dtv, pp. IX–XXVII.

Rojo, L. and van Dijk, T. A. (1997) ' "There was a problem and it was solved!" Legitimating the expulsion of "illegal" immigrants in Spanish parliamentary discourse', *Discourse and Society*, Vol. 8/4, pp. 523–67.

Römer, R. (1989)[1985] *Sprachwissenschaft und Rassenideologie in Deutschland*, Munich: Fink.

Said, E. W. (1978) *Orientalism*, Harmondsworth: Penguin.

Said, E. W. (1993) *Culture and Imperialism*, New York: Knopf.

Sarcinelli, U. (1998) 'Legitimität', in: O. Jarren, U. Sarcinelli and U. Saxer (eds) *Politische Kommunikation in der demokratischen Gesellschaft: Ein Handbuch*, Opladen: Westdeutscher Verlag, pp. 253–67.

Sartre, J.-P. (1994[1954]) *Überlegen zur Judenfrage*, Reinbeck bei Hamburg: Rohowolt.

Scharsach, H.-H. (1993) *Haiders Kampf*, Vienna: Kremayr & Scheriau.

Schiffrin, D. (1994) *Approaches to Discourse*, Oxford: Blackwell.

Schmitt-Beck, R. (1998) 'Soziale Bewegungen', in: O. Jarren, U. Sarcinelli and U. Saxer (eds) *Politische Kommunikation in der demokratischen Gesellschaft: Ein Handbuch*, Opladen: Westdeutscher Verlag, pp. 473–81.

Schrammel, W. (1997) 'Ausländerbeschäftigung', *ecolex*, Vol. 9, pp. 724–27.

Silverman, M. (1994) *Rassismus und Nation: Einwanderung und die Krise des Nationalstaats in Frankreich*, Hamburg: Argument.

Simmel, E. (ed.) (1993) *Antisemitismus*, Frankfurt am Main: Fischer. [English: Simmel, E. (1946) *Anti-Semitism: A Social Disease*, New York, Boston: International Universities Press.]

Sivanandan, A. (1982) *A Different Hunger. Writings on Black Resistance*, London: Pluto Press.

Sivanandan, A. (1990) *Communities of Resistance: Writings on Black Struggles for Socialism*, London: Verso.

Slembek, E. (1983) 'Individuelle Identifikation und soziale Bewertung von Gesprächs- partnern durch Sprechausdrucksmerkmale', in: B. Sandig (ed.) *Stilistik Band 2: Gesprächs- stile*, Hildesheim: Olms, pp. 199–222.

Sokop, H. W. (1991) *Wiener Woikerln: Gedichte in Wiener Mundart*, Wels: Verlag Welsermühl.

Sokop, H. W. (1996) *1000 Jahre Österreich: Eine Wienerische Reimchronik*, Vienna: Österreichische Verlagsgesellschaft C. & E. Dworak.

Sondermann, K. (1995) *O Deutschland! Oi Suomi! Vielgeliebtes Österreich! Zur politischen und gesellschaftlichen Karriere vorgestellter Wesen*, Universität Tampere: Forschungsinstitut für Sozialwissenschaften.

Sornig, K. (1986) *Holophrastisch-expressive Äußerungsmuster. Anhand der Onomasiologie und Semasiologie der interjektionellen und expressiven Ausdrucks- und Darstellungsmittel der trivial-narrativen Gattung 'Fumetti'*, Graz: Institut für Sprachwissenschaft der Universität Graz (Grazer Linguistische Monographien 3).

Sornig, K. (1989) ' "Modische Interjektionen" oder der Fall GULP (anhand der trivial-narrativen Gattung "fumetti")', in: H. Weydt (ed.) *Sprechen mit Partikeln*, Berlin: de Gruyter, pp. 524–35.

Spörk, I. (1996) 'Das Phantasma vom "Anderen": Überlegungen zu Genese und Aktualität des Fremdbildes am Beispiel der "Juden" ', in: K. Hödl (ed.) *Der Umgang mit dem 'Anderen'. Juden, Frauen, Fremde*, Vienna: Böhlau, pp. 23–30.

Stern, F. (1991) *Im Anfang war Auschwitz: Antisemitismus und Philosemitismus im deutschen Nachkrieg*, Gerlingen: Bleicher.

Stern, F. (1993) *The Whitewashing of the Yellow Badge Antisemitism and Philosemitism in West Germany*, London: Sage.

Szymanski, A. (1985) 'The structure of race', *Review of Radical Political Economics*, Vol. 17/4, pp. 106–20.

Taguieff, P.-A. (1987) *La Force du Préjugé: Essai sur le Racisme et ses Doubles*, Paris: Editions La Découverte.

Tajfel, H. (1981) *Human Groups and Social Categories: Studies in Social Psychology*, Cambridge: Cambridge University Press.

Tajfel, H. and Turner, J. C. (1985) 'The social identity theory of intergroup behaviour', in: S. Worchel and W. G. Austin (eds) *Psychology of Intergroup Relations*, Chicago, IL: Nelson-Hall, pp. 7–24.

Tannen, D. (1989) *Talking Voices: Repetition, Dialogue, and Imagery in Conversational Discourse*, Cambridge: Cambridge University Press.

Titscher, S., Wodak, R., Meyer, M. and Vetter, E. (1998) *Methoden der Textanalyse*, Opladen: Westdeutscher Verlag.

Toulmin, S. (1969) *The Uses of Argument*, Cambridge: Cambridge University Press.

Toulmin, S. (1996) *Der Gebrauch von Argumenten*, Weinheim: Beltz Athenäum.

Trappel, J. (ed.) (1991) *Medien, Macht, Markt: Medienpolitik Westeuropäischer Kleinstaaten*, Vienna, St. Johann/Pongau: Österreichischer Kunst- & Kulturverlag.

Turner, J. C. (1981) 'The experimental social psychology of intergroup behaviour', in: J. Turner and H. Giles (eds) *Intergroup Behaviour*, Oxford: Blackwell, pp. 66–101.

Turner, J. C. (1985) 'Social categorisation and the self-concept: A social cognitive theory of group behaviour', in: J. Lawler (ed.) *Advances in Group Processes*. Vol. 2, Greenwich: JAI Press, pp. 77–102.

Turner, J. C. and Giles, H. (eds) (1981) *Intergroup Behaviour*, Oxford: Blackwell.

Turner, J. C., Hogg, M. A., Oakes, P., Reicher, S. and Wetherell, M. (1987) *Rediscovering the Social Group: A Self-Categorisation Theory*, Oxford: Blackwell.

Ulrich, W. (1992) 'In defense of the fallacy', in: W. L. Benoit, D. Hample and P. Benoit (eds) *Readings in Argumentation*, Berlin and New York: Foris Publications, pp. 337–56.

van Dijk, T. (1984) *Prejudice in Discourse*, Amsterdam: Benjamins.

van Dijk, T. (1987) *Communicating Racism: Ethnic Prejudice in Thought and Talk*, Newbury Park: Sage.

van Dijk, T. (1990) 'Social cognition and discourse', in: H. Giles and W. P. Robinson (eds) *Handbook of Language and Social Psychology*, Chichester: John Wiley and Sons, pp. 163–86.

van Dijk, T. (1991) *Racism and the Press: Critical Studies in Racism and Migration*, London: Routledge.

van Dijk, T. (1993) *Elite Discourse and Racism*, Newbury Park, CA.: Sage.

van Dijk, T. (1998a) 'Context models in discourse processing', in: H. Oostendorp and S. Goldman (eds) *The Construction of Mental Models during Reading*, Mahwah, NJ: Erlbaum, pp. 123–48.

van Dijk, T. (1998b) *Ideology. A Multidisciplinary Study*, London: Sage.

van Dijk, T, (2000, in press) 'Critical discourse analysis', in: D. Tannen, D. Schiffrin and H. Hamilton (eds) *Handbook of Discourse Analysis*, Oxford: Blackwell.

van Dijk, T., Ting-Toomey, S., Smitherman, G. and Troutman, D. (1997) 'Discourse, ethnicity, culture and racism', in: T. van Dijk (ed.) *Discourse as Social Interaction*, London: Sage, pp. 144–80.

van Eeemeren, F. H. and Grootendorst, R. (1992) *Argumentation, Communication and Fallacies: A Pragma-Dialectical Perspective*, Hillsdale, NJ: Lawrence Erlbaum.

van Eeemeren, F. H. and Grootendorst, R. (1994) 'Rationale for a pragma-dialectical perspective', in: F. H. van Eeemeren and R. Grootendorst (eds) *Studies in Pragma-Dialectics*, Amsterdam: International Center for the Study of Argumentation (Sic Sat), pp. 11–28.

van Eemeren, F. H., Grootendorst, R. and Kruiger, T. (1987) *Argumentation: Analysis and Practices*, Dordrecht (Holland): Foris.

van Leeuwen, T. (1993) *Language and Representation: The Recontextualization of Participants, Activities and Reactions*, Sydney: University of Syndney, unpublished PhD.

van Leeuwen, T. (1995) 'Representing social action', *Discourse and Society*, Vol. 6/1, pp. 81–106.

van Leeuwen, T. (1996) 'The representation of social actors', in: C. Caldas-Coulthard and M. Coulthard (eds) *Texts and Practices: Readings in Critical Discourse Analysis*, London: Routledge, pp. 32–70.

van Leeuwen, T. and Wodak, R. (1999) 'Legitimizing immigration control: A discourse-historical analysis', *Discourse Studies*, Vol. 1/1, pp. 77–122.

Voigt, R. (1990) *Politik und Recht: Beiträge zur Rechtstheorie*, Bochum: Universitätsverlag Brockmeyer.

von Eichborn, R. (ed.) (1994) *Deutsch-Englisch. Englisch-Deutsch, Die Sprache unserer Zeit*, Wörterbuch in 4 Bänden. Third Volume.

Wagnleitner, R. (1984) *Understanding Austria*, Salzburg: Herold.

Wallerstein, I. (1979) *The Capitalist World-Economy*, Cambridge: Cambridge University Press.

Wallerstein, I. (1990)[1988] 'Ideologische Spannungsverhältnisse im Kapitalismus: Universalismus vs. Rassismus und Sexismus', in: E. Balibar and I. Wallerstein (eds) *Rasse, Klasse, Nation. Ambivalente Identitäten*, Hamburg, Berlin: Argument-Verlag, pp. 39–48.

Walzer, M. (1990) *Kritik und Gemeinsinn: Drei Wege der Gesellschaftskritik*, Berlin: Rotbuch [English: 1987].

Weiss, H. (1987) *Antisemitische Vorurteile in Österreich*, Vienna: Braumüller.

Weiss, G. and Wodak, R. (2000a, forthcoming) 'European Union discourses on employment strategies of depoliticising unemployment and ideologising employment policies', *Concepts and Transformation*, Vol. 5/1, pp. 29–42.

Weiss, G. and Wodak, R. (2000b, forthcoming) 'The EU Committee regime and the problem of public space. Strategies of depoliticising unemployment and ideologising employment policies', in: P. Muntigl, G. Weiss and R. Wodak (eds) *European Union Discourses on Unemployment. An Interdisciplinary Approach to Employment Policy-making and Organisational Change*, Amsterdam: Benjamins, pp. 185–205

Welzig, E. (1985) *Die 68er. Karrieren einen rebellischen Generation*, Vienna, Böhlau.

Wengeler, M. (1997) 'Argumentation im Einwanderungsdiskurs: Ein Vergleich der Zeit-räume 1970–1973 und 1980–1983', in: M. Jung, M. Wengeler and K. Böke (eds) *Die Sprache des Migrationsdiskurses: Das Reden über 'Ausländer' in Medien, Politik und Alltag*, Stuttgart: Westdeutscher Verlag, pp. 121–49.

Westwood, S. (1994) 'Racism, mental illness and the politics of identity', in: A. Rattansi and S. Westwood (eds) *Racism, Modernity and Identity: On the Western Front*, Cambridge: Polity Press, pp. 247–65.

Wetherell, M and Potter, J. (1992) *Mapping the Language of Racism: Discourse and the Legitimation of Exploitation*, New York: Harvester Wheatsheaf.

Wiederlin, E. (1997) 'Die Einreise- und Aufenthaltstitel nach dem Fremdengesetz 1997', *ecolex*, Vol. 9, pp.719–23.

Wiegel, G. (1995) *Nationalismus und Rassismus: Zum Zusammenhang zweier Ausschließungspraktiken*, Köln: PapyRossa-Verlag.

Wiener Integrationsfonds (ed.) (1996) *So regle ich als Zuwanderer/in meinen Aufenthalt in Österreich*, Vienna: Wiener Integrationsfonds.

Wiener Integrationsfonds (ed.) (1997) *Bericht über das Jahr 1996*, Vienna: Wiener Integrationsfonds.

Wiener Integrationsfonds (ed.) (1998a) *Bericht über das Jahr 1997*, Vienna: Wiener Integrationsfonds.

Wiener Integrationsfonds (ed.) (1998b) *A Brief Information on the Law on Aliens 1997 ('Integrationspaket')*, Vienna: Wiener Integrationsfonds.

Wiener Integrationsfonds (ed.) (1998c) *How to Establish Residence in Austria*, Vienna: Wiener Integrationsfonds.

Wieviorka, M. (1991) *The Arena of Racism*, London: Sage.

Wieviorka, M. (1994) 'Racism in Europe: Unity and diversity', in: A. Rattansi and S. Westwood (eds) *Racism, Modernity and Identity: On the Western Front*, Cambridge: Polity Press, pp. 173–88.

Willems, H. (1997) *Rahmen und Habitus: Zum theoretischen und methodischen Ansatz Erving Goffmans. Vergleiche, Anschlüsse und Anwendungen*, Frankfurt am Main: Suhrkamp.

Wippermann, W. (ed.) (1997) *'Wie die Zigeuner': Antisemitismus und Antiziganismus im Vergleich*, Berlin: Elefanten Press.

Wistrich, R. S. (1991) *Antisemitism: The Longest Hatred*, New York: Pantheon Books.

Wistrich, R. S. (1996) 'Antisemitism in the New Europe', in: K. Hödl (ed.) *Der Umgang mit dem 'Anderen': Juden, Frauen, Fremde*, Vienna: Böhlau, pp. 31–46.

Wodak, R. (1986) *Language Behavior in Therapy Groups*, Los Angeles: University of California Press.

Wodak, R. (1989) 'Judeus ex machina: Diskussionen bei der Mahnwache, Wien 1987', *Grazer Linguistische Studien* 32, pp. 153–80.

Wodak, R. (1990a) 'Opfer der Opfer? Der "alltägliche Antisemitismus" in Österreich – erste qualitative Überlegungen', in: W. Bergmann and R. Erb (eds) *Antisemitismus in der politischen Kultur nach 1945*, Opladen: Westdeutscher Verlag, pp. 292–318.

Wodak, R. (1990b) 'The Waldheim Affair and antisemitic prejudice in Austrian public discourse', *Patterns of Prejudice*, Vol. 24/2–4, pp. 18–33.

Wodak (1990c) 'Alltag bei der Mahnwache: Alles schon mal dagewesen?', in: A. Holl (ed.) *Wie werden aus Menschen Monstren? Manuskripte*, 109/90, Graz, pp. 35–46.

Wodak, R. (1991a) 'Jedem Österreicher seine Krone – jedem Österreicher sein Vorurteil: Wie Vorurteile sprachlich hergestellt und vermittelt werden', in: P. Bruck (ed.) *Das Österreichische Format*, Vienna: Edition Atelier, pp. 108–27.

Wodak, R. (1991b) 'Turning the tables: Antisemitic discourse in post-war Austria', *Discourse and Society*, Vol. 2/1, pp. 65–83.

Wodak, R. (1994) 'The development and forms of racist discourse in Austria since 1989', in: G. Graddol and S. Thomas (eds) *Language in a Changing Europe*, Clevedon: Multilingual Matters, pp. 1–15.

Wodak, R. (1995) 'Critical linguistics and critical discourse analysis', in: J. Verschueren, J-O. Östman and J. Bloomaert (eds) *Handbook of Pragmatics: Manual*, Amsterdam: Benjamins, pp. 204–10.

Wodak, R. (1996a) *Disorders of Discourse*, London: Longman.

Wodak, R. (1996b) 'The genesis of racist discourse in Austria since 1989', in: C. Caldas-Coulthard and M. Coulthard (eds) *Texts and Practices*, London: Routledge, pp. 107–28.

Wodak, R. (1997a) 'Das Ausland and anti-semitic discourse: The discursive construction of the other', in: S. H. Riggins (ed.) *The Language and Politics of Exclusion*, London: Sage, pp. 65–87.

Wodak, R. (1997b) 'Others in discourse. Racism and anti-semitism in present day Austria', *Research on Democracy and Society*, Vol. 3, pp. 275–96.

Wodak, R. (1997c) 'Austria and its new East Central European minorities: The discourses of racism', in: L. Kurti and J. Langman (eds) *Beyond Borders*, Boulder, CO: Westview Press, pp.132–51.

Wodak, R. (2000) 'The rise of racism. An Austrian or an European Problem', *Discourse and Society*, Vol. 1/2000, pp. 2–3.

Wodak, R. and de Cillia, R. (1988) *Sprache und Antisemitismus: Ausstellungskatalog*, Vienna: Mitteilungen des Instituts für Wissenschaft und Kunst 3/1988.

Wodak, R. and Matouschek, B. (1993) ' "We are dealing with people whose origins one can clearly tell just by looking": Critical discourse analysis and the study of neo-racism in contemporary Austria', *Discourse and Society*, Vol. 4, pp. 225–48.

Wodak, R. and Reisigl, M. (1999) 'Discourse and discrimination. European perspectives', *Annual Review of Anthropology*, Vol. 28, pp. 175–99.

Wodak, R. and Reisigl, M. (2000) 'Discourse and discrimination', in: Wodak, R. and van Dijk, T.A. (eds) *Racism at the Top. Parliamentary Discourses on Ethnic Issues in Six European States*, Klagenfurt/Celovec: Drava, pp. 31–44.

Wodak, R. and Sedlak, M. (1999) ' "We demand that foreigners adapt to our life-style...": Political discourse on Immigration Laws in Austria and the United Kingdom', revised version of the paper delivered to the Conference 'Affirmative Action: A Model for Europe', Innsbruck, 16–17 September 1998.

Wodak, R. and van Dijk, T. (1997) *Racism at the Top: Discourse Analytical Strategies of Political Exclusion*, Vienna/Amsterdam: Project Application for the Austrian Ministry of Education.

Wodak, R. and van Dijk, T. (eds) (2000) *Racism at the Top. Parliamentary Discourses on Ethnic Issues in Six European States*, Klagenfurt/Celovec: Drava.

Wodak, R, de Cillia, R., Reisigl, M. and Liebhart, K. (1999) *The Discursive Construction of National Identity*, Edinburgh: Edinburgh University Press (revised and shortenend translation of Wodak, R, de Cillia, R., Reisigl, M., Liebhart, K., Hofstätter, K. and Kargl, M. 1998).

Wodak, R, de Cillia, R., Reisigl, M., Liebhart, K., Hofstätter, K. and Kargl, M. (1998) *Zur diskursiven Konstruktion nationaler Identität*, Frankfurt am Main: Suhrkamp

Wodak, R., Menz, F., Mitten, R. and Stern, F. (1994) *Die Sprachen der Vergangenheiten: Öffentliches Gedenken in österreichischen und deutschen Medien*, Frankfurt am Main: Suhrkamp.

Wodak, R., Pelikan, J., Nowak, P., Gruber, H., de Cillia, R., Mitten, R. (1990) '*Wir sind alle unschuldige Täter!' Diskurshistorische Studien zum Nachkriegsantisemitismus*, Frankfurt am Main: Suhrkamp.

Wodak, R., Titscher, S., Meyer, M. and Vetter, E. (1997) *Sprache und Diplomatie*, Vienna: Projekt report (FWF).

Woods, J. (1992) 'Who cares about the fallacies?', in: F. H. van Eemeren, R. Grootendorst, J. A. Blair and C. Willard (eds) *Argumentation Illuminated*, Amsterdam: International Society for the Study of Argumentation (ISSA/SICSAT), pp. 23–48.

Würtenberger, T. (1982) 'Legitimität, Legalität', in: O. Brunner, W. Conze and R. Koselleck (eds) *Geschichtliche Grundbegriffe: Historisches Lexikon zur politisch-sozialen Sprache in Deutschland*, Stuttgart: Klett-Cotta, pp. 677–740.

Zerger, J. (1997) *Was ist Rassismus? Eine Einführung*, Göttingen: Lamuv.

Zimmerman, E. N. (1989) 'Identity and difference: The logic of synecdochic reasoning', *Texte. Revue de Critique et de Théorie Littéraire*, Vols 8–9, pp. 25–62.

Index